Max Siporin, D S W

INTERVIEWING IN SOCIAL WORK

A Sociological Analysis

BY

PAULINE V. YOUNG, Ph. D.

*The University of Southern California, Author of
Pilgrims of Russian Town*

INTRODUCTION BY

JOANNA C. COLCORD

Russell Sage Foundation

FIRST EDITION
SEVENTH IMPRESSION

McGRAW-HILL BOOK COMPANY, INC.

NEW YORK AND LONDON

1935

Composition by the Maple Press Company, York, Pa.
Printed and bound by Comac Press, Inc., Brooklyn, N. Y.

To

ERNEST W. BURGESS

TEACHER AND FRIEND

PREFACE

Interviewing is the tool par excellence of the social worker. It is the most constantly used of all social work techniques. Whether with clients, fellow-workers, executives, or public officials, social workers are constantly using some form of interviewing. They find themselves frequently under the necessity of inducing people to talk fully, freely, and truthfully; they must explore the experiences, attitudes, and opinions of a wide variety of personalities. The facility with which interviewing is carried on often means the difference between good and bad social work.

Interviewing is a difficult and delicate art. Failure to secure needed information, invasion of the interviewee's personality, conflict, and hostility occur only too frequently even with experienced interviewers.

Fortunately interviewing has proved to be a communicable technique. The inexperienced can learn from the experienced, and the professionals can pass on to each other much of the skill they have acquired. True, an indispensable minimum of desirable personal traits is needed. The taciturn, sullen, or cynical interviewer or the unimaginative, dull, insensitive interviewer, as well as the talkative, thoughtless, or scatter-brained, can hope to accomplish little beyond carrying on formal questioning and the mere filling out of schedules and face-sheets, however much they may "know" academically of the sociology and psychology of interviewing processes. On the other hand, the sympathetic, cultured, sensitive worker may fail for the reason that he does not understand how to deal with a nervous or unresponsive or deceptive interviewee. For such interviewers a social psychological analysis of interviewing processes and a careful study of the experiences of other interviewers have much to offer.

In the present state of the social sciences and of social work in particular a volume on interviewing cannot pretend to deal with all the possibilities suggested by so broad a subject. Professional literature on interviewing is still in a nebulous state. So far as it is available the author has drawn heavily upon it. Where there are gaps she has been compelled to fall back upon her own experience and information.

Since interviewing is in many respects inseparable from general case work, it has not been possible to avoid considerable discussion of case work problems.

The present treatment is for several reasons sociological. Interviewing as here conceived is itself a phenomenon in the general field of social interaction, and the problems which it faces have to do for the most part with social situations. Furthermore, such competence as the author may have lies in the field of sociology.

The needs of both practitioners and students have been kept in mind in the preparation of this volume. That is, logical as well as pedagogical considerations have governed the organization of the material. However, much of the critical evaluation of the material presented is left for the students to grapple with under the guidance of the instructor who knows their academic background. The author has sought to avoid dogmatic attitudes on controversial matters and indoctrination of the student in case work, and has endeavored to supply the bases for independent judgment.

PAULINE V. YOUNG.

LOS ANGELES, CALIF.,
February, 1935.

ACKNOWLEDGMENTS

The author wishes to express indebtedness to the following publishers, who generously gave permission to quote extensively from many books published by them:

The American Association of Social Workers, New York
The Atlantic Monthly, Boston
The Family Welfare Association of America, New York
Harper & Brothers, New York
Henry Holt & Company, New York
Houghton Mifflin Company, Boston
Journal of Social Forces, Chapel Hill, N. C.
Little, Brown & Company, Boston
The Macmillan Company, New York
New Republic Publishing Company, New York
G. P. Putnam's Sons, New York
Russell Sage Foundation, New York
Charles Scribner's Sons, New York
Sociology and Social Research, Los Angeles
University of Chicago Press, Chicago
University of North Carolina Press, Chapel Hill, N. C.
University of Southern California Press, Los Angeles

The author has drawn heavily from articles published in *The Family* and the *Journal of Social Forces* and wishes to express gratitude to Miss Margaret Rich and Professor Howard W. Odum, respective editors, for ready permission to quote from their publications. Gratitude is also due Mrs. Ada E. Sheffield, a masterly writer on the interviewing technique, for her personal interest in the present volume and her suggestions as to bibliographical selections. Dr. Arthur E. Briggs, member of the Los Angeles Bar, has prepared especially for this volume the article "Legal Interviewing," and Mr. Floyd Covington, Executive Secretary of the Los Angeles Urban League, has written "The Negro and the Interviewing Process." Miss Louise Drury, Executive Secretary of the Children's Protective Association of Los Angeles, has prepared an outline for the interview with the unmarried mother, and Mrs. Eleanor McCreery, Secretary of Family Service, Council of Social Agencies of Los Angeles, has made many helpful suggestions in the selection of the social case history outlines in family case work. They deserve special mention for their ready and cheerful consent to prepare material on very short notice.

Special mention is due Miss Margaret Rinde for her painstaking care in typing the manuscript.

To her son, Clarence, and daughter, Harriet, the author is deeply indebted for constant inspiration and eager help in various mechanical details incidental to the preparation of the present volume.

To her husband, Dr. Erle F. Young, her obligation is unending for his numerous suggestions and critical discussion as to the theoretical treatment and for the examination of the manuscript.

The author wishes to express indebtedness to Dr. E. S. Bogardus —her first teacher in interviewing as a social process—for his generous consent to quote extensively from his book, *The New Social Research*, which still remains the best text on methods of social research, and for his suggestions as to the organization of the material.

P. V. Y.

Los Angeles, Calif.,
February, 1935.

CONTENTS

CHAPTER XV

CHAPTER XVI

CHAPTER XVI

APPENDIX A

APPENDIX B

INTRODUCTION

Sociology differs from the exact sciences in its reliance upon the method of the interview to secure the materials upon which it works. Interviewing is by no means the only tool of the social scientist, but it is undoubtedly one of the most important in his kit. The pure scientist, however, looks down his nose at the method of the interview.

Students of physical science up to and including biology cannot interview the objects of their study. But the interview as a scientific method is defective, they say, first, because we cannot interview the dead, but only the living, so that comparison of the present with the past is denied us by this method; and second, because, as Wells put it, we are no longer dealing with objects "too innocent to lie." He means, of course, that when we come up the scale to the sciences dealing with human beings, we find for the first time that the material with which science is dealing may modify the study by its own conscious volition. Crystals, asteroids, eggs, do not consciously participate in what is being done to them. Men do. Crystals, asteroids, eggs, develop helplessly in accordance with laws over which they have no control. Men actively and consciously oppose the action of those laws. So that in the study of mankind there are new and unpredictable elements to contend with. . . . We have to admit that the elements of free will and determination, as it used to be called in religious controversy, of the power of conscious deception and of unconscious self-deception, of the complexity of all the causes that affect human life, do most powerfully handicap the use of ordinary scientific methods now in the study of society. . . . [1]

When we come to social work, as distinguished from sociology and social research—or at least that form of social work which deals with individuals in some sort of trouble—we are even more inexorably confined to the interview as practically our sole means both of acquiring knowledge of that individual's peculiar situation and problems and of applying treatment. The process does not stop with the client himself—skill in interviewing is demanded of the practitioner in all his contacts, not only with clients but with other sources of information concerning them. It is perhaps most of all demanded of him in those special "treatment interviews" in which he essays to make his position clear to uninformed and often critical members of the general public.

[1] JOANNA C. COLCORD, "Case Work and Social Research," Chap. X, *The Art of Helping*, Association of Volunteers in Social Service, New York, 1924.

Besides the interview, what tools have social workers, indeed, except letter-writing and the examination of documents, most of which are themselves secondary results of some type of interview? Diagnoses of bodily and mental ills we must have, of course, but social workers must secure these not by any technique of their own, but by *interviewing*, verbally or by letter, the practitioners of another profession.

It seems extraordinary, in view of the extent to which this process of face-to-face discussion is relied upon in social work, that so little attention has been paid to it, comparatively speaking, in the literature of the profession. *Social Diagnosis*, to be sure, devotes much space to the purposeful development of the interview; the pamphlet *Interviews*, prepared by a committee of the American Association of Social Workers, gives verbatim examples of how definite results may be brought about; while a more recent book tells how development of the interview by the interviewer may be masterfully though passively avoided. Many books which cover various phases of social case work treat incidentally of the interview. But in reading the exhaustive bibliography appended to Dr. Young's volume, one is struck by two facts: first, that a large proportion of the material listed comes out of other disciplines than that of social work; and second, that the material which actually grew out of social case contacts is overwhelmingly in the form of short periodical articles.

It is, therefore, a real and important service that Dr. Young has performed in drawing together all these scattered accounts of theory and practice, these opposing views as to the right methods to be pursued, giving each author his due hearing and welding the whole together into a scholarly discussion of the methods, purposes, and techniques to be consciously followed or avoided in the most exigent and ever recurring test of skill that social case workers have to meet.

A social worker may be trained, he may be experienced; but unless he is also a good interviewer, with all that the term implies—unless he can come to terms easily with all sorts and kinds of human beings and make his will to service felt by them— he cannot lay claim to that much higher qualification than conveyed by the words *trained* or *experienced*—"a social worker of proved ability."   JOANNA C. COLCORD.

CHARITY ORGANIZATION DEPARTMENT,
    RUSSELL SAGE FOUNDATION, NEW YORK,
        February, 1935.

INTERVIEWING IN SOCIAL WORK

CHAPTER I

NATURE AND OBJECTIVES OF INTERVIEWING

Interviewing serves a variety of purposes and enters into many social situations. It is as old as the human race and as extensive as the leading professions of the day. The priest, the journalist, the detective, the physician, the lawyer, the anthropologist, the salesman, the employment manager, the psychiatrist, the psychoanalyst, the research worker, and the social worker regularly use the interview in daily practice.[1] Therefore, no single, formal, inclusive definition of interviewing is feasible.

Definition of the Interview.—Noah Webster defines the interview as "a mutual view or sight; a meeting face to face; usually a formal meeting for consultation; for a conference; for eliciting information by questioning; an interview is a visit for the purpose of obtaining particulars respecting a person or his opinions" and attitudes. Such synonyms as "meeting," "conference," "consultation," "questioning," "visit," "conversation," "discussion" are very useful in indicating the scope of the interview.

From a common sense point of view interviewing seems to be a specialized form of conversation, by means of which we exchange experiences, reveal our attitudes, and express our views. Ordinary conversation is generally informal, more or less spontaneous, and its subject matter is often of a general nature; it is controlled chiefly by convention, and each participant in the conversation is influenced by the attitudes and the views of the other.

When the participants in a conversation find common experiences, interests, and attitudes, they may lay aside many of their conventional reserves and drift toward the intimate and personal.

[1] *Cf.* E. S. BOGARDUS, *The New Social Research*, p. 78.

1

Confidences may be exchanged, self-revelation and even con‹ fession may follow. This form of social intercourse generally occurs where there are only two participants, though it also occurs in small, intimate, primary groups, such as religious sects.

When conversation is purposive and deliberate, and when at least one of the participants seeks to explore the mind of the other, the parties to the conversation pass from the status of mere talker and listener to the status of interviewer and interviewee. The tendency is for interviewing to assume the form of questions and answers—the interviewer supplying the form and the interviewee the content, as one journalist has expressed it. This form of interviewing generally tends to revolve around certain clearly defined subject matter, and the approach is apt to be direct. The freedom and spontaneity of ordinary conversation are lacking.

In social case work the interview is often regarded as " . . . a method through which most of the information used in social diagnosis is secured and through which most of its results in treatment are insured."[1] In the process of both diagnosis and treatment the interview is in reality an interplay of dynamic personalities which constantly act and react to each other's questions and answers, to each other's gestures, facial expressions, manners, and even dress. Generically an interview is a mutual view of each party by the other; a view of each other's thoughts, feelings, and actions. The interviewee, therefore, is as apt to influence the interviewer and guide the course and outcome of the interview as vice versa. Furthermore, the thoughts and feelings which prevailed at the outset of such an interaction may be so completely changed in their course that new and unforeseen moods and mental content may come to dominate the situation; that is, the interview conforms to the *circular response pattern*.[2] Dr. E. S. Bogardus writes:

Interviewing as a Social Process.—Interviewing is a series of interacting relationships between two or more people. At every stage of the process the interviewer-interviewee situation changes, the reactions

[1] AMERICAN ASSOCIATION OF SOCIAL WORKERS, *Social Case Work, Generic and Specific*, p. 24.

[2] See E. S. BOGARDUS, "Personality Clash and Social Distance," *Journal of Applied Sociology*, XI (November–December, 1926), 168.

EDUARD C. LINDEMAN, *Social Discovery*, p. 177, where he discusses behavior of the group as a stimulus response relation.

of both tend to change from moment to moment according to each successive stimulus in the process. This process may be called the *circular response*.[1] In other words, there is stimulus and response, with every response becoming a stimulus for another response. Interviewer and interviewee generally stimulate each other in new ways as the interview proceeds step by step.

Perhaps this process may more accurately be called a *spiral response*, because after each round of stimulus and response the interviewer and interviewee occupy a more advanced position of knowledge about each other and about the social situation under consideration than they did at the beginning of said round of interaction. After each stimulus-response step a new level of relationship is attained by the interviewer and interviewee jointly.

The circular or spiral response concept of interviewing tends to do away with the set of pre-determined questions, and supersedes the notion that the interviewee is "a well" from which facts are to be pumped. It challenges the belief that the interview is to be conducted chiefly by the interviewer.

Following the circular or the spiral response principle of interviewing, most of the work is after the interview starts. It means that the interviewer will need to change his rôle and no longer act chiefly as a questioner. He will right about face, forsake his previously conceived primary rôle of a questioner for an entirely different one of being an associate and a joint-student with the interviewee. The resultant product will be of inestimably greater value than if the question-answer method is followed.

As a questioner he may often put the interviewee "on the spot," on the defensive, on the witness stand as it were. As an associate and a joint student he and the interviewee sit down to talk over an important situation together. When the circular or spiral concept does away with the somewhat formal question-answer type of interview, it gives the interviewer the new rôle of being "on his toes" every minute of the interview. He secures his clues as the interview moves along. He picks up new threads of thought and experience at every stimulus-response step. He becomes a collaborator. Together he and the interviewee in rapport work together to unravel tangled skeins of conflicts and problems. Hand in hand, or mind in mind they may jointly search for truth regarding a mutually interesting problem. Paraphrasing a statement by Mary P. Follette, we may say: We must learn to think of interviewing not as a struggle but as an experiment in cooperation.[2] It is important to observe the community principle in interviewing, "never to work with individuals as individuals," but to

---

[1] MARY P. FOLLETTE, *Creative Experience*, p. 61.
[2] *The New State*, p. 97.

work in terms of that higher social relationship which results when two persons begin an interview.[1]

Not only "answers" from the interviewee, but also many of his questions, may become highly important. Not his formal yes or no and "replies" but his expressions of feeling, his gestures, his silent reactions assume primary importance. Not the number of his forced answers but the degree of his spontaneous participation is a criterion of a successful interview. . . .

If this interpretation of the interview as a social process, as an interacting process, as a process of stimulus and response, of give-and-take, of two persons together *en rapport* upon a given problem is accepted, then our whole terminology needs to be revised. The terms interviewer and interviewee as involving an aggressive person probing into the affairs of a person on the defensive become grotesque. The term interview, however, may still be kept if we will accept its original meaning in the French, where it connoted "visiting each other" and "having a mutual insight."[2]

In general it may be said that an interview is a systematic method by which one person enters more or less imaginatively into the inner life of another, who is often a comparative stranger to him. In intimate, face-to-face social groups in which both physical and social distances are at a minimum, there is little that is personal or peculiar to the individual. His life is an open book which all members know. In such primary groups[3] there is little occasion for formal interviewing. In modern secondary society, however, experiences are varied; few share a common lot; attitudes and values are very divergent. The individual finds it possible to live an increasing share of his life within himself; he lives much of his life in private, and learns to wear a mask before strangers or intruders. He is oftentimes to a large extent emancipated from neighborhood, family, and other traditional groups in which a warm, personal, and intimate life is shared. It becomes the task of the interviewer to penetrate behind the mask of conventionality and to arrive at an understanding of the underlying attitudes and values and the unique experiences of the person. An understanding of the social

[1] *Ibid.*, p. 79.

[2] E. S. Bogardus, "Interviewing as a Circular Response," manuscript prepared especially for this volume.

[3] For a systematic discussion of primary and (by implication) secondary group relations see C. H. Cooley, *Social Organization*, pp. 23 *ff.*

attitudes is the keynote in the treatment of personal and social problems.

Varieties of Interviewing

1. Newspaper Interviewing.[1]—The journalist was one of the earliest exponents of interviewing as an art. The exigencies of newspaper work required the reporter to deal frequently with those who, intentionally or otherwise, distorted the actual happenings in the telling. Many times great skill was required to arrive at even simple facts. The real test of the journalistic interviewer came when he undertook to match his wits with the statesman, industrial magnate, social reformer, orator, scholar, artist—men who are themselves accomplished interviewers and not easily induced to reveal themselves. Newspaper men have also often collaborated with the police in crime detection and have occasionally secured confessions from criminals. It is in part due to their methods that the older, crude, "third degree" of the police has taken a form which more nearly approximates cross-examination on the one hand and confession on the other.

The journalist . . . is handicapped because he is not sent for, as is the doctor or lawyer. He must make his own *entrée* into the interviewee's personal life. He must often overtake persons who are shunning him, and secure a "story" from them against their wishes. As a symbol of publicity he is evaded by many different types of people as different as the timid and the guilty. . . .

Both his difficulties and his desire for news are urgent and so he often goes to extreme lengths in forcing an interview, even using threats. . . .

He may even try to make the interviewee angry, and thus to "give away" important secrets unintentionally and impulsively in self-defense. . . . [2]

Moreover, "He has a nose for news and manifests a quick perception of news values in even chance remarks."[3]

It is clear that the social worker can rarely use the methods of interviewing employed by the journalist. The social worker

[1] For a bibliography on "The Interview in Journalism" see

Walter V. Bingham and Bruce V. Moore, *How to Interview*, pp. 302–304 and Chap. X.

W. S. Maulsby, *Getting the News*.

[2] E. S. Bogardus, *The New Social Research*, p. 85.

[3] H. F. Harrington and T. T. Frankenberg, *Essentials in Journalism*, p. 119.

must win the confidence of his client in a manner which maintains and prepares for further relation. The social worker's task with a client is of long duration, while that of the journalist often only that of a chance encounter. Neither does the journalist undertake to readjust the interviewee to his social environment.

2. Business Interviewing.[1]—This form of interviewing is widely used in various fields of business administration. The salesman, the credit manager, the vocational and personnel director rely on the interview to establish and maintain satisfactory relations with their clientele and personnel. As soon as the employee is regarded as something more than a hand and the credit customer as something more than a risk it becomes necessary to use an interviewing strategy which deals with them as more than abstractions. Dean Olson says:

> The personal interview is not a modern adaptation of ancient requisitions, nor a financial third degree; it is a business call, friendly and helpful in spirit, during which the credit manager is enabled to secure, not only those basic facts which he afterwards checks with business agencies, but also that "indefinable something" which gives evidence of character. . . .
> It is necessary that the debtor be made to feel not only that the crediting house is friendly in its attitude but that the friendliness shown has a basic sincerity.[2]

3. Formal Investigation.[3]—Census enumeration employs the "yes" and "no" or simple answer type. This method when employed in social work strips the situation of all surrounding circumstances and generally makes it impossible to arrive at the true character of the person or to understand his interests and motives. It rarely secures more than simple facts and generalizations. There are some types of investigations which involve

[1] See E. K. STRONG, *Psychology of Selling and Advertising.*

H. G. KENAGY and C. S. YOKUM, *The Selection and Training of Salesmen,* Chap. X.

NATALIE KNEELAND, "The Interview in Training Salespeople," *Personnel Journal,* VIII (1929), 47–52.

WALTER V. BINGHAM and BRUCE V. MOORE, *op. cit.,* Chaps. IV, V, VI, XIV, XV, and XVI.

[2] EMERY E. OLSON, *Credit Management,* pp. 64–65.

[3] See ARTHUR L. BOWLEY, *Elements of Statistics,* 3d ed., pp. 18 *ff.*

F. STUART CHAPIN, *Field Work and Social Research,* Chaps. V and VI.

VIVIEN M. PALMER, *Field Studies in Sociology,* pp. 47–54.

simple factual material—"Are you under fifty years of age?"
"Have you lived in this state for twelve consecutive months?"
"Were you born in the United States?" and the like in which
it is perhaps good practice to confine the inquiry to questions
which can be answered by "yes" or "no." Yet the significance
of an answer may be completely altered when the "yes" or
"no" has been properly qualified or the concepts used have been
carefully defined. "Yes, I think I am under fifty years of age,
but I have no record of my birth; I may easily be two or three
years younger or older." "Am I afraid of the dark? Well, it
depends on where I am, whom I am with, how I feel." "Have
I paid my rent? Well, yes and no. I painted the landlord's
house and he gave me credit for it." A given datum can thus
be interpreted only when other related data are taken into
consideration and its significance in the social setting understood.[1]
When the qualifying circumstances in the case and their social
setting are overlooked, persons are reduced to isolated atomistic
units. In reality persons are members of organically interrelated
and closely interwoven social groups: family, church, industry,
school, club, and so on, and can be best understood in relation
to the total social situation of which they are a part.

4. Crime Detection.[2]—The detective has become most ingenious—in his own way—in extracting information from people
who wish to withhold it. "He resorts to all types of deception
in order to attain his ends. In the most unexpected ways he
appears on the scene as a lucky fisherman in the mountains,
in the guise of a 'prominent citizen' at a banquet, or even a
kindly stranger doing a friendly deed."[3] The social worker
cannot trail his subjects and he is not interested in obtaining
information at all costs. It is frequently wiser to forego an
interview than to compromise one's dignity in this fashion.

5. Legal Interviewing.[4]—The lawyer depends on the personal
interview to obtain highly confidential matters, often damaging
to the client, who is not infrequently in a state of social and

[1] E. W. BURGESS, "Statistics and Case Studies as Methods of Sociological
Research," *Sociology and Social Research*, XII (November–December, 1927),
103–120.

[2] G. S. DOUGHERTY, *The Criminal as a Human Being.*

[3] E. S. BOGARDUS, *The New Social Research*, p. 86.

[4] For a bibliography on "The Interview for Legal Evidence," see WALTER
V. BINGHAM and BRUCE V. MOORE, *How to Interview*, pp. 305–307 and Chap.
XI.

mental collapse. Dr. Arthur E. Briggs, of the Los Angeles Bar and Dean of Metropolitan University Law College, writes:

The interview is a highly technicalized procedure in the legal profession. The characteristics of the art of direct and cross-examination in the trial courts are well known. Less understood, but equally important is the less formalized interviewing work preparatory to the trial which requires a high degree of professional artfulness.

Sociologically the problems of the legal interview are:—(1) the translation from raw individual experience which is a psychological fact (that is the content of the interview proper) into the social or institutional fact of the law; (2) the eliciting through the interview of the matter of the psychological conflict, the clash of individual personalities (which is the second or intermediary phase of the interview), and the translation of that conflict into the formal representation thereof as a legal issue or issues; (3) the presentation in court of the selected primary data obtained as aforesaid into immediate statement or exhibition of purely sensuous data from which is excluded all legally irrelevant and inadmissible matters (this in formal questions and answers is the final stage of interviewing in the course of the lawsuit), from which primary data of interviewing legal inferences of fact by the jury or of law by the court may be had. Thus in the legal interview a complete social cycle is expressed; the first of which is on one side or other the relationship of attorney and client; the second involving the additional relationship with the adverse party for the defining of issues; and the third including the supposedly disinterested and impartial arbiter, the court, as representative of the public, to determine and settle the conflict of individual interests as public policy and social welfare may seem to render desirable.

In the latter stage there is a kind of interview which is not strictly such, but which as direct intercommunication performs all the functions and obtains all the results of the interview. This is the argument of attorneys to the court or jury. Although the lawyer may do most of the talking, it is *to* and *with* and not *at* his auditors. Skillful lawyers make most of that interchange of ideas. By subtle signs unconsciously communicated they read the minds and hearts of courts and juries and by altruistic understanding persuade. All successful interviewing must elicit by such persuasion. For the experiences of the arbiters of law and fact do and always must contribute some facts (their own experiences) to the social ultimum. These are artfully produced by the arguments of counsel and so constitute a very real type of interviewing. . . .

In the work preparatory to trial and in the manifold relationships of practitioners of law the interview is a most necessary instrument of law practice. It deals with a twofold relationship. This grows out of the social and psychological conflict. There is the basic conflict of interests and emotional attitudes. This is represented and expressed by the terms "plaintiff" and "defendant." It is the function of the lawyer as representative or advocate of one or the other side to obtain by interview not only facts on the side which he advocates, but also to discover those favoring the opponent. To know the other side's case is as much or more important than to know one's own side.

A further difficulty is the need to translate the raw facts of a particular social experience or event into the peculiar legal facts or logical formulae of law. For the most part the interviewer obtains the raw facts from those who have no knowledge whatsoever of the legal form and implications thereof. He is confronted also by a very complex set of obstacles which conspire to thwart obtaining the truth about the situation, the parties involved, the relationships, and the actual facts which occurred. For example, the interviewee desiring to justify himself often unintentionally and to his own injury distorts or fails to disclose pertinent facts. To overcome such handicaps tries the skill of the legal interviewer.

How then should he proceed? The infinite variety of human nature makes the manner of approach and method of procedure no simple one to which fixed rules may be applied. However, a dignified, easy, friendly manner on his part may disarm the reticence or intrigue of the suspecting interviewee. By invitation to tell the story and by cautious, sympathetic questions a first viewpoint may be gained. Tact sometimes demands of the interviewer much consideration for irrelevant details irrepressibly flowing from a garrulous person. The interviewer is not entitled to expect from the interviewee the performance of his own work which is primarily to extricate essentials from a mass of immaterial matters.

Verification of pertinent facts is a next step in interviewing procedure. This may be documentary evidence or demonstrative evidence. The latter is a term to describe those facts which are presented directly to one's sense perceptions. Important corroboration may be gained by further interviewing of other persons to check up or compare various items of fact and out of the agreement or disagreement are drawn inferences of probability. It may be, after preliminary work of first interviewing and subsequent verification, that the whole case must be worked over again. The interviewee should not be wholly depended upon to provide a clear statement and relationship of facts or events. It may become necessary for the interviewer out of the fragmentary data at hand to construct a theory and therefrom to build a case which will truthfully represent the primary facts. In many situations the obvious or apparent fact is not the true fact which it is the true purpose of the interview to arrive at.

Throughout the course of the interview the interviewer must keep in mind those ultimate facts of a legal character which are defined as constituting legal causes of action upon which a suit may be maintained. In this he must think for himself and be guided by his legal knowledge. The ultimate facts are logical rather than sensuous and differ in form of expression from the purely evidentiary matters upon which they rest. The sociologist is especially interested in this translation from individual or purely psychological facts into the folkways or institutions of the law. This procedure is analogous to what takes place in social case work and indeed in every scientific investigation of an inductive sort. It is a method of proceeding from particulars to generals. Although the legal interview is wholly made up of the evidentiary particulars, it is necessarily related to the scientific generalizations of the law. . . .

It has been seriously proposed to eliminate "the battle of wits" going on in these different types of interviews and to require the parties to write out at length the evidence on their respective sides, and, after exchanging such data and striking out the matters of agreement or resolving same into a stipulation or statement of agreement on facts, the agreements and disagreements are presented finally to the judge or court for decision. This proposal quite overlooks and disregards the value for discovery of truth by sudden and artful attack upon an unwilling or dishonest witness through the lawyer's methods of examination and cross-examination, which often put quite a different aspect upon the facts than if time and opportunity were given to the interviewee to carefully prepare and therefore disguise the true facts of the situation and relationships.

In certain courts such as the juvenile court and domestic relations court and in quasi-judicial bodies like commissions, much of the formalism of legal interviewing method has been eliminated. But even there it has been admitted by such sociological authorities, not in the law, as Miriam Van Waters, that much of the most technical rules of legal evidence should be retained because those rules tend both to expedite the trial and safeguard the rights of the individual by confining the issues to those of fact free from the bias and prejudices arousable by extraneous or side issues. So it has been found convenient and desirable in trials even before a trained trier of facts such as is a judge to keep to those principles and rules of evidence which were formulated and developed in Anglo-American courts for the purpose of keeping from the unprofessional jury of laymen matters likely to mislead it, to be misused by it to the prejudice of a party, or which complicate a case unnecessarily, or which are slight, remote or conjectural in significance.

Not only the rules of logic but also the most technical rules of exclusion of evidence are of vital importance to the legal interviewer because they set the standard of his procedural method from the start to the completion of his task as interviewer.

However, even appraising highly the considerable amount of literature on the subject, it must be admitted that the art of legal interviewing consists more largely in the empirical skill of the interviewer gained through his experiences than through any nicely formulated science describing the art of the legal interview.[1]

From a sociological standpoint the problems of legal interviewing, as outlined by Dr. Briggs, are not vastly different from those in social case work. The lawyer must view his client's experiences, needs, and problems from the point of view of the institution of the law, while the social worker must take into account the accepted practices, folkways, and mores of the social institutions of the family, the community, and the larger social groups of which the person in question is or is to become a member. Furthermore, it is the social worker's task to learn of the conflicts and clashes of individual personalities and groups not only because of personal differences, but because of conflicts of group standards, customs, and culture patterns. The social worker, on the other hand, is spared the necessity of presenting in a court or before a jury any data obtained from the client in order to settle an issue or a conflict of individual differences. The social worker, however, must frequently select primary data from the interviews held with clients and present them to a case committee which aims—through collective planning—to suggest next possible steps to be adopted by the worker.

Likewise, we recognize the lawyer's preparatory stage[2] of interviewing—the friendly, sympathetic, cautious approach to the interviewee, the obtaining of essentials, and the verification of pertinent facts—as the case worker's procedure in interviewing.

The lawyer's battle of wits must necessarily be supplanted in case work interviewing by the skillful discussion of the situations involved and by the sympathetic insight into problems leading to a desire to disguise facts, if the interviewer intends to establish *rapport*, win the confidence of the client, and carry out a plan of social therapy.

6. Direct Examination and Cross-examination of Witnesses.[3] The courtroom uses a highly specialized form of interviewing. The fallibility of legal testimony has long been recognized by examiners of witnesses. Hugo Münsterberg,[4] through his

[1] ARTHUR E. BRIGGS, "Legal Interviewing," manuscript prepared especially for this volume, January, 1934.
[2] See Chap. III.
[3] FRANCIS L. WELLMAN, *The Art of Cross-examination.*
J. H. WIGMORE, *The Principles of Judicial Proof.*
[4] *On the Witness Stand.*

extensive experiments on the mind of the witness and his perceptive judgments, points to the illusions, tricks of memory, emotional coloring, and suggestion to which the witness is subjected.   To arrive at the true facts of the case the cross-examiner must possess a thorough knowledge of the psychology of testimony and keen insight into the personality and mental processes of the witness.[1]   So uncertain is the witness in his report as to what he says he actually saw and heard that judicial proof is now beginning to lean more heavily on physical evidence. The physical and social settings of the courtroom frequently inhibit the witness or create a desire to defeat the purposes of his questioner.   Many antagonistic interests are present which may further invalidate the accuracy of the response.   An examination of the courtroom situation reveals the dangers associated with this variety of interviewing.   Cross-examination in particular is apt to create a conflict situation and cannot, therefore, be efficiently employed in social work.

Many men in the witness box feel and enjoy a sense of *power* to direct the verdict towards the one side or the other, and cannot resist the temptation to indulge it and to be thought a "fine witness" for their side.   I say "their" side; the side for which they testify always becomes their side the moment they take the witness chair, and they instinctively desire to see that side win, although they may be entirely devoid of any other interest in the case whatsoever.   It is characteristic of the human race to be intensely interested in the success of some one party to a contest, whether it be a war, a boat race, a ball game, or a lawsuit.   This desire *to win* seldom fails to color the testimony of a witness and to create fallacies and inferences dictated by the witness's *feelings*, rather than by his *intellect* or the dispassionate powers of observation. . . .

Cross-examination requires the greatest ingenuity; a habit of logical thought; clearness of perception in general; infinite patience and self-control; power to read men's minds intuitively, to judge of their character by their faces, to appreciate their motives; ability to act with force and precision; a masterful knowledge of the subject matter itself; an extreme caution; and above all, the instinct to discover the weak points of the witness under examination.[2]

The statement of Richard Harris, noted authority on legal interviewing, is to a large degree applicable to social work interviewing:

[1] See Chap. XIII, "Psychological Problems of Interviewing."
[2] Francis L. Wellman, *op. cit.*, pp. 149–152.

. . . One fact should be remembered to start with, and it is this: the witness whom [the advocate] has to examine has probably a plain, straightforward story to tell, and that upon the telling it depends the belief or disbelief of the jury, and their consequent verdict. If it were to be told amid a social circle of friends, it would be narrated with more or less circumlocution and considerable exactness. But *all the facts would come out;* and that is the first thing to insure, if the case be, as I must all along assume it to be, an honest one. I have often known half a story told, and that the worst half, too, the rest having to be got out by the leader in reexamination, if he have the opportunity. If the story were being told as I have suggested, in private, all the company would understand it, and if the narrator were known as a man of truth, all would believe him. It would require no advocate to elicit the facts or to confuse the dates; the events would flow pretty much in their natural order. Now change the audience; let the same man attempt to tell the same story in a court of justice. His first feeling is that he must not tell it in his own way. He is going to be examined upon it; he is to have it dragged out of him piecemeal, disjointedly, by a series of questions—in fact, he is to be interrupted at every point in a worse manner than if everybody in the room, one after another, had questioned him about what he was going to tell, instead of waiting till he had told it. It is not unlike a post mortem; only the witness is alive and keenly sensitive to the painful operation. He knows that every word will be disputed, if not flatly contradicted. He has never had his veracity questioned, perhaps, but now it is very likely to be suggested that he is committing rank perjury.

This is pretty nearly the state of mind of many a witness, when for the first time he enters the box to be examined. In the first place, then, he is in the worst possible frame of mind to be examined—he is agitated, confused, and bewildered. Now put to examine him an agitated, confused, and bewildered young advocate, and you have got the worst of all elements together for the production of what is wanted, namely *evidence.* First of all, the man is asked his name, as if he were going to say his catechism, and much confusion there often is about that, the witness feeling that the judge is surprised, if not angry, at his not having a more agreeable one, or for having a name at all. He blushes, feels humiliated, but escaping a reprimand thinks he has got off remarkably well so far. Then he faces the young counsel, and wonders what he will be asked next.

Now the best thing the advocate can do under these circumstances is to remember that the witness has something to tell, and that but for him, the advocate, would probably tell it very well, "in his own way." The fewer interruptions, therefore, the better; and the fewer questions, the less questions will be needed. Watching should be the chief work; especially to see that the story be not confused with extraneous and irrelevant matter. . . . The most useful questions for eliciting facts are the most commonplace, "What took place next?" being infinitely better than putting a question from the narrative in your brief, which leads the witness to contradict you. The interrogative "Yes?" as it asks nothing and yet everything is better than a rigmarole phrase, such as, "Do you remember what the defendant did or said upon that?" The witness after such a question is generally puzzled, as if you were asking him a conundrum which is to be passed on to the next person after he has given it up.[1]

Helen Myrick observes that in order to determine the relation of facts to life it is necessary to sift a mass of evidence by means of cross-examination. In social work such sifting is best carried on by means of the diagnostic and treatment interviews held privately and with no concern for convincing a judge, jury, or the public of the truth. The art of the cross-examiner is immediately decisive but the social worker's is more prolonged; in many instances it continues as long as the case is under care.[2]

7. Religious Confession.[3]—The priest penetrates deeply into the inner life of the sinner who has sought out the father confessor and unburdened his soul to this trustworthy confidant—the physician of souls. The assurance that his secrets will not be violated helps to create an urge to tell the whole truth. Frequently the confessant is "stirred to tell all, for he cannot escape the Eye which seeth in secret and knoweth the innermost thoughts." However, the confessional is often an unsatisfactory place for a detailed interview, and the priest may not be able to get far with the questions of motive, of environment, of past habits, and of conditioning factors. In the hands of many confessors the whole ceremony remains formal and ritualistic.

What they [the sinners] really want is not the Sacrament of Penance . . . but an easy means of mental or spiritual direction, with what I call the "protected approach," making it possible for the disturbed individual to seek and find help, understanding and wisdom from some authoritative human being, without having to give his or her name, without the necessity of "making a definite appointment" and the

[1] RICHARD HARRIS, *Hints on Advocacy*, p. 29. Quoted by J. H. WIGMORE, *op. cit.*, pp. 497–498.

[2] HELEN L. MYRICK, "Cross Examination and Case Work Interviewing: An Art," *The Family*, VII (June, 1926), 121.

[3] ANNA ROBESON BURR, *Religious Confessions and Confessants, passim.*
JOHN R. OLIVER, *Psychiatry and Mental Health*, Chaps. I and II.
CASPER E. SCHIELER, *Theory and Practice of the Confessional.*

danger of establishing with the person consulted a confidential contact that might later on prove unpleasant or mortifying.[1]

The priest or minister has command of more powerful social sanctions than does the social worker, a state of affairs which enables him to act more surely when he comes to the treatment of sick souls.

8. Interviewing Primitive Peoples.[2]—The interview has been highly developed as a scientific method by certain anthropologists and ethnologists. They are concerned not only with external observations of the material culture, but also with "manners and morals, beliefs, avoidances, repugnances, enthusiasms," and cultural norms. However, their task is somewhat simplified because (1) much of the cultural tradition is homogeneous and simple enough to be contained within the memory of an average adult member of the group; and (2) because much of their investigation concerns itself with those aspects of the primitive life which can be arrived at by an analysis of the culture itself: religious beliefs, sex habits, methods of discipline, social aims.[3] Their experiences have much to contribute to social work, in particular the efforts they make in order to get into the situation they seek to understand. Margaret Mead observes:

The anthropologist . . . has devoted a great deal of time to the study of different primitive societies and the analysis of the social forms which are most characteristic of them. He has studied non-Indo European languages so that his mind will adjust easily to linguistic categories which are alien to our own. He has studied phonetics so that he may be able to recognize and record types of sound difficult for our ears to distinguish and even more difficult for our organs of speech to pronounce, accustomed as they are to different phonetic patterns. . . . In addition, he is willing to forsake the amenities of civilized life and subject himself for months at a time to the inconveniences and unpleasantness of life among a people whose manners, methods of sanitation, and ways of thought, are completely alien to him. He is willing to learn their language, to immerse himself in their

---

[1] JOHN R. OLIVER, *op. cit.*, pp. 13–14. Life adjustment clinics are now being created in some of the Protestant congregations which aim to serve as means of mental and spiritual direction through this protected approach of the personal interview.

[2] MARGARET MEAD, *Growing Up in New Guinea*, particularly "Appendix."
KNUD RASMUSSEN, *Across Arctic America, passim.*
JOHN ROSCOE, *At the Back of the Black Man's Mind.*

[3] MARGARET MEAD, *op. cit.*, p. 280.

manners, get their culture sufficiently by heart to feel their repugnances and sympathise with their triumphs. In Manus, for instance, it was necessary to learn a very real horror of the meeting of two tabu relatives, to guard one's tongue against ever uttering a tabu word and feel embarrassed contrition if one had made a slip; to learn to greet every news of illness or misfortune with the question of what spirit was involved. Such investigations as these involve a fairly drastic rearrangement of thought and daily habit.[1]

In a broad sense, the social investigator is doing an anthropological job. He is investigating some phase of culture. Usually he is studying the culture of his own group, and feels some concern himself as to how the facts are going to turn out. The bias of the investigator is very apt to generate a bias in the informant and so to color the data obtained. The anthropologist in his typical job has the advantage of studying an alien culture with which he has no personal concern. It is comparatively easy for him to take an objective, fact-finding attitude, without fear or favor.[2]

9. Psychoanalytic Interviewing.[3]—The psychoanalyst uses the interview as a means of uncovering emotional strains, dreams, the forgotten, the repressed. It explores the memories, wishes, motives—"hidden beneath the threshold of consciousness." It subtly injects suggestion and stimulates the patient to revive past experiences, thoughts, and feelings, which are believed to account for the present difficulties. Psychiatrists and psychoanalysts "secure from their patients what the doctor and lawyer ordinarily do not get, and what a priest may only approximate, a picture of the innermost feelings and thoughts."[4]

But the secrets of the mind are not generally exposed for the mere asking. Repression is a powerful motive and device which protects one from those disturbing impulses which must fre-

[1] *Ibid.*, pp. 281–282. Reprinted by permission of William Morrow & Co., Inc., New York.

[2] R. S. WOODWORTH, "Psychological Experience with the Interview," *Journal of Personnel Research*, IV (1925), 163.

[3] J. J. DEJERINE and E. GAUCKLER, *Psycho-neuroses and Their Treatment by Psychotherapy*, Chap. XX.

S. ALEXANDER, *Psychoanalysis of the Total Personality, passim.*

HAROLD D. LASSWELL, "The Prolonged Interview and Its Objectification," *Psychopathology and Politics*, pp. 210–212.

SMITH ELY JELIFFE, *The Technique of Psychoanalysis.*

For a bibliography of "The Interview in the Mental Clinic," see WALTER V. BINGHAM and BRUCE V. MOORE, *op. cit.*, pp. 299–301.

[4] E. S. BOGARDUS, *The New Social Research*, p. 91.

quently be excluded from the mind with almost unreflecting violence.[1] Professor Lasswell writes:

The interview necessitates the reactivation of the individual's struggle with his antisocial impulses. This happens, be the subject sick or well, for every individual possesses more or less active and powerful antisocial drives. Every personality displays some pathology in the form of remainders of the Oedipus phase of growth. The socially adjusted portion of the personality takes up the battle again against the unsublimated drives, and considerable amount of neurotic anxiety is generated in the process. The problem is to encourage the subject to face these unadjusted remnants frankly, to bring them to full focus of waking consciousness, and to discharge their bound energy. This comes to pass in the roundabout way of recapturing the original episodes in which the neurotic solution was invented. The work of reminiscence is the preliminary to liberation and understanding.

The interview substitutes the talking-out for the acting out of personality drives. One learns to recover the critical points in one's past history by watching the present for clues to the full meaning of the present situation, and this includes the inspection of reminiscences. A reminiscence is always relevant to a present situation, and serves the double role of annotating the present and reporting the past. The interview experience is long and arduous, and the subject learns very slowly to deal with himself as an object in a world of objects and to free his judgment more and more from the distorting effects of primitive psychological structures. . . .

Fortunately for the investigator, there are many advantages to the participant which sustain and fortify his conscious purpose to persevere until understanding has been substantially deepened. [The interviewer] treats every manifestation of the personality, no matter how trivial, with respectful interest. This is exaggerated unconsciously by the subject, who greatly overestimates the personal affection which the interviewer has for him. Some of the energy of the personality is always free to begin new object attachments, and this energy is concentrated upon the interviewer. The subject is permitted to talk at length about himself, and when the interviewer listens attentively and patiently, the subject identifies himself with the listener on the basis of a common attitude of interest in a beloved object. The interviewer's ascendancy in technical knowledge (his authority) resembles the authority of adults who were once supposed to possess unlimited knowledge. The day-by-day solicitude tends to reinstate the emotions of the early family situation in which the child could play irresponsibly, under the watchful, responsible care of the adult. The subject relaxes

---

[1] S. Alexander, *op. cit., passim.*

the effort to keep bawdy, disloyal, mean, and revengeful thoughts from welling into his mind. The frank expression of these thoughts in ordinary social life would bring down punishment upon his head, or mark him out as a victim of mental disorder. The subject is enabled to welter in unsocial or antisocial ravings and imaginings, and the process of developing these symptoms in the presence of another person becomes an absorbing part of his daily, weekly, and monthly existence. The subject intensifies his warm emotional interest in the one who exempts him from society's code of reticence. This is a mark of the analyst's tremendous power, and also of the analyst's special interest in the subject. The free-fantasy procedure even exempts the individual from abiding by the ordinary forms of logic and grammar. He is also able to enjoy the pleasure of impressing someone else with the brillance of his language. From time to time, new insight comes into old habits and worries, and the zest of intellectual comprehension is added to the other pleasures.[1]

It is not perhaps within the province of the social worker to explore the weird caverns of the human mind by the light of the clinical psychoanalytic interview and introspective interpretation, but he needs to recognize the fact that the present of human beings is composed to a large extent of the memories and emotions from the past and that prevailing attitudes and behavior patterns can be traced to earlier experiences.

The social worker can also profit by the psychoanalytic method of interviewing by association. The subject talks freely about things of interest to him and the interview revolves around clues and issues immediately related to the matters under consideration.

10. Social Research.[2]—Interviewers in the fields of personality, family relations, and personal and social disorganization make considerable use of the data accumulated in the files of social agencies in which are recorded direct observations and the results of a vast number of interviews, frequently extending over a long period of time. However, the social research student must generally supplement these data by interviews leading to a

---

[1] HAROLD D. LASSWELL, op. cit., pp. 209–212. Reprinted by permission of the University of Chicago Press.

[2] E. S. BOGARDUS, The New Social Research.

F. STUART CHAPIN, op. cit.

WILSON GEE (Editor), Research in the Social Sciences, Chap. I.

VIVIEN M. PALMER, Field Studies in Sociology.

See also Chap. II, "Types of Interviews in Social Case Work."

study of the inner person or of the innermost recesses of group life which condition the life of the person.

The social research interview . . . aims particularly at discovering human attitudes and adequate bases for interpreting these. The research interviewer is a social reporter, seeking first of all an accurate account of human experiences; of the experiences in which attitudes, opinions, prejudices, are embraced; of experiences that lie behind conflict and accommodation situations alike, of experiences that are different. To make personal experiences objective is the main problem. To get what is in the back of persons' minds out into the open is the chief task. To find out what is behind the faces of the people one meets is the goal. It is important to get pertinent experiences put down in writing by persons concerning themselves,—to get individuals "to pour out their souls."[1]

Objectives of Interviewing

The objectives of the social case work interview vary widely with the type of problem presented, with the type of interviewee visited, and with the interviewer's philosophy of social work and his conception of what is involved in the total social situation. In general terms it may be said that the object of the so-called diagnostic interview is to find (1) the social and personal problems an individual is facing, (2) the cause of these problems, (3) their effect upon the personality, (4) the social setting in which the interviewee most vitally lives; persons or social groups which have influence over him; conditions under which he attains the satisfaction of his desires, impulses, and social wishes; groups or sets of social conditions which give him the feeling of "belonging" and "create the stimulating flush of loyalty."[2] The object of the treatment interview is to help the interviewee become incorporated into these groups and to stimulate attitudes and behavior patterns which will ultimately make for a socially satisfactory life.

According to Mary Richmond, the objects of a first interview are fourfold:

1. To give the client a fair and patient hearing.
2. To establish, if possible, a sympathetic mutual understanding, a good basis, that is, for further intercourse.

[1] E. S. BOGARDUS, *The New Social Research*, p. 107.
[2] EDUARD C. LINDEMAN, *Social Discovery*, pp. 177 *ff*.

3. To secure clues to whatever other sources of information will give a deeper insight into the difficulties of his situation and their possible solutions.

4. To begin even at this early stage the slow process of developing self-help and self-reliance, though only by the tonic influence which an understanding spirit always exerts, and with the realization that later the client's own level of endeavor will have to be sought, found, and respected.

These apparently separate and sometimes apparently conflicting tasks are four parts of one purpose. We wish to serve, and we desire to influence in order to serve, but influence exerted in a mistaken direction would be worse than futile; we wish to serve, and we wish to know in order to serve, but knowledge is an impotent thing in the hands of one who has lost, through impatience, the chance to use it. Consideration of this aspect emphasizes the difficulty. The way out of the difficulty is to see clearly that frank and informal talk can be a help both in winning a common understanding and in securing clues to the coadjutors who can help us to understand still better.[1]

Dr. Bessie A. McClenahan summarizes the objectives of the first interview as follows:

i. To discover the social problems and immediate·needs.

ii. To establish mutual understanding between social case worker and client.

iii. To win confidence of client.

iv. To give client a feeling of security in the fact that someone is interested in him personally; and a sense of being treated as a person who has a definite social place.

v. To give client opportunity for emotional release in the telling of his story; to help him arrive at a clearer appreciation of his own situation, to gain insight into his problems and some of the causal factors related to them.

vi. To give client an understanding of the services which he may expect from the agency which the worker represents. (Care, however, must be taken that the agency and its machinery of operation do not come between the client and the worker during the interview and as a consequence, the relationships become too impersonal and official; for example, "I must consult my supervisor;" "We can't tell you what we can do until we complete our investigation.")

vii. To lay a basis in the client's attitudes to help him meet future problems.

[1] *Social Diagnosis*, p. 114. Reprinted by permission of Russell Sage Foundation.

viii. To relieve immediate needs and initiate efforts to solve problems.
. . .

ix. To give client something definite to do which he feels and sees will help to improve his situation.[1]

x. To secure clues to other sources of information.

xi. To protect client against a feeling of self-humiliation.

xii. To close the interview in such fashion that the client feels more hopeful and convinced that it is worth while to struggle, and that, figuratively speaking, the door is left open for the visitor's return.[2]

Helen L. Myrick and Ada E. Sheffield state that the objectives of a treatment interview are

. . . to stimulate attitudes and habits which will turn the client's attention upon the total situation (*i.e.*, all the facts which should be taken account of in deciding what to do); on the other hand she [interviewer] must help client to get such an understanding of her situation as will help to maintain those attitudes and habits which make for socially satisfying behavior.[3]

Dr. Richard C. Cabot approaches the subject from still another angle by maintaining that the objectives of the social case work interview are not "economics, nor neighborliness, nor a general desire for social amelioration," but rather a "study of character under adversity and of the influences which mold it for good or ill."[4] Information regarding the environment, diet, daily activities, companions, amusements, etc. must be supplemented by a knowledge of the strong and weak points of character and the forces which govern in general a particular behavior pattern. "The first thing that I try to discover," says an able executive, "is the type of person I deal with."

It may even be said that questions of economic relief and dependence—in normal times—are subordinate to the main objectives of the interview, since the interviewer must concern himself chiefly not with the immediate problems of need but with the causes of the client's distress—assuming that the causes

---

[1] Miss Richmond calls this the process of "self-help." See *Social Diagnosis*, p. 114.

[2] Bessie A. McClenahan, *Social Case Work—Theory and Practice* (mimeographed), p. 34, revised ed., 1934.

[3] "Reflective By-products of a Social Treatment Interview," *Journal of Social Forces*, III (May, 1925), 663.

[4] See *Social Service and the Art of Healing*, pp. 55–56, 58–62.

are within his control, such as overwork, arrogance, alcoholism, ignorance, discouragement, a paralyzed will, narrowed mental horizon.

In the field of problem children, for instance, the objectives of interviewing are not only the offenses the children committed but also the discovery of the causes of these offenses: are these children in trouble because of excess vitality, or "moral flabbiness," or inferior mentality or lack of proper social and spiritual guidance and training, and so on. We must aim to see the child, the offender, as well as the offense.

Furthermore, the interviewer aims to discover—through observation and communication—not only the physical aspects of disease and maladjustments (the conditions of tenement houses and the outstanding problems of the family group) but also the influences of the social and economic machinery which exert pressure upon the life of the family group, of the spiritual effects of the communal forces and the means of social control which the family group or individual persons accept. The object of the interview is to visualize the person or group in his relation to the other members, to his local community, and to the larger social machinery which has any bearing on his life, and to understand the individual as a closely interwoven unit in a complex constellation of social forces.

Suggestions for Further Study

1. Suggest several synonyms for "interview" and indicate in each instance the essential differences of the terms.

2. How does interviewing differ from ordinary conversation and in what respects is it like a conversation?

3. Which of the definitions of interviewing given in the text do you favor most? Why?

4. Formulate your own definition of interviewing and indicate its relation to social case work and to sociology.

5. Why is Dr. Bogardus' discussion of the "circular response pattern" fundamental to the understanding of social case work interviewing?

6. In what respects can the social worker profit by (a) the journalist's approach to interviewing, (b) business interviewing methods, (c) formal investigation, (d) legal interviewing, (e) direct examination and cross-examination, (f) anthropological interviewing, and (g) psychoanalytic interviewing?

7. What precautions must the social worker take when he uses the above techniques?

8. What is the relation between social case work interviewing and social research interviewing?

9. What methods used in other fields not mentioned in the text should the social worker consider?

10. Compare critically the objectives of interviewing as summarized by (a) the Committee on Interviews of the American Association of Social Workers, (b) Mary E. Richmond, (c) Dr. Richard Cabot, and (d) Dr. Bessie A. McClenahan.

11. What important social and psychological factors does the first summary of above objectives fail to take into account?

12. How do you interpret Miss Richmond's statement: " . . . give client a fair and patient hearing"?

13. Under what circumstances is it possible to achieve the objectives of the first interview outlined by Dr. McClenahan?

14. Make a careful classification of objectives in the above lists, indicating which ones fall under the objectives of the "diagnostic interview," which are under "treatment interview," and which under "research interview." (Consult chapter on types of interviews.)

15. Is it advantageous to formulate objectives before knowing the circumstances of the case? If so, why? Specifically, which objectives are most helpful?

16. Formulate your own objectives of interviewing in the field of your special interest.

17. State the objectives of any of the illustrative interviews cited in the text.

18. State the objectives of some interviews recorded in the case records of the agency with which you are connected.

Selected Bibliography

1. AMERICAN ASSOCIATION OF SOCIAL WORKERS: *Interviews: A Study of the Methods of Analyzing and Recording Social Case Work Interviews*, 1931.

2. BINGHAM, WALTER VAN DYKE, and BRUCE VICTOR MOORE: *How to Interview*, 1931.
   A very good discussion of the uses, techniques, and reliability of the interview, as used in employment, business, education, social work, mental clinic, journalism, legal evidence. An account of the researches in the use of the interview for industrial fact-finding. An excellent annotated bibliography on interviewing in the various fields.

3. BOGARDUS, E. S.: *The New Social Research*, 1926.
   A lucid sociological discussion of the new methods used in social research, of the value of the personal interview, of the varieties of interviewing.

4. CABOT, RICHARD: *Social Service and the Art of Healing*, 1928.
   Stresses close relation between physician and social worker. Discusses objectives of social case work.

5. FAMILY WELFARE ASSOCIATION OF AMERICA: *Interviews, Interviewers and Interviewing in Social Case Work*, 1931.
   Articles reprinted from *The Family* on the interviewer's attitude toward client, on the varieties of interviews, on techniques, analyses, processes, on methods of social treatment; brief illustrative interviews.

6. HARRINGTON, H. F., and T. T. FRANKENBERG: *Essentials in Journalism,* 1912.

   Interviews in journalism.

7. MAULSBY, W. S.: *Getting the News,* 1925.

   Stresses the importance of discreetness and of ability to listen sympathetically and understandingly to interviewee's language and mind. A good treatise on various techniques of interviewing.

8. RICHMOND, MARY E.: *Social Diagnosis,* 1917.

   An extensive treatise on social case work, social exploration, social evidence, testimony, processes involved in diagnosis, treatment, analysis. Chap. VI discusses and illustrates the steps in the first interview.

9. WIGMORE, J. H.: *The Principles of Judicial Proof,* 1913.

   Principles of judicial proof discussed in the light of logic, psychology, experience, and actual court trials.

CHAPTER II

TYPES OF INTERVIEWS IN SOCIAL CASE WORK

Three major functional types of interviews may be distinguished in social case work[1]: (1) the diagnostic, (2) the research, (3) the therapeutic interview. These are rarely mutually exclusive; elements of the diagnostic interview frequently enter into the therapeutic interview or into the research interview, and conversely. Social therapy, on the other hand, may start even with the first question of an interview which aims primarily to secure information, and the securing of information may not be complete even at the final therapeutic interview. The following classification has, therefore, chiefly theoretical value.

The Diagnostic Interview.[2]—This type of interview, as already stated, aims primarily to determine symptoms requisite for the treatment of the situation; to discover the needs, resources, and possibilities of each case.[3] The diagnostic interview involves the

. . . attempt to make as exact a definition as possible of the situation and personality of a human being in some social need—of his situation and personality, that is, in relation to the other human beings upon whom he in any way depends or who depend upon him and in relation also to the social institutions of his community. . . . [4]

Frequently in periods of economic crisis, under the stress of heavy case loads, of inadequately trained case work personnel, the diagnostic interview tends to degenerate into merely securing face-sheet data (names, ages, addresses, relatives who can help, size of income, amount of rent, occupation, birthplace, length

---

[1] Frequently the interviewer secures life histories and confessions, or he resorts to cross-examination and other forms of interviews. For a discussion of these consult the index. Here the discussion is confined to functional types of interviews.

[2] See E. R. Mowrer, *Domestic Discord*, pp. 54–58, for a discussion of the diagnostic interview in domestic discord cases.

[3] For a more thorough discussion of the aims of the diagnostic interview, see F. Stuart Chapin, *Field Work and Social Research*, pp. 74 *ff*.

[4] MARY RICHMOND, *Social Diagnosis*, p. 357.

of time in state and county, etc.). Such questions of "what," "when," "where," and "how much" may be very important parts in the diagnostic interview but they cannot be considered as the significant data by which problems of personality, of group relation, philosophy of life, and general pattern of life organization may be defined and treated. The ideal way of securing face-sheet information is to await the time when the interview is naturally guided toward the question of relatives who can help, the size of income, the length of time in state or county, etc.

An interview which stops short of securing the data which will enable the worker to understand the interviewee's motives, attitudes, social wishes, the environment, past and present, frequently gives little insight into the fundamental needs of the client, and even social economic issues cannot be intelligently decided upon. A complete diagnostic interview tends, therefore, to be very long.[1]

The following is one of a series of first interviews[2] held and recorded by Clifford R. Shaw with the father of a delinquent, Milton Walker, in an attempt to secure all the available material which might throw light upon the boy's delinquent activities, upon the attitudes of the father, upon the problems of the family as an interacting social unit, and upon the personality problems and the emotional relation within the family group—factors frequently neglected in many social case histories:

(The family consists of four members: the father, 38 years of age; the mother, 36 years; Milton, 14 years and nine months; and William, 13 years. . . . The father is a tall, thin man, with a rather definite and reflective manner. . . . He affects a jovial manner. . . . He has always begrudged any time or money spent on recreation. He dreads Sundays "because of the anticipation of a day of loafing," and he never takes a vacation because he does not know what to do with himself. Likewise, he refuses to allow his wife to take a holiday to visit her own relatives. He seldom goes to a movie. There are occasional bridge games with his wife [because she likes it] but his favorite pastime is discussing abstract subjects such as "What stimulates thought?" or "What is personality?" He will never, however, accept the opinion of other persons in any of these discussions.)

Interview with Father (Mr. Walker).

Interviewer: It is certainly very nice of you to come to the office to-day to talk over your son's difficulties. Because of your special training, I am

---

[1] For a social case history guide, see Chap. V.

[2] Face-sheet information and all identifying material was secured in a previous interview at the intake desk.

sure you can give us considerable help in understanding his problems and formulating a plan of treatment. However, before discussing his problems, I would like to become better acquainted with you. To this end, I wonder if you would be kind enough to tell us something of your own experiences, beginning with your earliest memories.

Answer: Well, no; not at all. Should I begin at the very first?

Interviewer: If you please.

Answer: Well, I was born in the city of X; my father died when I was two months of age and my mother had to go to work to care for us. When I say us, I mean me and herself. She was very proud and independent and refused to seek assistance from her relatives. As a result I was placed in the care of a housekeeper who was very strict with me. We lived in a rooming house and I was kept indoors most of the time. I had no outside associates until I was at least nine or ten years of age.

Interviewer: Didn't you have any contact with other children during that period?[1]

Answer: None that I recall.

Interviewer: Now, will you please tell me more about your childhood?

Answer: My mother being strict didn't want me to associate with other children, so she arranged for me to get my education under a tutor. I had private instruction instead of going to the public school. I recall that I was fond of blocks, puzzles, and solitary games, but my mother was adverse to children's playthings so I very early took to reading. I can safely say that I had read, at about 10 years of age, all of Dickens, some of Scott, Hugo, and Thackeray, and many other such books. My mother had quite a library of high-class books and was quite adverse to trashy books. It was in this way that I developed my preference for the superior type of literature. She didn't make me read, but I naturally took to it. I was imaginative and entered into the stories that I read. My chief interest was in reading and I think that I spent almost all of my time in that way. I played a little in the yard, but never in the street. When I was 10 years of age, my mother remarried. At that time I began to go out more and had more social experiences and this lessened my reading activity somewhat.

Interviewer: Will you please tell me something about your family life after your mother remarried?

Answer: It was most unpleasant (in a very low voice).

Interviewer: What was that?

Answer: It was most unpleasant.

Interviewer: Tell me something about it, will you?

Answer: Well, mother, of course, felt that there ought to be a father in the house for the sake of my development, and for that reason alone she married. My step-father was an impressive type of person. On first acquaintance you would take him for a bond salesman; but in reality he only had the mentality of a stock clerk. But for various reasons, among them the fact that he had a little fund of money at the time, he created an impression. But his funds were soon exhausted and my mother's savings didn't last long, so they began to have difficulties. She became sickly, contracting tuberculosis, and died when I was thirteen years of age.

[1] [Note that the questions which can be answered by "yes" or "no" brought very short replies. P. V. Y.]

Interviewer: Tell me more about your experiences with your step-father. Have you a definite memory of the way he behaved and of your attitudes toward him?

Answer: Yes; I felt that he was a chap who had married wrongly. I think that if he had married one of his own type, a woman not as superior as my mother, there would probably have been a very happy family. But as it was, he developed the loafing disposition which was probably an attempt to feel superior to my mother. So in that way, even as a youngster, I felt that he was out of place with my mother.

Interviewer: What were your attitudes toward him?

Answer: I was not bitter toward him, but when my mother died, I felt free to leave him. He meant nothing to me. I had no definite attitudes or feelings with regard to him. Consequently, after the death of my mother I went out on my own responsibility, feeling no ties for my home. Since that time I have made my own way without any assistance from anyone. I studied hard and completed one year of college. I became greatly interested in technical subjects, especially electrical engineering, and studied very hard to improve myself in that field. I took a position with a telephone company in the South and it was while working at that position that I met my wife. We became very fond of each other and married in a short time even though her parents were opposed to her marriage, at so young an age.

Interviewer: Will you please give an account of your experiences following your marriage? Did you and your wife have difficulties?

Answer: My wife and I have never been exactly happy together. Soon after we married I found that we had few things in common and had very different views about a number of things. For example, I found soon after we were married that her taste in literature was quite different from what I would like to have had it be. She had a preference for novels, magazines, and very trashy literature. I suggested that she select books that were more elevating. I tried to get her interested in technical books and classic literature. Instead of accepting my suggestion she was provoked. After some discussion in this connection I let things go and in that way we drifted apart in our taste for literature.

Interviewer: Will you please continue?

Answer: We had differences of opinion also on the question of religion. As you know, I do not follow the Christian Church, having found something far superior. I was interested in intellectual pursuits. My beliefs, of course, were incomprehensible to my wife. It was difficult for her to accept my ideas so she occasionally reverted back to her early education in the Lutheran Church. When we had discussions about our religious beliefs, they usually ended by her accusing me of being critical. In reality I was only trying to help her.

Interviewer: Will you please continue?

Answer: I made attempts to improve her vocabulary, but that led to antagonism also.

Interviewer: Will you give specific examples, please?

Answer: More in the matter of her southern accent. I did not try to correct her, but rather her pronunciation of words. I felt that her difficulty was largely a question of lack of training rather than a question of accent.

Her poor pronunciation embarrassed me in the presence of other persons, so I tried to correct her, but this only provoked antagonism.

Interviewer: Were there any questions concerning which you and your wife held different views?

Answer: Yes; it was difficult for me to accept her friends. I was always interested in selecting friends of intelligence and would associate with them for the educational benefit which I would derive. But my wife seemed to select friends simply because she liked to be with them. Consequently, we never went out much together. I spent most of my time studying my work. I tried to get her to read intellectual books instead of the cheap, trashy novels, and to make fine distinction between the things she read, but my effort in this respect only led to more antagonism.

Interviewer: Were there any points concerning which you had difficulty?

Answer: We were quite different in disposition. I am inclined to plan and deliberate before I act, but she acts on the impulse of the moment. I have tried to teach her to act more deliberately. I am inclined to be very precise and accurate and hold to a rational plan of life; on the other hand, she is careless about details and is more emotional and religious. She is likely to be sentimental about the children and make concessions to them while I am inclined to be firm. That has led to much trouble between us, especially during recent years. Her views about children are quite different from what I would like them to be. When I am inclined to punish, she wants to shield them. These differences finally led to a divergence of our interests, and more recently we have had little in common. The tensions are quite strong on many points.

Interviewer: Are there any activities in which the family as a group engages?

Answer: I am afraid not. There is too much tension and debating about everything. We never go to church, seldom attend movies or social affairs together. Being more or less of a hermit in type and not being inclined to converse on the topics in which the others are interested, I have little to say. Consequently, we seldom engage in conversation as a family, not even around the table at dinner. I usually more or less selfishly occupy myself with my own interests; my wife with hers, and the boys with theirs. We have had a little common interest in local community work of late, but that is only infrequent. Strictly, we have little common interests at home or outside. If there is a little conversation it usually ends in a heated argument and leads to antagonism.

Interviewer: Now, will you give me a detailed description of the difficulties which you have had with Milton?

Answer: The first thing that we noticed was his tendency to run away from home, which began when he was quite young, perhaps five or six years of age. He always seemed to have an overabundance of nervous energy that required some outlet. To think and deliberate is unbearable to him. Since it is necessary for me as a parent to teach him and restrict him, antagonisms follow and frequently he is wilfully disobedient. He replies by saying that he has "a mind of his own" and implies that he feels that he should be permitted to do as he wishes. He has always had a great spirit for adventure. He has read many detective stories and stories of the wild west and underworld stories. At various times he has undertaken what I hoped would be a hobby, such as chemistry, biology, geology, etc. As soon as he skims the content of the subjects and finds that considerable effort must be made to master the subject, he drops it quickly but after he has dropped it he will pretend to others that he is very conversant with the subject. He has done quite a large amount of acting and impersonating and has built himself a pedestal on which he sits in self-complaisance. But, as I have frequently told him, the pedestal is very frail. Recently he asked to join a radio club. I told him that I would be very pleased, but that he should know something about the technical aspects of the subject before entering the club. But when I have attempted to instruct him in the hope of giving him at least some simple knowledge of technical subjects he has always avoided it. We have obtained books in which there would be information on various subjects, but after a glance of probably not more than fifteen minutes, he would be finished. I have always tried to stimulate his interest instead of forcing him to become interested in technical subjects. But it is usually necessary for me to initiate these meetings and they usually end in difficulty between us. I have not found anything that he will devote himself to. I think sometimes that he realizes some of his difficulties, but in his attempt to feel that he is of more importance, he will associate with inferior companions who cater to him so that he can feel a certain degree of importance.

To go back to the evening when he came home from high school and asked to join the radio club, I tried to show pleasure and at the same time hide my apprehension. I said it would be a very nice thing for him to enter into more activities at school, but suggested that it would be necessary for him to have a better knowledge of the subject of radio before entering the club. Then I carelessly reminded him that it was best for him to gain that knowledge without my assistance. As usual he only evaded my suggestion. I tried to point out some of the problems involved. For example, I said that there was a strong possibility that he might not fit in well with the other members of the club. I did that for two reasons: First, to destroy part of his feeling of superiority, and secondly, I thought it might spur him to investigate the technique of radio. But, so far, he has not consulted a single book on the subject.

He is always searching for big returns without effort and work. I have tried in various indirect ways to find out how he was getting along with his school work, but he will not volunteer information to me. He will not come for assistance, most likely because his mistakes are certain to be found out. When I point out his errors, he becomes antagonistic. To give another example: He may bring a stone from school and be highly interested in its color, composition, etc. But I try to get him to appreciate the stratification and history of the stone, and in order to lead up to the subject I will open a book and look over the pages on the formation of the earth, at first trying to get his eye interested and then hoping later to lead him to the more technical terms. But he becomes forced immediately when he finds there is so much to be known about the subject. All of which illustrates a discouraging superficiality and carelessness about essential things.

At various times I have tried in subtle ways to discourage his absorbing interest in cheap novels, newspapers, and movies. But when I try to restrict him, he only develops a sulky and snarling expression which usually brings reproof on my part. My wife, due to her own nervous troubles, lacks self-control and a certain firmness which is essential in training children. When I attempt to be firm and to advise and correct in a constructive manner, the boys go to her for direction and that leads to conflict. So any constructive efforts which I make act like sandpaper on the youngsters; it only irritates them. So the youngster is in an awful fix, isn't he? My wife is very adverse to corporal punishment. On several occasions I have suggested corporal punishment, and she has been very resistive, although she continually asks to make the boys behave. On these occasions I have pointed out to her that it was necessary to try new methods of discipline, since all her methods had failed.

Interviewer: Will you tell me more about the methods of discipline which you have used in the family?

Answer: Largely I have tried to make our discipline objective, to create a desire within the boys to do right things rather than to force them into it. I have tried to encourage interest in a hobby. For example, at one time he expressed an interest in chemistry. I purchased a set and let him try to develop it. We had all the plans made, but as soon as he opened a book and I indicated some of the more important parts of the subject, he dropped it. I had waited a few weeks to see what he was going to say and began to question him. I asked him what the difference was between a molecule, an atom, and an electron, and his expression was a perfect blank. Having failed to stimulate an interest in him by taking a friendly attitude, I then tried ridiculing him. I asked him if he was an infant and wanted to shake a rattle and make a noise, or whether he really wanted to do more genuine work. That caused him to pack up the set and put it away, and he has never had it out since.

A few weeks ago he came rushing home from high school one evening energetic and enthusiastic about a card game which he had learned. Hoping to stimulate a little seriousness I asked him if he had not passed the infant stage and was not becoming a man. We started to play the game and when I pointed out some of the tricks and how much there was to be known about the game, he lost interest and antagonism resulted.

Interviewer: Did you observe that any changes took place in Milton's behavior after you moved into the present community?

Answer: Yes; we noticed several very definite changes in his behavior. First, in the tone of voice. He developed sort of a snarling, hard-boiled type of expression. He began to swagger and took a more haughty attitude toward us. There was a tendency toward vulgarity and swearing which we had never noticed before. He was afraid to use such language around the house, but on many occasions it slipped out unconsciously. He began to use such phrases as "The world owes me a living," "I have a mind of my own," "Other children are allowed to go to the movies more often and be out after dark," and such other expressions, which annoyed me very greatly.

After moving into this community he became less particular about the way he dressed. He seemed to take more pride in being dirty and untidy. Also, it was at this time that he began to steal and stay out all night in the dugout with his gang. When we began to learn about his stealing, he became more deceitful and secretive. I tried to influence him against his companions by objective reasoning and pointing out the pitfalls. I told him what a mistake it was for him to pretend to be something that he was not, that he was not only deceiving others but deceiving himself, but it was very annoying to find that he would protect his companions in crime and lie to us. His repeated deceitfulness has led us to distrust him, and at present it is almost impossible to place any confidence in what he says.

Interviewer: Is there any difference between your relationships to Milton and William?

Answer: Yes. It is necessary to correct Milton much more and, therefore, possibly he feels that we are partial to William. But, as a matter of fact, William is the one that is given the least credit to as an individual because what he does is done with less effort; just comes natural to him as a product of the formation of the brain. William is, furthermore, very much more deceitful in a sweet and angelic manner. He also gets out of more difficulties and misdeeds because he knows how to cover them more smoothly and provokes less reaction on our part. And Milton, who carries out his misdeeds crudely, probably feels that he is picked on. We try to discuss the matter with Milton and show him that his continued disobedience has made it necessary for us to correct him more. But he, nevertheless, feels abused and that we are very partial—especially me.

Interviewer: Now, I wish to ask you some very personal questions. In the first place, do you feel easy in the presence of other persons?

Answer: I usually feel quite uneasy. When I enter a Pullman, for example, I feel at a loss in trying to keep up with the conversation which is usually about athletics, the stock market, and other current events; I try to keep up my end by asking questions. By keeping the others talking I relieve myself of embarrassment somewhat. I have the same feelings in the presence of my employers; that is, it is difficult for me to make conversation and to be sociable. I am all right so long as the conversation is about our work. When it drifts to current topics then I am lost again.

Interviewer: How do you react when other persons attempt to give you advice or orders?

Answer: If they appear logical, I am not so likely to resent them; however, on several occasions I have caused ill feelings where I work because I stood too rigidly on my ground.

Interviewer: Do you feel that you are inclined to impose your ideas on other persons?

Answer: I am certain that I do.

Interviewer: Have you attempted to regulate your family life according to your own notions?

Answer: Yes; I have definite ideas about how the house ought to be run and I try to see that it is run properly. I have wanted to see Milton be more orderly and his mother, too, but that is out of the question.

Interviewer: Supposing your scheme is not accepted readily, what is your reaction then?

Answer: I am inclined to stick rather firmly to my position. Speaking broadly, I would say that I am too dictatorial; not so much to have my own way, but for the sake of the method. I think in most respects I am justified in my attitudes in the home because our family needs discipline.

Interviewer: Do you find it difficult to be sociable and easy in youɪ relationship to your children?

Answer: My own lack of ability to be a pal—much as I would like to be— makes it impossible for me to be sociable and to be a mixer with them. Much as I try, my social desires die out. I am altogether too rigid and dictatorial and find it impossible to carry on a free and easy conversation or to show enthusiasm in their (children) interests and activities. By sheer effort of will I sometimes show a little enthusiasm, but with all my trying it only lasts a short time and I revert back to my hermitlike existence.[1]

Mr. Walker came to the interviewer anticipating a prolonged interview; consequently he was prepared to talk freely and intimately, and to all appearances needed little stimulation. The interviewer set himself to learning sufficient of the family background to be able to account for the tensions and conflicts arising between Milton and his father, of the father's experiences, attitudes, and philosophy of life, and of the role each member plays in relation to each other. Subsequent interviews with the mother and Milton provided a cross-section picture of the attitudes and interrelations of a home in constant conflict.[2]

On the basis of such an interview it is possible to understand Milton's failure to develop a stable life organization and to see Milton's needs for a feeling of security, the desirability for getting away from the domineering attitude of the father, and the boy's need for stimulation, response, and recognition.[3] In view of such diagnostic data it is possible to outline a plan of treatment which might ultimately help to solve the emotional tensions, personality problems, and delinquencies of Milton Walker.

The following interview with Mrs. Brown has many diagnostic elements and illustrates how face-sheet information may be secured in the natural process of the interview:

Interview with Mrs. Brown.

Case Referred: By neighbor, stating woman extremely ill and in need of financial assistance.

(Visitor[4] met at door by friend of woman)

Interviewer: Good morning, I am Miss Davis from. . . . I understand that Mrs. Brown is ill and would like to talk with me. Would she be able to see me now?

[1] CLIFFORD R. SHAW and HENRY McKAY, *Social Factors in Juvenile Delinquency* (National Commission on Law Observance and Enforcement, Vol. II, No. 13), pp. 293–302.

[2] *Ibid.*, pp. 303–343.

[3] *Ibid.*, p. 343.

[4] Interview held and recorded by Priscilla Ann Davis, Los Angeles, Calif.

Friend: Oh yes, you can see her.   She is much better now.   Come inside. You must be careful not to get her excited though.

Interviewer: Thank you.

Friend: (Upon entering bedroom) Mrs. Brown, this is the Welfare lady you were expecting   She says that one of your neighbors called her.

Mrs. Brown: What is your name, and where are you from?

Interviewer: How do you do, Mrs. Brown?   I am Miss Davis from . . . and I understand that you would like to talk to me.

Mrs. Brown: I don't know whether I do or not.   I have heard so much about Welfare workers and the red tape and questions they put everyone through.   Besides, I am used to living on beans by now.

(Before an answer could be made by interviewer woman's friend interrupted.)

Friend: That's true, Mrs. Brown.   And then the only people who get anything are Mexicans or alien ones.   It's too bad our tax money has to be spent like that, and paying high salaries.

Interviewer: I know just how you feel Mrs. . . . (Visitor paused long enough to allow friend to give her name.)   In fact, I felt just as you do before I knew anything about this work, but now I am able to see both sides.   If you like, I could call to see *you* as soon as Mrs. Brown and I have had our talk.   Perhaps then I could answer some of *your* questions.

Friend: All right, I'll be expecting you.   I guess I better go now.   I'll see you later, Mrs. Brown.

Mrs. Brown: Mrs. G. has been a mighty good friend to me ever since I have been ill.

Interviewer: How long have you been ill?

Mrs. Brown: I've been in bed for several weeks this last time.   But I have really been on the verge of a nervous breakdown ever since coming to California.   Worry over money is the biggest cause of my trouble.   I really don't know just what to do next.

Interviewer: It is hard when a person is sick to try to plan.   Perhaps we could discuss some of your problems and find a solution for them.

Mrs. Brown: Well, I certainly have enough of them.   It is real nice of you to be interested though.   Here I am sick in bed, with no money, and myself and Edward, my son, to take care of.   He is sixteen and goes to P. High School.   He is very good to me but, of course, he cannot find any work, so what can I do?   My husband—well, he might just as well be dead.

Interviewer: Does he know that you are sick, Mrs. Brown?

Mrs. Brown: Oh yes, I have written to him and he says that he will do what he can, but I know that won't be very much.   He used to have a good position as salesman with the main plant of the Ford Motor Company, but I guess he is only working part time now.

Interviewer: Your home was in Detroit, Mrs. Brown?

Mrs. Brown. Why yes, that is where Mr. Brown is now.   He and I were both born in Detroit and grew up there.

Interviewer: You must have many pleasant associations connected with that town.

Mrs. Brown: Yes, we do.   We didn't marry though until we made our first trip to California in 1915.   He and his father came together, and I with my mother (you see my father died when I was a small child). After our marriage we only lived in California a short time and then went back to Detroit to make our home. I have always lived there until coming to California in 1928. The only reason I came was because the children had asthma so bad. Mr. Brown had to stay in Detroit because of business.

Interviewer: Then you have more than just Edward to think about.

Mrs. Brown: Yes, I have three boys, including Edward. One of them is in the M. Home for Boys. He is only six but certainly is a bright one. Don't let me get started on my children. I think the world of them. The other boy, Fred, lives with Mother in Los Angeles. He is going to High School there.

Interviewer: You should be proud of your children. Could your mother or some other member of your family help take care of Edward until you can get on your feet again?

Mrs. Brown: No, I have no near relatives at all. You see I was an only child. I know Mother could do nothing for me now. She just lost her job at B. Bros., where she has been for a number of years. Besides, she pays $15 a month for Edwin's care in the M. home. She is also boarding Fred. I really can't expect her to do any more. As I told you, Mr. Brown can't help me. In fact he has only sent me $2 a month during the past two years. Mother has practically supported us since we came back from Arizona.

Interviewer: Why did you go to Arizona, Mrs. Brown?

Mrs. Brown: I took the children to Arizona for their health and while I was there decided to take a course in beauty culture, so that I could do something to support myself. However, the course was too expensive and we were there only six months when Mother had to send us money to come back. I do wish I could be independent as I hate to ask for charity.

Interviewer: You know that this is only temporary until you can get well again. Then when you are able to work, you can reimburse us for any aid you receive. Why not consider this money just a loan, to be repaid as soon as you start working?

Mrs. Brown: I want to pay back every penny as soon as I find work.

Interviewer: The first thing to do is to get well again. You said you had no relatives who could help you. Perhaps your church or lodge could do something for you. They are usually willing to aid in time of sickness.

Mrs. Brown: Well, I don't belong to any church. We used to be good Methodists, but since coming out here I have scarcely attended church. As to lodges, well, I have no money to pay dues and have not been a member of any organization since I belonged to the Eastern Star back in Detroit.

Interviewer: May I offer another suggestion, Mrs. Brown? Do you have any insurance on which you could borrow or which carries a sick benefit?

Mrs. Brown: No, I had to drop all of my insurance. Now, Miss Davis, just what do you think can be done for me? Will they take me to the hospital?

Interviewer: That will depend entirely upon the doctor's report as to whether he feels you should be in the hospital or in a rest home. Do you have a family physician?

Mrs. Brown: No, I just called Dr. P., one of the doctors in town here. He has been here two or three times but has not charged me anything. He said that as far as he could see, all I needed was proper food, care, and rest. . . . His name is Dr. P., and he can give you a report on my condition.

Interviewer: I shall be glad to talk with Dr. P. and see what he recommends. In the meantime, how would you like to have one of our doctors call and make a recommendation as to the care that he feels you need?

Mrs. Brown: That would be fine. I will be glad to do whatever he tells me to. If I leave home, though, some plans will have to be made for Edward.

Interviewer: Perhaps your friend, Mrs. G., could take care of him.

Mrs. Brown: Yes, I would like to have Edward stay with her, and I know she would be glad to have him. She is very fond of him and she has a lovely home. When you go to see her, tell her that I want to see her and make some plans.

Interviewer: I shall, Mrs. Brown. We shall also have the doctor call sometime this afternoon. As soon as he tells us of his decision, I shall let you know. We can then make some definite arrangements. Will it be possible for Mrs. G. to stay with you until tomorrow?

Mrs. Brown: Yes, I am sure she will be glad to help me out. I do appreciate your interest and kindness. Be sure and come back tomorrow.

Interviewer: I shall call tomorrow, in all probability. In the meantime would you like to have me write to your husband? Perhaps he doesn't realize how serious your financial condition is.[1] Maybe a letter from our agency would help. What do you think?

Mrs. Brown: I would like to have you write to him. Look on the dresser and get his address from the envelope there.

Interviewer: I hope you will not be tired out after our visit. I hope to see you tomorrow. Good-bye.

Mrs. Brown: I am not a bit tired. You don't know how much I appreciate your kindness. It's nice to know some one cares. Good-bye.

The Research Interview.—The research interview is more concerned with the analysis of the fundamental processes involved in social situations, social problems, and human behavior than with their diagnosis.[2] The research interviewer, as such, has little or no immediate interest in practical problems and does not undertake to find solutions for them. The following excerpts from an interview with John Yablokoff, a seventeen-year-old Russian Molokan boy, illustrate the social researcher's approach to the understanding of the cultural background and the social position

[1] Because of the woman's illness and her friend's warning "not to get her excited" the interviewer deemed it wiser to leave discussion of the husband until tensions were released.

[2] Social diagnosis is regarded here as primarily concerned with the determination of causative factors in order to decide upon treatment, whereas social analysis is mainly concerned with the formulation of scientific law.

of an American-born boy in the old traditional home of a Molokan patriarch:[1]

Interview with John Yablokoff.

Interviewer: John, I have come to you to get some information about Molokan customs and traditions which have interested me for a long time. Won't you tell me something about your home life and your religion?

John: Why do you want to know about us?

Interviewer: I have come in contact with many Russian boys; their behavior and thinking make me believe that their home life must be vastly different from that of the rest of us.

John: You sure have to know all about Russian history, Molokan religion, and family to understand what we try to practice. I can tell you that my parents are very religious and they practice the Christian life the best they can in the city. Saturday nights my father reads out of the Bible to us about children's duty to their parents and parents' duty to their children. It gradually grows upon you how to respect your home and your people. I think the gatherings at the house teach though a young fellow more than the parents can tell him.

Interviewer: What is the nature of these gatherings?

John: Once some visitors came from Mexico, and we entertained them. Special prayers were held. My parents and all nine of us children knelt down before them praying. My father and mother lay prostrated on the floor in deep prayer, and soon some of us kids fell to the floor too. They prayed long, and all the guests were on their knees. My father and mother even asked our forgiveness if they were ever too harsh with us or unreasonable. That touched me to the core. I couldn't bear my father's bow to me. If a fellow is attached only to himself, such gatherings sure take a lot of pride and selfishness out of him. You can't stand on your knees and pray for forgiveness and kiss everybody as your brother, and still be haughty.

Interviewer: Do you go to church with your parents?

John: Sure, I go to church with my parents. They want me to go, and my father is after me, so I go. Sometimes I tell him I am sick, I have a headache, I am tired, and he lets me off; but many times he says, "Oh, those are old stories," and makes me go. On Sundays my father does not want to talk about school or business or anything else. He wants to rest and go to church. Sometimes my father will talk about the olden times when he was a boy. . . . You see, my father is not an educated man. He was a Russian peasant and lived a very simple life, but he stuck to his religion and has many good ideas. My mother had no schooling either. She wants us to go to school and learn a trade. Oh, I have a good mother. She says she does not want to disappoint us. She works pretty hard, and she is very good to us.

Interviewer: And how do you get along with your father?

John: Well, my father is kind and good too, but he is a hot-tempered man, and when he gets mad he forgets himself. Oh, yes'm, he gets mad; and when he gets mad, he grumbles and goes off by himself and talks himself out. I can get along with my dad—we only had two arguments; but my big brother

[1] For a full treatment of the culture, of American experiences and the present status of this group, see Pauline V. Young, *Pilgrims of Russian Town*.

was always in wrong with him.   When my brother was working in my father's grocery store, and worked hard, he thought he had the right to tell my father how to run the business.   He said, "Don't I earn money for you? Can't I have a voice, too?"   But my father could not stand for that.   Now my brother has a business of his own.

Interviewer: What do *you* and your father argue about?

John: Once my father and I got into an argument because when I was driving our Dodge the wheel came off the car and broke.   It was not my fault.   My father said I didn't grease it.   I would not contradict him so I told him I forgot to grease it.   He said: "What do I sent you to school for— to forget?"   He was mad, but he did not punish me.

Interviewer: How does your father pay you for your work?

John: Our father never pays us for our work, but he always gives us what we need.   When I graduate from school, I'd like to continue in my father's business.   It's established and it's a good business, and I have been working in it for many years.

Interviewer: Does your father intend to move from Los Angeles?

John: I never heard my father say that he will move from Los Angeles. As for me, I don't see what's the use of changing around.   I was born here. I am used to it, can have a business here—so why change around.[1]

In this interview the research worker succeeds in learning the attitudes of the boy towards himself and his family, which are a direct outgrowth of his cultural background.   John brings into the open personal experiences in an objective manner and indicates the sources of cultural conflict and accommodation in a traditional Molokan family.

The Therapeutic Interview.—The therapeutic or treatment interview seeks to redirect the behavior of individuals through a change of attitude.   The following excerpts are an illustration of a therapeutic interview with a woman who is antagonistic to the school and to the medical clinics which her children should attend.[2]

Interview with Mrs. Burton.

(Mrs. Burton had consistently ignored notes from the school nurse to take her daughters to the medical clinic for an examination.   The attendance officer calls at the home.   After rapping the door opened a little way, disclosing a partially dressed, pleasant-looking woman about fifty years old, who immediately became a brusque, irritated person.   She assailed me with a volume of talk, but I let her "get it off her chest.")

Interviewer: Good morning.   Is this where Mrs. Burton lives?

Mrs. Burton: Yes.

Interviewer: Does Charlotte Burton live here?

Mrs. Burton: Yes.

Interviewer: Are you her mother?

[1] *Cf.* Pauline V. Young, *Pilgrims of Russian Town*, pp. 110–113.

[2] Interview held and recorded by Mrs. Gretchen Couch, Glendale, Calif.

Mrs. Burton: Yes, ma'am (irritated).

Interviewer: Mrs. Burton, I am Mrs. C. of the Child Welfare and Attendance Department of the City Schools. Charlotte has been absent from school a great deal lately. I called to see——

Mrs. Burton: I wish you school people would let me alone. You're always wanting excuses, and excuses, and you expect me to do my share, and a whole lot more that I'm not able to do. Charlotte's not well, and neither is Margaret. They haven't shoes, nor clothes fit to be seen in. The plain truth is they don't have even enough to eat some days, and then they are expected to go up there to school every day and be as self-respecting as the rest. Instead of being kind to them, those teachers say, "Why don't you get to school every day? How do you expect to pass when you're out so much?" I tell you, I can't stand any more. (Bang!—the door slammed shut.)

(I decided to wait on the porch a minute. When it seemed quiet, and she had time enough to realize, I hoped, that I had not personally injured her, I rapped again. No answer. I waited another minute, and then I sat on the steps, fumbling through a pack of visitation cards as if to organize my schedule for the next call, and then just sat looking into the street. I decided to rap again. She opened the door wide, but with a cold what-do-you-want look.)

Interviewer: Mrs. Burton, I'm sorry if I've caused you any unpleasantness, but you are a patron of our city schools, a parent of three children worthy of an education. I have called entirely in the interest of those three children. If the school has not met its obligations through its instruction or its management to provide equal opportunities to your children as to other patrons' children, it is time we got together and came to some common understanding of where the trouble lies.

Mrs. Burton: I see, won't you come in?

Interviewer: As a representative of the school, I wish that we could discuss the matter thoroughly, and see what can be done for these girls. I may be taking time from you now that is very valuable, but if you will allow me to call at another time which is entirely satisfactory to you, I shall be glad to come after supper . . .

Mrs. Burton: That's kind of you, Mrs. C. No teacher would go out of her way like that.

Interviewer: I can see, Mrs. Burton, that you haven't met some of our fine teachers, and let me say that it was a teacher who has been concerned over Charlotte's rapid falling off in health as well as her studies, who asked me to call on you.

Mrs. Burton: I'll bet it was Miss G. Charlotte never said anything especially about her.

Interviewer: Your guess is right. Would you want to come to school some time and discuss the whole situation there with her teachers, the nurse—everyone who has contact with Charlotte—or, shall we work out some of the difficulties here first?

Mrs. Burton: Has Charlotte been in any trouble in school?

Interviewer: No, ma'am! We believe that she needs our kindest and most considerate understanding, and realize that she's burdened too heavily with something that is rapidly tearing her down, physically and socially. What is it, Mrs. Burton? What do you think?

Mrs. Burton: (Cries) Children just can't help worrying over troubles in the family, can they?

Interviewer: No, Mrs. Burton, they unconsciously take on the family burden. . . .

Mrs. Burton: . . . Margaret is so irritable, she finds fault with Bobby, and then with Charlotte. But Charlotte just keeps quiet, and does something nice for me when she can do it unnoticed.

Interviewer: Mrs. Burton, what seems to make Margaret so irritable?

Mrs. Burton: Oh, honey, she has a bad ear. She has trouble every winter. That's one reason why I came out here to California. She catches cold so easily, and then that ear, her left one, just gathers up inside like a boil, and her neck swells inside from her ear way down to her collar bone. It hurts her to talk, it hurts her to eat, and she can't even lie down to sleep.

Interviewer: Poor child! That's enough not only to make her irritable, but also to drive her mad. What does the doctor say about it?

Mrs. Burton: I haven't seen a doctor for a long time, 'way last fall. We've hardly had enough to eat, let alone having doctor bills, and she's afraid he'll do something to make it hurt worse.

Interviewer: What does her father think about it?

Mrs. Burton: Her father? He's a brute. He's earning good money. He won't do a thing for one of them because I have them. He made life miserable for all of us back there and I wasn't well after Bobby came. (He's eleven years old now.) I couldn't put up with him any longer with his hot temper and lack of interest in his own children. I've had to support myself all these years, and now that I'm sick and lost my job—there's no income. So you see how much their father cares about them. And then the school expects me to do my part and his too.

Interviewer: You have a heavy burden, Mrs. Burton, and I know that I express the sentiment of the school in personal hope that every legitimate arrangement be made to help you carry this load. . . . Would you be interested in Margaret's having a thorough physical examination at the Health Clinic downtown? That is one of the benefits to which every person in our community is entitled, for the sake of public health. One free thorough examination a year. . . .

Mrs. Burton: I don't want any charity, you understand.

Interviewer: It isn't a charity proposition. Like your mail, it's there for you, but you must go to get it yourself. You see, it safeguards the public health indirectly; if people with ailments which need diagnosis wish to do their part not only to safeguard their own future health and efficiency, but at the same time to remove possible carrying of disease in society to some less fortunate, we soon overcome certain diseases. . . .

Mrs. Burton: What's the use of such a general looking over?

Interviewer: If the general examination shows need of a more thorough special examination, for eye or ear trouble, lung condition, kidney infection, the examining physician recommends such further examination by the specialists in that field. . . . So Margaret will no doubt be recommended to one of our eye, ear, nose, and throat specialists to determine her condition and what attention she needs. . . . Whatever the specialists recommend, you're at liberty to follow or not, as you think best. Should he recommend an operation, and you felt unable to pay the price for it, the Clinic may take it up with the medical social adviser.

Mrs. Burton: I've hated to ask for any such help. I've paid my bills and never ran any except as I knew that I could pay. If I knew I would have work soon . . .

Interviewer: Don't you rather question the advisability of letting Margaret's condition ride much longer without knowing what the Clinic doctors find in their diagnosis of her condition? There could be a long time afterward for one to regret that even this much, which is possible now, hadn't been done to guide proper action in her behalf.

Mrs. Burton: How can I take care of this matter?

Interviewer: If it would help matters any for you, I shall be glad to give you a card of introduction to the Clinic. Once introduced, you'll be directed from then on by them. . . .

Mrs. Burton: I'll take Margaret down tomorrow morning. What should I do now about Charlotte?

Interviewer: Why don't you take her with you? You say she's not well. The school nurse finds that she's losing weight.

Mrs. Burton: No better time than now. Thank the Lord, Bob's all right. While I'm there I'll ask about my shoulder muscles. That's why I lost my last job. (Weepy.) My arms and hands seem to paralyze, and I dropped too many dishes and broke them. The rent is due now, and I don't know what to do if I can't even earn our food. . . .

Interviewer: Maybe a thorough physical examination will help you get at the cause of it. And, if your finances don't permit bare living costs, why not call on Miss L. of the A. Welfare Department, and ask if there is a way to be tided over to a time when your good health will permit you to hold a job again. (Left card of introduction to Miss L.) Your family's health is of first importance now, rather than the question "When shall I work again?" . . . There are a few other matters about adjusting the girls' programs at school which I'd like to discuss with you at another time. Wouldn't you think it best that we clear up these health matters first, and ways will open for adjusting the school situation later?

Mrs. Burton: (Assent.)

Interviewer: If you wish, I shall notify the school that the girls will not be there tomorrow, and that your conference with the doctors will probably determine all that shall be best for the girls' school progress? (Agreed.) May I call to see you regarding this, after your clinical visit?

The interviewer through careful and patient planning was able to explain to Mrs. Burton the source of the girl's difficulties, to indicate the advantages of a medical examination and to change her attitude towards the school and free clinics. The social treatment in this interview lies primarily in (1) providing an opportunity for mental release through sympathetic interest; (2) in supplying certain information to the client which served as

a basis for seeing the situation in a different light; **and** (3)
in motivating the client to meet an urgent medical problem
promptly.

The Group Interview.[1]—The group interview or, as it is
sometimes called, the "collective interview,"[2] is frequently used
in social case work and social research work alike when the
interviewer informally gathers together several members of a
family or a social group to discuss common problems. Group
discussion may bring out points which otherwise might not
have come to the surface, and the information obtained may
come much more quickly and with fewer inhibitions than if
each member had been interviewed separately. The group
interview may disclose either uniformity and harmony of thought
and action or diversity and disharmony. The extent of either
may best be gauged during the interaction of the various members present. Thrasher points out also that in gang activities
suggestion by the interviewer and a few leading supporters are
likely to turn the gang in any direction during the collective
interview. Change of attitude in such an interview "grows out
of intercommunication which proceeds at a rapid rate in such a
group until unanimity on some particular policy is arrived at."[3]
Thus the group interview may be used for diagnostic, research
or treatment purposes. The following interview, reported by
Clifford R. Shaw, is an illustration of the group interview with
several relatives of a delinquent boy. In this interview the
interviewer seeks to establish the significance of the relation
between the various members of the family and the delinquent
boy:

Interviewer: Mr. . . . , I have come here to see you in regard to Nick.
I understand that you are having some difficulty with him.

Father: Nick is a ver' bad boy. I have ten kids (pointing to the children
who were standing in the room), but Nick causes lots of trouble. He run
away, fights, steal, and wants to play all day. He lazy, won't work, and
. . .

Married Daughter: Nick is awful bad. He swears at me and hits me and
talks awful bad. He swears at his mother and won't do a thing she tells

---

[1] E. S. BOGARDUS, *The New Social Research*, pp. 92–106.
[2] F. M. THRASHER, "How to Study a Boys' Gang in the Open," *Journal
of Educational Sociology*, I (January, 1928), 244–254.
[3] *Ibid.*, p. 253.

him. He fights her, even strikes her and calls her names, something awful. You should hear him cussing and swearing at his mother and father. You wouldn't believe it if you wouldn't hear him. Yes, and he steals; he stole two dollars and bought a ball glove once. He took the money from his mother. He's always running off with other boys without askin' his ma. Now, what can you do with such a boy? He's got a good job working in his uncle's restaurant, but we have to beat him to make him work there, and he whines and complains that the work is too hard and he don't want to work there. He's stubborn and bullheaded and lazy. It's a good job and he could learn the business and the uncle would treat him swell. He only makes excuses not to work, but pa beats him and makes him work.

Mother: I have a big family and have to work hard washin', but Nick he want to loaf around and run away with other boys. I lick him, but he swears back and runs off again. I afraid he be learning to steal with them. He don't work; my husband has heart trouble and can't work much. He lies lots and steals. Maybe you scare him, mister, so he work.

Married Daughter: You can't believe a word he says. He's a big liar and—

Boy: (Interrupting). Yes! You're the liar. You don't need to stick in. Why don't you go home and take him (pointing to brother-in-law) with you? You make me—

Married Daughter: You see how he talks back. You should hear him when he swears at his mother. It's awful the way he swears at his parents.

Boy: Shut up, you hain't got anything in this. You don't live here. Why don't you go home where you belong?

Married Daughter: He was always wanting me to cook him a good dinner. One day I told him I would cook him a good meal. He wanted to help and asked if he couldn't go to the store for me and acted so nice. But as soon as he'd got his belly full then he began to cuss me and talk mean to me. That's the way he is. He can be awful nice if he wants you to do somethin' for him, but then he turns around and cusses you afterwards. I won't have anything to do with him.

Boy: She lies. I don't want anything to do with her either. I never will make up with her.

Mother: And the worst part is, Eddie who is only twelve do everythin' just like Nick do. Eddie is a good boy now, but I afraid he learn bad things if Nick keep on being bad.

Boy: Yes; you just think Eddie ain't bad. What did he do to Irish the other day? He tripped him and hurt his face when he fell and then Eddie just laughed. I guess he's just as bad as I am. You all think the other kids are angels and that I'm the only one that's bad. You're all against me.

Married Daughter: We wouldn't be against you if you would be good and work. You're always fighting and cussing. You're the cause of all the trouble around the house.

Boy: You're always talking against me and making fun of me. Nobody likes me here. You're all against me. I don't want to stay around here. I can't do anything I want to do. Irish (a chum) don't have to work. He can do anything he wants to. Nobody always hollers at him. I don't see why I can't play ball and not work in an old restaurant all day.

Married Sister: (Sarcastically). Why, you've got an easy job. You don't have to do much. It don't amount to much, what you do. You're just lazy and want to play all day. What do you care what Irish does? He's a bum and you'll be just like him.

Boy: (Retorting). Oh, you don't know anything about my work. You wouldn't think it was easy if you had to do it all day. Why don't you do a little work? You're always sticking your nose in. You've got a big mouth.

Married Daughter: Have I? Well, I'll slap yours, if you get too fresh. If I can't, my husband can. You're too fresh, you little bum. You're just like the lazy bums you run with. You're good to them but cuss your own father and mother. You need a good beating. Everybody's too good to you.

Brother-in-law: He (referring to Nick) talks too much, don't know how to mind. He needs somebody with a strong arm to handle him a while. His parents let him play with them. He's got a hot head. I'd take it out of him if I lived with him. I have beat him a few times, but you'd have to kill him to break him. But he needs it.

My father was strict with me in the old country. He knowed how to lick. There the kid has to mind or be killed by beating. My father's word was the law there.

There the married sons usually live at home with the father. It is like one big family, but the father rules everything. Believe me, he rules, too. Mine did. All the money that is earned is turned over to the father. The father is very strict and whips his kids lots if they don't mind. If I had done like the kid (referring to Nick) my father would beat me to death. That's the reason they obey there and don't steal and get into trouble. They are afraid of the father. I was terribly afraid of mine. When the old man dies, the oldest son runs things. If he is good and the brothers like him they stay, but if he is too mean or their wives don't like to obey him, they will leave.

There the boy has to work. Why should this kid (Nick) play ball all day and not work and help his father? If we don't beat him he won't mind and will grow up to be a thief or kill somebody. He already is a bum. I've tried to help the parents out by whipping him. I've given him several good beatings for quarreling and fighting. He needs more of it and harder.

Boy: Yes! You are not my boss. You have no right to whip me. I don't have to mind you. You can't make me mind you. I'm not going to be bossed around by you. Why don't you go on home and take care of your own business? You're always sticking your nose in.

They are all against me. They hate me around here. They don't want me to have any fun, just work. This hain't like any home. They are all against me. (Boy cries.)

Married Sister: You baby, you'd better cry. It'll be better for you to cry instead of stealing and fighting so much.

Boy: Shut up. You're always sassing.

Married Daughter: I've seen you cry before; it doesn't worry me. You'll be beating somebody the next minute.

Mother: Mister, see Nick has a hot temper. He fight and quarrel with everybody, like you see.

Boy: Oh! you're all against me.   You make me feel like killing somebody. You don't want me here.

Married Daughter: Yes; you'll be a murderer, running with them little Irish bums.   What did we tell you?   You're just like them, want to be a lazy bum.   We don't want you to disgrace our family.   You're the only bum in the family.

Brother-in-law: He seems to think that he doesn't need to work, but just bum off of the family.   He ought to have my father for a little while in the old country.   He'd make a man out of him.   They're too easy with him here.   He runs everybody around here but me.   I gave him a good trimming the other night.

Boy: I'll get you some of these days!   If I were bigger, I'd get you now. I'll lay you out!

(At this point everybody laughed, and Nick became very angry and rushed out of the house into the back yard.   As he was leaving he cursed his parents and said: "You are all against me and hate me!   I'll kill you! I'll run away and never come back!")

Married Daughter: You see how mean he is.   He is liable to kill somebody.   He's dangerous!   Won't you have him arrested?

Mother: Mister, please scare Nick.   He very bad boy.   We no can make good boy him.

Father: I lick him many times hard with club.   Think sometimes I kill him.   No good.   He very bad.   Just like Irish bum kids.   No work, wanta play.   That is bad.

Mother: Mister, I got ten kids, work hard, lots a' worry.   I lick Nick hard every day.   Father lick him; brother-in-law lick him; sister lick him; everybody lick him.   Still he bad boy; say he kill all us.   Mister, he bad boy; scare him, Mister, please.   Tell him, "Nick, work or I'll put you in jail for long time."   Then he be good, maybe![1]

Dr. Park's remarks on the above type of interview are of importance:

. . . The materials upon which Shaw's study were based were elicited in what amounted to an informal trial, in which the members of the family were the accusers and the delinquent boy the accused, the investigator acting in the role of the court.   As a matter of fact, the procedure in getting the materials for case histories of this sort is not unlike the more formal proceeding of the French criminal courts, where the accuser and the accused are brought face to face and invited to substantiate, by question and answer, each his own side of the case.   Under circumstances such as these, in which all the actors are actively engaged, not only the language but the accents and gestures of the participants are significant, and, as far as possible, made a part of the record.

The difference in the procedure begins after the informal court has adjourned and the record is completed.   Since inquiry thus instituted

[1] CLIFFORD R. SHAW and HENRY McKAY, *Social Factors in Juvenile Delinquency*, pp. 15–19.

is not a judicial proceeding and the "family interview" is not evidence but merely a record of behavior, it is not made the basis of a legal proceeding, but, together with the mental tests and psychiatric record, furnishes a basis of a social diagnosis.[1]

Suggestions for Further Study

1. Differentiate between functional types of interviews and nonfunctional types.

2. Secure a diagnostic interview and indicate what data are essential to the understanding of the needs, resources, and possibilities of the case.

3. Secure a diagnostic interview in which all face-sheet information was obtained indirectly in the course of conversation regarding the general social situation of the interviewee.

4. Write a critique of the interview with Mr. Walker, pointing out (a) whether the interviewer's questions actually aimed at securing diagnostic information, (b) whether the questions were tactful and noncompromising, (c) and whether the interviewer failed to follow up important clues which came to the surface in the process of the interview.

5. Point out the essential differences between this interview and those held by members of your agency (provided the latter are reported in similar form).

6. Write a sociological analysis of the interview with Mr. Walker.

7. In what essential respects does the interview with Mr. Walker differ from that of John Yablokoff?

8. Write a critique of the interviewing technique used in the interview with John Yablokoff.

9. What social factors enter into the interview with Mrs. Burton which did not appear in the above two interviews?

10. Write a critique of the technique used in the interview with Mrs. Burton and note particularly: (a) Is the interviewer participating in the thinking of Mrs. Burton? (b) Is Mrs. Burton participating in the planning? (c) Does Mrs. Burton fully understand the proposals made to her? (d) Are the proposals and plan consistent? How could the interviewer motivate Mrs. Burton to lay her own plans?

11. Obtain a treatment interview, record it carefully in dialogue form. Indicate the treatment elements used and their degree of success in accomplishing your goal.

12. Find diagnostic factors in the treatment and research interviews and treatment factors in the diagnostic and research interviews listed above.

13. What is an interview of persuasion? Find instances of persuasion in the above three interviews.

14. Read Jean Lucas' "The Interview of Persuasion" and Porter Lee's "A Study of Social Treatment" (consult general bibliography), then secure a verbatim interview of persuasion and indicate the executive and leadership phases of treatment.

15. What outstanding features do you observe about the group interview reported by Clifford R. Shaw?

[1] Wilson Gee (Editor), *Research in the Social Sciences*, pp. 45–46.

16. Are Dr. Park's remarks applicable to the diagnostic interview held with Mr. Walker?

Selected Bibliography

1. BOGARDUS, E. S.: *The New Social Research*, 1926.
   Chap. IV, "The Group Interview," is a means to the study of public opinion, race relations, and social distance between social groups, between social work leaders and community leaders.
2. LUCAS, JEAN: "The Interview of Persuasion," *The Family*, V (July, 1924).
   The interview of persuasion—through effective leadership of worker—is a key to treatment.
3. MOWRER, E. R.: *Domestic Discord*, 1928.
   Chap. V, "The Interview Process," is a good discussion of the types of interviews in social case work.
4. RICHMOND, MARY E.: *Social Diagnosis*, 1927.
   Chap. XVIII, "Comparison and Interpretation," is a good discussion of the logic of the diagnostic interview.
5. SHAW, CLIFFORD R., and HENRY McKAY: *Social Factors in Juvenile Delinquency* (National Commission on Law Observance and Enforcement, Vol. II, No. 13), 1931.
   Presents excellent verbatim interviews of the research and group types. Pp. 4–20; 109–130; 200–253; 285–343; 347–480.
6. THRASHER, F. M.: "How to Study a Boys' Gang in the Open," *Journal of Educational Sociology*, I (January, 1928).
   Points to an approach to the study of gang life on a collective basis.
7. YOUNG, PAULINE V.: *Pilgrims of Russian Town*, 1932.
   Shows character of life history material secured by confessional interview.

CHAPTER III

THE TECHNIQUE OF THE INTERVIEW

The Traditional First Interview[1] and Changing Conceptions in Social Case Work.—The first interview[2] is frequently regarded as a means of getting the history of a person's or family's background, relations, problems, social attitudes, and values. Too little *rapport* and confidence can be won, however, at a first meeting to eliminate direct questioning and the eliciting of information regarding the events of a lifetime. Furthermore, an applicant for financial relief is required to give references of employers, landlords, relatives, etc. Being scarcely acquainted with the interviewer, many applicants feel that they are regarded with suspicion. "The really intimate and enlightening revelations are given when the client feels a need to reveal himself,

---

[1] The following suggestions regarding the technical use of the interview are necessarily general. Their applicability to specific situations needs to be checked in the light of particular circumstances governing each case. It may be remarked that there are as many interviewing techniques as there are interviewing situations. Miss Richmond points out the following circumstances which modify the technique of the first interview:

(*a*) The nature of the task about to be undertaken, whether probation work, family work, protection from cruelty, etc.

(*b*) The origin of the application or request for service; whether from an agency or individual already interested, or from an applicant on his own behalf.

(*c*) The place of the interview, whether in the client's own home or at the social agency's office.

(*d*) The recorded experience available. Any possible previous record in the agency's files concerning either the person applying or others of his family. (Search should be made for such a record before the First Interview and again after its close.) *Social Diagnosis*, p. 132.

[2] See Mary E. Richmond, *Social Diagnosis*, pp. 103–133.

Beatrice Z. Levey, "The Extent of the Intake Interview," *The Family*, XIV (December, 1933). See also *Interviews, Interviewers, and Interviewing in Social Case Work, passim.*

Louise Odencrantz, *The Social Worker*, Chap. II.

Bessie A. McClenahan, *Social Case Work—Theory and Practice* (mimeographed), pp. 34 *ff.*

Helen P. Kempton, "The First Contact," *The Family*, XIII (June, 1932), 111–115.

when he perceives that solution of his difficulty hinges on a mutual understanding of past events; or they are offered spontaneously when he knows and trusts the worker."[1] This may occur during the first visit though in reality it is rarely the case.

It would appear, therefore, that the first interview, particularly where serious problems are involved, should be a means of getting acquainted, of providing the client with an opportunity to understand the objectives of the interview, the policies of the agency, and the value of the own story, and of giving the visitor a chance to understand the tempo of the client. It is of interest that the psychoanalytic interviewer, though dealing with people under tension and often ready to talk, does not plan to inform himself regarding the patient's past in the first visit. In recent years, a client's total conception of his rôle, of the relations he maintains with others, of his attitudes and values, wishes and ambitions—conditioned by his environment past and present—has assumed far greater significance than a recital of isolated events, often elicited by direct questioning and colored by the emotional situation of a first encounter.

Miss Richmond pointed out a long time ago that "there are no short cuts to diagnosis" and that the longest road, paradoxically enough, is often the shortest. Diagnostic information may be secured in a first interview, but more frequently it is wiser to defer the securing of such information until subsequent visits.

The following discussion of the technique of interviewing has little or no reference to the order of interviews, as it is quite conceivable that what might be accomplished in the first contact with certain types of interviewees and in certain types of interviewing situations must be left for subsequent contacts in other instances. Certain general stages, however, are found to be present in many interviewing situations; there is a preparatory phase for the interview, the interview proper, the closing of the interview, and so on.

Preparatory Thinking.—It is best to plan each interview, whether diagnostic or treatment, in advance, according to its unique circumstances. "Plan your interview, but keep mind and plan flexible," says Mary Brisley.[2] Accidental findings and

[1] ELEANOR NEUSTAEDTER, "The Rôle of the Case Worker in Treatment," *The Family*, XIII (July, 1932), 153.

[2] "An Attempt to Articulate Processes," *The Family*, V (October, 1924), 158.

new developments may prove to be as important as those which have been foreseen. The interviewer needs to know very clearly the specific reason for interviewing particular persons; he needs to plan in advance what he is going to ask. Dean Dunham of the Harvard School of Business quotes a salesman's remark:

> I would rather walk the sidewalk in front of a man's office for two hours before an interview than to step into his office without a perfectly clear idea of what I am going to say and what he—from my knowledge of his interests and motives—is likely to answer.[1]

Just as a successful teacher maps out in advance the course a class discussion should take, so the investigator in any field of endeavor will find it advisable to anticipate the probable course of the interview, to pin down at least the main topics to be covered and the ways in which they are to be approached. They all economize time and get better results by planning the interview carefully.[2]

Before going out on a case it is best to concentrate on such facts as one may already know and give attention to: the problems of personality (egocentric, introvert, extrovert, etc.); habitual modes of response (opposition, defense mechanism, give and take, etc.); the social problems (poor health, lack of regular income, or limited intelligence of parents); the assets (interested relatives, loyal children, strong ties between husband and wife); the liabilities which may handicap readjustment (lack of confidence in medicine, work shyness, lack of desire to improve, etc.)

Neighbors reported that Mrs. D. was cruelly abusing her fourteen-year-old boy and suggested an investigation by the Child Welfare Department of the X Agency. Before going out on the case I learned from the school that (1) the boy, Almo, was "one of their most brilliant and promising students," that (2) Mrs. D was "hard to deal with" because she is "suspicious," "egocentric," "always on the defensive"; that (3) the family are poverty stricken and in need of food which (4) they will not accept from "charity."

How does one prepare himself to interview this type of family? It had been suggested to "file on the mother" for cruelty to her child. Obviously, this type of procedure is unreasonable for: (1) the report of the neighbors may be false; (2) the mother may

---

[1] "What to Do If You Want to Sit at the Boss's Desk," *American Magazine*, XCIII (February, 1922), 73.

[2] Walter V. Bingham and Bruce Moore, *op. cit.*, p. 17.

think she is performing her highest duties to the boy by means of severe punishment; (3) court procedure may destroy all possible future constructive dealings with the mother; (4) personal, friendly relations may accomplish more than legal action.

Having weighed these factors carefully one still asks: "How am I going to approach Mrs. D. and what am I going to tell her as to the reason of the interview? I can't bluntly tell her of the neighbor's report?"

It was decided to approach Mrs. D. on the basis of the school's interest in the brilliant boy: "Your boy has distinguished himself at school. He is doing excellent work. . . . But our experience is that these brilliant youngsters are hard to handle at home. . . . There is generally some problem which they present. . . . Tell me, if you don't mind, what problems does Almo present?"

In view of the fact that Mrs. D. is hard to deal with, the interviewer took special precautions to be friendly, to be tactful, to overlook defense mechanisms, and to phrase her statements in such a way as to eliminate any possible feeling on the part of Mrs. D. that she is to blame for any friction with her son.

The interviewer through her preparatory thinking created an impartial—though highly friendly—attitude toward Mrs. D. and by the time she arrived at the home of Mrs. D., the interviewer felt more or less acquainted with the problems of the family and could discuss them with a certain degree of sympathetic insight.

Gathering Clues.—Wherever possible the interviewer should fortify himself in advance with as much information about the interviewee as is available to him. In the case of families known to social agencies, their case histories should be carefully read (1) to avoid duplication of work on the part of the interviewer, (2) to relieve the families from the embarrassment of going over the same ground, which in some instances may induce the family to frame a set story. However, previous case histories should be read with caution as biases and prejudices against a family may have been accumulated in the course of long contact with several visitors, each one of whom might have viewed the problems of the family from a different standpoint. The interviewer may carry the facts in mind but he should be free of any emotional coloring and he should be ready to reevaluate the facts. Of course, the source of information should not be disclosed to the interviewee, as numerous compromising situations might result.[1]

I find it valuable to get a "line" on a family from case records of social agencies, keeping in mind, however, only certain concrete facts, pointers, so to speak and thereby I could find my way more easily when talking to them. . . . I guard myself against jumping to conclusions and against being prejudiced in any way toward the interviewee by what I may read in a court record or a social case history. I never disclose my source but proceed in the usual manner. In most instances it saves time to read a previous case-history, and intelligent follow-up work is thus made possible.[2]

When interviewing executives, officials, or persons of reputation, biographical sketches in such works as *Who's Who* may be consulted. If they have written on the subject under investigation, the interviewer will find it expedient to acquaint himself with their points of view.

Executives and people of note are hard to interview because they know how to evade the question which they do not like to answer. If I am acquainted with their point of view, their hobbies or accomplishments, I can approach them from different angles and can often "pin them down" to something which they will talk about.[3]

It is said of Colonel Edward House, "the silent partner" of Woodrow Wilson, that he

. . . was able to gear his every word, his every action to the man he wanted to win. He understood *all* the points of difference which set him apart from others:
The traits of his character, his capacities—
The things he wanted: his problems and his prejudices—
His special interest, his achievements and his hobbies.
It is no wonder that the German was swept off his feet.
He yielded to Colonel House's strategy, to his "personality," as hundreds of other men had yielded before him—in the same way and for the same reason.[4]

The Place of the Interview.—It is generally agreed that the best place for the interview is where "the sense of strangeness

[1] See Chap. IX. See also

BEATRICE WEBB, *Methods of Social Science*, Chap. VI, "The Spoken Word."

[2] Statement by a family welfare worker.

[3] Statement by a research worker.

[4] E. T. WEBB and J. B. MORGAN, *Strategy in Handling People*, pp. 151–152.

may be worn away most quickly." Mary Richmond
observes:

The place in which the First Interview is held depends in part upon
the nature of the task and its origin, but not wholly upon these. Societies dealing with questions of family relief and, in these later days,
with family rebuilding, have changed their policy several times with
regard to the place of the interview. Following the line of least resistance, the older type of worker usually conducted First Interviews at
his office desk, with record form before him and pen in hand. He asked
each question in the order indicated by the items on the form, and filled
in a short summary of the perfunctory reply before going on to the next:
Assistance asked? "Coal and groceries." Cause of need? "Out of
work." Any relatives able to assist? "No."

As a reaction against this stupid compiling of misleading items, many
American case workers have abandoned the office interview, except in
emergencies and in dealing with the homeless. It is their practice to
take only time enough, when application is made at the office, to assure
themselves that treatment is probably needed, and then promptly to
make a visit to the home, where, in an unhurried talk, the basis is laid
for further acquaintance.

The arguments in favor of holding the First Interview in the home
instead of in the office are, in family work, (a) Its challenge to the case
worker at the outset to establish a human relation, at the risk, if he
fail, of coming away without the simplest and most elementary data.
In the office, clients are on the defensive and justify their visits by their
replies. In the home, the social worker is on the defensive; the host
and hostess are at their ease. (b) Its avoidance of the need of so many
questions, some of which are answered unasked by the communicative
hostess and by her surroundings. To the quiet observer the photographs on the wall, the framed certificates of membership in fraternal
orders, the pensioner's war relics, the Sunday school books, the household arrangements are all eloquent. And far more revealing than these
material items are the apparent relations of the members of the household to one another—the whole atmosphere of the home. (c) Its provision of natural openings for a frank exchange of experiences. "The
great facts of birth and death alone are sufficient to make the whole
world kin," and these and the universally interesting comparison of
diseases form a good basis for that kind of informal intercourse which
belongs to the fireside. Then, if some of the children are present for a
part of the time at least, there is a good chance for comparing notes
about brothers and sisters, their ages, names, namesakes, etc. (d)
Its further emphasis upon the personal side when there has been no
visit by the client to an office, but when his situation has been reported

there instead by others; its relegation of official paraphernalia and attitudes, in such instances at least, to the rear. . . .

Some interviews are best held on neutral ground, as at a settlement or some other neighborhood center. A children's worker describes a painful interview with a domestic who had applied to have her child boarded out, held in the front room of the house in which she was at service. It happened to be a doctor's office, and she was so fearful of the return of the doctor that it was impossible to get her to talk freely. The interview should have been postponed to some other time and place. . . .

The preoccupation of the client with the immediate crisis is one of the things to be avoided in the choice of a place; no conditions should interfere with our efforts to lead his mind back to the events that will reveal the deeper-seated difficulties of his life, and forward to the possible ways out. In so far as the home and its familiar objects suggest the more normal aspects of his life, they are a great help. Some places in their very nature emphasize the crisis—a court room does, or the waiting room of a busy relief bureau. This emphasis is a barrier between case worker and client.[1]

Jessie Taft, whose interviews are leisurely and informal, is in favor of the office interview since the subject is thereby removed from practical situations in which he is involved.[2] Practically all writers on the technique of interviewing advocate strict privacy, with no one else present, and with few distracting articles in the room. Clifford R. Shaw, however, holds his interviews, both with single individuals and with several members of a family, in the presence of a stenographer—whose function he explains to the interviewees. Judging by the character of the life histories obtained one may conclude that Mr. Shaw has been highly successful in his approach to the interview. Psychiatrists also specify not only strict privacy but also relaxation, comfort, quiet, and the use of formal office environment.

Pertaining to the privacy of the interview, Beatrice Webb, famous English investigator and writer on labor problems, states:

Regarded as a method of investigation the process of interviewing is a particular form of psychoanalysis. From within the consciousness or subconsciousness of another mind, the practicioner has to ferret out

[1] MARY E. RICHMOND, *Social Diagnosis*, pp. 106–110. Reprinted by permission of Russell Sage Foundation.

[2] JESSIE TAFT, "The Function of a Mental Hygienist in a Children's Agency," *Proceedings of the National Conference of Social Work*, 1927, pp. 392–399.

memories of past experiences—"orders of thought"—corresponding with "orders of things." . . . You may easily inhibit free communication, or prevent the rise to consciousness of significant facts, by arousing suspicion. . . . Except in cases in which your client is not merely according an interview but is consciously cooperating in your investigation, it is a mistake to bring a secretary or other colleague. Caution is increased when a man perceives that his words are being "witnessed." . . .

Bear in mind that it is desirable to make the interview pleasing to the persons interviewed. It should seem to him or her an agreeable form of social intercourse. I remember, in one of my early adventures in "wholesale interviewing" with a whole party, even telling fortunes from their hands, with all sorts of interesting results! Without this atmosphere of relaxation, of amused interest on both sides, it will often be impracticable to get at those intimate details of daily experience which are the most valuable data of the sociologist. Hence a spirit of adventure, a delight in watching human beings, as human beings quite apart from what you can get out of their minds, an enjoyment of the play of your own personality with that of another, are gifts of rare value in the art of interviewing; and gifts which are, I think, more characteristic of the woman than the man.[1]

George A. Lundberg observes:

For most interviews, privacy is highly desirable, though the importance of this varies with the nature of the interview. When personal data are sought, the presence of other people is almost always inhibitory. For such interviews, the office of the interviewer is an inhibitor through the suggestion of officialdom. Where personal revelations are desired, places most removed from the social hitchings of the informant—the camp, woods, etc. yield the best results. There are other types of interviews which can best be carried out in the office of the person interviewed, where records and corroborative material are available. The place and environment in which the interview takes place must be governed by the nature of the interview and the practical considerations involved.[2]

Proper Introduction.—The interviewer owes the interviewee a proper introduction of himself and of the agency represented, and whenever possible he should tell why the interview is sought. It may be sufficient to telephone or write directly to the interviewee and arrange to be expected. Appointments previously made should be as specific as possible. The interviewer need

[1] BEATRICE WEBB, *My Apprenticeship*, pp. 424 *ff*.
[2] *Social Research: A Study in Methods of Gathering Data*, pp. 152–153.

then only arrive at the agreed upon time and place to be recognized as soon as he gives his name. An appointment

. . . avoids the antagonistic attitude which is frequently, and justly, aroused by the attempt of anyone to "break in" when the prospective informant is engaged in other work. Ordinarily, a request by letter for an interview is preferable to a request by telephone, as the former permits a more adequate statement of the purpose for which the interview is desired, the auspices under which the inquiry is undertaken, and other matters designed to insure the granting of the interview and a favorable reception. . . . [1]

Some knowledge of the daily routine of the interviewee is essential if a proper time and place are to be chosen. Preoccupation with other immediate interests and interruptions are to be avoided. It must not be assumed that, when dealing with workmen or with housewives, it is not necessary to consider carefully questions of convenience and convention. Even those who have time and who place little weight on convention will generally appreciate the gesture of politeness. The necessity of postponing a given interview to a more convenient time should be foreseen by the interviewer, and the proposal should originate with him. Readiness to withdraw, to forego the interview entirely, frequently brings proposals to proceed with the interview immediately; at least, a foundation can be laid for a subsequent interview.

Many of my research interviews were held with immigrant boys at the school, whose parents I did not know. If the latter were to be interviewed later, I told the boy that I should like to meet his parents. I was anxious to meet them, I said, because I too was an immigrant, had my struggles when I came to this country, and added that I can speak their language. "Why, sure, come along. My parents will be glad to see you." But that was not sufficient for an invitation into the home. I gave the boy my telephone number asking him to let me know *when* his parents could see me. Only in two instances did I fail to hear from the boy or the parents. In the case of the older people whom I could not reach through the school-boy I asked a previous acquaintance to introduce me, or speak of me, or I came to church services and made my appointments on a wholesale scale. In each case I was expected.[2]

[1] GEORGE A. LUNDBERG, *op. cit.*, p. 152.
[2] Statement by a research interviewer.

The interviewer should make certain that he has been properly identified by the interviewee. Formal credentials, such as to-whom-it-may-concern letters, should be used sparingly, but means for positively but gracefully identifying oneself should not be neglected.

Manner of Greeting.—Frequently field investigators, seeing many people in the course of one day, forget that their visit may be the only one paid to a particular client in a period of several days, and neglect to greet him in a more than cursory businesslike manner. Clients have volunteered the following information:

I like this visitor because she always makes me feel as if she were glad to see me.

She kind-a cheers you up. . . .

I'd rather talk to her than anyone else, because she starts me out right by her warm greetings. . . .

You kind-a feel she won't "high-hat-you" or snub you when she shakes hands with you so heartily.

Interviewers who aim to influence others can hardly afford to be fastidious, or to use forced smiles or assume a forced cordiality. It is said that Theodore Roosevelt's great popularity was attributed to his ability to "beam all over" and be "dee-lighted" as he greeted each farmer and shoemaker as a long lost friend.[1]

Journalists who must constantly face strangers agree that nothing can take the place of a smile in showing people that you intend to be cordial. "A smile often counts for more than a thousand words a minute." Experienced investigators maintain that with a cordial, friendly smile they can often discuss difficult personal problems with reticent interviewers. Richard Harris gives the following hints to cross-examiners:

. . . With regard to manner, a man should imitate the best. The most eminent are as a rule the most unaffected, and the quiet, moderate manner is generally the most effective. I do not intend to imply that bluster and a high tone will not sometimes unnerve a timid witness, but this is not cross-examination or true advocacy. It is not art, but bullying—not intellectual power, but mere physical momentum. Nor would I say that an advocate should at all times treat a witness with the gentleness of a dove. Severity of tone and manner, compatible with self-respect, is frequently necessary to keep a witness in check, and to draw or drive the truth out of him if he have any. But the severity will lose none of its force, nay, it will receive an increase of it,

[1] WILLIAM LAWRENCE, *Henry Cabot Lodge*, p. 109.

by being furnished with the polish of courtesy instead of roughened with the language of uncompromising rudeness.   Instances of the latter kind are extremely rare at the English bar.   But they do occasionally appear, and are usually followed by a public outcry against them; they do not, however, cast discredit on the great body of a profession which is as jealous of its high reputation for courtesy and honor as it is deserving of it.[1]

Facial Expression.—Some interviewers maintain that they find it best to use a "poker face," which reveals few or no traces of their emotional reactions to the story; others, however, have found that such a rigid poise is irritating to the person who searches in the listener's face for traces of interest.

It is curious and interesting that this character which we call human should be so intimately connected with expressiveness.   Human interests, as we ordinarily use the phrase, attaches to anything that is "expressive," that is, to anything that suggests, symbolizes or reveals sentiments and passions in others of which we are immediately conscious in ourselves.   The faces we know have no secret for us.   For that reason, if for no other, we feel secure and at home with them as we do not among less familiar faces. . . . One of the first and most important discoveries that one who meets an alien people for the first time is likely to make, is that, different as they seem, most strange people, when we come to know them, turn out to be human like ourselves.   It always requires an effort of the imagination to realize this.   It is because their faces are for us not expressive; and we, in turn, do not respond to sentiments whose expression we are not able to read.[2]

The problem of facial expression must be viewed from two standpoints: (1) Will the expression of face tend to alter the story, or (2) will it tend to stimulate the narrator to disclose himself and lay aside the mask behind which his true self is hidden?   In every case, however, definite interest in the story should be shown.

The interviewee's facial expression must be closely watched. An embarrassed blush, an unconscious wince, or an argumentative tone of voice often disclose sore spots which should be either carefully avoided or tactfully explored.   The interviewer who can tell by the interviewee's face when to leave or what points

[1] *Hints on Advocacy* (Amer. ed., 1892), p. 29.   Quoted by J. H. WIGMORE, *The Principles of Judicial Proof*, p. 501.

[2] ROBERT E. PARK, "Behind Our Masks," *The Survey Graphic*, LXI (May, 1926), 138.

to stress or what to omit from the interview is indeed very fortunate. Such reading of faces can be cultivated by prolonged interviewing experience.

Personal Appearance.—The interviewer must pay some attention to personal appearance. Within considerable limits it is possible for the interviewer to adopt a mode of dress suitable to the particular situation. The attention of the interviewee should not be attracted to the interviewer's dress or manner. Peculiarity of dress, manner, speech may be not only distracting but irritating to some interviewees. Outward appearance may serve as an external symbol by which we often classify and judge each other. It should serve to identify the interviewer in the interviewee's mind as his own kind.

It is not necessary for the worker to dress dowdily, but extremes of fashion, sleeveless dresses and exaggerated skirt lengths, pronounced make-up, etc. will alienate the public to such an extent that good work simply cannot compensate for it. Work day clothes may be suitable to business and at the same time stylish and attractive. Party gowns are evidence of poor taste when worn in the working world, particularly so when the worker is doing social work. Ultra-expensive garments, even though entirely suitable to the street, seem out of place in such work as ours.[1]

The Interviewing Approach

In interviews in which the interviewer has been sought out, the problem of approach is at times made difficult by what may be called the application complex. The story which the interviewee believes will secure him needed assistance is already framed up in his mind, that is, his relation to the interviewer is more or less sharply defined in his own mind. Considerable skill will be required in such cases to bring the interview to the level of easy and free conversation. It may be wise for the interviewer at first to take the active lead in the conversation, spending time on conventional matters, turning attention to subjects not immediately connected with the subject at hand. Exchanging experiences or discussing incidental happenings may serve to get the interviewer accepted in a more casual, friendly manner.

All the men and women we meet, no matter how important, no matter how humble, enjoy the *right kind* of compliment. It gives

[1] Adapted from *Office Manual*, Los Angeles Travelers' Aid Society.

them an increased sense of power, of achievement and of self-confidence. It offers an effective way to influence them.

We have all, of course, seen compliments and flattery fall flat, arouse suspicion or even disgust.   But the art of complimenting rests on very simple precautions. . . .

Nearly all men . . . have . . . pet vanities—matters about which they are a little uncertain, yet in which they would like to shine and be approved.   When they are praised on one of these points the compliment clicks. . . . [1]

"Men have various subjects in which they may excel, or at least would be thought to excel," says Lord Chesterfield, "and though they love to hear justice done to them where they know they excel, yet they are most and best flattered upon those points where they wish to excel and yet are doubtful whether they do or not. . . . "[2]

You will easily discover every man's prevailing vanity [says Lord Chesterfield] by observing his favorite topic of conversation: for every man talks most of what he has most a mind to be thought to excel in. Touch him but there, and you will touch him to the quick.[3]

It is by giving a thought to the victim that able men make their humor effective in creating good will.   They take care that their thrusts inflict no damage which they may regret.   Kindly humor charms people and puts them at ease.   It is perhaps unequalled as a means of relieving tension and drawing people together.[4]

The Interviewer's Attitude.—On the subject of the worker's approach to the client Miss Brisley and the senior visitors of the Minneapolis Family Welfare Association agreed that a worker should

. . . maintain a professional attitude, and guard against emotion on her own part, or at least keep her own emotion in the background. Hard and unsympathetic?   Not at all.   Understanding and sympathetic she must be, but freedom of emotional response is a luxury which is apt to blur her reasoning ability and submerge her judgment so that she becomes just one more pitying or impatient friend.   The statements, "we never adopt a defensive attitude and are willing to discuss misapprehensions and prejudices frankly," "we avoid evasion," "we

[1] E. T. Webb and J. B. Morgan, *op. cit.*, pp. 173–174.
[2] *Ibid.*, p. 174.
[3] E. G. Johnson, *Best Letters of Lord Chesterfield*, p. 61.
[4] E. T. Webb and J. B. Morgan, *op. cit.*, p. 241.

are willing to admit the possibility that we may be in error," might, if taken seriously, save bad moments for the visitor who is still laboring under the tremendous burden of the necessity for always being right; as might the suggestion that she "assume co-operation from the client" help the over-fearful. . . .

"Do nothing which will lower the client's self-respect;" "never humiliate him before others;" "do not put him on the defensive;" "do not use detective methods nor take advantage of your own position of authority;" "do not coerce people mentally;" and—one which some of us who are over-earnest may need—"after proving an excuse inadequate, drop the subject and do not nag. . . ."

"Agree with the client whenever possible" was one of the processes formulated, "show approbation, and say nice things when you can sincerely;" "pick out the favorable elements of the situation;" and "let the client know that you have a picture of him at his best."[1]

When the interview is kept on a strictly businesslike basis, limited to the immediate issues involved, it will seldom secure more than superficial data. Even though the interviewee is wholly agreeable to a direct approach, resort to some method of indirect approach will almost invariably be required in order to release the tensions associated with ordinary interviewing. Leisurely, but not dilatory, methods of approach, as already indicated, are, paradoxically, most rapid.

The problem of approach is a difficult one, particularly when the interviewer is not expected or when previous experience with certain types of social workers and investigators has prejudiced the interviewee. It is often necessary to break down a good many barriers before one receives attention, let alone confidence. Indeed, it may require quick action to get a hearing at all, as the following experience illustrates:

I visited a mother referred to me by a social agency. The agency had telephoned her that someone was coming to visit her. When I came I told her whom I represented, and without opening the door she said: "Yes?" I proceeded: "I should like to talk with you . . . " "Yes?" I felt worse than a book agent in whose face the door is shut. I knew I had to win her confidence immediately, so I said: "You know, Mrs. F., I want your help in regard to the Black Street gang." "My help? Why sure! Come right in; I can tell you enough about them to write a book." I did not write a book but I did secure her social case history and that of her boy in whom I was chiefly interested. She

[1] *Interviews, Interviewers, and Interviewing in Social Case Work*, pp. 36–37.

later sent the boy to talk to me, and even telephoned to learn if I needed more *help*, which, of course, was thankfully solicited.[1]

The Indirect Approach.—In interviews where a definite appointment does not seem advisable, the approach can best be made during leisure time, or at the club, church, or factory, or during a conventional call at the home or when inquiring about some general matters regarding the district. Community leaders may be best approached through these channels. The following illustrates a successful approach to a leading immigrant family, and through them to the entire community:

While engaged in a piece of research work I always regarded everyone as a possible source of information. Our family physician happened to call at the house. I told him of my desire to be introduced to an immigrant colony where investigations abound to the sorrow of the inhabitants. This physician volunteered to send a friend of his to see me who was a member of a Club which had some relations with the colony. This member introduced me to the chairman of the Club, who in turn introduced me to an ex-advisor of the colony, who had many friends there. He in turn introduced me to one of the influential members of the colony, who had a young married daughter living in the home of a leader of the group. This leader invited me to attend the church services where I made many acquaintances and even friendships. Thus I gained entrance into these immigrant homes and subsequently into the community as an interested friend, and not merely as an "investigator."[1]

Purely accidental interviews where neither has approached the other, of course, require little resort to a strategy of approach. For this very reason they are exceedingly desirable, and relaxation and detachment are more apt to be secured.

Relaxation and Leisurely Pace in Interviewing.—Mary Brisley, in describing the experiences of the senior visitors of the Minneapolis Family Welfare Association, states:

We establish a sympathetic atmosphere . . . we let the client know that we are at ease and that we have time to listen and to consider. How often, I wonder, does the almost pathetically earnest young visitor defeat her purpose by sitting upright on the edge of a wrong chair and proceeding directly to the "heart of the matter!" "Be able to put yourself in the background, especially when there are two other

---

[1] Statement by a social research worker.

people present or when the client is weeping or trying to gain his composure" and "wait until the client is ready to talk" are other suggestions made. The use of different tones of voice to make ourselves understood, was agreed to be important—especially, for example, employing a clear, low tone instead of opposing our shouts to an angry client's.[1]

Mary Richmond also strongly advocates absence of hurry to ease the strain, but observes that "a slow, steady, gentle pressure" is required to reach the goal set by the interviewer. She further remarks:

Giving the client all the time he wants often leads to that fuller self-revelation which saves our time and his in the long run. Pressure of work! Lack of time! How many failures in treatment are excused by these two phrases! But, wherever else the plea of lack of time may be valid, it is peculiarly inappropriate at this first stage, for no worker ever has leisure enough in which to retrieve the blunders that result inevitably from a bad beginning. Save time, if need be, at some stage of treatment, but not at the First Interview.

"The physician who comes in like a gust of wind," says Dr. Paul Dubois,[2] "looks at his watch, and speaks of his many engagements, is not cut out to practice this psychotherapy. It is necessary, on the contrary, that the patient should have the impression that he is the only person in whom the physician is interested, so that he may feel encouraged to give him all his confidence and peace . . . "[3]

GAINING RAPPORT

"*Rapport*," observe Park and Burgess, "implies the existence of a mutual responsiveness, such as every member of the group reacts immediately, spontaneously, and sympathetically to the sentiments and attitudes of every other member."[4] *Rapport* may be achieved by means of showing interest, attention, or admiration, by identification, by observance of conventionalities, by listening, by meeting people on their own grounds, by heightening their social status, by eliminating social distance, and numerous other means. H. A. Overstreet states the situation as follows:

In trying to analyze my contact with people I believe I follow three more or less definite steps.

[1] *Interviews, Interviewers and Interviewing in Social Case Work*, p. 36.
[2] *Psychic Treatment of Nervous Disorders*, p. 242.
[3] MARY E. RICHMOND, *Social Diagnosis*, pp. 115–116.
[4] *An Introduction to the Science of Sociology*, pp. 893–894; *rapport* in imitation, *ibid.*, p. 344.

First, I try for a "transfer," to make the person I'm talking with, feel my genuine interest in him; by

(*a*) concentrated attention with the impression that my time is his entirely for as long as he wishes;

(*b*) establishing some bond of common interest or experience;

(*c*) finding something about the person's looks, manner, or experience that I can conscientiously admire.

Second, I try to have him feel my desire and ability to help or advise him; and

Third, I try to make him feel I believe in him and make him believe in himself.

My chief failures have come when I was fatigued, and when it became an effort even to simulate interest. The person talked with felt the break, the effort; and the responsive chord was not awakened.[1]

The interview proper does not need to begin until a considerable degree of *rapport* has been established. In accidental and casual interviews this is a natural conversational development, and little conscious effort to secure it need be made. In service interviewing, and particularly in the more formal type, it may require some patience and cleverness to secure it. If social proprieties suitable to the situation have been observed, the basis for *rapport* is laid. To greet a man in his native tongue using the accustomed idiom may be sufficient to cause his face to light up and his manner to become cordial. A casual reference to personal experience may serve as a bond of identification. However, the interviewer must avoid talking about himself beyond the point which will interest interviewees or will serve to identify him with them. Anything said beyond these points serves only to distract the attention of interviewees and may be regarded as boasting, scatterbrain talk, or defense.

I recently went to an agency to advise me regarding vocational training for my son. The worker told me she had been to Europe to study methods of vocational guidance. At first I was fascinated, but as she continued with her tale I became impatient since she was forgetting to advise me about John. Why do you suppose she would try to impress me with her trip to Europe?[2]

Reference to some person or object with which one's life is identified may perform the service when the greeting has failed. An object on a whatnot in the corner, a badge or a button the interviewee wears, his dog, a family picture on the wall, a child, a

---

[1] Quoted by H. A. OVERSTREET, *Influencing Human Behavior*, pp. 289–290.
[2] Statement by an interviewee.

meeting with a mutual friend, the neighborhood, any such matter as may be of genuine interest to him will serve. A rapid survey of the room or the person himself almost invariably will yield an opening. Capacity to take a genuine interest in these matters—capacity to appreciate their significance in his life—is a sure means of attracting the interviewee. William James's dictum that a man feels himself to the end of his walking stick can perhaps be applied: he feels himself to the limits of his furthest possession. Exploration of his personality includes the study of his personal values—in them his attitudes are to a large degree revealed; through them he expresses his life interests.

Identification.—The above methods are chiefly ways of getting attention. They offset indifference and incipient hostility. More than this, however, they serve in a measure to identify the interests of the interviewer and the interviewee. The most useful touchstone is probably the mutual discovery of common experiences. Ability to speak the native tongue, the professional jargon, the argot of the other's group must be supplemented by the ability to match personal experiences. For this purpose vicarious experiences—those of a friend, or one reported in a book—even fiction—may be quite as useful as an actual experience. The more widely read the interviewer, the broader his sympathies are apt to be. Through actual or vicarious common experiences each enters imaginatively into the life of the other. Common experiences tend to arouse in each corresponding emotions, attitudes, tendencies to act. It is a short step thence to becoming brothers-in-arms, to complete identification.

In interviewing social workers for research purposes I frequently found it helpful to use scientific terms thus meeting them on their own ground. As a rule I succeeded in securing their attention, and the ten or fifteen minutes originally begrudgingly alloted for the interview stretched into an hour and fifteen minutes or more. In the case of medical agencies, nurses and physicians, it's very essential that one use the accepted scientific or medical terms which have currency in the group. I found that unless I had some command of their terminology I was not getting serious consideration from physicians. I felt that they thought that "social work" or "research" was only a fad with me. I never talked of syphilis as a "social disease." There are many social diseases, and he wants to know specifically what I am talking about.[1]

[1] Statement by a social worker.

A still more important function is served by intimate knowledge of the world in which the interviewee lives. Beatrice Webb observes:

Technical terms and technical details, relating to past as well as present occurrences and controversies, are so many levers to lift into consciousness and expression the more abstruse and out-of-the-way facts or series of facts; and it is exactly these more hidden events that are needed to complete descriptive analysis and to verify hypotheses.[1]

The lives of the interviewer and interviewee probably never lie so far apart that nothing in the one can be matched by anything in the other. Sympathy grows rapidly as the area of common experiences widens. Later in the interview when dealing with experiences strange to the interviewer—the very data that is being sought for—an attentive attitude, an interested manner, a sympathetic expression will suffice to keep the story going on the momentum acquired during the earlier stages of the conversation.

It is remarked that there are two general types of interviewers: (1) those who dominate other human beings and show little interest in the problems as the interviewees see them, and (2) those who project themselves into the situation and create a consciousness of kind, a fellow feeling, and maintain interest and show consideration to all kinds of problems.

I am deeply interested in what the interviewees tell me. I can sympathize with them, however, without sobbing over them. One can show interest by merely listening patiently to the narrative without making any comments. Interviewees can quickly enough sense the presence or absence of interest. . . .

I usually say that I had a similar experience, and thus we have common grounds. I cannot over-emphasize the importance of understanding, taking an interest, and showing an appreciation of their difficulties if one is to secure confidence.[2]

A sure way to win people's good will is to tell a joke on yourself or criticism of yourself is often an effective means of gaining attention and good will and of disarming hostility.

This powerful type of strategy is seldom used by the "small" man. He is too anxious to assert his own importance, to turn the laugh on someone else, or to prove that he himself is exceptionally clever and competent.

[1] *My Apprenticeship*, p. 424.
[2] Statement by a social worker.

But the genuinely able leader, as we have already observed, takes the long view. His purpose is to control others, to establish his influence over them. And one of his methods is to let the *other fellow* do the strutting.[1]

Often interviewers avoid the gloomy, serious-minded, complaining type of interviewee. "Laugh and the world laughs with you, weep and you weep alone," remarks one overburdened client, "and that holds true even of the social worker, who comes to spread charity and peace." Everybody seeks out the person with a smile, but the disheartened, discouraged, and gloomy need the interest and attention of the interviewer more than anyone else.

Observance of Conventions.[2]—Once entry into the home or office has been gained it is necessary to observe all the social graces and conventionalities which produce the desired atmosphere.

While in a home I govern myself like a Roman among the Romans and never question its customs. I try to make myself one of the family. It was difficult for me (in certain research work) to sit down and have a meal with some of the immigrant families every time I came around, but if I declined it would have reflected upon the hospitality of the housewife. I ate and drank jam and tea, sipping the tea from a saucer. I broke bread and salt with many a host, and carried away many tokens of real friendship. Some of my most useful information was gained over the tea-cup. They are symbols of hospitality and intimacy. . . .
I rarely sit down without being invited to do so by the interviewee. If, however, I am convinced that he has overlooked the invitation because of excitement and that he might become embarrassed once he discovers that I am still standing, I quietly and inconspicuously move toward a chair and sit down without being asked. If the interviewee does not intend to invite me to sit down I do not presume my welcome but cut the visit as short as possible, indicating that I would like to come back some other time or invite the interviewee to come to see me.[3]

Face-saving.—Loss of status is so painful and disorganizing to the person that special precautions need to be taken in interviewing to avoid situations in which interviewees may suffer loss of face. One's status is conventionally defined in many ways. Being in trouble, or coming to the charities, or having to tell one's

---

[1] E. T. Webb and J. B. Morgan, *Strategy in Handling People*, pp. 121; 120.
[2] See G. S., "How We Behave in Other People's Houses," *The Survey*, LXIX (June, 1933), 218–219.
[3] Statement by a social worker.

life history may of themselves be regarded by many as degrading or compromising to their self-respect. Furthermore, at any point in the story the interviewee may feel called upon to justify his behavior or attitude. All one's actions are subject to social and moral evaluations and they may seem at times to be in conflict with group standards or not consistent with one's own better self.

In the course of the interview there is a constant risk that the interviewee will feel at any given moment that he has inadvertently given himself away. The consequent embarrassment is apt to be very real and the interviewee may then seek to explain away what he has said. In the presence of anyone whose opinion is valued the interviewee may make a desperate effort to retrieve the esteem he feels he has lost. The interviewer needs to be keenly sensitive to this motive and may even help the person to create a face-saving formula. Only after the person's sense of security has been regained can it be hoped to deal satisfactorily with him.

The necessity for face-saving in an interview arises when the interviewee feels that his attitudes are in conflict with those of the interviewer. That is, it is evidence that *rapport* has not been fully established. Effort spent in overcoming the personal and social barriers between the interviewer and interviewee will greatly reduce the necessity for face-saving. Merely passing it over may not be good tactics since the situation rankles in the mind of the interviewee. He is apt to be especially disturbed by the question of just how much note the interviewer made of the embarrassing incident or statement and how much weight he is giving it in appraising the situation.

CHAPTER IV

THE TECHNIQUE OF THE INTERVIEW (*Concluded*)

Creative Listening.—Frances M. Potter maintains that social workers, whose very occupation makes them more than "ordinarily assertive and expressive in a positive way," must take pains not to overpower the weaker persons. Social workers must turn off the outgoing current, so to speak, if they are to get the incoming current from clients. "This means a conscious putting aside of self and its experience . . . a giving of one's consciousness completely to the other person. . . . In this atmosphere the mind of the client is released, and he talks of things that are vital to him."[1] An interview should actually be the "interviewee's moment" and he should be allowed to tell his story in his own way. Interviewers need to center their attention upon the interests, attitudes, and activities of their client and orient themselves only with regard to their interests, wishes, and behavior patterns.[2] Nannie Deihl and Robert Wilson hold listening to be a case work art:

A certain amount of listening is conceded as effective in every interview. It seems necessary, however, to distinguish the interview in which listening is a consciously predominant part and not incidental to the case work process. If we should try to characterize the kind of listening which seems to give respite to personality-strain and worry, we might get such terms as: "expectant," "understanding," "poised," "non-emotional," "casual." The silence of the listener is a receptive silence. It both invites and respects disclosures. The sense of intimacy is in the type of the disclosures rather than in the character of the relation—the listener retains a certain degree of impersonality. She fills a dual rôle of confidant and stranger, of participant and outside observer. The interviewing relationship presents, it would seem, a curious paradox of such apparently contradictory terms as nearness and remoteness, animation and casualness, intimacy and impersonality,

---

[1] FRANCES M. POTTER, "Subjective Elements in Interviewing," *The Survey*, LIX (November 15, 1927), 226.

[2] JESSIE TAFT, *The Dynamics of Therapy in a Controlled Relationship*, *passim*.

rapport and professional distance, understanding yet comparative absence of expression of sympathy.

The rôle of listener describes a far more dynamic relation to the person in trouble than the passivity ordinarily associated with the term. In the listening interview the one receiving the disclosures gives a curious impression of aliveness. Passive silence gets only the client's speech, a kind of surface behavior. Dynamic listening connotes listening to the client's total personality. Listening of this character seeks the subtle meaning—hints of motivations, reactions to experience, interpretations painful to articulate—conveyed by non-verbal gestures (such as movements or expressions of eyes; posture; pitch, inflection, and speed of voice; hand movements) as much as by speech. . . . [1]

When the interviewee is an executive or an employer it is equally important that the interviewer recede from the center of the stage. It is often observed that successful men have taught themselves to listen and expect others to do likewise.

We are beginning to appreciate the value of silence [says Miss Neustaedter]. A listening attitude and inactivity on the part of the worker frequently throw the burden of proof on the client. He feels the need to explain in order to make his position clear instead of leaving it to the worker to find out what she can about him.[2]

The client reveals himself in many ways if we but give him the opportunity—by his attitude toward us, by his manner of talking, by the things he says, and by his reticence, responsiveness, or resistance to our suggestions. If we obtrude by asking too many questions, by figuring too prominently in any way, we will blur the picture of the client as a unique individual; if, on the other hand, we show by an interested, sympathetic attitude that we are willing to listen, if we give encouragement when this is indicated, if we let the client occupy the center of the stage, we give him the opportunity to be himself, and to offer us material quite as important as the information we deliberately seek in the course of the interview. Indeed, we have come to feel that our ideal standard for investigation is to get information only in so far

---

[1] NANNIE E. DEIHL and ROBERT S. WILSON, "Can Listening Become a Case Work Art? *The Family*, XIV (June, 1933), 100. Reprinted by permission of *The Family*.

See also ELTON MAYO, "The Human Effect of Mechanization," *American Economic Review*, XX (March, 1930), 171–173. Dr. Mayo discusses the effects on the output of industrial workers of being supervised by a man who listened to their personal affairs.

[2] "The Rôle of the Case Worker in Treatment," *The Family*, XIII (July, 1932), 153.

as our client gives it willingly, and that our test of skill lies in the ability to release him to the point where he talks because he wants to, and not because we want him to. If we achieve this end, the act of talking is in itself therapeutic, and we leave our client relaxed and benefited instead of keyed to a high point of tension as the result of our visit.[1]

As a therapeutic measure listening becomes highly important when dealing with emotional clients who are given the opportunity to release their pent-up feelings, which oftentimes hamper their thinking and their behavior. "It is not easy [to listen] in the pressure of throngs of waiting clients [during the unemployment crisis]: certainly it calls for all the philosophy we can muster, for the self-application of our case work principles, for some degree of detachment in the midst of the whirl."[2]

Meeting People on Their Own Terms.—Silence on the part of the interviewer also implies meeting people on their own terms— on their own playground, so to speak—and a respect for their interests and for the choice of whatever they wish to tell him. When dealing with children it is possible to bring into the contacts more of action than verbalization, but with adults the reverse is often true. However, throughout the verbalization process the interviewer can display his sincere esteem for the other's point of view, for his plans, problems, habits, and attitudes; and any new ideas should be presented in terms of the other's experience. It is pointed out that much of the power of the great man comes to him chiefly because he can meet people on their own playground:

Taft displayed his sincere respect for the other fellow's customs by himself adopting one of them.

So also Calvin Coolidge made his bow to the farm vote by posing for photographers in his overalls, pitchfork in hand; complimented our Indians by donning a feathered headdress. . . .

William Wrigley, Jr., the salesman who has made himself a millionaire captain of industry, literally built his career around this type of strategy. "Wherever I went to sell goods," he recently told the authors, "I got the atmosphere of the town and the people and talked to dealers in their own terms. . . . "[3]

[1] HELEN P. KEMPTON, "First Contact and Social History," *The Family* XIII (June, 1932), 111–112. Reprinted by permission.

[2] JULE S. DRISCOLL, "Are We Doing Case Work?" *The Family*, X (November, 1929), 236. For a further discussion of this topic see Chap. XIV, "Sociological Problems in Interviewing."

[3] E. T. WEBB and J. B. MORGAN, *op. cit.*, pp. 19–21.

Assuring Security.—Interviewees seldom reveal themselves fully because of fear of being ridiculed, compromised, scolded, or misunderstood.   If an interviewee senses the feeling, however, that the interviewer's attitude is one of sympathetic insight, his reserves and fears will be greatly minimized and often completely overcome.

I always assure the interviewee at the outset that he need not tell me any more than he wishes, and make it clear that should I unwittingly ask disconcerting questions he has the right to ignore them.   Being assured that I respect his "spiritual private property," he generally tells me many things which he did not intend telling at the beginning. If, however, an interviewee does withhold too much informatoin essential to the understanding of his situation, I make that fact plain to him and indicate that my only interest in his private life is to understand the total situation, and I solicit his help.   The few individuals who persist in silence, I press no further, but await a future chance of finding them in a more responsive mood.[1]

It is essential to show respect not only to the interviewee himself but to the customs of the group of which he is a member. This is particularly true in the case of an immigrant, where primary group relations and ties of solidarity are still strong.

I generally try to show that I know something of the culture of his group, and what I do not know I would like to learn.   One Russian boy once said to me: "But when you learn that my parents jump in church, you won't have any more respect for us."   When I explained to him that all customs, and particularly the ritualistic ones, have a sacred origin, and that I admired his parents for the tenacity of their religious beliefs, he unburdened to me a life of perpetual culture conflict.[1]

The Golden Rule in Interviewing.—"I make it a practice to deal with all my interviewees in a manner in which I would expect others to treat me," reports a successful interviewer.   "I never ask questions which—under similar circumstances—I would resent answering about myself, or my husband, or my child.   We must think of human dignity first even if it means that we must forego certain information."

If we ask a client if her husband drinks, or abuses her, or how much her income is, we must stand prepared to answer the same questions about ourselves.   Interviewing clients should not be different from interviewing any of our other equals.

[1] Statement by a research interviewer.

Skillful interviewers are observed to win and inspire confidence by their frank and confidential way of relating their own personal experiences. They talk with their interviewees as if they were their close friends, and thus largely eliminate social distance. It is observed that shut-in or introverted personalities—those not able to share their own experiences—rarely make good interviewers.

Honesty in Interviewing.—Some interviewers advocate shrewdness, subtle diplomacy, or even outguessing, outwitting the interviewee, and extracting the needed information through clever tactics; other interviewers stoutly uphold the policy of straightforward honesty not only because of ethical considerations but because of expediency.

Sidney and Beatrice Webb point out that the difficulties presented by an interviewee who is either unable or unwilling to reveal the truth might be overcome by clever tactics and maneuvers or by appealing to subexecutives who are less on guard and who more easily commit themselves than their superiors.[1] We can conceive of some situations where, for the general good, these authors might be justified in resorting to the above measures for securing information; the social worker, however, is rarely put in a situation where he can afford to ignore the consequences which subordinates might suffer when they are induced to commit themselves.

Walter Bingham and Bruce Moore say that the above procedure is not only an undemocratic exchange of ideas, but a positive danger to a free give-and-take process. The clever detective tactics may produce results but they fail to obtain confidence and cooperation; they induce deceit and misunderstanding. Furthermore, when the interviewer tries to be more clever than his interviewees, he overlooks the fact that he induces the same effort in them. Such strategy proves a boomerang when it puts the interviewee on the defensive.[2]

Sincerity in the interviewer is easily sensed by the interviewee. Mere promises, or lip service, or rationalizations without the genuine belief in what the interviewer is expostulating to his listener are incapable of lasting and influential relations. If the interviewer finds it impossible to be sincere under certain conditions, he will find it far more expedient to withdraw.

[1] *Industrial Democracy*, pp. ix–xviii.
[2] *How to Interview*, pp. 8–9.

Seeking Help.—The interviewer's function in the last analysis is to enable the interviewee to make his own social adjustment. The most far-reaching help may come from those who may make it appear that they are aided by those whom they aid. Clients often seek out the visitor who makes them feel that they do him a service by talking to him. Persons who are in need of help regard themselves as having lost social status or the world as being against them. If they can be made to feel that no matter what their social or economic situation is they can be of service to someone, that the interviewer is looking up to them, and that he recognizes their ability and potentialities and appreciates their judgment, it will not only aid them to maintain their customary status but prevent them from relying on others in matters for which they can assume responsibility. Undoubtedly, there are many ways in which clients needing help could help others.[1] In recent years particularly many competent persons were obliged to seek help, both material and personal.

I always tell my staff never to greet a client with "Well, what can I do for you?" While this expression is quite conventional, it may stress to the unfortunate that we know before hand that they need help and that we take it for granted that we can help them.[2]

To a large extent we, social workers, pauperize clients by our matter-of-factness and our ready offers to help them, to dictate to them, to order them around and to shape their lives for them without taking stock of what they can do for us, for themselves and others in the community. It is no accident or "inborn" trait cropping out when some of our clients lose initiative and begin to show signs of moral as well as economic dependency after they have been in contact with a welfare agency for some time. We have not given them an opportunity to be independent.[2]

A client should rarely be refused to render any help which he believes he can extend. If there is nothing he can do at the moment for the particular agency to which he volunteers his services, a church club, a ladies' aid society, a parent-teacher's group may be urged to solicit his help to sew, to embroider, to make sandwiches or artificial flowers, or to exploit any of his

---

[1] VIENNIE BORTON, "Partnership in Relief Giving," *The Family*, XIV (January, 1933), 302–304.

[2] Statement by a social work executive.

capacities at disposal. Many times difficult persons have been thus rendered enthusiastic and loyal supporters. Miss Book's experience with the Andrews family is in point:

After my first few visits to the home and subsequent interviews with Mr. and Mrs. Andrews separately, it was clearly indicated that we were dealing with a frustrated family. I interpreted their touchiness and exaggerated sense of pride as the only means left to them of safeguarding their personal identity and a screen to shield themselves from further encroachments. Their life had become static and, to them, barren. First, there was little hope of Mr. Andrews' having work because of his age and technological changes in his trade. Mrs. Andrews was cut off from her relatives and in ill health. Olive was at a standstill in school, with no hope for the career she had planned. Anna was doing poor work and fighting with her teachers. Dan's college education and preparation for the ministry were now impossible. I began to think of ways by which some of the family's plans could be realized. My efforts were directed toward giving the Andrews individually a sense of achievement. To Mrs. Andrews I was an appreciative audience when she related details of everyday happenings in the home. She felt my admiration and respect for her ability to manage so well on the budget and began to give me much practical advice on the subject. We exchanged ideas on child training. Mr. Andrews was given the opportunity to develop his latent leadership abilities by membership in our clients' committee where his opinion was respected. Through vocational guidance it was made possible for Olive to pursue her ambitions— she and Mrs. Andrews making the choice of school. Anna and Dan had the chance to expand through camp experiences. Because of the family's increased self-confidence and security with us, they gradually were able to take on interests outside the home. Spontaneously they offered their services to the organization. Anna volunteered free clerical service in order to meet her family's obligations. She now reports regularly to work in our office and works with enthusiasm, feeling that she is gaining much in experience. "You know," she said recently, "I am glad we had to come to you though I hate the money part of it. Everything is better at home and besides it has given me new ideas." She sees their problems in proportion. . . .

Mrs. Andrews says that she took on outside interests when she began to feel that she could hold her head up. We had strengthened her sense of importance to her family. By insisting upon her capabilities as a mother and household manager, she was led to accept responsibilities for other families we knew. I turned to her for help in demonstrating budgeting to an extravagant, mentally dull American widow. Mrs. Andrews was too excited and exhilarated to sleep the night before her first visit. This enthusiasm persists as she works with the family and her own family is glad to release her from the home for this, though Anna laughingly remarked the other day, "I have to hunt for clean handkerchiefs and sometimes wash them myself, now that Mother is so busy with other things." Conscientiously Mrs. Andrews uses methods with these families once employed successfully by us with her. She takes a professional attitude and will not discuss the work with her own family for fear of betraying confidences. She stresses the importance of tact, remembering that it worked in her case.[1]

Meeting Objections.—When it becomes necessary for a social agency to reduce the meager cash allowance of an impoverished client, or to send a favorite child to an institution or commit a mate to an insane asylum, the social worker must be prepared to meet objections. Objections should be anticipated as far as possible and the client should be prepared for any drastic changes by mere hints at first, by telling of similar circumstances in other cases (without giving identifying information), or by asking the client's suggestions on the subject.

It may be necessary to watch for the opportune moment when the idea can be implanted without any direct reference to the interviewee's situation, thus charting in advance a course of action which he is expected to follow later: "Well, according to the general feeling times are not getting any better. It's a wonder that the social welfare agencies are able to hold their own so long. It may be necessary for them to reduce budgets and rations." Thus the unpleasant news is gradually broken and time allowed to make the adjustment. "When I am able to anticipate the objections of the interviewee I make them the cardinal points in the interview. 'Of course it is poor policy to issue standard packages,' to 'cut wages,' 'to keep men in idleness,' but 'what else can be done under the circumstances?'"—relates a social worker of her experience in such situations.

In cases where it is necessary to remove a member from the home an appeal can be made in behalf of his best interests: "I know how hard the parting must be for you, but, of course, I know that you want the best for your child (or wife)." When points of view clash, the interviewee may be made to see differently by discussing in general the advantages gained in cases known to the interviewee, or one reported in the newspapers, thus bringing the issue directly within the experience of the

[1] MARY VIRGINIA BOOK, "As the Andrews Family Sees It," *The Family*, XIV (January, 1934), 308–310. Reprinted by permission.

interviewee without, however, stressing personal problems or interests.

Often it may be possible to allow the objector to voice his aversions without taking any action until he has forgotten about them or discarded them or changed his mind. It is best not to press him as pressure will tend only to exaggerate and color his feelings more forcibly. The remarks of Webb and Morgan and of George Hopkins are of significance:

We all know such men and women who are fortified against other people's suggestions. Psychologists have a special name for them. They call them "negativistic"; people who are "negative," who like to say "No" and think "No."

When such people are exceedingly clever and cultured, like Wilson, we say they have "analytical" minds. Otherwise we say they are just plain "ornery." . . . [1]

Each sales prospect presents a different kind of human problem and only the congenital dub will treat all alike. A good salesman will sell the close trader on how to make more money with less effort; he will sell the purse-proud fellow on how big a man he is; he will rush the snap-judgment buyer through to a conclusion; but he will not try to sell the analytically-minded prospect at all—he will just give him the information in the form best suited and look in the next day for the order. [2]

When the interviewer is convinced that it is for the best interests of interviewees to abandon their objections they must not be given the chance to commit themselves to the point where it will be compromising to change their minds. Several writers believe that it is far more important to move in the affirmative than in the negative direction:

The psychological patterns [involved in the "yes" and "no" response] are quite clear. When a person says "No" and really means it, he is doing far more than saying a word of two letters. His entire organism —glandular, nervous, muscular—gathers itself together into a condition of rejection. There is, usually in minute but sometimes in observable degree, a physical withdrawal, or readiness for withdrawal. The whole neuro-muscular system, in short, sets itself on guard against acceptance. Where, on the contrary, a person says "Yes," none of the withdrawing activities take place. The organism is in a forward-moving, accepting, open attitude. Hence the more "Yesses" we can, at the very outset,

[1] E. T. WEBB and J. B. MORGAN, *op. cit.*, p. 137.

[2] GEORGE HOPKINS, "The Real 'Star Salesman' in Modern Business," *American Magazine*, XCIII (April, 1922), 70.

induce, the more likely we are to succeed in capturing the attention for our ultimate proposal. . . . Get a student to say "No" at the beginning, or a customer, child, husband, or wife, and it takes the wisdom and the patience of angels to transform that bristling negative into an affirmative. . . . [1]

Most people hate to admit that they are wrong, and it takes time for them even to realize that this could possibly be the case. Once they have taken a position, it is hard for them to retreat: Their *ego* is at stake. If we start by trying to prove that their attitude is unsound or silly, we do the one thing that will certainly egg them on to maintain it. But if we show that we respect their position and understand how they happened to get there, we make it easy for them to come down off their perch and agree with us. . . . [2]

It is best not to argue with an interviewee. He should be made to feel that he is entitled to his point of view and that it will be respected. A particular point of view can rarely be changed by argument, rather by altering the conditioning circumstances. However, if he fears that he is not worth arguing with, the tactics he expects should be adopted. "It is disastrous to 'show off,' or to argue: the client must be permitted to pour out his fictitious tales, to develop his preposterous theories, to use the silliest arguments, without demur or expression of dissent or ridicule," says Beatrice Webb. The competent social investigator will not look bored or indifferent when irrelevant information or trivial details are offered him, any more than a competent medical practitioner will appear wearied by his patient's catalogue of imaginary symptoms. [3]

It is best for the interviewer not to defend himself when interviewees find fault with him. Silence in these matters is often most effective.

I either acknowledge my regrets and lay the blame to the fact that I am "only a queer human" and that all of us have lots to learn or keep strictly silent regarding mistakes, differences of opinion or misunderstandings, and thus do not draw further attention to them. . . . [4]

Lending one's ear to grievances may not be sufficient in cases where a concession is expected. Without endangering the main

[1] H. A. OVERSTREET, *op. cit.*, p. 17–18.
[2] E. T. WEBB and J. B. MORGAN, *op. cit.*, p. 98.
[3] BEATRICE WEBB, *My Apprenticeship*, p. 425.
[4] Statement by a research interviewer.

issues a form of strategy, known in business as "the law of minor concessions," may be employed.

Mrs. E. was eager to tell of her sex experiences, but since she had practiced certain perversions she insisted on telling her story not to a social worker but to a psychiatrist who would give her "professional sympathy." I made it clear to her that I would be happy to make all the arrangements for an interview with a psychiatrist at which time I would not be present. I was not interested in who got her story as long as it was gotten.[1]

This worker was willing to withdraw and sacrifice details in order to win principles; otherwise there is danger that the interviewee may go to the logical extreme and a conflict may result.

At times disgruntled interviewees take their complaints directly to the executive or to the head of the organization without mentioning any dissatisfaction to the field visitor. On subsequent interviews, it is best to overlook these acts and not to let any strained relations inhibit further contacts. It must be remembered that people in trouble generally turn their thoughts mainly upon themselves and become alarmed over matters which may appear trivial to the interviewer. If they can get help or mental relief behind the interviewer's back, so to speak, he must learn to turn his back frequently. It remains with the executive or head of the organization to explain to the interviewee why matters should be taken up first with the field investigator whenever possible.

At times it may be necessary to meet resistance head-on, but it must be remembered that by trampling roughshod over the other man's ideas and flatly refusing help for his wants little can be accomplished.

Mrs. D. insisted that we were unfair to her because we could not grant her a piano. "Why, Mrs. D., I am surprised at you, you seem an intelligent person, how can you even mention a piano when we can hardly keep head above water in our attempts to supply enough bread and milk to the thousands of families without any means of subsistence." Of course, she knew what other clients were facing during their long periods of unemployment, but she sensed that I considered her unfair. The piano was never mentioned again, and before requesting other things, she generally asked if I thought it would be fair to ask for them.[1]

---

[1] Statement by a family welfare worker.

Facing the issue with an interviewee, informing him of the difficulties involved, revealing to him the underlying reasons often avoid drastic action and eliminate hard feelings.

Not long ago a group of radicals came storming into my office, demanding more relief for their hungry children. I invited them to sit down and told them I was grateful for their coming, as I too had this problem on my mind. "Do you think it is easy for me to allow you meager rations? But what am I to do? I have exactly so much money at my disposal and so many families on the list. It's a matter of pure paper-and-pencil work. It's a matter of sharing the loaf. . . . If I allow your children more I have nothing left for your neighbor's children." They saw I was sincere and they recognized my own predicament. I reasoned with them the same as I would with my superior.[1]

This executive put complete faith in their honor and good judgment and undoubtedly averted a serious clash. Artful suggestion is another way of implanting ideas without arousing objections.

Not long ago I interviewed an executive who was suspected of neglecting to take steps to stop a leakage in trust funds. When we cautiously came to the subject I said: "Of course, I am convinced that you would not tolerate dishonesty in your subordinates." Indeed he "would not." Thus by suggestion I perhaps indicated a course of action. Had I openly told him of the gossip without showing respect for him, I would have only succeeded in putting him on the defensive.[2]

Controlling the Interview

It is at times necessary to control the course of the interview to some extent. After *rapport* is established and the conversation becomes free and easy, it is apt to travel on a tangent to the subject of the inquiry. While always on the alert to discover important bypaths, it may be necessary to check the flow of the story, to hark back to the point of departure, to encourage the interviewee to retrace a line of thought. Many methods will suggest themselves.

When the conversation begins to drift too far I take part in it, trying to steer it along more definite channels. I usually say: "You know

[1] Statement by a county welfare executive.
[2] Statement by a family welfare executive.

has probably proceeded too rapidly, or by his manner he has suggested the need for deception or dissimulation. Checking back on the story, therefore, needs to be very carefully done. To catch an interviewee in a deliberate misstatement will inevitably destroy *rapport*. It requires great tact and mental dexterity to overcome the resulting embarrassment and confusion.

I usually listen pretty closely to the interviewee's story and can, therefore, determine whether he is consistent, or posing, or misinformed. I can tell whether his statements coincide. I frequently ask the same question a second time later in the interview to compare answers and then say: "Did I understand you to say before, so and so? Is that what you really meant?" I watch the time and place elements pretty closely. They are good indicators of a consistent story. In some instances it is important to know whether what the person says is an actual fact. If he takes it to be a fact and acts accordingly, then the fiction is as real to him as fact, and that is what counts.

It is best, of course, to avoid giving any opportunity for lying. This may be accomplished by informing the interviewee that the true facts of the case are known.

One boy tried to lie to me about his name. I emphatically called him by his correct name throughout the interview.

If a boy has actually stolen something, I never ask him if he has stolen or not. I ask him what led him to steal, or where he has hidden the goods.

If a mother tells me that she never has any difficulty with her boy who is a problem to everybody else, I ask her to tell me how she has been able to avoid it since all mothers have problems with growing children. . . . I have with mine. . . .

The interviewer must distinguish between (1) lies as defense mechanisms; (2) pathoformic lies; (3) conventional lies or so-called white lies; (4) lies due to mental conflict;[1] (5) seeming lies which arise in differences in viewpoint regarding matters; (6) accidental lies, due to tricks of memory, illusions; (7) lies due to a desire to control the situation. Professor Cooley remarks:

Even telling the truth does not result so much from a need of mental accuracy, though this is strong in some minds, as from a sense of the unfairness of deceiving people of our own sort, and of the shame of being detected in so doing. Consequently the maxim, "Truth for friends and lies for enemies," is very generally followed, not only by

[1] See WILLIAM HEALY, *Mental Conflicts and Misconduct.*

savages and children, but, more or less openly, by civilized people. Most persons feel reluctant to tell a lie in so many words, but few have any compunctions in deceiving by manner, and the like, persons toward whom they feel no obligation. . . . "Conscience is born of love" in this as in many matters. A thoughtful observer will easily see that injustice and not untruth is the essence of lying, as popularly conceived.[1]

Closing the Interview.—There is probably a natural closing point to each interview. It is rarely advisable to complete the entire story at a single sitting. A second or third interview may be necessary. In that case the best results will be secured if the first interview breaks off at a time when the interviewee is still fresh, still has something important to say, and himself proposes another talk. If both have arrived at a stage of physical or nervous strain, or if the story has run its course, there may not be enough momentum to carry over into a second sitting. It is well to share the responsibility of getting a complete account with the interviewee and to ask: "What have we omitted?" or "What have we failed to touch on?" or "What else would you like to tell me?"

There is apt to be a reaction on the part of the interviewee if confessional material has been given. The interviewee may check himself with the statement: "I didn't intend to tell all that." In that case it is very important that *rapport* be reestablished before the interview is closed. Miss Richmond observes:

In our effort to build a solid foundation we may have had to ask some embarrassing questions and touch a nerve that is sore. It is most important, where this has been the case, that in the last five or ten minutes of the interview we dwell upon hopeful and cheerful things, and leave in the mind of the client an impression not only of friendly interest but of a new and energizing force, a clear mind and a willing hand at his service. Dr. Meyer is quite right. If we know how to do it, the patient's statements can usually be obtained not only fully but with an actual feeling of relief on his part, and a distinct gain in the relation between client and worker. . . . [2]

Interviewers at the conclusion of an interview at times expect the client to show a sense of gratitude or to thank them for their time and efforts. Thanks and appreciation must be taken for granted. Often the client is bewildered and confused and forgets

---

[1] CHARLES H. COOLEY, *Human Nature and the Social Order*, pp. 388–389.
[2] MARY E. RICHMOND, *op. cit.*, pp 130–131..

the niceties of polite conversation. "Nothing can be less charitable on the part of a social work interviewer," says an experienced executive, "than to expect gratitude or 'thank you, ma'am' from a client whom we degraded to the point of accepting our services. . . . The more merciful thing is for us to thank the client for giving us an opportunity to be of service."

THE TEST OF A SUCCESSFUL INTERVIEW

Miss Richmond observes that the test of a successful interview is twofold: (1) "We must have succeeded in getting enough of the client's story and of the clues to other insights to build our treatment solidly upon fact"; (2) "and we must have achieved this, if possible, without damage to our future relations, and with a good beginning made in the direction of mutual understanding."[1] However, the client's story might have been secured against his will or knowledge, for as Miss Richmond further remarks, "Interviews which have covered every item of past history and present situation with accuracy and care can be total failures." At the close of each interview it is well to take stock of oneself, so to speak, and to ask the following questions regarding the success of the interview:

1. Have I rendered the interviewee articulate; have I put him at his ease and given him an opportunity to express himself freely?

2. Have I seen and understood the interviewee's problems and position from his point of view?

3. Have I conducted myself in such a manner that it will be possible for the interviewee to cooperate with me or the agency, or have I failed to secure his cooperation?

4. Have I succeeded in learning his attitudes as well as opinions, defenses, or rationalizations? Did I enter his inner life? Did he lay his mask aside?

5. Have I enlarged his social world and provided the practical ways and means for readjustment fully?

6. Have I invaded the personality of the interviewee or secured his story against his will or his knowledge?

7. Did I secure important data to enable me to understand the problems involved?

8. Did I learn the cause of his behavior?

[1] *Social Diagnosis*, p. 30.

9. Did I impose my views and plans upon the interviewee or did I create sufficient opportunity for him to exercise his own judgment and his own will and follow his own plans?

Summary

Skillful interviewing does not depend upon rules and maxims, but a knowledge of certain principles found helpful by a large number of interviewers may provide some suggestions which can be utilized in a large number of cases:

I. Preparation for the Interview:
1. Understand why the interview is held.
2. Be prepared to be viewed by the interviewee and to answer any questions he may wish to ask.
3. Gather all possible clues and concentrate on each one to see which might be best utilized toward a successful approach to the interviewee.
4. If time is limited and problems are pressing formulate tentative objectives for your interview or chart its course as far as possible.
5. Keep in mind the unique problems of each case and relate them to the total social situation in which the interviewee finds himself, as far as is possible under the circumstances.
6. "Size up" your interviewee from whatever clues you may possess but keep your mind flexible when you are in contact with the interviewee.
7. Make appointments whenever possible, thus showing respect for the client's time.
8. Provide privacy, comfort, and agreeable surroundings.
9. Be modestly and suitably dressed for each occasion.
10. Introduce yourself to the interviewee, explain the function of the agency you represent, and state briefly the purpose of visit.
11. Extend cordial greetings.
12. Observe conventionalities of the interviewee's home and social group.

II. The Interview Proper:
13. Show interest in everything the interviewee wishes to tell you. Make the interview "his moment."
14. Be at ease with the interviewee, thus helping him to be at ease with you.

15. Adopt a leisurely pace to give the interviewee the feeling that you consider his situation seriously.
16. Allow sufficient time to learn the facts which will enable you to understand the problems involved.
17. View all problems confronting the interviewee from his point of view.
18. Make suitable allowances for your preconceived notions about his problems, for your biases and prejudices.
19. Meet the interviewee on his own terms.
20. Gain, keep, and deserve the interviewee's confidence.
21. Identify yourself with the interviewee through similar experiences, points of view, mutual likes or dislikes.
22. Gain sympathetic insight into problems confronting the interviewee.
23. Assign social status to the interviewee, remembering that status is one of his most priceless possessions.
24. Ask only questions which you would not resent answering about yourself under similar circumstances.
25. Ask questions which are easily understood.
26. Ask questions which do not imply their answers.
27. Take care not to sound insinuating or impertinent.
28. In asking questions be frank and straightforward rather than cunning.
29. Avoid "getting around" the interviewee or extracting information against his will or knowledge.
30. Allow the interviewee to tell his story in his own way and to take his time in telling it.
31. Allow the interviewee to think for himself and give him time to think his situation through.
32. "Make your minds meet"; that is, be sure that you understand what the interviewee says, what he wants and what his culture complexes are and he yours.
33. Listen with interest.
34. Follow up every important clue of interest to the interviewee.
35. Seek to understand source, cultural setting, and development of the interviewee's behavior patterns.
36. Meet objections in a way which is satisfying to the interviewee.
37. Avoid ordering-and-forbidding techniques.
38. Allow for face-saving.

39. Lessen tensions by assigning status, by soliciting help, by complimenting good performance, etc.

III. Controlling the Interview:
40. Check the story in your own mind to see if there are any inconsistencies.
41. Deal with inconsistencies as misunderstandings.
42. Remember the saying that the truth is told to friends and lies to enemies.
43. Eliminate opportunities which an interviewee might seize upon to deceive you.
44. If you sense that an interviewee is going to falsify start out by stating the facts of the case as far as they are known to you.

IV. Closing the Interview:
45. Close the interview before you have worn out your welcome.
46. Close the interview when the interviewee is at ease emotionally.
47. Close the interview when the interviewee has caught the desire to manage his own affairs.
48. If subsequent interviews are necessary close when you still have something important to talk about.
49. At the close of the interview ask if there is anything else the interviewee wishes to talk about. "What else would you care to tell me?" "What didn't we touch on?"
50. Test the success of your interviews.

Suggestions for Further Study

1. Examine several case records of a family welfare agency and indicate in how many instances a prolonged first interview was held when the case was opened by the intake department or by the visitor in the home.

Indicate under what circumstances the prolonged first interview was successful in laying the foundation for confidential relations.

In the cases examined could you suggest a different approach to the family than the one followed by the visitor?

2. Under what circumstances are suggestions regarding the technical use of the interview helpful to an experienced worker? to a student in training?

3. Indicate in what ways it is dangerous to do preparatory thinking regarding a case.

4. Indicate the dangers and pitfalls in gathering clues regarding a case which the interviewer contemplates visiting.

5. Examine several case records of a family welfare agency and indicate whether the home, the office, or some neutral ground was found most suitable for interviewing. (Note type of client interviewed and problems entering the situation.)

6. How do you account for the fact that psychiatrists prefer the office interview while family welfare workers favor the home interview?

7. Under what circumstances does the interviewer not need to introduce himself to the interviewee?

8. What manner of greeting have you found most appropriate in your types of interviews?

9. When should the interviewer adopt a "poker face" and when should he reveal his inner feelings?

10. Read R. E. Park's discussion "Behind Our Masks," *Survey Graphic*, *LXI* (May, 1926), and indicate its significance to case work interviewing.

11. Analyze the methods you have found most helpful in the approach to different types of interviewees. Indicate their degree of success and explain the cause of success or failure.

12. What is meant by "the right kind of a compliment"? Why does a compliment "break the ice" in the approach to the interviewee?

13. Examine several case records and interpret the interviewer's attitude in his approach to a client.

14. Explain when and why honesty, sincerity, modesty should be adopted by the interviewer even at the risk of delaying the story or even of foregoing it altogether. Is honesty the best policy in dealing with different types of clients?

15. Search in the sociological literature for an adequate discussion of *rapport*. Why should the case work interviewer be concerned with *rapport* as it is understood from the sociologist's point of view?

16. Examine several case records and analyze the methods of gaining *rapport*.

17. Read E. T. Krueger's and Read Bain's contributions to the study of *rapport*. How do these two men differ? From a social work angle which of the two discussions is more fruitful? Why?

18. What is meant by identification?

19. Can the interviewer maintain impersonal and objective standards when he identifies himself fully with an interviewee?

20. Explain Burgess' discussion of the sense of the dramatic in the light of your understanding of identification. (See index.)

21. What methods of securing identification have you found most successful?

22. What forms of identification are dangerous; under what circumstances?

23. Discuss identification in terms of degree of social distance.

24. Webb and Morgan say: "A sure way to win a person's good will is to tell a joke on yourself." Have you ever used that method? Under what conditions is it dangerous to follow such a procedure?

25. What methods of observing conventionalities have you found most helpful? dangerous?

26. Examine several interviews and indicate the amount of listening the interviewer did during the contact with the client.

27. When is listening to a client undesirable?

28. Discuss listening in terms of mental catharsis.

29. When is it undesirable to meet people on their own grounds?

30. Explain the therapeutic value of meeting people on their own grounds.

31. What are the best means of assuring security to an interviewee? How does social security differ from economic security?

32. Read W. I. Thomas' or Park and Burgess' conception of status and indicate the importance of their discussion to a case work interviewer.

33. Explain the therapeutic value of heightening an interviewee's social status.

34. What are the best methods of heightening an interviewee's status?

35. What methods of controlling the interview have you used to advantage? Read the recent literature on the subject and examine the newest methods used.

36. Discuss report on the Andrews family from the standpoint of partnership in relief giving.

37. What dangers are involved in such a procedure? How can you best prevent gossip? unprofessional attitudes? How can you remedy the results of the mistakes of an untrained interviewer? Under what conditions can the procedure used by Miss Book be used to advantage?

38. Analyze your own methods of meeting objections of interviewees. Analyze the most recent proposals to deal with objections of clients.

39. Examine the advantages and disadvantages involved in meeting the objections in a manner advocated in the text. Cite cases where the opposite procedure should be followed.

40. Explain the term "artful suggestion" from the standpoint of social therapy.

41. Should an interview be controlled? Compare Mary Richmond's and Jessie Taft's conceptions regarding the control of the interview. Explain the standpoint of each.

42. Cite interviewing situations which are inadvisable to control; which are inadvisable not to control.

43. What methods of controlling the interview have you found most successful?

44. Read in psychological literature discussions of pathological lies, lies due to mental conflict, to tricks of memory, to illusions. Classify the lies you believe your interviewees have told you. How do you account for being deceived? How do you deal with lies?

45. What methods of closing the interview have you found most successful?

46. What do you consider a test of a successful interview.

47. Analyze critically the tests of successful interviewing discussed by several writers and cite cases which do not fall under the stated categories.

Selected Bibliography

1. BINGHAM, WALTER VAN DYKE, and BRUCE V. MOORE: *How to Interview*, 1931.
   Numerous helpful suggestions on how to approach an interviewee and how to hold a successful interview in many professional fields.
2. *Interviews, Interviewers and Interviewing in Social Case Work*, 1931.
   A collection of articles many of which deal with the technique of the interview.
3. CRAWFORD, C. C.: *The Technique of Research in Education*, 1928, Chap. IX, "Interviewing Technique."
4. RICHMOND, MARY E.: *Social Diagnosis*, 1917.
   See particularly part II, "Processes Leading to Diagnosis," discussing the technique of the first interview.
5. TAFT, JESSIE: *The Dynamics of Therapy in a Controlled Relationship*, 1933.
   Sets forth the newer methods of interviewing by allowing the interviewee to control the course of the interview.
6. WEBB, BEATRICE, *My Apprenticeship*, 1926, "Appendix."
   Suggests methods of approaching the interviewee.
7. WEBB, E. T., and J. B. MORGAN: *Strategy in Handling People*, 1930.
   Offer many helpful suggestions in interviewing executives and important personages, which are at times applicable to social work situations. The authors do not always advocate "handling" people.

CHAPTER V

THE CONTENT OF THE INTERVIEW

"What outstanding facts should a complete interview or a series of interviews with a person, family, or small group include?" is frequently asked by both social workers and social research investigators. Before answering this question at least two other basic questions must be considered: (1) What is a fact? (2) What basis should we use for the selection of facts?

Definition of Fact.—Park and Miller in their discussion of social heritages and of immigrant groups state:

It is one of the ordinary experiences of social intercourse that words and things do not have the same meanings with different people, in different periods of time, in different parts of a country—that is, in general, in different contexts. The same "thing" has a different meaning for the naive person and the sophisticated person, for the child and the philosopher. The new experience derives its significance from the character and interpretation of previous experiences. To the peasant a comet, a plague, an epileptic person, may mean, respectively, a divine portent, a visitation of God, a possession by the devil; to the scientist they mean something quite different. The word slavery had a connotation in the ancient world very different from the one it bears to-day. It has a different significance to-day in the Southern and Northern states. "Socialism" has a very different significance to the immigrant from the Russian pale living on the "East Side" of New York City, to the citizen on Riverside Drive, and to the native American in the hills of Georgia.

The meaning any word has for an individual depends on his past experience, not only with the thing the word means, but with many other things associated with it in his mind. For example, the concept evoked in his mind by the word "food" is determined not only by the kinds of food he has eaten, but also by the normal state of his appetite and digestion, the ease or difficulty with which he secures his daily ration, whether he grows, hunts, or buys it, whether or not he prepares it, whether he has ever been near starvation, and so forth. No two people have exactly the same experience by which to define the same word, and sometimes the resulting difference in meaning is

92

immeasurably great. This is the meaning of the saying of the logicians that persons who attach different meanings to the same words and the same things are in different "universes of discourse,"—that is, do not talk in the same world.

All the meanings of past experience retained in the memory of the individual form what is called by psychologists the "apperception mass." It is the body of memories with which every new item of experience comes in contact, to which it is related, and in connection with which it gets its meaning. The difference in the interpretation of words is merely an example of the fact that persons whose apperception masses are radically different give a different interpretation to all experience. The ecclesiastic, the artist; the mystic, the scientist; the Philistine, the Bohemian—are examples of classes not always mutually intelligible. Similarly, different races and nationalities, as wholes, represent different apperception masses and consequently different universes of discourse, and are not mutually intelligible. Even our forefathers are with difficulty intelligible to us, though always more intelligible than the eastern European immigrant, because of the continuity of our tradition.[1]

Thus it is evident that the investigator is not so much concerned with the facts per se as with the meaning these facts assume in the life of the interviewee or with the role they play in his life organization. Ada Sheffield throws further light on the subject by her discussion of the fact and the key conception, indicating that facts assume significance only when seen in a network of interrelations:

How are we to determine whether a given fact in a given case has value or significance? We must first inquire what we mean by "significance," what relationships for the fact constitute its significance. A fact gets its significance from some larger idea to which it points, and since that larger idea is a variable factor, the fact's significance must vary accordingly. For instance, a keen and experienced worker was called in consultation on the problem of a widow with two children who had been receiving an allowance for some years. The woman had steadily declined to move from an unsanitary and inconvenient tenement, giving one reason and then another for not availing herself of better quarters that were found for her, or of moving expenses that were promised. The consultant worker urged that careful inquiry be made into the woman's character. She remarked that in all her long experience she had never known an instance in which the explanation of a woman's apparently unaccountable obstinacy in holding on to an undesirable dwelling place had not finally come to light as being

[1] ROBERT E. PARK and H. A. MILLER, *Old World Traits Transplanted*, pp. 265–267. Reprinted by permission of Harper & Brothers, New York.

something discreditable in her mode of life. At the same time she recognized at least two other explanations as being possible: one the home sentiment, the other inertia. Many a woman and man has come to feel the sentiment of home for a spot to which no one else can see anything but drawbacks; and everyone at some time in his life clings to outworn ways rather than go to the trouble of change. Immoral conduct, home sentiment, inertia are all then possible "larger ideas" or "concepts" in relation to which the bare fact of this woman's not moving may take on significance. Now the "significance" which each of these concepts gives consists in the linking of this fact to other facts or ideas which are thereby brought under view. . . .

In order to grasp the full significance of a fact, the thinker must first have identified the whole group of items that each conception relates it to. His conceptions, that is, must be full and distinct. A partly trained investigator, for instance, noting the fact that a child is pale, may at once associate it with her as yet incomplete conception of bad personal hygiene, within which paleness is related to sleeping with closed windows, lack of exercise, and underfeeding. She may thereby miss the items actually operative in the case of the child in question— say *insufficient* sleep and feeding upon *innutritive* bakery stuffs—because her conception of bad hygiene has been lacking in one item about sleep and vague in the item about feeding. An investigator, therefore, can count on grasping a fact's significance only when her training or experience has supplied her with conceptions so copious and exact as to focus all the fact's relations.[1]

Selection of Facts.—Owing to the complexity of life situations the interview, and more especially the subsequent recording of the interview, must be a selective process. Of course, the more details we have regarding a person's life the better we may be in a position to understand his life processes. Just what this selective process should be is dependent upon the unique circumstances governing each case. However, there is some basic information which is generally essential for the understanding of each case, apart from its unique elements.

Following the line of reasoning advanced by Charles H. Cooley in his profound discussion of "The Roots of Social Knowledge,"[2] the interviewer is concerned with two major types of data:

[1] ADA E. SHEFFIELD, *The Social Case History*, pp. 21–24. Reprinted by permission of Russell Sage Foundation.

[2] The following discussion, exclusive of illustrations, is based on Professor Cooley's article, "The Roots of Social Knowledge," *The American Journal of Sociology*, XXXII (July, 1926), 59–79. Note also that this discussion is closely connected with the problem of sympathetic insight.

(1) Spatial or material—pertaining to things—which come to us primarily through the various sense perceptions (personal appearance of interviewee, tone of voice, outward circumstances of home, and other external data which are self-recording). Perhaps a series of photographs could just as well supply most of the information needed. In addition, certain identifying data generally appearing on face-sheets may be included under this category: name, address, date and place of birth, nationality, addresses of interested persons, employers, etc. (2) Social and personal—information, obtained chiefly through contacts with the minds of others (through communication), reveals a complex inner life not primarily sensuous. This inner life does not present itself as a unified whole. It reveals itself in part through: (*a*) "flashes of visions" as to how a person would look, how he would speak, or what he would do in a particular situation, for example, how he would act when his income is exhausted, when his child becomes wayward or seriously ill, or when his mate deserts. It is by such flashes that we gain a conception of his bravery or his cowardice, of his generosity or his selfishness, of his excitement or poise, of his ability or inability to adjust and to think rationally; (*b*) inner sentiments which one feels in some degree when thinking of others in their particular situations. "It is these latter sympathetic elements which make the difference between our knowledge of man and our knowledge of a horse or of a dog."[1] Without a measure of true sympathy there is no penetration, no distinctively human insight, no sharing of psychic processes, and our information becomes largely external or behavioristic. "This is also the process by which we come to understand the meaning of a word, and through such understanding make ourselves at home in that vast realm of meanings to which words are the key. We may know words as mere behavior, as when a man speaks to us in a strange tongue, but in that case they do not admit us to the realm of meanings. To have human value the word and the inner experience that interprets it must go together."[2]

LIFE HISTORIES

A complete life history of a person or group is the most important part of the interview, since it is most likely to illumine

[1] CHARLES H. COOLEY, *op. cit.*, p. 64.
[2] *Ibid.*, p. 65.

various aspects of social and moral life which we may have
known hitherto only indirectly through observation, bits of
conversation, or disconnected statements.[1] "In the one case,"
says Dr. Robert E. Park, "we are like a man in the dark looking
at the outside of the house and trying to guess what is going on
within.   In the other, we are like a man who opens the door and
walks in, and has visible before him what previously he had
merely guessed at."[2]   The life history is an account of a person's
or group's experiences, attitudes, and values on which he has
placed the highest importance; it "exhibits casual sequences in
the mental life of the individual which might not be detected in
the organized interview"[3] and shows behavior in its social setting
at each stage.   Dr. Park further observes:

In the study of contemporary life the sociologist has one point of
attack and one device for exploration of his subject which is not to the
same extent available to the historian nor the anthropologist.[4]   He can
interview the individuals who have participated in and are themselves
a part of the social order he is seeking to investigate.   He can, by means
of interviews or by the use of intimate personal documents, build up
what is called, technically, life histories.

The relation of the individual to the society in which he lives is probably much more real and intimate than has hitherto been assumed, even
by those who have been the first to direct attention to it.[5]   It is inevitable that people who live together, even on the most casual terms,
should eventually come into possession of a common stock of memories, a
tradition; that they should acquire some common standard of decency,
some accepted forms of intercourse, etiquette, manners, and social
ritual, even when the deeper motives and interests of life remain relatively untouched.   It is just as inevitable that continued intercourse
should reduce personal habits to conventional forms, and that these
should assume, in time, the character of binding social customs. . . .

[1] WILSON GEE (Editor), *Research in the Social Sciences*, p. 47.
[2] *Ibid.*, p. 47.
[3] STUART A. RICE (Editor), *Methods in Social Science: A Case Book*, p. 562.
[4] The difficulties of the anthropologist in studying primitive peoples are
not merely the ordinary difficulties of language.   A special difficulty is
due to the fact that the primitive man is not sophisticated and articulate,
and he has no words for the subtle meaning of things—things that are to
such an extent taken for granted that he does not speak of them except,
perhaps, in symbolic and expressive language.—See the paper by Bronislaw
Malinowski in *The Meaning of Meaning*, by C. K. Ogden and I. A. Richards.
[5] CHARLES H. COOLEY, *Human Nature and the Social Order*.

It is by non-conformity, nevertheless, that the individual develops his personality and society ceases to be a mere mass of inert tradition. He may distinguish himself and become ambitious. He may fail; he may cheat; he may do the unpardonable thing and suffer the pangs of remorse. In any case, as a result and to the extent of his collision with the existing social order he is likely to become acutely conscious of himself. The ultimate effect of this is to create that inevitable personal reserve which constitutes his private life. This reserve, which, by the way, little children do not possess, assumes in time, and under certain circumstances, the character of something sacred and terrifying. The individual himself conceives it as something wholly, or almost wholly, inaccessible to other minds. Society is composed of such self-conscious personalities, and these brooding, subjective, inscrutable egos are apparently just as much a product of personal association as are the traditions, customs, and objective forms of social life over against which, in their inaccessible privacies, they set themselves as a contrast effect. . . .

If, now, one asks, What facts in the personal history of an individual are for most or all purposes genuinely significant, it seems to me that we are bound to say that the most important fact about any person is this:

What is it that habitually engages his attention?

What are the subjects of his dreams and reveries?

And what is the rôle in which he conceives himself?

What his acts have been and what his habits are, we can know.

In addition to these facts of his history, it is important to know, however, his incompleted acts: what he hopes; what he dreams; what his vagrant impulses, "temptations," are. . . . [1]

Clifford Shaw—in his discussion of what "the own story"[2] reveals—implies that the social investigator is concerned with:

1. The interviewee's point of view—that is, personal attitudes, feelings, interests, the role the person conceives himself to play in relation to others and the interpretation he places on the social situations in which he lives.

2. The social and cultural world in which the person lives. Human behavior can best be explained in relation to the social and cultural context in which it occurred. This milieu reveals not only the traditions, customs, moral standards of the group to which the person is subjected but also "the manner in which

[1] Wilson Gee (Editor), *Research in the Social Sciences*, pp. 38–40, 47–48. Reprinted by permission of The Macmillan Company.

[2] *Cf.* Clifford R. Shaw, *The Jack Roller*, pp. 3–16.

these cultural factors become incorporated into the behavior trends of the child" or person. The Gestalt psychologists refer to this social milieu as "the frame of reference" or "configuration" which supplies meaning in the life experience of the person or group. To study a person apart from his social environment is to study him in a vacuum, and not as an individual who has acquired status in a group, who has established many social or group relations.

For the purposes of therapy it is essential to learn the person's "moral struggles, his successes and failures in securing control of his destiny in a world too often at variance with his hopes and ideals";[1] his social complexes, his sentiment and attitudes, which cooperated with other factors to create his personality. It is essential to know the prestige and incentive to a particular form of behavior.

3. Sequence of events. Early experiences and influences shape and direct the course and behavior trends of a person. The interviewer seeks to visualize the process involved in the fixation of a particular behavior trend, as the successive events of life. The value of the life history and the manner in which this sequence of events contributes to a particular behavior trend is illustrated by one of the numerous "own stories" reported by Shaw:

When I was eight years old I did my first job in the racket. This job was the biggest thrill I ever got in my life. It happened in April. That day I was hanging around with my oldest brother and his gang. They had been playing baseball all afternoon and I was watching them.

When it got too dark to play ball we all went into the alley to have a smoke and tell stories. The big guys got to talking about stealing, and my brother said he had a good place spotted where we could get some easy "dough" (money). The place was a butcher-shop in Thirty-first Street. The big guys planned everything, and I only listened. These guys were seven or eight years older than me and had pulled off a lot of big jobs before. They would never let me go with them on big jobs; but this night I went along and they didn't say a word. We all went to the butcher-shop about 11:30 o'clock. It was very dark and everything was quiet, and I was nervous and stayed close to my brother. We all slipped around into the alley behind the butcher-shop and my brother and another big guy went up to the building to see if the doors

---

[1] E. W. BURGESS, "The Family and the Person," *Personality and the Social Group*, p. 133.

were unlocked. My brother had been in the place a few days before to see how to get in and where the cash register was; and so he led the way. I and two other guys waited close to the alley between two buildings. We were going to give "jiggers."

In a little while my brother came back and said everything was locked tight. The owner lived over the butcher-shop, so we couldn't make much noise by breaking the glass or jimmie the door. We all went up to the back door, and then my brother got a box and stood on it, and tried the transom—and it opened. It was too little for my brother or the other guys to get through. Then I was thrilled when they said I'd have to crawl through the transom. That was the kick of my whole life.

I was only eight and always was very little so I could get through the transom easy. I was scared but made up my mind to go through anyway. I was too thrilled to say no.

My brother lifted me up on his shoulders and I crawled through the transom. I hung down on the inside and stood on an ice-box and then crawled down on the floor. The door was locked with a padlock and chain, but I was able to unlock the window and let the big guys in that way. The big guys looked for money first and found twenty-two dollars. Then we all got everything we wanted to eat and several cartons of cigarettes and ditched the place.

When we got out, my brother divvied up everything and I got four dollars and a lot of cigarettes. I felt like a "big shot" after that night and the big guys said I could go with them every time they went robbin'. Almost every night we went robbin' and many times I had to crawl through transoms and one time through an ice-box hole. That's why the big guys called me the "baby bandit."[1]

Summarizing, we may say that a comprehensive life history tends to reveal: (1) an accurate account of human experiences; experiences which reveal attitudes, wishes, plans, fears, likes, and dislikes—material to be analyzed with a view to social treatment; (2) an understanding of the mind of the interviewee and insight into his mental processes; (3) a picture of the social setting in which he lives and which determines his life organization; (4) a formulation of a common plan for possible ways and means of social readjustment.[2]

[1] CLIFFORD R. SHAW and HENRY McKAY, *Social Factors in Juvenile Delinquency*, Case No. 25, pp. 252–253.

[2] For a discussion of the doubtful values of life history documents (written) see Read Bain, "The Validity of Life Histories and Diaries," *The Journal of Educational Sociology*, III (November, 1929), 150–164.

THE SOCIAL CASE HISTORY OUTLINE

A series of social case history outlines is here presented merely as suggestive of the variety of data the interviewer seeks to explore in his attempt to understand a given social situation or a given personality. Frequently social workers cease their exploration as soon as they have hit the cause of the trouble, even though they know little about all of the attendant circumstances. It is usually dangerous to proceed to treat the trouble when only isolated, often disjointed bits of information have been secured, without knowing their specific relation to the whole configurations. Furthermore, diagnosis is a process of elimination. The interviewer cannot rest satisfied when he has discovered something that ails the client at the moment. He must explore further until he has secured a reasonably complete account of the client's total experiences. Such exploration might continue over a long time, but once insight is gained, much time, effort, and money might be saved in arriving at a consistent plan of treatment. Furthermore, it is quite as important to know what is not wrong as to know what is wrong.

As repeatedly stated, the success of the interview depends not so much on the specific questions asked as on satisfactory relations' being established between interviewer and interviewee. The outlines merely indicate the scope of the territory theoretically to be covered in the exploration of a given social situation. It must be remembered that these outlines are at best mere *skeleton guides* in the exploration and not questions to be asked of an interviewee.

Experience of the various professionals who have prepared these outlines shows that the mature student more readily masters the entire scope of the outline when he reclassifies the various points and details under those major headings best suited to the particular needs and problems presented by the interviewee. In other words, these outlines will be useful only in so far as the investigator thoroughly digests them and reshapes them according to his ability to use them.

It follows that these skeleton outlines should never be taken into the home of a client, nor should they be in evidence when interviewing him at the office. It must also be remembered that there is no intention to fix the order of the interview in terms of the order of the questions in the outline. Strictly speaking, there is no definite order applicable to all types of interviewing situations. The reserved or timid interviewee may be best approached by securing from him routine data—names, dates, places of residence, birth, etc.—first, and the story later. The experience of skilled interviewers indicates that generally it is best to proceed from the less formal to the more formal, from the less personal to the more personal, from the concrete to the abstract. However, there are situations which at times seem to defy any calculated system or predetermined order, and the interviewer must adopt an order of interviewing which best fits the exigencies of the situation.

E. R. and Harriet Mowrer maintain that the material pertaining to the early life and community contacts or background material should come first, since (1) a person talks more freely and with fewer reservations about his childhood happenings and memories and his community contacts than about the more intimate contacts within the family circle; (2) a person can detach himself from the immediate social situation more easily if allowed to review the more or less distant past than if he were to discuss the emotional conflicts which upset him at any given time; (3) reviewing the past, the person has an opportunity to see and take cognizance of his life process as a whole—which fact also has therapeutic value. They further maintain that "If the person is allowed to talk about the immediate situation first, he either refuses to give other information or becomes impatient when asked to."[1]

Some of the following guides are from the point of view of the practicing social case worker, some from the clinical and some from the research point of view, and in some instances they overlap. The reader is asked to compare these guides and to note the shifting emphasis from investigation of sources, background, verification to the newer interests on the dynamic, propelling attitudes, interrelations, and the individual's own story. "It is the inside, and not the outside story which we care most about learning."[2]

[1] E. R. MOWRER, *Domestic Discord*, pp. 63–64.

[2] ELIZABETH McCORD, "The Value of the Psychiatric Approach for All Children's Case Workers," *Proceedings of the National Conference of Social Work* 1928, p. 112.

The Social History Outline in Case Work

The nature and content of the social case history obtained by case work interviewers—whether in its diagnostic or treatment aspects—is generally determined by the policies of the agency, by the intake of cases, by the available trained personnel, by the cooperative relations maintained with and the division of work assumed by kindred agencies, by legal responsibilities and restrictions particularly in the case of public agencies and so on. Furthermore, it must be remembered that the social case worker in his contacts with interviewees is primarily concerned with social treatment; he approaches social problems from the standpoint of the art of helping people out of trouble. The following are samples of standard outlines used by family case workers:[1]

The Social Case History Outline of a Family[2]

A star (*) indicates that the answer to the question may be found in, or confirmed by, public records.

I. General Social Data.
1. Family's name? Wife's given and maiden name? Husband's given name? Full names of children? Names of all other members of household, and their relation to the family?
2. What was the birthplace of husband, of wife, and of each child? Nationality of each of the four grandparents?
3. What was the date of birth of husband, of wife, and of each child?*
4. What were the conditions, economic and moral, in the husband's childhood home? The wife's? What was the effect of these conditions on his or her health, character, and industrial status?
5. How long have they been in the city, the state, and the country? Reason for each migration? Do they both speak English?
6. What was the date and place of their marriage?*
7. What previous marriages had either contracted, if any?*
8. Has there been any divorce or legal separation and if so on what grounds?* Have any of the children been placed under guardianship?* Adopted?*
9. What relatives outside the household have husband and wife (including married and unmarried children) and children by

---

[1] For an outline of information to be covered in a minimum record, see Margaret Rich, "A Study of Case Work Processes," *The Compass*, December, 1923.

[2] Mary E. Richmond, *Social Diagnosis*, pp. 378–381. Reprinted by permission of Russell Sage Foundation. See also

Report of the Milford Conference, *Social Case Work—Generic and Specific*, pp. 20–21.

Louise Odencrantz, *The Social Worker*, pp. 20–21.

previous marriages)? What are the circumstances of these relatives, their interest in the family, degree of influence with the family? Names, addresses, degrees of relationship?

10. What is the point of view of such other natural sources of insight as friends, former neighbors, former tradesmen, and landlords, priests or pastors, fellow-workmen and lodge members, etc.?

11. Has the trend of the family life been upward or downward? What characteristics of husband or wife, or what circumstances of health, employment, etc., have determined this trend? What were the family circumstances and characteristics when the family was at its best? How do these compare with its present standard?

12. What is the attitude of the members of the family toward one another? Do they hang together through thick or thin or is there little cohesion?

13. Have the parents good control over the children? Have they their confidences? Are the children taught consideration of the rights of others?

14. What are the children's aptitudes, chief interests, and achievements?

II. Physical and Mental Conditions.

15. Did the parents or other relatives of husband or wife have marked mental, moral, or physical defects? Unusual gifts or abilities? What facts, if any, about the husband or wife or their parents would indicate physical or mental dangers to be guarded against or special capabilities to be developed in the children?

16. How many children have they had? Did wife have any miscarriages? How many children have died? When and from what causes?

17. What attention is given to personal hygiene and health in the family? Are there regular meal hours? Do the food expenditures give a sufficient and well-balanced diet? Is the importance of regular sleep, bathing, care of the teeth, and regular action of the bowels appreciated?

18. If there is a baby, how is it fed, where does it sleep, how much is it in the open air during the day? If the wife is pregnant, is she receiving good care?

19. What is the present physical condition of each member of the family, including also bodily and mental defects?

20. What treatment has been and what is now being given the various members by physicians and medical agencies, and with what results?

III. Industrial History.

21. What is the business or employment, both previous and present, of each worker in the family? What are the names and addresses of employers, previous and present? Between what dates was worker employed by each? What were his earnings, maximum and usual, when regularly employed? What was his work record at these places for speed, accuracy, regularity, sobriety? What

were his reasons for leaving? To what trade union, if any, does he belong? Is he in good standing?

22. At what age did each member of the family go to work, what was his training, and what was his first occupation? Have his occupations since been, on the whole, a good fit? If not, is he capable of developing greater skill at something else?

23. What was the occupation of the wife before marriage, if any, and wages then?

24. Is present occupation of each worker regular, seasonal, or occasional? Is there any chance of advancement? If out of work, how long and why?

25. Are the conditions under which each member of the family works good? If not, in what way bad?

IV. Financial Situation (exclusive of charitable relief).

26. Income. What are the present wages and earnings? What proportion, in each case, goes into the family budget? Is this proportion too large or too small? Present income from other sources, including lodgers, boarders, pensions, benefits, contributions from relatives, etc.? Is the present income adequate? Could the present income be increased in any wise way?

27. Outgo. What are the monthly expenditures for food, rent, clothing, fuel, insurance, carfare, recreation, sundries? What is the amount of debts, to whom, for what? Are any articles in pawn, where, amount due? Are any articles being purchased on the installment plan? Weekly payments? Amount still to be paid? With what insurance company are members of family insured? What is the total of weekly premiums? Are they paid up to date? Could the present expenditures be decreased in any wise way? Should they be increased, and how?

28. Is there any court record of inheritance, of property, of insurance, of damages recovered?* Has the family, or did it ever have, savings? When, where, and how much? Do any members belong to benefit organizations? Amount of dues, possible benefits?

V. Education.

29. What was the education of parents? At what ages did they and the older children leave school? Did the children have any vocational training? How does the education of each member of the family compare with the standards of the community in which each was reared?

30. What is the school and grade of each child of school age? His teacher's name? School evidence as to scholarship, attendance, behavior, physical and mental condition, and home care?

VI. Religious Affiliations.

31. What is the religion of each parent? Name of church? What signs are there of its influence?

32. Do children receive religious instruction in Sunday schools, or otherwise? Where and from whom? Where were they baptized?

VII. Recreation.
33. What social affiliations have the various members of the family? Do any of them belong to clubs or societies—church, settlement, fraternal, political, or other? What forms of recreation do the family enjoy together? What separately? How does each member employ his leisure time?

VIII. Environment.
34. Does family occupy a whole house? If so, has it a yard? A garden? If not, on what floor do they live? At front or rear? How many rooms? Name and address of landlord or agent?
35. Are the rooms adequately lighted and ventilated? What are the toilet and water facilities? The general sanitary condition of the house?
36. Are the rooms comfortably furnished? Are they clean, or sordid and dirty?
37. What is the character of the neighborhood? Has it undesirable physical or moral features? How many other families in the house? Their general character?
38. How long has family lived at present address? At what previous addresses has family lived? When and how long? Character of each neighborhood and house?

IX. Relations, If Any, with Social Agencies.
39. Have any social agencies or institutions had relations with the family? If so, of what kind and with what results? If first contacts have been with the wife, is the husband known also, or vice versa? To what extent has the family received charitable aid, if at all?

X. Basis for Treatment.
40. What are the family's plans and ambitions for the future? What moral and temperamental characteristics and what aptitudes of each member can be reckoned with as assets or must be recognized as liabilities in the shaping of that future?

Miss Richmond includes all of the face-sheet information in the outline for the family history. As already stated, experienced investigators maintain that it is more expedient to secure this material during the general course of the interview and in vital relation to other desired data than to set it apart as separate items to be asked in more or less routine manner.[1] Miss Richmond's outline is very comprehensive, but it must be remembered that the interviewer is concerned not only with an account of the cultural background or family traditions of his interviewees, not only with an account of the economic and social conditions in which they live, and not only with the things they do or fail to

---

[1] Face-sheet material as an administrative convenience can be prepared later from the body of data obtained in the interview.

do, the things they have or do not have, etc., but with the role
their cultural and family backgrounds play in their lives, with the
meaning their activities, attitudes, or possessions assume in their
life organization, and with the conditioning of their attitudes by
the social setting. Unless the interviewer is at all times concerned with social relations, with the meaning and the effect of
the physical, social, and intellectual worlds upon the person, the
investigation tends to degenerate into a sterile history which
throws little light upon the central problems and the personality
under consideration. It is more important, for instance, to ask,
"What effect does a person's occupation, education, family life,
etc. have upon him?" than "What is his occupation, education, or
the status of his family life?" In the first instance we secure
an outside story; in the second instance, an inner view of the
life organization and the personal attitudes. As stated before,
human behavior cannot be understood unless social attitudes are
brought to the surface. The social case history of a family as
tentatively presented by Professor E. W. Burgess "aims to discover the nature and meaning of the social processes by which
families maintain their unity" and by which they succeed in
adjusting their members to society's requirements. The outlines
by Miss Richmond and Dr. Burgess are perhaps complementary.

Tentative Social Case History Outline of a Family[1]

I. Location and Extent in Time and Space. Family History.
   1. Genealogical tree as retained in the family memory: (a) chartered;
      (b) emphasis upon ancestry; (c) family history.
   2. Map showing geographical distribution and movement: (a) of large
      family group; and (b) of small family group.
   3. Mobility of the family: (a) home ownership or tenancy; (b) number
      of times moved; (c) number and kind of books, magazines, and
      papers in home; (d) automobile, etc.
II. Characterization of Members of the Family.
   1. Mentality.
   2. Temperament: (a) choleric; (b) sanguine; (c) phlegmatic; (d)
      melancholic.
   3. Social reaction pattern: (a) objective (direct, enthusiastic, explosive,
      emotionally unstable); (b) introspective (indirect, secretive, evasive,
      psychopathic, psychic inferior).
   4. Character (stabilized, unstabilized).
   5. Philosophy of life: Philistine, Bohemian, religious, idealistic.

[1] Prepared by E. W. Burgess (mimeographed).

III. Family Economy.
1. Location: (*a*) urban; (*b*) rural.   (Include also description of physical structure of home.)
2. Occupation and its effects: (*a*) of husband; (*b*) of wife; (*c*) of children.
3. Division of labor between members of family.
4. Family communism (illustrations).

IV. Family Traditions and Ceremonies.
1. Family traditions: (*a*) family romances; (*b*) family skeletons; (*c*) family name; (*d*) family lore (album, pictures, superstitions, family proverbs, and expressions).
2. Family ceremonies and symbols: (*a*) family prayer, family altar, grace at meals; (*b*) story-telling; (*c*) family ritual (demonstration of affection, terms of endearment, greeting father on return from work, habitual forms of behavior, as father's chair, family circle around hearth, etc.).

V. Family Organization and Control.
1. Typical forms of organization: (*a*) patriarchy; (*b*) matriarchy; (*c*) paidocracy; (*d*) consensus (describe with illustrations of mechanism of authority and type of family complex); (*e*) relation to larger family group (consultation with members of larger family group, relatives with prestige, poor relations, etc.).
2. Conflicts and accommodations: (*a*) what are type of conflicts; (*b*) what are social distance; (*c*) family factions.
3. Family education: (*a*) general; (*b*) economic; (*c*) religious; (*d*) sex instruction.
4. Family control and discipline: (*a*) control by imitation and suggestion (direction of attention, *rapport*, gesture, facial expression, ridicule, etc.); (*b*) physical punishment; (*c*) appeal to self-respect or pride; (*d*) appeal to conscience; (*e*) persons as control; (*f*) proverbs and family sayings as control.
5. Family events: (*a*) reunions; (*b*) picnics; (*c*) family recreation; (*d*) holidays; (*e*) birthdays; (*f*) Sundays.
6. Family solidarity: (*a*) family *esprit de corps;* (*b*) family morale; (*c*) family objectives; (*d*) effect of family crises; (*e*) sense of success or defeat in life.

VI. The Family, the Community, and the Person.
1. Familism: (*a*) family ideals and sentiments; (*b*) social sufficiency of the small family or the large family group; (*c*) family life analyzed by the four wishes (security, response, recognition, and new experience).
2. The family and the neighborhood; (*a*) status of family in the neighborhood and community; (*b*) participation of family in neighborhood activities (in school, church, recreation centers, as a family or as individuals); (*c*) extent to which leisure of family or its members is spent outside of neighborhood.
3. The family and the person: (*a*) family as stimulus to the person; (*b*) personality of its members (as developed or retarded by the family).

The Social Case History Outline of an Unmarried Mother[1]

The preliminary social questions regarding the husband and wife contained in the questionnaire regarding Any Family, those regarding names, ages, nationality, religion, language spoken, length of residence in city, state, and country—may be assumed to apply to the Unmarried Mother, and (in cases in which she is sure who he is) to the father of her child. This is not a schedule to be filled out nor a set of queries to be answered by a social agency's client or clients. It is merely a list of queries which, when gone over by the social case worker with a particular case in mind, may bring to his attention, out of the many presented, a possible four or five that may contain suggestive leads.

I. The Mother.
  A. Her Family and Home.
    1. Did or does she live with her own parents? Is she legitimate? Adopted? Did she ever live in an institution, and if so, when, how long, and why? What is the standing of parents in the community? Are they self-supporting, self-respecting people? Is the home clean and respectable looking? Was her parents' marriage forced? Did her mother or sisters have illegitimate children? Were these children kept with their mothers, or what became of them?
    2. Are (or were) parents fond of children? Even-tempered or irritable? Faithful to church? Earnest or indifferent as to moral standards? Lax or firm in control (for instance, are they conscientious in overseeing their daughters' recreations; did the mother teach her daughters housework, instruct them in sex hygiene)? Or oversevere (for instance, are they reasonable in allowing pleasures and part of earnings)?
  B. Her Community.
    3. What is the character of the city quarter or town in which the girl or woman grew up—in size, race, religion, general moral standards, faithfulness to church, predominating occupation (if any), recreations, and social life? Is it a factory town, farming region, or what is its industrial character? Has it distinct foreign colonies?
    4. If she came from a small town or village, is it within easy distance of a large city? Do her companions have local amuse-

[1] Prepared by Ada E. Sheffield and quoted by Mary E. Richmond, *Social Diagnosis*, pp. 414–419.

For a discussion of the problem of unmarried mothers, see ALICE S. CHEYNEY, "Study of 200 Unmarried Mothers," Philadelphia Children's Bureau, 1910.

MARY F. SMITH, "Changing Emphasis in Case Work with Unmarried Mothers," *The Family*, XIV (January, 1934), 310–317.

PERCY G. KAMMERER, *The Unmarried Mother.*

LOUISE DRURY, "Milestones in the Approach to Illegitimacy," *The Family*, VI (April, May, June, 1925) 41–42; 79–81; 98–99.

ments or do they go to the city for them? Are their pleasures supervised?

5. Are the schools good from academic, vocational, and social standpoints?

6. Are the local police alert towards loose behavior on the streets? Are saloons, dance halls, etc., regulated well? Are they numerous in proportion to the population? Is the judge in the local police court interested in the welfare of boys and girls?

7. What is the proportion of illegitimate births in the girl's or woman's native town or country?* Does custom there treat the offense as a slight one, or is ostracism relentless? Do pregnant girls frequently leave to hide their conditions and dispose of the child elsewhere? Is this region equipped to care for such girls? If not, why? If it is, what cooperative understanding has been established with local agencies?

8. Are the local doctors and clergymen (if a small community) awake to the problem? What attitude do they take in regard to young unmarried mothers' keeping their babies?

C. The Mother Herself.

9. What was her health as a child? At what age did she mature? Has she any physical peculiarity or deformity? Is there any evidence that she is mentally deficient or abnormal?

10. Did her parents say that she was troublesome as a child? If so, how? Did she disobey her parents, fail to heed their advice, was she disrespectful to them? Did she frequent candy, ice cream, or fruit stores for diversion? What sort of associates did she have while she was growing up? How have they turned out? Can her parents throw light on the reasons for her behavior, if loose? Of what sort are her present girl or women friends?

11. When her parents learned she was pregnant, what, if any, plans did they make for her?

12. What grade in school did she reach? What do the teachers who knew her best think of her? In what studies did she excel? What vocational training, if any, did she receive?

13. What do her employers say of her work? How long has she held her positions? If she was employed in a factory, how much judgment did her work call for? Was it mechanical? If as a domestic, what are the things that she does well, what ill? For instance, can she make good bread, season vegetables? Is she neat and clean about her person and her work? Can she wash and iron? Does she wait on table smoothly and quietly? Has she done ordering for her mistress? How much did she know when her mistress took her? Does she improve—rapidly or slowly? Does she remember directions, or do they have to be repeated? What does she do best, heavy work or light? Is she good with children? Is she capable enough to hold a place with her child?

14. What do her employers say of her character? Is she honest, of a good disposition, industrious? If a domestic, has she been

discreet with tradesmen who come to the house? Has she had men callers, one or many? Have they been accustomed to go at a proper hour? Has she been given to staying out very late? Does she dress conspicuously?

15. When did girl's or woman's sexual experience begin? Under what circumstances—was it with a relative, an employer, an older man, a school boy? Had she accepted money from any man or men for unchastity, or has she received only a good time—theaters, dinners, etc.—or board? Has she lived for any period as the wife of any man or men? Has she supplemented her income through men, or has she made her whole livelihood in this way? If so, for how long and when? Has she been a common prostitute, has she had a succession of "friends," or has she been intimate with but the one man? Has she a court record?* From what she, her relatives, friends, and employers say, does she seem to seek wrongdoing, or does she merely yield when evil approaches her?

16. Has she had another child or other children by a different man or men? When were the children born and where? How long did she nurse them? If they did not live, at what age and of what disease did they die? If they are alive, where are they—with her, with her family, with the man's family, boarded out, or adopted? If the latter, through whom was the adoption brought about? What does she know of the character and circumstances of the adoptive parents of her child or children? Has she any child in charge of a society or institution? Was it placed out in a family? How often has its mother seen it? Is it under supervision? If she is separated from her child, what has seemed to be the effect upon her character? If she kept it with her, what?

17. Has she ever been under treatment for syphilis or gonorrhea? When and by whom?

II. The Father.[1]
  A. His Family.
    18. What is or was the standing of the man's parents in the community? Did the father instruct his sons in sex hygiene? Did his influence in this direction tend towards high-mindedness, towards cautiousness in pleasure, or towards unabashed laxity in morals? Did the mother and sisters take a double standard for granted? (See in addition same topic under The Mother for questions that apply.)
  B. His Community.
    19. What is the character of the community in which the man grew up? (See same topic under The Mother for questions that apply.)

[1] To be used only in cases where the mother is sure who is the father of her child.

C. The Man Himself.

20. Was he troublesome to his parents as a boy? Respectful and obedient, or the reverse? What sort of associates did he have while he was growing up? How have they turned out morally? Have any of them got girls into trouble? If so, do they boast of it, or have they the average moral scruples? Where do they draw the line as to the things "a fellow can't do"?

21. Did he spend any part of his childhood in an institution? If so, how long was he there, at what age, and why? What was his record while there?

22. What grade in school did he reach? Why did he leave, and at what age? What have his teachers to say of his character and ability? In what studies did he excel? Has he attended a trade school or a night school?

23. Is he single or married? Is he still living at home? If not, at what age and for what reason did he leave? How has he lived since? What type of associates has he chosen?

24. At what age did he first go to work? With what employer and at what occupation has he worked longest? Where is he now working and how long has he held this place? What do his employers say of the quality of his work? How much judgment does it call for?

25. Does he drink to the point of intemperance? Use drugs? Gamble? Is there any evidence that he has been dishonest?

26. What is his record as to sexual morality? Has he been known as a loose liver? Involved in scandals? Or has he, on the other hand, borne a good reputation, and is this the first affair with a woman in which he has been involved?

27. Has he ever been arrested? At what age and for what offense? If imprisoned, for how long? What was his record at reform school or prison?*

28. Is he of the same social status as the mother of his child?

III. The Situation, Past and Present.

A. Man and Woman.

29. What is the girl's or woman's explanation of her going wrong? Was she engaged to the man? Was she in love with him? If not, was it loneliness, drink, ignorance, force that led to her "shame"? Where and when did she meet the man? Was she living at home at the time? With relatives, friends, in a lodging house, or at service? Had she known the man steadily or was he a passing acquaintance? Did she live with him for any time as his wife? Did he promise marriage? Do her family or friends know of his seeing her often at about the time of conception? Had they been expecting that he would marry her? Has she letters from him that go to show his probable paternity? Has the man known her family, called at her home? Does she know his family?

30. Does the man acknowledge paternity? Does he acknowledge having had relations with her? Does he claim that others had

also? If so, who? Did she live in a lodging house, or were there men lodgers in the same house or tenement? Is there any evidence that she was intimate with any other man at about the time of conception? Any evidence (such as that of the physician who confined her, regarding earlier abortions, miscarriages, or births) to prove her previous unchastity?

31. What is the man's opinion of the girl's character? What suggestions, if any, has he made to her regarding her plans? Did he suggest her consulting any illegal practitioner? Did she follow his advice? Name of the practitioner?

32. Do the man and the girl wish to marry? If so, why have they not done it before? Are they both such human material as to make marriage advisable? What are the man's health and habits? Has he had a medical examination? By whom? Was it clinical only or with laboratory tests? Does marriage in the mother's home state legitimize a child, or must its parents adopt it?

33. Have the couple lived together for several years and had more than one child? (Consult, in Mary E. Richmond, *Social Diagnosis*, as circumstances of the case demand, the questionnaires regarding Any Family, a Deserted Family, or a Neglected Child, pp. 378, 395, and 405.)

34. If the man is married, does his wife know of his relations with the girl or woman? Has he legitimate children to support? If unmarried, has he relatives whom he must help?

35. Has the man property? Has he a steady place? What is his income? Would his employers bring pressure on him to help his baby, or would they abet him in eluding his responsibility? Is he a man who would readily leave for another state if prosecuted? (See in Mary E. Richmond, *Social Diagnosis*, the Deserted Family questionnaire, p. 395.) How much should he pay?

36. Is there evidence beyond a reasonable doubt as to the man's paternity? Has he a lawyer? If so, who? Will the man settle out of court? Is it desirable that he do so? Why? Can he get bonds? If not, is he likely to keep up weekly payments, or is he so unreliable that a lump sum is wiser? Would his family do anything for the baby? Has his father property?

37. Has the mother a lawyer? If so, who? Has she taken out a warrant, started or completed proceedings? If the latter, what was the settlement?* Has the man paid her anything towards the expenses of confinement, etc.? Did she sign a release paper?

38. Is it better that the man pay the money to the girl, or to a trustee who would hold it for the child? In your opinion, is the purpose of payment in this case to punish the man, to help the girl, or to provide for the baby's future?

B. Mother and Child.

39. If this is the girl's or woman's first child, does she appreciate the seriousness of her act and of its consequences? Did she

leave her home to hide her "shame"? To give her baby to strangers so that her misconduct might remain unsuspected at home? Does she love her baby? Does she want to keep it?

40. What preparations did she make for the child? How long before confinement did she stop work? What sort of work was she doing during the previous months? What was her physical condition at this time? Did she have instruction in prenatal care and did she follow it?

41. Was she confined in a hospital? How long did she stay? Did she receive after care? If not confined in a hospital, where? Was she attended by a physician or by a midwife? (Name and address of either.) How soon after confinement did she go to work?

42. Is the child's birth correctly recorded?* Has the child been baptized?

43. Have the mother and her baby been examined by a physician? What is his name and address? How soon after confinement did the examination take place? Was it clinical only or was it accompanied by laboratory tests? Is the mother or her child under treatment? What is the physician's report of her health and of the child's, and what is his advice?

44. Does she nurse the baby? If not, is it by a doctor's advice? Can she get pure milk? Does she understand the preparation of food? Has she had instruction in the general care of an infant? Is she capable of profiting by such instruction? Can she easily get a nurse's visits or take the baby to a clinic?

45. Do her parents know of her situation? Are they so circumstanced that they can help her by taking her home with the baby, by tending the baby while she goes to work, by adopting the child, or by showing their sense of responsibility in any other way? Do they feel that their younger children should be kept in ignorance of her story?

46. What are the unmarried mother's plans for herself and child?[1]

The following outline or guides in the interview, by Miss Louise Drury, with an unmarried mother differ in many respects from those presented by Mrs. Sheffield:

First Interview Outline with an Unmarried Mother[2]

The first interview with an unmarried mother is particularly difficult because of the very delicacy of the situation, and because often she has planned to tell a story which she thinks will lessen her difficulties and keep the true facts a secret. The interviewer, therefore, must use specialized skill and tact to gain the confidence of the girl. This is necessary not only in order to give help, which must be based on an understanding of the true

---

[1] Quoted by MARY E. RICHMOND, *Social Diagnosis*, pp. 414–419.

[2] Prepared by LOUISE DRURY, Children's Protective Association, Los Angeles, 1934.

facts, but also to begin treatment, which will give the girl a feeling of security and confidence in the ability of the agency to help her make satisfactory plans for herself and her baby.   It is important to start as soon as possible the process of giving the unmarried mother more insight into what is involved in her situation and of replacing her emotional attitude with one of objective planning.[1]

The same detailed information, understanding, and treatment is needed whether the girl comes to the agency early in her pregnancy, asking help in making plans for her confinement, or whether she comes after the birth of her baby, wishing to establish paternity and secure support or wishing to place her baby in a foster boarding home or give it for adoption.

If, in the course of the interview, it is obvious that the girl is telling a fictitious story, the interviewer should never even imply criticism but rather sympathetically let the girl know that she understands the reasons for her reticence but that she will be able to help her only if the real facts are understood.   She should encourage a fresh start on the true story.

I. Family History.
1. Unless the girl has been married, she should be studied as a member of her own family group, covering the same data which is secured for all family cases, including the interrelations of the individual members and their attitudes toward each other, especially toward the girl.[2]
2. If she has been married, secure in addition the full family history of her husband and legitimate children.

II. The Unmarried Mother.
1. Personal History.
Chronological history of the mother's life, including growth, development, health, sex education, school experience, recreation, employment, religious affiliation, and social adjustments.   Secure details of all previous sex experiences and other illegitimate children, where born, paternity, and present care.
2. Relation with "Alleged Father." (Term changed to "father" when paternity has been established.)
Date, place, and circumstances of first meeting.   Date and place of first intercourse.   Dates of subsequent acts of intercourse. Names of other men with whom intercourse occurred during this period, giving dates and places (very important for legally establishing paternity).   Were contraceptives used?   Date of last menstruation.
3. Basis of Sexual Relations.
Were they engaged?   Were they in love?   Why did she submit to illicit relations?   Did they live together as man and wife?   Was there a promise of marriage in case of pregnancy?   Was he free to marry?   Was money offered and accepted?
Has man been told of pregnancy?   What was his reaction?   Has he admitted paternity?   To her alone?   Before witnesses?   Does

---

[1] See Chap. XIV particularly section on sympathetic insight.
[2] See "Social Case History Outline of a Family," by Mary E. Richmond, pp. 102–105, and by E. W. Burgess, pp. 106–107.

she understand that the father is legally responsible for the support of his illegitimate child? What is the girl's present feeling towards him?

III. **The Alleged Father.** (Omit if the girl has been promiscuous or had relations with more than one man during the period of conception, usually considered the alleged month of conception, the month before, and the month after.)

 1. Name, address, age, religious affiliation, school history, employment, earnings, health, make-up of family. Standing of man's family in community and home life, so far as known to girl first-hand.

 2. Is he married? Living with his wife? Has he legitimate children? Is marriage apparently happy? Is he divorced? Is he responsible for support of wife? Of children? What amount?

 3. Is girl willing that the father be visited by the agency in order to establish paternity legally and secure support for the baby?

IV. **Mother and Baby.**

 1. What members of girl's family know of her pregnancy (or about the baby, if born)? If no one knows about it, persuade her to confide in some close relative whom she believes to be understanding and helpful. Explain the mental hygiene value of sharing a distressing secret with someone in whom she has confidence. Explain also that relatives are almost always kind and resourceful when called upon in a difficult situation, and feel it their right and responsibility to offer help.

 2. Place, date, and name of physician who made prenatal examination. Was special care advised? Extent of prenatal care. Were laboratory tests made for venereal disease? Results? If recommended, what treatment has been secured?

 3. Have plans been made for confinement and nursing period? Can she be confined at home? If not, can she stay at home until delivery, go to a general hospital, and return home with her baby after ten days in the hospital? Would she like to enter a maternity home where she may receive care until confinement, and where she can remain through the nursing period?

 4. If the girl thinks she wishes to give her baby for adoption at birth, suggest to defer any decision until after the nursing period, when she will have recovered from the physical and emotional strain and knows what resources are available to help her care for the baby. Reassure her that the agency will help her make a satisfactory plan for herself and the baby when that time comes. It is wiser to proceed one step at a time, because the majority of mothers desire to keep their babies when the emergency is past and when they realize that help and guidance is available as long as they need it.

 5. If marriage is being considered, is there mutual affection? Would the marriage have been consummated without the complication of pregnancy? Is there reasonable assurance of a stable home for the child? Is the girl sure that marriage is not being considered merely to give the baby a name? Such marriages cannot be advised, because they so often result in neglect, desertion, infidelity, and divorce.

6. What are the girl's plans and hopes for her future? Education?
Employment? Care of her baby?

V. Summary of Interview.

Before closing the interview, sum up with the girl the next steps to
be covered by worker and girl before their next meeting. Emergency housing, appointment for prenatal examination and tests (if
not already done), confiding in a member of her family to pave the
way for worker's eventual contact. Plans of seeing the alleged
father and for the next interview.[1]

Medical Social History Outline[2]

I. Interpretation.

A. Of Hospital to Patients.

The social worker interprets the patient's disease or injury to him
if of an age to cooperate in treatment and always to his parents,
explaining the meaning of it; what may be expected in the future;
how to carry out the doctor's orders; and what agencies in the
community may help him.

B. Of Patient to Hospital.

Social history varies with the type of case but in general the
interpretation of the patient to the hospital involves the interpretation of all of the contributing factors of the disease and whether
or not the doctor's orders will be carried out and the hospital
treatment augmented in the home. . . .

C. Interpreting Patient to His Family and Social Agencies.

In order to make adequate plans for the future of the family, the
family or the social agency interested in the family needs to know

1. What is the matter with the patient?
2. What usually happens in a case of this kind?
3. What is going to happen in this individual case?
4. Is he going to be partially or entirely disabled?
5. Disabled for a week, a month, a year, or forever?
6. Disabled in physical endurance or mental capacity?

II. Social History Outline.[3] . . .

III. Making the Social Diagnosis.

A. After the information regarding the medical and social situations
is secured, the analysis is made and the following factors determined.

1. How long is the patient going to be acutely ill?
2. How long is the patient going to be disabled.
3. How much of a drain the family budget can stand for:
(a) convalescent care; (b) medicine; (c) special diet; (d) appliances.
4. The state of the family finances.
5. What help can be expected from relatives?

---

[1] LOUISE DRURY, "First Interview with an Unmarried Mother," manuscript adapted especially for this volume, 1934.

[2] Adaptation from Richard C. Cabot's article in *Hospital Social Service*,
October, 1928, 269–320, by Perle Dow, Children's Hospital Society, Los
Angeles, for the guidance of the Hospital Social Service Department.

[3] See pp. 102–108.

    6. What help can be expected from social agencies?

    7. The strength and weaknesses of the family:

       (*a*) material; (*b*) traits of character.

  B. Thus a social diagnosis or medical social decision is arrived at, based on the medical findings and social situation of the patient. The decision as to the patient's ability to look after himself is based upon

    1. The seriousness and complexity of the medical problem.

    2. The patient's background and character.

    3. The family situation.

    4. The economic situation.

    5. Available resources in the community.

  C. It must be emphasized that the medical social worker must fill a need that cannot otherwise be filled; that she is not to do what the patient can do himself or that his family can do for him; that the efficient worker helps the patient to help himself.

IV. The Social Service Plan.

In collaboration with the doctor, the medical social worker sets up a goal considering the assets and liabilities of the family and keeping in mind the medical and social prognosis.

 V. Medical Social Treatment.

Medical social treatment is the social worker's part in the plan for helping the patient. The social service department may carry the responsibility entirely or share it with an outside agency. Where no funds for relief are available, a large percentage of the cases may be carried jointly with another agency.

VI. Follow-up.

Any scheme for follow-up which fails to put the interests of the patient first is complicating to the patient and may fail ultimately because of the patient's lack of cooperation. When social service enters the field of medical follow-up it does so because the follow-up of the patient's disease and its cure is only a part of a well-thought out plan for an all around medical-social solution of the patient's life problems. The method and frequency of follow-up depends upon the problems involved in the individual case. Follow-up for the purpose of completing a record is discouraged.

The outlines presented above—whether in the field of family case work or medical social service—give sufficient concrete detail of the varied possibilities in case work to enable the interviewer to utilize at least a few suggestive leads. But it must be remembered that rarely do cases come systematically arranged, or, as Dr. Richard Cabot observes, "They are generally presented to us from an angle, and with one symptom, generally a misleading one, in the foreground. From this point of view we must reason our way back into the deeper processes and more obscure cases which guide our therapeutic endeavor."

It might be asked: "To what extent are the data outlined above applicable to or true of everybody?" Miss Richmond says:

We all have a birthday and a place of birth, and have or have had two parents, four grandparents, etc., with all that this implies by way of racial and national characteristics, of family inheritance and tradition, and probably of family environment. Our place of birth (assuming here and elsewhere the conditions of a modern civilization) was a house of some kind, and we have continued to live in this or in a series of other houses ever since. The characteristics of these houses, their neighborhood and atmosphere, have helped to make us what we are.

We all have bodies that need intelligent care if we are to keep them in good repair. Their condition has influenced our minds and our characters, though it is equally true that these, in turn, may have influenced profoundly our bodily health.

We have all had an education, whether through instruction in the schools and in the churches, or through means less formal.

We have all had some means of subsistence, whether through gainful occupations of our own, through dependence upon the gainful occupations of others, or through assistance public or private.

We all modify, and are in turn modified by, our material and our social environment. The body of social traditions, institutions, equipments of every sort that man has built up has left a deep mark upon him. This implies, among other things, an emotional responsiveness to the society of our fellows—responsiveness whether shown in marriage and the founding of a second home (in which case, of course, all of the foregoing things are true also of the one married), or in other associations of personal loyalty with our fellows, individually and in groups. These attractions imply repulsions. We are remoulded by the discords of the one, the concords of the other.

We are all going somewhere and have not yet arrived. Our character is "not cut in marble," but is the sum of our past experiences—a sum which is to be changed, inevitably, by our future experiences.[1]

---

[1] *Op. cit.*, p. 377. Reprinted by permission of Russell Sage Foundation.

CHAPTER VI

THE CONTENT OF THE INTERVIEW (*Concluded*)

The Social Case History in Clinical Procedure

The social case history obtained in clinical procedure stands midway between the one obtained by the social case worker and the one obtained by the research interviewer. The clinical interviewer is interested in every conceivable factor which theoretically is assumed to have some bearing on the behavior of the person. The clinic inquires into the organic constitution, the mental constitution, the personal characteristics, the physical factors, the social factors, and so on. It generally engages the services of several scientists, and each is expected to contribute information on the case pertaining to his field. Like the case worker, the clinician utilizes as far as possible available scientific findings in arriving at a diagnosis and, like the research worker, he is constantly studying his materials in the hope of new discoveries.

The Social Case History Outline of an Individual Delinquent[1]

I. Family History.
   1. Racial and national characteristics of forebears.
   2. Marital conditions in the family.
   3. Industrial and financial history of the family in its general bearings on the problem.
   4. Account of siblings.
   5. Abuse of alcohol or drugs by father and mother before conception and by mother during pregnancy.
   6. Specific defects or diseases of father and mother, particularly such as may have debilitated germ plasm or affected embryo, including hereditary diseases.
   7. Mental aberrations or defects on the part of forebears; peculiar traits of disposition in the family.

[1] Summary of outline prepared by William Healy, *The Individual Delinquent*, pp. 53–61.

See also D. A. Thom, *Habit Clinics for the Child of Preschool Age*, Children's Bureau, U. S. Department of Labor, 1924.

Walter C. Reckless, "Suggestions for the Sociological Study of Problem Children," The *Journal of Educational Sociology*, II (November, 1928), 156–171.

8. Mental and physical defects or disease in siblings which may throw light on hereditary tendencies.
9. Mental, moral, and other traits in ancestors, siblings, and ancestral side lines.

II. Developmental History.
1. Conditions of disease, use of intoxicants, or debility of either parent directly prior to conception.
2. Antenatal conditions of health, hygiene, and occupation of mother during pregnancy.
3. Mental condition of mother during pregnancy, including aberrations, worries, shock.   Note illegitimacy and its effects.
4. Injury or accident to mother during pregnancy.
5. Attempted abortion.
6. Birth.
7. Infancy and childhood.
    Full history of all diseases or nutritional disturbances, including anything in the way of convulsions or disturbances of consciousness.
    Sex habits, in detail, if possible.   Fright or shock.   Habits of sleep.

III. History of Environment.
1. Changes of living through immigration.   Other residential changes.
2. Effect of various languages used in the family.
3. Effect of disordered marital conditions.   Harmony in family.
4. Education and mental disposition of parents which may influence child in environment.
5. Housing and financial conditions in detail.
6. Recreational facilities.   Occupation outside school hours.
7. Family control, and influence of neglect.   Mother working or away from home.
8. Companionship.   Opportunities afforded by relatively good or bad associations.   Amusements in detail.
9. Opportunities for religious culture.
10. Occupational opportunities.   Character of places worked in.
11. Institutional life in detail.
12. Efforts to assist individual before or after custody.
13. If married, complete history of home life.

IV. Mental and Moral Development.
1. School history in detail with individual's own reaction towards it.
2. Effect of companionship, beginning with earliest associations.
3. Were bad companions voluntarily sought or were associations forced?
4. Character of associations with the opposite sex.
5. History and character of reading.
6. Use and development of special talents, in music, art, mechanics, athletics, etc.
7. Occupation or employment history, with detailed account of success or failure.

8. History of the home life and the development of the individual in it.
9. General behavior, with detailed characteristics.
10. Disposition and mental traits. Detailed history of any changes taking place in these.
11. Habits with regard to alcohol, tobacco, drugs, sex, etc.
12. Effect of coming into the hands of the law.
13. The effect of incarceration, sentence, or probation.
14. The effect of institution as compared with the opportunities and training while there.

V. Anthropometry.
VI. Medical Examination.
VII. Psychological Examination.
VIII. Delinquency.
    1. Description of special acts and types of misconduct.
    2. The cause of delinquency in the opinion of relatives and friends.
    3. Attitude of delinquent towards court, probation, institution, etc.
    4. Official record, police, court, institutional.

The Social History Outline[1] [Concerning Problem Child]

I. Identifying Data.

Name	Address
Date of Birth	Birthplace
Color Sex	Religion
School Grade	Present School
Name of Father	Address
Name of Mother	Address
Names of Siblings	Addresses
(brothers and sisters in order of birth)	

Referred by
Reason for requesting examination.
Sources of information.
    List informants seen, giving names, addresses, relation to child, and date of contact. Describe briefly for each the attitudes and circumstances which facilitated or interfered with the interviews and note inquiries which provoked an emotional reaction of any sort.

II. Personal History (Chronological Account of Child's Life).
    A. Problem.
        Give a detailed account of all behavior, such as:
        1. Asocial behavior: Stealing, truancy, lying, destructiveness, cruelty, overt sexual activities, etc. Give court record if there is one.

---

[1] DOROTHY BRINKER, Social History Outline (Bulletin No. 1, New Series), State of California Department of Institutions Bureau of Juvenile Research (December, 1929), pp. 1–5. Adapted in part from history outlines used at: Institute for Juvenile Research, Chicago; Institute for Child Guidance, New York; and Colorado Psychopathic Hospital, Denver.

2. Personality traits: Seclusiveness, timidity, fear, excessive imagination, habitual whining or crying, temper tantrums, overactivity, teasing, show-off behavior, inability to learn, failure to profit by experience, etc.
3. Habits: Sleep disturbances, capricious appetite, thumb-sucking, nail-biting, enuresis, masturbation, speech defects, etc.

Give age at first occurrence of problems, ways in which such behavior developed, attitude of parents, teachers, and others concerned. For example, in case of stealing, what was taken; from whom stolen; alone or with companions; age and sex of companions; what was done with articles stolen; methods used in treatment and child's reaction.

B. Personality.

Describe by giving illustrations the child's attitudes and reactions to his parents, his brothers and sisters, his home, his associates, his duties, those in authority (teachers, employers, etc.), his own interests, himself (*i.e.*, self-reliance, self-pity, conceit, etc.), and life in general (amount of daydreaming). It is important to have a picture of the child's reactions in terms of satisfactory and acceptable behavior, as well as in terms of unsatisfactory or unacceptable behavior.

C. Developmental History (Covering First Two Years of Life).
1. Date and place of birth.
2. Pregnancy—Health of mother and emotional reactions, attitudes of parents toward each other, wanted or unwanted child?
3. Delivery—Normal or difficult, weight at birth, any injuries or malformations. Influence of any abnormalities on attitude of mother toward child.
4. Feeding—Breast or bottle fed; regularity; length of nursing period; difficulties at weaning.
5. Age of dentition, walking, talking. Any peculiarities? When were toilet habits established? Methods used? Tendency for right- or left-handedness.

D. Health.
1. Give ages of occurrence, duration, severity, and after effects of: illnesses, accidents, operations.
2. Inquire particularly as to: spasms, St. Vitus' dance, sleeping sickness, infantile paralysis, meningitis, fainting spells, ear infections, eye trouble.

E. Habits.
Food, sleep, elimination, cleanliness.

F. Sex Development.
1. Sex interests or activities. Sex information given, age, and child's reaction. Any sign of puberty?
2. For girls: first menstruation, what preparation, emotional effect.

G. School History.
Chronological account of school progress (age of entrance, grades skipped or repeated, schools attended, etc.). Give results of any intelligence or achievement tests. Attitude of child toward

his school work, his teachers, and his schoolmates. Attitude of teachers toward child. —

H. Work History.

Kind of work done, amount and use of earnings. Child's attitude and parents' attitudes toward his work.

I. Recreation.

Chief interests and kinds of recreational activities. Does child have a regular allowance to spend as he chooses?

J. Companions.

Types. How does he get on with them? What is family's attitude toward them? Are they welcome in the home? etc.

III. Family History.

A. Immediate Family.

1. Parents (Father and Mother).

Name, age, place of birth, present residence, and present occupation. If foreign born, reason for emigration and citizenship status. Outstanding facts regarding health, education, and work history.

Place in his or her own family group (youngest, oldest, etc.). Relation to own family group (spoiled, dependent on either parent, antagonistic toward parents or brothers and sisters, etc.). Kind of discipline received as a child.

Marital history. Any previous marriages? If so, at what age, when and why terminated? Preparation of each parent for marriage, *i.e.*, degree of independency of own family, sex information, etc. Were children wanted? Present marriage adjustment. Any friction? In case of mother, attitude toward each pregnancy or any miscarriages.

Attitude toward problem child's difficulties.

2. Substitute Parents   (Secure same information as for parents.)

3. Siblings (Brothers or Sisters).

List in chronological order all pregnancies including miscarriages or abortions. Give for each child born—name, birthdate, and place, present grade in school or occupation and adjustment, health, past and present reactions to the problem child and latter's reaction to each of the siblings.

4. Step- or Half-brothers and Sisters. (Secure same information as for siblings.)

B. Background.

1. Paternal and Maternal.

Grandfather, grandmother, uncles, aunts.

Information regarding relatives is of value because of conditioning factors to the other members of the group. Obtain significant facts such as name, age, birthplace, education, work history, special aptitudes, health, nervousness, "queerness," mental disease, violent temper, suicide, use of drugs or alcohol, criminality, etc.

IV. Home.

A. Former Addresses.

Reasons for change.

B. Present Neighborhood.
    Describe.   How long here?
C. Physical Conditions of Home.
    Describe as to rooms, sleeping arrangements, furnishings, etc.
D. Economic Conditions.
    Sources of income.
E. General relations (Within the Family Group and to the Outside
    World).
    Members of the present family group—solidarity, affection, com-
    mon interests.   Language used.   Recreational facilities in the
    home.   Club connections.   Religious interests.   Attitude on edu-
    cation, ambitions, etc , with special reference to attitudes toward
    the problem child.

V. Social Resources Available for Treatment.
A. Agencies.
    Past work of all agencies who have dealt with family.
    Agencies at present interested and what they are prepared to do.
B. Neighborhood Resources.
    Church, school, recreational, etc.
C. Family Resources.

The Social Research Interview Outline

The social research interviewer has an advantage over practicing social case workers in so far as he is not hampered by unlimited
intake of cases.   He can select his cases and limit the intake in
accordance with the available resources for exploration and
analysis.   Furthermore, his primary interest is in social discovery
and not in social treatment.   He accumulates facts about persons, groups, and social situations with a view to analyzing the
meaning of social facts.   His aim is to understand human
behavior, social attitudes, public opinion, social institutions, and
social change.   He studies social processes involved in the
development of social attitudes and social values with a view
to developing a science of social relations.

While the ultimate aim of social research is prediction and
control of human behavior and of social problems, the immediate
interest of the research interviewer is not social treatment or
social reform—unless he studies these from the point of view of
social experimentation—but social discovery.   For this reason
he may pursue the unique and the unusual while the social
worker is apt to be concerned with the typical.   The social
research interviewer in the strict scientific sense is confined to
investigation based on hypotheses which are being tested.

The Social Case History Outline of a Boy[1]

(By a social history of a boy is meant an account of his conflicts and accommodations within the home, neighborhood, school, church, play and occupational activities, and of the resulting problems as he sees them. A social history is a social-psychological picture of one's world, of one's human associations as one sees them himself. . . .)

I. Heritage.

What was the boy's social heritage? What were the traditions of his parents? Their attitude toward religion, toward racial and national values, toward education, toward industrial activities? What is their type of family life? What was their equipment for training boys, including their handicaps and advantages? What difficulties occurred within the home in matters of adjustments between parents? What were their hopes and ambitions for this particular boy?

What brothers and sisters did he have? What have been their outstanding traits? Their influences upon his life?

What musical and artistic tendencies has he?

His age, birthplace, race?

II. Early Life.

What was the nature of his earliest distinctive tendencies? The trend of his earliest interests and habits? His earliest conflicts? The first handicaps that he brought on himself? What were the earliest fears that he can recall, and his earliest joys? How were his earliest conflicts settled?

III. Social Contacts.

Which parent seems to understand him best? Which parent is he most like? What routine work does he do at home? How far do he and his parents associate in their amusements? If he lost his parents what would he do? What books, outside school books, did he read? What magazines? What did he read that he liked most?

Who are his chums? Describe their likes and dislikes. Has any of them gotten into trouble and if so in what ways? Does he bring his pals into the home?

How often does he go to motion-picture shows, to public dance halls, and to pool halls?

What girls has he known well? How intimate has been his friendship with them? What are his parents' attitudes toward the one or ones he likes best? What are their likes and dislikes? What does he do in his leisure time; how much leisure does he have and during what hours of the day? With whom does he come in contact at these times?

To what organizations, such as a boy's club, a gang, a church club or class has he belonged? What was the nature of the activities of each? Has he been a member of a Sunday School, of the Boy Scouts, of any similar organizations? Has he dropped out of any of these? Under what conditions? Does he smoke cigarettes? Why? or why not? His parents' attitude?

In what ways does he get along well at school? In what ways poorly? His parents' attitude?

[1] Prepared by E. S. Bogardus, *The New Social Research*, pp. 165–168. Reprinted by permission.

Has he been a leader in any of these clubs? In what ways did he lead well, and in what did he fail, and for what reasons?

IV. Conflicts and Accommodations.

What difficulties has he had in the home, with either parent, of long-standing nature? What conflicts has he had with other members of his family and what has happened?

What outstanding difficulties has he had with his playmates? Any fights he remembers? Have him describe the history of any boyhood feud that he was a part of for any length of time.

Did he have any difficulties with the older people of the neighborhood? With the parents of other children?

Under what conditions does he remember most distinctly being punished? What activities does he seem to conceal from his parents? Is the home atmosphere one of peace or conflict? Of economic pressure?

What conflicts has he had at school, with any teachers, principals, truant officers, or with other boys at school?

Did he ever run away from home or school? Why and what were the reactions?

Has he a car? Any problems? His parents' attitude toward his use of it? What picture shows does he like best? Least?

Did he ever "swipe" anything, and if so under what conditions? Did he ever get "pinched"? His experiences in this connection? Ever been in jail? Experiences. Ever been on probation, either in school or in connection with the Juvenile Court? Experiences.

Has there been any breaking off of love affairs? What daydreams has he had? Has he had any troublesome dreams? Has he ever had imaginary companions?

In what ways does he feel that he has been treated most unjustly? Has he ever felt hampered, and wanted to upset things generally? What important questions does he decide for himself? How does he get increased independence?

In what ways does he feel that he has been most misunderstood? By whom, and under what conditions? Any disagreements with his parents regarding money, clothes, the automobile, girls, chums? What things does he ask permission to do?

Under what conditions has he experienced pangs of conscience? Does he remember feeling distinctly sorry for something?

Has he ever had any religious problems or conflicts or "been converted"?

Has he ever worked for wages? Has he ever wanted money and couldn't get it? Has he ever saved and why? What kinds of work does he like best, and what least?

V. Philosophy of Life.

What was his first or earliest choice of a vocation, and what changes have occurred along this line? What are his greatest ambitions today? His occupational expectations? Does he have any money-making ambitions, and what are his reactions to making money and becoming rich? What is his life aim? Do parents agree with it?

What are his religious beliefs? Does he believe that one political party is better than another? Does he believe in racial equality? Is he interested in more than one race or nation? What does he consider to be the leading public questions of the day? Does he have any idea of social responsibility and social service, and if so, how did they arise?

If he could have one wish above all others granted, what would it be?

The Social Case History of the Delinquent as a Person[1]

The following outline offers a scheme for studying behavior in terms of individual and personal traits.

Outline for the Study of Individual and Personal Traits

I. Study of the Individual.
  1. Physical examination.
  2. Mental tests.
  3. Affectivity score.
  4. Will profile.
  5. Temperamental type.
II. Study of the Person.
  1. Participation.
    a. Extent of membership in groups.
    b. Intimacy of membership (social world).
    c. Role in groups.
  2. Character.
    a. Stabilized.
    b. Unstabilized.
  3. Personal behavior pattern.
    a. Objective or direct.
      (1) Equable, (2) enthusiastic, (3) frank, (4) aggressive.
    b. Introspective or indirect.
      (1) Imaginative, (2) secretive, (3) sensitive, (4) inhibited.
    c. Psychopathic or perverse.
      (1) Eccentric, (2) egocentric, (3) emotionally unstable, (4) psychic inferior.
  4. Social type.
    a. Practical or Philistine.
    b. Liberal or Bohemian.
    c. Idealistic or Religious.
  5. Philosophy of life.

Thus Professor Burgess seeks to learn not only the qualitative but the quantitative aspects of social participation, of personal behavior patterns and social types. Regarding the threefold classification of personal behavior patterns he further seeks to learn " . . . the characteristic types of the behavior of the person fixed in the matrix of social relations in infancy and childhood." He recognizes the potency of original differences in

---

[1] Prepared by E. W. BURGESS, "The Study of the Delinquent as a Person," *The American Journal of Sociology*, XXVIII (May, 1923), 665–666.

mentality, in temperament, and in volition but he aims to discover the degree of social influence upon them, the modification they have undergone by education and social interaction in the play group and the family. What are the earliest social forces which mold a personality; what social influences are at work in shaping a philosophy of life; what are the social copies which the person takes for models; what appears to him to be the realization of his most ardent wishes?[1]

The Social Case History Outline of a Boys' Gang[2]

(The social history of a boys' gang refers to its origin in the desires of the boy and in the stimuli or the lack of stimuli in the social environment, to the description of the dominating desires of its personnel and of the conflicts as a group with other social institutions.)   Data of the following kinds are useful:

I. Ecological.

What are the hang-outs of the gang? Addresses of the homes of the members.

General nature and range of activities of the gang?

The geography of the community under which the gang ranges?   Topography, railroad tracks, industrial properties, manufacturing establishments, types of stores?   A map carefully drawn would be valuable.

Locate the moving picture shows, poolrooms, dance hall, cabarets, soft-drink establishments, penny arcades, in the neighborhood which serve as a center of the gang's activities.

Locate the parks, playgrounds, athletic clubs.

Locate the schools, libraries, settlements, churches, missions.

What are the types of houses, the degree of sanitation?

What is the distribution of races?

II. Personnel.

Get as complete a social history as possible of each of the ringleaders of the gang throughout its history and of any members who have played a peculiar or significant role.   (Use "The Social Case History Outline of a Boy.")

III. Origins.

Date of the club's earliest known activities, and dates of all outstanding experiences of the club as such; for example, its clashes with other gangs, with the police, or its marauding expeditions.

What is the time of the gang's regular meetings, and also of its irregular meetings?   What are the main places of meetings?   What main changes in personnel have occurred in the history of the gang?   How far are its present principles the same as at the outset?   Under what conditions have changes in personnel and principles occurred?

---

[1] *Ibid.*, pp. 657–680.

[2] Prepared by E. S. BOGARDUS, *The New Social Research*, pp. 169–171. See also F. M. THRASHER, *The Gang*. Reprinted by permission.

IV. Organization.

What is the basis of membership? What written laws? What unwritten rules, agreements, understandings?

Does the gang have a constitution, by-laws, a charter?

What property does it possess, equipment, paraphernalia?

What words, signs, symbols, whistles are characteristic of it?

Does it exist in the form of a secret fraternity in connection with the schools? If so, what conflicts has it had with the school? What is the attitude of the parents of the members toward it, and of the teachers and principals toward it?

V. Group Activities and Conflicts.

What are the activities within the group, such as fighting, "chewing the rag," gambling, drinking, smoking cigarettes, sex practices?

What conflicts with other groups has it had? With other gangs? With truant officers and the police? With neighborhood people or storekeepers?

What mischievous activities characterize it? What malicious delinquency? Stealing? Assaults? Destruction of property? trespassing? pickpocketing?

Who has dropped out of the gang? Under what conditions?

What new interests have arisen?

VI. Philosophy.

How do the members account for their destructive activities as a gang? What are their attitudes regarding good citizenship? What are their reactions to organized religion? What sense of respect do they have toward their respective homes? Toward establishing homes of their own? Toward having money? Toward becoming community leaders?

R. L. Whitley points out that "Interviews with delinquent boys reveal the fact that these boys have very decided attitudes towards their problems, towards the way they are treated, and that they have wishes which in most cases are well formulated in their minds."[1] The interviewer, therefore, should seek to explore the mind of these boys and learn their conception of the relations they maintain with the social world around them, whether that social world is the city street, the back alley, or the boys' home. In view of Whitley's findings, it may be said that the interviewer should aim to learn of the methods of social control which these boys recognize and acknowledge, or with which they come in conflict. What are the reactions and experiences of boys who have spent some time in institutions? What phase of education in the institution did they find most profitable? Which method of control most advantageous? What are their reactions to the social conditions in the community in which they live?[2]

[1] "Interviewing the Problem Boy," *The Journal of Educational Sociology*, V (October, 1931), 89.

[2] *Ibid.*, pp. 89–90.

The most complete outlines or schedules for different types of interviews are perhaps those worked out by the clinicians for the study of problem children. William Healy, Louis Bisch, the Child Guidance Clinics at present stress family and personal history of the patient, psychological and physical examinations, the private talk with the child—or "own story," heredity chart, observation of home and neighborhood conditions, educational, school, vocational records, personal habits and interests, etc. D. A. Thom stresses a detailed family history but gives major attention to personal history, habits, interests, discipline, play life, intellectual life, religion, relation to other members of the family.

The schedules planned to aid the social work interviewer stress social problems and maladjustments and seek possibilities for social and personal rehabilitation. Little information is generally secured regarding a person's attitudes, his personality traits, his conception of his role in the group, cultural patterns, personal experience. The sociologist maintains that a worker who attempts to integrate an unadjusted person in his social group needs to secure an accurate account of the origin and development of social attitudes, of the role and effect of folkways, mores, social institutions, and relations on the development of personality, as well as an account of the physical environment and the mental life of the person.

The social worker inquiring about the mobility of a family seeks to learn names and places of landlords and residences, amount of rent paid, number of rooms, etc. The sociologist is interested in the mobility of the family to learn not so much the movement through space and time as the range and frequency of social contacts and psychic stimulations which the person experiences. He seeks to learn if the person is capable of establishing roots and becoming integrated in a given group. In view of the psychic stimulation and social contacts, what type of personality has the person developed?—Bohemian, Philistine, creative? How will he respond to change or to lack of change?

The sociologist studies the family economy from the standpoint of occupational attitudes and types, of the interrelations developed within the family group, of the habits and the modes of satisfaction, the standards of success and failure, of the social status assigned or assumed.

The family traditions and ceremonies are perhaps the best means for tracing the development of a particular personality type or a behavior pattern. The strength of family solidarity, the degree of personal individualization and of responsiveness are best understood in relation to the familial soil which nurtured them.

A knowledge of family organization and control throws light upon the social and personal influences the person is subjected to. Furthermore, the sociologist stresses the necessity of knowing not only the family group but the community—the larger social forces which shape the destiny of both the family and the person.

It is obvious that without a thorough knowledge of the social forces which mold habits and create behavior patterns, without an understanding of the social soil which nourishes personality, without an understanding of the interaction and interrelations between the various members of the family or group, it is exceedingly difficult if not well-high impossible to influence or motivate individuals to work out a consistent plan of treatment. The history of the social worker under these circumstances is adequate for sociological analysis only in so far as it depicts social attitudes and interaction between various members of the group in a particular social setting.

Suggestions for Further Study

1. Formulate your own definition of "fact." When does a fiction become a fact?

2. Read Charles H. Cooley's article "The Roots of Social Knowledge" and indicate its value to the interviewer. Supply concrete illustrations from personal interview data to clarify the conceptual analysis of Professor Cooley. Does he try to show how we know that we know?

3. What are the essential differences between a life history and an autobiography? Read E. T. Krueger's article "Technique for Obtaining Life History Documents," and show its value to the interviewer. (See index.)

4. What are the most important facts in the life history as stressed by the clinician, the research worker, the social worker? What is the basis of their selection?

5. Compare Shaw's conception of a life history with that of Bogardus and Healy; of Mary Richmond and Burgess.

6. What are the relative strengths and weaknesses of the social case history outline?

7. For what purposes is it suitable? Under what conditions is it usable?

8. Analyze the outlines used in standard case work and indicate the degree of stress laid upon the study of social attitudes. Which questions are best designed to secure information regarding personality development, philosophy of life, and social control?

9. Compare critically the two outlines of information cited in the text required for securing a family history. Indicate the basis for your judgment.

10. To what extent should these outlines be modified for emergency relief purposes?

11. Analyze the social case history outline for securing information regarding an unmarried mother, in terms of social heritage, social contacts, conflicts, accommodations, philosophy of life for both the man and the woman.

12. Indicate probable plan of treatment in view of the information outlined by Mrs. Sheffield; by Miss Drury.

13. In what essential respects are the outlines prepared by Mrs. Sheffield and Miss Drury different? Which outline is more adaptable to the treatment of the unmarried mother?

14. In what essential respects does the medical social history outline differ from that used in clinical procedure? in family case work?

15. What are the outstanding features of the outline prepared by a Child Guidance Clinic?

16. What is the significance of Bogardus' social case history outlines of a boy and a boys' gang? Read F. M. Thrasher's *The Gang* and show relation between Bogardus' and Thrasher's conceptions of what a life history of a boy should include.

17. Define all concepts Burgess uses in his social case history of the delinquent as a person.

18. Develop an outline of your own suitable for your purposes in securing a life history of a client of your agency.

19. Construct an outline of your own to be used in securing a medical social history and send it to your staff physician for comments.

20. Construct an outline suitable in clinical procedure and compare with one used by the Child Guidance Clinic in your community.

21. Construct an outline to be used in the sociological study of the family. (Consult some texts on the family, for example, Groves, Nimkoff, Reuter.)

22. Secure a life history of a family bearing in mind the points stressed in the outlines by: (*a*) E. W. Burgess; (*b*) Mary Richmond; (*c*) Mrs. Sheffield; (*d*) E. R. Mowrer; and evaluate your results.

23. Secure life histories of children, bearing in mind the points stressed in the outlines by: (*a*) Cyril Burt (*The Young Delinquent*); (*b*) E. S. Bogardus; (*c*) William Healy; (*d*) E. W. Burgess; and evaluate your results.

24. Prepare a diagnostic syllabus for interviewing (*a*) persons with physical handicaps; (*b*) parents of children with subnormal intelligence; (*c*) hoboes; (*d*) newly arrived immigrants; (*e*) runaway children; (*f*) alcoholics; (*g*) drug addicts.

Selected Bibliography

1. Bain, Read: "The Validity of Life Histories and Diaries," *The Journal of Educational Sociology*, III (November, 1929), 150–164.

Life experience materials secured by social workers are a "unique, subjective, non-generalized" form of art, but "they are valid techniques for investigation, diagnosis and treatment" when desired results are obtained, and the test of validity is the approval of the clientele. Life history documents and diaries have many shortcomings, are less objective and more unverifiable than case work records.

2. BOGARDUS, E. S.: *The New Social Research*, 1926.

Chapter VII provides comprehensive interview guides for obtaining life histories from native Americans, Oriental children, problem boys, boys' gangs, boys' work leaders, boys' welfare agency.

3. CABOT, RICHARD C.: "Medical Social History Outline," *Hospital Social Service*, October, 1928.

A comprehensive discussion of the type of data a medical social worker needs to gather from patients for social service and medical purposes.

4. RECKLESS, WALTER C.: "Suggestions for the Sociological Study of Problem Children," *The Journal of Educational Sociology*, II (November, 1928), 156–171.

Studies objective data: habits of child, disposition, participation, and social status; family background, organization, control, conflicts, and tensions; neighborhood forces, agencies, organization. Subjective data: child's life as told by him, his world, his neighborhood, his conception of his role, dominant wishes and ambitions. Points out briefly what can be secured in the first, second, and third interviews with the child and with the mother; suggests ways of recording.

5. RICHMOND, MARY E.: *Social Diagnosis*, 1917.

See particularly Chap. XX, "Social Disabilities and the Questionnaire Plan of Presentation."

CHAPTER VII

SPECIAL TYPES OF INTERVIEWING SITUATIONS

The Immigrant

Many interviewers state that the problems arising in interviewing people of their own racial, cultural, or language groups are much intensified when interviewing aliens. A distinct and peculiar state of mind seems to emerge in the contacts between members of different cultures or races. What these mental idiosyncrasies precisely are is subject to considerable difference of opinion. N. S. Shaler, late dean of Harvard University, who has made an exhaustive and lifetime study of the relations of strangers,[1] points out that when strangers meet it is not the individual that they see but the type.[2] The individual is in front of us, as it were, but we do not meet him. The individual Jew, or Negro, or Russian, or Chinese remains a strange representative of his race, not a neighbor. Dr. Park observes:

The most important, if not the most fundamental differences between nations and peoples, aside from physical characteristics, are reflected in their manners, their etiquette, and in the conception which they form of themselves. The characteristic traits of people are in other words, not so much innate qualities as group conventions.

The barriers to communication are not differences of language and of culture merely, but more particularly of self-consciousness, race consciousness, and consciousness of kind; not physical distances merely, but social distances. Whenever representatives of different races meet and discover in one another—beneath the differences of race—sentiments, tastes, interests, and human qualities generally that they can understand and respect, racial barriers are undermined and eventually broken down. Personal relations and personal friendships are the great moral solvents. Under their influence all distinctions of class, of caste, and even of race, are dissolved into the general flux which we sometimes call democracy.[3]

[1] *The Neighbor*, particularly Chaps. VI, VII, VIII, IX, and XI.

[2] See also RICHARD C. CABOT, *Social Service and the Art of Healing*, Chap. I.

[3] ROBERT E. PARK, "Behind Our Masks," *The Survey Graphic*, LXI (May, 1926), 137.

If the interviewer is not of the same racial and cultural group as the interviewees, he can do much in breaking down self-consciousness, extreme reserve, and even fear when he is able to show that he is conversant with their culture. Furthermore, familiarity with an alien culture enables the interviewer to identify himself with the interviewee and to understand the motives, interests, and wishes which control the behavior of the interviewee. The strange and outlandish become familiar, the queer and the peculiar become intelligible. Intellectual appreciation of an alien culture, however, needs to be further strengthened by an emotional tolerance of form, etiquette, and outward symbols of group behavior which may not find ready justifications in one's own cultural behavior patterns. But here is a dilemma: American democracy is relatively intolerant in matters of form and etiquette. Americans display "an impatient directness, a disconcerting candor of speech and manner, a lack of reserve,"[1] which is at times shocking to the foreigner. The average interviewer not only needs to guard against displaying such shocking traits when interviewing foreigners, but must take special precautions in preventing their ascribing these traits to him though he himself may not actually possess them.

My varied experience with American interviewers leads me to the conclusion that some not only do not take the trouble to acquaint themselves with the culture of the particular group they contact but they believe that it is not necessary to do so. They think that by this process they can "compel the foreigners to become Americanized." Little do they realize that their tactics are repulsive to the foreigner to such an extent that he will withdraw deeper into the protective fold of his own group and delay becoming Americanized. Furthermore, the American interviewer almost always assumes that he has to break down a "stubbornness" of the foreigner, which is largely imagined. The foreigner is not stubborn; he is more reserved with Americans than with members of his own group for obvious reasons. Some American social workers tell me that "it was impossible to pierce through the hard shell of the thickheaded and unemotional foreigner," but that particular foreigner in his own group is so responsive, imitative and so easily led that he becomes a victim of any and all schemes. Just watch him lay down resistance when a salesman with "soft" tactics approaches him.[2]

[1] *Ibid.*, p. 137.
[2] Statement by a foreign journalist.

Some American social workers state that foreigners are boastful and have "a fierce ego." Two things must be taken into consideration here: first that undoubtedly the approach of some social workers is so devastating to the foreigner that he must employ some defense mechanism not only to maintain his personal dignity but to preserve the status of his group—from which he rarely becomes fully emancipated and to which he often feels himself closely allied. Second, the foreigner is in the habit of stating facts about himself which may be complimentary to him, without the slightest intent to boast; he is in the habit of listening to facts about others without feeling that there is any intent to boast. Edward Bok's autobiography is distasteful to many Americans because they read into it an ego which few of Bok's countrymen would admit. To the latter to tell the truth about oneself is perfectly acceptable and is not interpreted as boasting.

Frequently American interviewers are rebuffed by the seriousness with which foreigners take themselves, or by their serious and even austere faces. The fun-loving Americans need to realize that a foreigner's serious countenance is not created especially for or during the contacts with them, but is the resultant of the sad social and personal experiences of the group of which he is a member. A foreigner generally regards life as a weighty and serious matter and does not understand the easy manner of the fun-loving American.

Park and Miller in their book *Old World Traits Transplanted* throw considerable light on the significance of immigrant heritages, immigrant institutions, and immigrant types in relation to changing social attitudes and to resulting social conflicts and accommodations,[1] which the American interviewer should take into account:

A certain identity of experiences and memories between immigrants and Americans is of main importance for assimilation, because, in the process of learning, a new fact has a meaning and makes an appeal only if it is identified with some previous experience, something that is already known and felt. Thus, when we appealed to the patriotism of our immigrants during the war, we found a ready response, because they knew what patriotism is. The Bohemians in a Cleveland parade carried a banner with the inscription: "We are Americans through and through by the spirit of our nation," and interpreted this by another

[1] See particularly Chaps. I, III, V, VII, VIII, and IX; also FRANK V. THOMPSON, *Schooling of the Immigrant, passim.*

banner: "Americans, do not be discouraged. We have been fighting these tyrants for three hundred years." . . .

This process of making warm and personal something that would otherwise remain cold, extraneous, irrelevant, and foreign, by identifying it with a body of sentiments that is already intimate and warm, is illustrated . . . by the case of the Italian boy. . . . [1]

All the time I hear about the grand city of New York. They say it is something to surprise everyone. I learn New York is twice, three, four, ten times bigger than Italian city. Maybe it is better than Milano. Maybe it is better than Naples.

"The land of the free and the home of the brave"—I am young and I think that is beautiful land. I hear such fine words like "liberty," "democracy," "equality," "fraternity," and I like this high principles.[2]

I go about the streets to find the great history, to feel the great emotion for all that is noble in America. I do not see how the people can think to compare the American city with the beauty of Rome, or Venice, or Naples. Even in big city like New York I do not find much monuments to the great deeds, to the great heroes, and the great artists. I was deeply surprised not to find the fountains. I do not find the great art to compare with the art of Italy. . . . But one day I see very, very big building. My mind is struck. With all I have seen in Italy, in Rome, in Venice, in Genoa, in Milano, in Florence, in Naples—I have never seen anything like that! I say, "There is the thing American. It is a giant!"[3]

The apperception mass of the immigrant, expressed in the attitudes and values he brings with him from his old life, is the material . . . we must work with, if we would aid this process [of adjustment]. Our tools may be in part American customs and institutions, but the substance we seek to mold into new forms is the product of other centuries in other lands. In education it is valuable to let the child, as far as possible, make his own discoveries and follow his own interests. He should have the opportunity of seeking new experiences which have a meaning for him when connected with his old experiences. A wise policy of assimilation, like a wise educational policy, does not seek to destroy the attitudes and memories that are there, but to build on them.

There is a current opinion in America, of the "ordering and forbidding" type, demanding from the immigrant a quick and complete Americanization through the suppression and repudiation of all the signs that distinguish him from us.[4] Those who have this view wish

---

[1] ROBERT E. PARK and H. A. MILLER, *op. cit.*, pp. 273–275. Reprinted by permission of Harper & Brothers.

[2] *Ibid.*, p. 46.

[3] *Ibid.*, p. 275.

[4] "Broadly speaking, we mean [by Americanization] an appreciation of the institutions of this country, absolute forgetfulness of all obligations or

the repudiation to be what the church fathers demanded of a confession of sin—"sudden, complete, and bitter."[1]

The Social History Outline of an Immigrant[2]

As already pointed out in connection with the social case history outlines in general, the social case history of an immigrant merely suggests the scope of territory theoretically to be covered in the exploration of the experiences and problems of an immigrant in America. It should be regarded as a skeleton guide and its use governed by the same considerations as stated previously in connection with the outlines of the social case history.

Life histories of immigrants are valuable in so far as they give us insight into the processes of the "melting pot." We seek to learn from these documents:

1. What the immigrant brings to this country as a heritage from the mother country. What are his hopes, ambitions, and his illusions in regard to life in America?

2. What does he bring in the way of equipment, education, technical training, industrial habits, etc.? How much of his heritage, his language, for example, and his traditions are a handicap to him? How far is he able to overcome these handicaps? How does he actually accommodate himself to American life?

3. What about the second generation, the children? How far do they seek to preserve the language, traditions, and habits of thought of the older generation? How far do they succeed? What is the effect upon them of the inevitable break between the customs of their parents and of the Americans among whom they live?

These are the questions to which we have in the past found, and must still seek, answers in the stories which the immigrants tell of their own intimate personal experiences in this country.

The following inquiries are intended to be suggestive merely. What is wanted is a narrative, concise, vivid, personal, with all the inflections and accents of the individual man or woman—and, so far as possible, in the first person.

I. Early Life.
1. What had been your life, *i.e.*, your place of residence, occupation, and ambitions before coming to America?
2. When did you first hear of America and what were your early notions and interests in regard to it?
3. What are the stories, legends, and general conceptions of America current in the part of the country whence you came?

---

connections with other countries because of descent or birth."—Superintendent of the New York Public Schools, *New York Evening Post*, August 9, 1918. Quoted by I. B. Berkson, *Americanization*, Chap. II (in press).

[1] ROBERT E. PARK and H. A. MILLER, *op. cit.*, pp. 280–281.

[2] Prepared by Robert E. Park and quoted by E. S. Bogardus, *The New Social Research*, pp. 133–136.

See also MARY E. RICHMOND, *Social Diagnosis*, pp. 387–394.

II. First Impressions of America.
1. What was the most interesting thing about America as you saw it for the first time?
2. What was most difficult to comprehend in your new experiences here?
3. What were your first and greatest difficulties in finding your way about and getting adjusted to America?
4. Did your fellow-countrymen look strange or disappointing out here, or did you feel immediately at home with them?
5. What shocked you most about America? What about the freedom of young women? The candor with which Americans discuss love affairs and sentimental matters in their daily conversation, in their newspapers, billboards, and movies?
6. How far have your own notions about the freedom of women, the independence of children, etc., changed as a result of life in America?
7. How about the younger generation? Does the freedom and independence of Americans bring them into conflict with their parents? Does it unfit them for life in the old country?
8. How have you or your people sought to meet the problem of the second generation?

III. Social Contacts.
1. How far have you been able to master the spoken and written language of America?
2. What newspapers, magazines, or books do you read in English? What book have you read that interests you most?
3. What acquaintances have you made among Americans and how intimate have your relations with Americans been?
4. To what organizations, church, social, or welfare, if any, do you belong which bring you in touch with Americans?
5. What, if anything, are your own people, independently or in association with others, doing to improve the condition of your neighborhood or your community?
6. How have the land laws affected your personal and family life? Have they tended to make you nomadic, unsettled, and restless? How do you propose to meet this difficulty?
7. Do your people have more family difficulties, divorces, and desertions in this country than in the old? If so, how do you explain that fact?

IV. Conflicts and Accommodations.
1. Have you had difficulties in finding a suitable home? Did your efforts to find a suitable home bring you into conflict with your neighbors? How did you manage to make peace and on what terms?
2. Has anything occurred in your experience to make you wish to avoid Americans, keep at a distance from them, or conceal your feelings regarding them?
3. If you had the one chance of your lifetime to express what you feel deepest about Americans, what would you say?

4. In what ways do Americans misunderstand, misjudge foreign peoples and especially your own?

5. Are you planning to return finally to your native country or to send your children back? If not, why?

V. Philosophy of Life.

1. How far have you realized the ambitions with which you came to America?

2. What illusions have you had in regard to life in America and how far have you become reconciled to life here as it is?

3. Are you an internationalist and a cosmopolitan? If so, do you think such an ideal is being, and is likely to be, realized?

4. What is or will be your ambition for your children?

5. Are you in favor of intermarriage now or ultimately? If that does not take place, how do you think the race problem is likely to be solved?

THE NEGRO

The contact of the Negro[1] and the white is apt to arouse much stronger prejudices than is the case of the foreigner of the Caucasian race, since the contact with the Negro is racial rather than cultural, and because the unusual differences of the racial uniform which the Negro wears at all times are noticeable at a glance.

Racial prejudice differs from prejudice generally in one important respect. One may change his politics or his religion; he may learn new languages and customs, or change the cut of his coat. If the change is successfully made, he may, in the course of time—depending on the length of men's memories—become fully assimilated into a new group. As he becomes identified with them he escapes the fire of prejudice directed against his former political and religious beliefs, his mother tongue, and the earlier style of his clothes. When, however, the prejudice is directed against the color of his skin, his features, or any other racial trait, he cannot avoid the effects of prejudices aroused by these traits. He is a marked man. The fact that these traits may be superficial weighs but lightly in the balance against the inescapable fact that he is different and cannot be assimilated except through racial amalgamation. At just that point, however, race prejudice runs highest.[2]

[1] See BERTHA REYNOLDS, "A Way of Understanding: An Approach to Case Work with Negro Families," *The Family*, XII (November, 1931), 203–208, (December, 1931), 240–244, (January, 1932), 267–272. CONSTANCE C. FISHER, "Some Factors in Understanding Negro Clients," *The Family*, XII (December, 1931), 245–247.

[2] ERLE F. YOUNG, "What Is Race Prejudice?" *Journal of Applied Sociology*, X (November-December, 1925), 139–140.

The Commission on Race Relations in its study of the conditions underlying the race riots in Chicago (July, 1919) have gathered and classified the common beliefs concerning Negroes which are found to prevail among American whites. Many people were found to have little or no personal experience with Negroes, but nevertheless they shared common beliefs, which were crystallized by years of unchallenged assumptions, that "the Negro loves to imitate," that "he has no originality and must be a follower," that "he is of subnormal mentality and low morality," that "he has never thrown off his slave ancestry," that "he is a sub-human character."[1]

The fact that the Negro has acquired the American culture, and has undergone a profound change in sentiment and attitude, does not make him less of a Negro in the eyes of many people, since he is not able to discard the racial uniform with the acquisition of the white man's culture; race prejudice is essentially a function of visibility.[2]

The Commission on Race Relations has also gathered considerable material which shows, among many other things, the Negro's viewpoint regarding his own situation. The following excerpts are in response to a question asked by the Commission:

What are some of the most pronounced mental complexes experienced in adjusting your personal desires and expectations to the present social system?

A constant haunting feeling when in the presence of white persons that they desire to shun me because of my color; that they are eager to use me to further their ends under the guise of piety or patronizing the "good-feeling-toward-your-people" attitude. I suffer from time to time an acute embarrassment because of uncouth conduct in the presence of white persons on the part of uncultured Negroes. Such conduct embarrasses me generally, but the presence of white persons who are supposed to be inimical seems to be the dominant element in the situation.

The most pronounced mental complex which I experience in adjusting my desires and expectations to the present social system is not the "inferiority complex" with which most Negroes are charged by the whites. I desire all that the social system affords; but as to expectation

[1] THE CHICAGO COMMISSION ON RACE RELATIONS, *The Negro in Chicago*, pp. 436–445.

[2] *Cf.* ROBERT E. PARK, "Behind Our Masks," *The Survey Graphic*, LXI (May, 1926), 135.

it is necessary for me to use auto-hypnotism to make myself expect it in order that I can present to the white man the front of optimism, the necessary air of expectancy to secure success. The shocks and disappointments which a Negro must constantly experience tend to get him in the attitude of expecting nothing. . . .

Personally, I am able to impersonalize my relation to the situation, and experience no mental perplexities. I try to preserve a rational attitude in an irrational environment and objectify cruelty, injustice and wrong. I know that I as an individual am not Jim Crow, or disfranchised or socially isolated; it is the race to which I belong. My only perplexity is how to remove these racial, not personal, disqualifications.

Determination to fulfill my personal desires in spite of the present social system; a loss of respect for the white man's sense of justice.

The arrogance of the poor ignorant white man and the snobbishness of the middle class. This is the stumbling-block for the future of our race to overcome.

Trying to get white persons, as employers, etc., to accept me as a man first of all, then to judge me on my merits, irrespective of my color. Trying to attain to the same degree of success and liberty of any other man of my training and experience in spite of the world in which I live.

Amused and almost cynical tolerance. A desire to reap the greatest possible advantages from the system, without permitting my intelligence to admit that it is right because it is personally advantageous.[1]

Floyd Covington, Executive Secretary of the Los Angeles Urban League, writes:

If the interviewer has learned well the principles of interviewing, the racial or cultural differences of the interviewee should present no "unique" or "special" problem to him. On the other hand, in the methods of interviewing there may be special helps which may aid the interviewer in dealing with such groups.

In America the Negro, because of his social background and the social conditions under which he lives, presents an anomalous situation which should receive careful consideration. Two problems concern us here: (1) What is the social situation in reference to the Negro as far as the

[1] THE CHICAGO COMMISSION ON RACE RELATIONS, *op. cit.*, p. 502. Reprinted by permission of the University of Chicago Press.

interviewer should know it; and (2) what special technique must be used in interviewing Negroes?

To answer either of these questions fully is to retraverse the general field of interviewing. . . . To the writer it appears that there are certain definite situations to be considered in the interviewing approach to the Negro:

I. Where both interviewer and interviewee are Negro.

II. Where the interviewer is racially different from the Negro interviewed.[1]

III. Where the interviewer is Negro and the interviewee is racially different from the interviewer, though this situation is, perhaps, the exception and not the rule under present conditions. . . .

I. Where the interviewer and interviewee are Negro, what is the social situation as far as the interviewer should know it?

The very fact that the Negro interviewer is racially "in-the-know" should, it would seem, establish almost immediate rapport—depending, of course, upon the personality and technical skill of the interviewer— between himself and his client. The converse, however, may be the case. The fact that the interviewer is Negro may at once establish between interviewer and interviewee very definite social barriers.

Hostility may arise since the two may be on the same economic and social level, may frequent the same places, and engage in the same activities, in short, may maintain the same general social status. If this is true, the interviewer may err in certain instances. Knowing something about his client, he may assume more than is really the case. Having similar social contacts, he may be prejudiced against the information given. He may read into the client's answers his own attitudes and opinions colored by his partial knowledge of the interviewee's life. In this particular situation the interviewer, having already had personal contact, may have to resort to an impersonal approach to establish rapport. The danger lies just here, since the interviewee may assume that the interviewer, because of his position, may be trying to snub or to "put it over" or "now that he has this job, he is becoming uppity."

In discussing this topic with several Negro social workers, this matter of being too much in-the-know suggests itself very definitely as one possible difficulty in interviewing racially alike clients.

The second limitation which may arise is the difference in color between interviewer and interviewee, though both are classed as

[1] We use the term "racially different" because we do not consider the word "white" an acceptable connotation, due to the large number of persons in America who are white of color, but are classified as Negroes racially. Furthermore, the interviewer could be Mexican, Japanese, Chinese, or Filipino. The word "colored" in reference to Negroes is equally a misnomer, because the term would be inclusive also of the above-mentioned groups.

Negroes. If the color of the interviewer is distinctly different from that of the interviewee, there is a possibility for the accentuation of social barriers. The interviewee may, if the interviewer be fairer or whiter than the interviewee, take the same attitude as if the latter were racially different. The interviewee may hastily conclude that the interviewer received his position because of favoritism toward color. In America white in color represents economic and social privilege and, therefore, "The darker the Negro, the less opportunity he has to move from job to job vertically. White, light, yellow, brown, and black Negroes find themselves competing against one another because of this color standard. . . . "[1]

If the social situation should place the interviewer in the opposite racial role, that is, darker in color than the interviewee, a reversal of attitude may follow. In this instance the American attitude which favors white in color may develop a superiority complex in the attitude of the interviewee. He may feel himself better than the interviewer and thereby create the mental attitude which expresses itself thus: "I should tell you my business? Humph!" . . .

Reactions involving color variations are tense, owing to the fact that "The Negro faces certain obstacles which are accentuated because of a color standard in his attempt to progress vertically in achieving social position."[2]

This condition is further accentuated owing to a "cultural lag"[3] from the period of our American slavocracy. Negro slaves were purposely prejudiced against each other by slaveowners seeking their own protection against slave insurrections. The slave of the "big house" was made to feel that he was of a higher social position than the slave of the fields. Furthermore, the large number of mulattoes born during the period of slavery stresses another difference—that between Negro and Negro extraction. . . .

The Negro interviewer's approach, therefore, is greatly aided by careful knowledge of his own racial background. It requires on his part a willingness to study his historical and social background from sources other than the ones usually provided for him by institutions of learning primarily set up for the cultivation of the non-Negro student. Being a Negro should naturally equip him with a knowledge and appre-

[1] Floyd C. Covington, "Color: A Factor in Social Mobility," *Sociology and Social Research*, XV (November–December, 1930), 151.

[This is probably more or less a direct consequence of the attitudes of Southern whites toward "color." That is, there is a noticeable attitude on the part of Negroes to react to each other as the whites react to them.]

[2] Floyd Covington, *op. cit.* See also

G. A. Steward, "The Black Girl Passes," *Journal of Social Forces*, VI (September, 1927), 99–103.

[3] W. F. Ogburn, *Social Change*.

ciation of the Negro's social and economic vicissitudes. No matter how white in color the Negro interviewer may be, because of the American racial classification of him, he may still think and feel Negro. That is to say, such an interviewer may have a distinct advantage over one who is racially different: he may be white and Negro at the same time and thereby sense and express the feelings, attitudes, and emotions of each racial strain; but a person who is white and racially different cannot be Negro in spirit or thought. . . . Therefore, all other things being equal, the Negro interviewer should be able to traverse with a greater degree of facility the social barriers of his Negro interviewee.

A similar point of view is expressed by Dr. Maurice Sullivan in his article "The Part of the Negro Doctor in the Control of Syphilis." In speaking of the clinics of the Flint-Goodridge Hospital of Dillard University he says: "In this hospital, under the direction of a white consultant staff consisting of men of recognized ability as practitioners and teachers in their special fields, the treatment and management of all syphilitic patients is conducted by the Negro staff of physicians, social workers and nurses. Each of the doctors in medical clinic is an individual of high standing and prestige in his community, wielding considerable influence among his people, capable of interesting his fellowmen in the rationale of a constructive program. *They speak the language of their brother, they know better than we his problems, his feelings, the soul of the black man. Their interest is an intimate, sincere, scientific and far-reaching endeavor asking only proper direction and instruction.*"[1]

II. Where the interviewer is *racially different* from the Negro interviewee, what is the social situation and what should the approach be?

The above discussion relative to the Negro interviewer should be of some assistance to the racially different interviewer in, at least, as far as it calls attention to the need for acquaintance with the social background of the Negro.

The Negro interviewer being in-the-know racially does not so easily err, being governed by traditional stereotypes in establishing relations with his client. The racially different interviewer, not in-the-know, may assume that he knows the Negro and, starting out on those premises, he may get from the interviewee only a reflection of himself. The Negro interviewee, then, makes only that reaction which the interviewer believes conforms with the stereotype of a Negro or of that Negro with whom the interviewer has had most contact.

In this social situation, therefore, the interviewer must beware of the influence of racial stereotypes, usually revealed by certain *lapsi linguae* to which the Negro interviewee may more or less be sensitive and by certain racial caricatures which may be suggestive of unpleasant experiences of his race.

[1] *Journal of Social Hygiene*, XIX (November, 1933), 442–443.

To what extent, then, does the racially different interviewer start with definite conditionings concerning what Negroes are like? Has he known enough of them to decide for himself how their emotional responses may be warped because of social pressure? For example, "Interview 12" of Chap. IV of "Interviews: A Study of the Methods of Analyzing and Recording Social Case Work Interviews," published by The American Association of Social Workers,[1] needs to be analyzed from this point of view. If accepted as a guide for interviewers who have had little contacts with Negroes or who have previous stereotyped conditionings about them, it is very likely to prove a hindrance rather than a help. It presents the case of Mrs. D., a "young colored girl, 19 years old. Ever since she was a small child she has always lied her way out of difficulties. . . . "

The writer bases his reactions on his contacts with social workers of both the public and private fields, many of whom had developed very definite categorical impressions of their Negro clients. Certain references concerning their black or mulatto clients have become to them stock phrases of truth. Beliefs that black of color, poverty, and dirt are synonymous; mulattoes are more immoral than the "native Negro;" "all Negroes are more susceptible to this, that, and the other," are but a few of the many. "None of them ever tell the truth" is perhaps among the most common stereotyped phrases. . . .

It may seem both trite and unnecessary to suggest here the numerous *lapsi linguae* so often committed when Negroes are interviewed by racially different interviewers. "I know and like your people because I had a black mammy when I was a girl." Such a statement is meant to establish rapport through achieving at least by inference social equality. To the Negro it reminds him of unpleasant slavery days; he smiles, appears flattered, and mentally hears no more.

The reaction of a Negro interviewee who had been in conference with a racially different interviewer is suggestive of what may be the aftermath of the reference to "darkey," "piccaninny," the "cullud story" for securing a humorous response, or the "Do you know our 'Auntie'? She's just the finest cook and laundress!"

In the instance cited, one of the above type of slips was used and the Negro interviewee remarked to a friend on relating the conference: "After that white woman said that, I never heard another word she said!" Too often does the interviewer lose the mental and emotional ear of the interviewee because he errs in presenting his own sentimental stereotype of what the Negro has meant to him. . . .

The Negro types presented by Amos and Andy, Aunt Jemima's Pancake Flour, Aunt Dinah's Old Fashioned Molasses, the Cream of Wheat Chef, with his red tie, are examples of the glorification of the

---

[1] *Studies in the Practice of Social Work*, pp. 76–77.

Negro type. If advertisers of these products are being subtly boycotted by some Negro buyers because of the slavery day reminders, is it not suggestive of the possible loss of rapport in the field of interviewing when similar reminders creep into the interview? More definite is the wide spread assumption that "real warm Southern dialect" is a characteristic of the Negro, whether he originates in Maine or Georgia, or whether he is a graduate of Yale or a one-room school in the South. . . . The glorification of the Negro servant, a so-called Negro dialect, and the Amos and Andy type of ornate vocabulary all create a stereotyped caricature of what the advertiser believes to be response-getting copy which, however, the sensitive Negro finds embarrassing. This is the social situation in which many a racially different interviewer may find himself unwittingly when interviewing Negro clients.

To strive for naturalness of approach, for a sympathetic understanding of the social anomalies of a racial group, and for the acquisition of the mental attitude that "I am your race" rather than "I know your race" should be within the art and science of the interviewer. . . .

The astute interviewer must strive to become at home and comfortable in the mental and emotional situations of either race. . . .

III. Where the interviewer is Negro and the interviewee racially different, what then of the social situation and approach?

If it were not a mere play on words, one might say far more easily and correctly that the Negro knows the white man than the converse. The Negro's having entered intimately into the varied family and social situation of his white slaveholder for some three hundred years, his "black mammy" suckling his young, and still his household servant of today should at least give him the advantage. The Negro has lived with the white man, but social convention has not permitted, except in few cases, that the white man should live with the Negro. The Negro, then, is quite naturally a reflection of that person whom he has served and catered to so long and is, therefore, better prepared to set the stage to release those reactions which produce the desired responses. I have heard employers of Negroes say, "I don't know why, knowing him as I do, but John can 'size up' or 'feel' many of my moods and thoughts."

Is it amiss to suggest, therefore, that perhaps the Negro interviewer might have the facility of gaining the rapport of the racially different interviewee? The writer has secured information from more than a thousand young white high-school and college Epworth Leaguers in connection with a laboratory experiment using a "Break-up of Prejudice" questionnaire. Our racial difference has been our advantage in getting responses rather than a disadvantage, despite the fact that the situation becomes that of teacher and pupil—the exceptional example in our American cities.

A more specific instance of how successful the reversal of our first situation can be appears in *Opportunity* for October, 1933.[1] The Family Welfare Association of Minneapolis had employed a Negro case worker for all Negro clients. The case load increased and a second worker was employed. Later the case load dropped, leaving only enough work for one worker. There was a need for a worker in an all-white district. "In the fall of 1928 we found ourselves with two colored workers with only enough colored families seeking advice to need the services of one worker and what was of greater importance from the viewpoint of this experiment—a vacancy in a district where the population was exclusively white. We placed Mrs. McCullough (Negro) in this district, where in the course of the next two years she came in contact with probably three hundred families, their relatives and friends. No exceptions were made as to people she was to visit, that is, she handled *all* the work for the clients under her care, regardless of where it might take her. . . .

"In September, 1931, a district secretary resigned and Mrs. McCullough was placed in charge of the district, both clientele and staff being white—though still with the title of Acting District Secretary. . . .

"This past spring our Board of Directors felt the experimental period was past and she was given the title of District Secretary. The case load at present is entirely white, the staff of three visitors and one clerical worker and district committee are white. White students in the Training School for Social Work are assigned to her. . . .

"We realize that personality has had much to do with the success of this experiment, but *that is true of anyone*."

And no less is it true that personality, training, and efficiency of the interviewer, be he Negro or racially different, is the chief approach to even the *especial* social situation.[2]

Sympathy with and understanding of the unique social complexes is of prime importance in contact with different cultural and racial groups. We must learn to think and feel Negro, think and feel Russian, or German, or Jewish, or whatever the case might be. We must enter into the problems and attitudes of alien groups and come to see the various situations from their point of view and evaluate them not through our foreign eyes, but from the standpoint of their standards, ideals, and purposes.[3] Patient and thoroughgoing inquiry into an alien culture seems inevitable if we are to penetrate beyond the superficialities of

[1] Editorial, "A Letter," Vol. XI, No. 10, 294.
[2] FLOYD C. COVINGTON, "The Negro and the Process of Interviewing," manuscript, 1934.
[3] PAULINE V. YOUNG, *Pilgrims of Russian Town*, p. 29.

their lives.   If the interviewer is unable to carry on this inquiry himself, he should at least acquaint himself with the existing accounts depicting the particular culture or history of the group with which he intends to come in contact.

Once we learn to "put ourselves into the other fellow's boots" we minimize conflicts and bridge social distance.   Interviewers successful in dealing with aliens remark:

I cannot always understand them, but I give them the benefit of the doubt in controversies. . . . I never attack their culture, their traditions and practices, no matter how outlandish they may seem to me.   Undoubtedly I seem just as queer to them and am convinced that I could not do half as well in their country as they do in ours. . . . I never take sides.   I never tell them: "You're in America now and must do as we do."   Democracy is founded on variety and these foreigners add a touch of color and spice to our life even though they also add many perplexing problems. . . . I never blame a foreigner for the sins of his fellow countryman.   I take it for granted that he is as ashamed of him as I am, and after all, while he is his brother's keeper he has no control over him.

In interviewing immigrants in general it is essential to inquire into the ties, traditions, and community backgrounds to which they are still responsive.   The average immigrant, particularly if he is still living in the area of first settlement, sees himself largely in relation to his group.   An understanding of group practices will explain personal behavior.

It is essential to remember that the immigrant in America is often confronted with many social and economic problems.   He may view these problems objectively and regard them as an inevitable consequence in adjustment to a new life.   He may view them, on the other hand, as a personal failure to control the new situation adequately.   In the first instance it may be wise to arouse the immigrant to a greater personal responsibility, in the second instance, to minimize the feeling of personal failure.

In interviewing immigrants I always ask: "Well, how have you been getting along in America?"   This question generally brings rapid and profuse responses.   If the immigrants "knock" American life, if they "curse Columbus for discovering America," and largely attribute their personal and social problems to the conditions in their new environment, I point out to them that what they say is undoubtedly correct, nevertheless there are other persons in their group, living practically under the same conditions, who have been able to make satisfactory adjustments. Frequently it is possible to indicate the specific conditions which help in the adjustment process. If, however, the immigrant is self-deprecatory, I strike a middle-ground and explain that the adjustment generally leaves in its wake problems over which a single individual has little or no control. In either case I try to resolve a complex on the basis of its origin.[1]

The Executive

Interviewing executives, professional men and women, civic leaders, employers, and so on is a very difficult task because frequently they themselves are accomplished interviewers and can anticipate the techniques and objectives of the interviewer; they are not easily induced to reveal themselves; they may be facing serious problems in connection with their organizations which will put them much on guard; they may be concerned over the status of their agency; their viewpoints and habits may be colored by occupational attitudes.

. . . accustomed to putting other persons to work or to instructing others, they are interested in getting others to give personal data but decline to offer help from their own experiences. The occupational habit of getting others to do things hinders free response on the part of the executive or teacher himself. . . . [2]

The interviewer must take all these problems of the executive into account and make him feel by manner—rather than word—that his problems are appreciated.

I generally say: "Of course, every organization has some problems, but we do not need to talk in terms of your problems, we can talk in general terms. You have a broader perspective by virtue of your experience and I will appreciate knowing your attitudes.[3]

Dean Donham of the Harvard Business School analyzes the situation as follows from the business standpoint:

Business is full of young men who seem to have ability, who work hard [but they do not progress]. . . . It is because they approach every problem from the standpoint of the little part of the business with which they are familiar; not from the viewpoint of the business as a whole, and not from the employer's standpoint. They never imagine themselves behind the boss's desk and ask, "What is he trying to

[1] Pauline V. Young, "Problems of Cultural Hybrids," manuscript.
[2] E. S. Bogardus, *The New Social Research*, p. 109.
[3] Statement by a research worker.

accomplish? What are the problems as he sees them? What would I be trying to do for this business if I had his responsibility?"[1]

If the executive sees fit not to reveal his personal experience, he should not be pressed for it. He is entitled to take whatever standpoint he wishes.

If I sense a fear in him that I am "skillful enough to get around him," I leave the particular subject under discussion strictly alone. In some casual way I remark that my policy is not to get information at "all costs" and I do not desire any data unwillingly disclosed. Of course, I make the purpose of my inquiry clear to him, my professional ethics, and those of the organization I am connected with; I indicate the desirability of having a complete personal as well as a general account, but I leave the decision of disclosing himself strictly up to him.[2]

Quite apart from ethical considerations, which will be discussed later, we must put the interviewee at ease so that we will not force our way into his secrets, which he for good reasons wishes to conceal. Frequently the executive, learning of this attitude in the interviewer, will confide many things which, of course, should remain confidential if he so desires. In order to dispel a fear that the interviewer is too shrewd he may have to talk considerably about himself and reveal his true self.

I am always afraid of people who listen to me intently and do not disclose any of their plans or attitudes. The shrewdest interviewers watch the other fellow and induce him to "open up," but they themselves sit and take it all in. I may open up once, but never again when I discover their game. . . .

I have watched the consequences of such tactics and find that the people who do not commit themselves but expect others to do so rarely make friends. Young "talkatives" will admire them because of the chance to talk themselves out, but the mature executive holds himself aloof from the "close-mouth." They do not play the game fairly.[3]

Physicians, attorneys, priests, peace and probation officers are legally protected as to confidences of clients and cannot be legally compelled to reveal them. Not so is the case of social

---

[1] Quoted by E. T. WEBB and J. B. MORGAN, *Strategy in Handling People*, p. 86.

[2] Statement by a research worker.

[3] Statements by social work executives.

welfare workers. This discrepancy in the professional standards may be compromising, but the interviewer should accept the situation with grace.

As has already been remarked elsewhere, the interviewer will find it expedient to acquaint himself with some of the scientific terminology of the interviewee's profession and thus identify himself in a measure at least through common use of terms.

When interviewing executives in various fields who know little about social work or who are antagonistic to it, their interest may be aroused or an appreciation created when social work situations are likened to situations in their own fields and within their own experience.

When I talk to business men I refer to the social case history in terms of "files" or "records." We are used to the term "case," but the business man confuses it with the "case" of the lawyer and while he may not say it he thinks in terms of the case of "the State *against* John Doe," and not "in the interest of John Doe. . . . "

To many business men "social work is a lot of red tape," but when I explain that we must investigate the same as he does when he makes an investment I am able to drive the thing home.[1]

Interviewers, even though they may be high-class executives themselves, cannot tell an interviewee-executive what he should do in a particular case, unless their opinions are solicited. Interviewers must assume that the executive is competent to know his job, and if he is not competent he will not tolerate being told. It is well to approach such an executive by saying: "You know, I have been thinking a good deal about what might be done in such and such case and just wonder what your reactions might be to my plan?"

Frequently it appears also that the interviewee-executive knows his job only tco well and needs no hints from outsiders, but the outsiders do not fully understand all the aspects of the whole situation of the executive and do not appreciate the various ramifications of his work, which are difficult to unify or coordinate. Neither can an interviewer directly undertake to correct a wrong viewpoint or attitude of an interviewee-executive.

Not long ago I was seeking aid in behalf of a child of poverty-stricken transients. The executive had prior to our conference obtained unfavorable information regarding the parents: "father had a bad reputation

[1] Statements by social work interviewers.

in the community," "child was reported illegitimate," "much dissension between maternal relatives." I was informed that "were it not for the facts in the case the child was entitled to help." I thanked the executive for the conference realizing though that I was bound by the policies of her agency. Several weeks later I contacted her regarding another case, but left enough time to go back to the first case. "I would like to ask your opinion on the following matters: Is it right to hold a child responsible for the misdeeds of his parents?" "No," was the reply, "the child is innocent and should be protected." "Should an illegitimate child of poverty-stricken parents be given aid in the form of school lunches and clothing?" "By all means; the child is *here* and should be helped to grow up a useful citizen," was the reply. "Should a child be aided when distant relatives who are able to help refuse to do so and quarrel over mother's past history?" "Why, the child cannot be held responsible for quarreling among relatives," was the reply again. Thus this executive corrected her own attitude and when we returned to a consideration of the case she revised her policy and granted the child temporary aid.[1]

Frequently an interviewer will plant an idea in the course of an interview with executives. The latter may develop it and in the process of growth may come to believe the idea was original with them. They are intent on the idea and may overlook its source. If the interviewer is interested in development of principles and not in credit for an idea, he will not object to having the executive believe that he was responsible for the idea and encourage him to develop it. Colonel House remarks about Woodrow Wilson:

After I got to know the President . . . I learned the best way to convert him to an idea was to plant it in his mind casually, but so as to interest him in it—so as to get him thinking about it on his own account. The first time this worked it was an accident. I had been visiting him at the White House, and urged a policy on him which he appeared to disapprove. But several days later, at the dinner table, I was amazed to hear him trot out my suggestion as his own. . . .[2]

Colonel House would come into an office and say a few words quietly, and after he had gone you would suddenly become seized by a good idea. You would suggest that idea to your friends or superiors and

[1] PAULINE V. YOUNG, "The Transient Problem in California," unpublished manuscript.
[2] ARTHUR D. H. SMITH, "A Collector of Friendships," *Saturday Evening Post*, CIC (August 28, 1926), 25; 69–74.

be congratulated for it. . . . But sometime as sure as shooting, . . . you would come to an abrupt realization that that idea had been oozed into your brain by Colonel House.[1]

Rex Stuart reports the views of a prominent executive regarding people who seize credit for ideas at the expense of their subordinates:

I'm thinking now of an executive who was always bringing new ideas to the managerial conferences of a store with which I was . . . connected. He paraded them proudly. He fought for them boldly. And we adopted a good many of them because they were essentially sound. This man seemed to be succeeding in his effort to create an impression.

Presently I discovered that he was getting nearly all these ideas from subordinates, to whom he failed to give a word of credit. The people under him learned the same thing and resented it. The morale of his department which had been excellent began to crumble. It was a bad mess all round.

Now suppose this executive had said to us: "Yesterday, I heard Bill Jones make a suggestion that I think is a corker. I'm passing it along." Why Bill Jones and all the other workers under him would have been tickled to death that he was "boosting them to the boss," and they would have worked their heads off. I would have congratulated myself that I had a department head who could inspire his people to think up things for the good of the business. And everyone would have been happy.[2]

THE EMPLOYER[3]

What has been said about safeguarding the interests of the executive holds equally true in the case of the employer. Many employers regard social workers coming to their offices as "Greeks who come bearing gifts." Many believe that social workers are either sentimentalists or hard boiled and in poor position to understand them and their situation. Miss Richmond says:

. . . The employer differs from the teacher and the doctor, however, in that he is farther removed in daily habit from socialized action, and is often controlled by quite another set of motives. Even when, as

[1] ARTHUR D. H. SMITH, *The Real Colonel House*, p. 120.

[2] REX STUART, "Getting the 'Extra Percentage' of Power out of People," *American Magazine*, XCII (August, 1921), 37.

[3] For systematic discussions of the various techniques used in the interview with employers see WALTER V. BINGHAM and BRUCE V. MOORE, *How to Interview*.

sometimes happens, his motives are completely social, this fact is not easily recognized, because he is hampered by imperfect forms of industrial organization. . . .

From what has already been said it is evident that personal visits to industrial establishments are far more fruitful than telephone messages or letters. . . .

Get the Employer's point of view before deciding how much can safely be told of a client's affairs, though more of what he knows will be revealed, usually, after he has been told a good deal. Often a reference to the foreman is the best result that can be had from the business office of a firm. . . .

Equally emphatic testimony is at hand as to the value of forewomen. One social worker believes that the forewoman of a factory has a rare opportunity to do constructive social work for girls, and cites instances of the influence of certain forewomen who are still the exception. . . .

Former employers can be consulted with far greater freedom than present employers, and the information that they are able to supply often (though not invariably) makes communication with the latter unnecessary. The most important former employer witnesses are those for whom a client has worked the longest in recent years.

In certain cases the evidence of present employers is essential. In non-support cases, for example, it is necessary to know exact earnings, duration of employment, number of times absent from work, supposed causes of absence, and number and amounts of wage attachments for debt.

As a rule, though there are exceptions, prospective employers should not be interviewed.

Personal visits to industrial establishments and interviews with foremen especially are far more fruitful than communications by letter, though some firms refuse to give information in any other way than by letter.

In accident cases not coming under the compensation law care it is necessary to avoid compromising the employee's interests.[1]

George Gill, Director of Indianapolis Employment Bureau, analyzes the approach to the employer as follows:

What can he [the prospective employee] do? says the semi-sympathetic employer to the case worker when approached in behalf of a client who needs a job. To answer this question it is obvious that the case worker must know something about the client's training and experience and that the more she knows the better she can talk about him and his

[1] *Social Diagnosis*, pp. 235; 247; 252. See also
WALTER V. BINGHAM and BRUCE V. MOORE, *How to Interview*, Chaps. 4, 5.

ability. Unless she is able intelligently to discuss her client with a prospective employer, it is well to postpone her interview until she has found out more about him.

In addition to knowing his age, marital condition, and other personal things about him, the case worker should have a record of his height, weight, physical condition (including handicaps and weaknesses), details concerning his schooling, a chronological report of the jobs held, and a record of what other people say about his character, experience and ability. . . . The occupational record is important: an account of how the client has spent his working hours for a number of consecutive years reveals much. . . .

One of the important observations which the case worker has a chance to make is the client's attitude toward people and things in general. It is obvious that the optimistic, good-natured person reveals an attitude which will get him further than the one who constantly complains that everyone has it in for him, that he has always had raw deals, and that luck is against him. These attitudes often remain hidden until brought forth by questioning. . . .

If the case worker feels that her client can be recommended she should talk about his positive qualities. The thing the employer wants to know is what the client can do for his company which would make it worth while from the company's standpoint to employ him. . . .

The case worker should be conversant with applied economics as well as with sociology. How well does she know her community and its economic resources? Can she discuss with both the owner of the small plant and the superintendent of the large one the problems which confront them in picking capable workers? Does she know how many local establishments have pension systems? Which ones have apprenticeship training? Has she ever made any effort to acquaint herself with the changes during the last few years in production methods which affect factory workers? . . .

The case worker who approaches employers in a spirit of cooperation will find them glad to enlighten her concerning their problems and their employment policies. They will tell her why they keep some workers and discharge others. The more she knows about employer's needs the more success she will have in placing "square pegs" in holes into which they will fit. She may not refer as many persons to jobs or to prospective employers, but her referals will be more intelligently made—resulting, perhaps, in more and better placements . . . [1]

The following is a verbatim report of an interview with a former employer in an attempt to reinstate a man in his employ:

[1] GEORGE E. GILL, "The Case Worker's Approach to Employers," *The Family*, X (June, 1929), 110–111. Reprinted by permission.

I came to get some information about Mr. Smith. I know you can help me.

Yes, what can I do for you?

Do you remember Mr. Smith well?

Enough; he loafed on the job.

Did you ever have a chance to learn something of his family life?

Well, I can't be concerned with it.

Yes, I know, you can't make a practice of it. But you will be interested in Mr. Smith. After all, a man's family life has a great deal to do with his skill and efficiency.

Well, what about his family life?

Did you know there was considerable illness in his family, his son ill, his wife ill? He lost sleep and weight. The son nearly died.

No, I did not know that.

If my boy was on the verge of death, I am sure I would loaf on the job too. Under those circumstances would you consider taking him back for a trial?

Well, I have no opening now.

May I call you next week about it?

Yes, if you will.

By the way, how much did Mr. Smith earn a week?

Twenty-two, I believe.

Well, thank you for your courtesy. I'll take the liberty to call on you again next week. Goodbye.[1]

It is of importance to note that the interviewer approached the employer for information and not directly for a job for Mr. Smith. The interviewer aroused the employer's interest and sympathy in the problems of his former employee, explained his failure on the job, and identified herself with his misfortune hoping that the employer would do likewise. The interviewer presented the employee not as a hand in the factory but as a person with obligations and family problems. The interviewer picked up the hint when the employer said that he had no opening now, by volunteering to call again and not leaving it up to him to get in touch with her. The question of the amount of money earned was left until the end. Courtesies extended, a foundation for a future appointment was laid.

Using a similar interviewing technique, but in a much more difficult case, the interviewer[2] was able to secure full cooperation from the employer:

Interview with Mr. Garland.

Interviewer: I am from the Restitution Office in the Probation Department, Mr. Garland, I've come to see you in regard to Mr. S., who was

---

[1] Reported by a student visitor.

[2] Interview held and recorded by **Mr. Robert Christenson, Los Angeles,** 1933.

ordered—as a condition of probation—to reimburse the Club for the bad checks he had passed.

Mr. Garland: Oh, yes, I remember the case very well. He is a bad character. He used to spend most of his time in the card room. (Mr. Garland then described in more detail than we need quote how Mr. S. started paying his losses in bridge by check, asking other members to hold same for a few days. One member would turn over a check to another member until it became a habit for all members to pay losses by check. Everybody would hold everybody else's check, and during this depression very little actual cash changed hands in the card room. These checks, one by one, found their way to the Club cashier, and when they had accumulated to $500.00 in S.'s case and had become a general nuisance all around, they decided to put a stop to these transactions by swearing out a complaint against S. to make an example of him.) He used to be a successful business man, but after the crash he did nothing but play cards. We even suspected him of cheating. What chance do you think we have of getting our money on those checks?

Interviewer: Prospects are not very encouraging at the present time unless we find a job for Mr. S. It's now two months since he was released from jail, and he has been unable to find a job of any kind. He has no income except what he might earn. He is living in a small room alone, his wife having left him. He is willing to do any kind of work, and we were wondering if it might not be possible that you would help us place him in some kind of a position with your organization—in other words, give him a chance to work off the claim.

Mr. Garland: I don't think that is possible. We all feel that he is a crook and it wouldn't do to have him working here. Besides, he would come in contact with his former friends and that would cause all kinds of embarrassing situations for the members.

Interviewer: Yes, I thought of that. You see, Mr. S. suggested that he be given a job as janitor, and I asked him how he would feel in such a position if he met some of his old friends. He—

Mr. Garland: (Interrupting) Do you mean that Mr. S. suggested this?

Interviewer: Yes, he did. He is very anxious to find work so he can start paying off his debt. He wants any kind of work. He realizes that it might be embarrassing both to him and the members, but he seems to think that he can stand it as long as he has a chance to earn an honest living and pay off the claim. I am sure the class of people you have here as members would understand.

Mr. Garland: (Thoughtfully) Maybe he is not as bad as I thought—of course, we employ a number of people who have no actual contact with the members. Do you think that he can be trusted?

Interviewer: I do, and I feel that someone will have to give him a helping hand soon if he is to be rehabilitated. He is almost at the end of his rope. He has tried everywhere to find work without results; you know how times are. He is behind in his room rent and he is continually worrying about not being able to comply with the Court order of restitution. I have talked to him and explained that we feel restitution is secondary, rehabilitation comes first, but he insists that paying back the money is the main issue. With your help we might be able to work out a plan whereby we can accomplish both.

Mr. Garland: (Slowly, thoughtfully) Maybe we were a little too hard on him, but we just had to stop those checks from floating around. We may be able to do something. (Briskly) What would you suggest?

Interviewer: I understand that you have several other places besides this Club. (Country Club, Beach Club, Yacht Club.) As this is where Mr. S. spent most of his time and is best known, I would suggest, if I may, placing him in one of the other clubhouses to avoid embarrassing situations as much as possible. He may not be a success as a laborer, but I am sure in an organization like this there is a place where his abilities can be used.

Mr. Garland: (Interested) That's so. We might be able to do just that. I'll call up our employment man and find out what the situation is at one of our other places. (Calls up Mr. H., who also remembers case. Has short conversation. Smiling.) I made an appointment for Mr. S. to see Mr. H. at 9 A.M. tomorrow morning. We may be able to use him at our Country Club.

Interviewer: That's mighty decent of you, Mr. Garland. I'll see Mr. S. this afternoon. I know that he will be delighted at the opportunity not only to pay off this debt, but also of the chance to show that he can come back. How do you wish to arrange the financial end of it?

Mr. Garland: Well, I don't really know—we could fix him up with a room down there and give him his meals at a reasonable charge, and then let the rest of his wages apply on his debt. That arrangement would save us sending the check to you every month and you returning it to us. That would save bookkeeping all around.

Interviewer: Yes, but he would need a little spending money. I have noticed no matter how blue he is, and he is quite broken in spirit, he still takes pride in his appearance. It might be an added incentive to show that you trust him by paying him like any other employee. That would make it seem more like getting a fresh start.

Mr. Garland: I see. I'll tell you what we better do then. We can send him down there with a letter of introduction, without explaining the case to them, and let them make their own terms. Afterwards he can make arrangements with you probation people about monthly payments on our claim. I don't care how you fix it. I am beginning to get more interested in getting him re-established in society than getting the $500.00 back. It certainly must be interesting work, this probation business. (Then followed a short conversation about the Probation Department, and a few thank you's and the interviewer departed.)

The above material when reduced to a case record entry took the following form:

4–26–33. Interviewed Mr. Garland, Room #123, ——Street, Los Angeles, who represents ——Club, the creditor, relative to having probationer work off claim. He seemed much opposed to such a plan at first, but before the interview terminated his attitude changed completely. He not only arranged an interview for probationer with Mr. H., who has charge of employment, but stated that after our little talk he was more interested in probationer's rehabilitation than the recovery of the money. Mr. S. was notified to see Mr. H. regarding work. Asked to let us know result.

CHAPTER VIII

SPECIAL TYPES OF INTERVIEWING SITUATIONS
(*Concluded*)

THE NEW POOR

A system of social diagnosis of the problems of chronic dependency and of personal and social disorganization has been in process of development for many years. The problems of the new poor are relatively recent phenomena. Few or no studies on a large scale have been made of the social and psychological reaction patterns developed by the new poor upon sudden loss of income. Since we know so little about the situation, we have not been able to devise satisfactory methods of analysis and therapy. So far trial and error methods have been largely employed. Only isolated experiences and fragmentary observations in dealing with the new poor have thus far been reported. The following typical experiences of employable and willing workers out of employment may provide the interviewer with some insight into the emotional, social, family, and economic problems of this group:

Story of Mr. Allamy.

I have been unemployed for a year and a half. I am a machinist by trade. I never thought I would be idle more than a month. This is the first time in my working life when I had to sit around and do nothing. The time drags until you count not the days but the hours and minutes. Have you ever been idle when you had no desire to do so? It's nothing short of a plague. Let me tell you, too, I had little patience with people who seemed radical, revolutionary; but those thoughts force themselves upon you when you sit at home, income cut off and demands for food, clothing and shelter remain the same, to say nothing of the things which we had to give up as "luxuries," but which we were forced into using "to raise our standard of living."

When I quit working we fell back on our savings. These have lasted several months. Then my wife went to work as a housekeeper and I was left as cook and homemaker for our three children. You can imagine the state of affairs at the house. When the wife returns Sundays she puts us straight for the week. She makes $50 a month and we live on that.

We gave up meats and fish and started a vegetarian diet. Then we gave up our house and moved into a shack for $12 a month. It's no place to

160

raise children in.   When the wind blows it makes little difference whether we are in-doors or out-of-doors.   On cold nights it is impossible to remain warm and we must heat up bricks and flat irons to put in the children's beds, but the worst of it is when it rains.   Well, you get what you pay for, and we can pay only $12 a month.

When I worked I was able to support my widowed mother.   I had to send her to my niece; but she again had to send her to my sister, and the poor old lady is driven every month somewhere else.

The women folks lose respect for you when you have to look into their hands for a dollar.   Well, maybe they don't, but I am too sensitive and it's getting too much for me.   I tell you I cannot stand this idleness much longer. I will either smash my head or that of somebody else.   It is not right for those of us who want to work and can work to sit and sit and gradually go down the scale.

Before long nobody will want me.   I am losing my skill and muscle and heart.   Things in the shop are changing, and I am losing out fast.

My wife is so discouraged nothing matters much to her.   Live or die, health or sickness—have lost their distinctions.   She is cynical and sees no sacredness in life.

The children were always a great pleasure to her.   She took pride and joy in raising them.   They were greatly attached to her.   She is away now most of the time.   The children can hardly find themselves without her.   I try to do for them all I can, but I can't give them the tenderness which their mother gave them.   The children have lost a great deal of their joy and laughter.   They are too serious and feel lonely, heart-hungry, you might say.

I must admit that I am growing more and more resentful toward the world. Something is wrong someplace, if a man of my experience, a man who can and wants to work, must kill time doing nothing.   I resent doing woman's work at home and it's very hard for me to do it.   We dropped our life insurance policies.   Should anything happen to us, we must be buried like paupers.[1]

Story of Mr. Mason.

My greatest difficulty is a severe inferiority complex.   I often reason with myself that I am not the only man out of work, not the only head of a family without funds for the necessities of life, not the only worker without a real job for three years, but many things around me indicate that I am a failure, if I am to speak frankly to you.   You start a discussion with a man who has a job or even with a welfare worker and he will tell you that most men out of work are "borderline-cases," whatever we are to understand by that. I've come to believe it.   The country must have some 10 million "borderline cases."

At home, the women folks look down on me; I have failed to function as a man, as a provider.   I am still the husband, the father, the "man of the house," but my opinion does not count; my presence is often too much for them.   They are used to see me off in the morning and back in the evening. The household is not organized to see an idle man around all day, under

[1] CALIFORNIA STATE UNEMPLOYMENT COMMISSION, *Report and Recommendations*, 1932, p. 109.   Interview held and recorded by Pauline V. Young.

their feet. I appreciate their situation, but what should I do with myself. It costs money to go places.

And let me tell you, the kids get notions in school that if their fathers are unable to provide for them, they will be provided for just the same. My influence over them is greatly diminished; my word doesn't count with them. Perhaps, I haven't the power in my voice when my head is down. I know my boy can get a job easier than I can.

What do you think all these things do to me? They certainly don't add to my self-esteem, to my happiness. At times I boil inside, but most of the time I feel licked. I never imagined that the peace of my home and the control over my children depended on my job. Why, the job just rules your life. Oh, we are still a family, but the ties are greatly weakened.[1]

It is pointed out by various agencies who recognize the problems of the new poor that mere giving of relief or any makeshift plan which these families may adopt fails to provide them with that sense of security and that feeling of self-respect which comes from holding a job. They become seriously discouraged when they wander aimlessly and fruitlessly in search of employment. Margaret Rich observes that an interviewer "who shows a man that she recognizes his personality, that she respects him, will help him endure many hardships which might otherwise be totally destructive."[2]

Many interviewers coming in contact with the new poor found such a philosophy as voiced by Miss Neustaedter quite helpful:

Perhaps our first contribution to those whom we are attempting to assist comes through a recognition of the fact that the problem is beyond us in that we have not resources to meet the entire need. We must make the best of a bad situation; there will be suffering which we cannot relieve, hardship that we cannot soften. When we have accepted that fact we become less tense and are more free to do that which is of the essence of case work—to individualize those who come to us for help. Moreover, when we admit that we cannot cope with the situation in its entirety, we have no need to deaden our sympathies and rationalize our failure to do the work that we would like to do by projecting responsibility for our overcrowded offices on to the applicants; we need not say, "We are getting the dregs of the community now." Let us relax, let us admit our limitations, and, as we look at our waiting rooms—with standing room only for unhappy people—let us do the

[1] PAULINE V. YOUNG, "What's on the Mind of the New Poor," manuscript.

[2] *The Administration of Relief in Unemployment Emergencies*, p. 20, pamphlet. See also

CALIFORNIA STATE UNEMPLOYMENT COMMISSION, *Report and Recommendation*, "The Human Cost of Unemployment," pp. 87–146.

thing for which we are especially trained, individualize them and see not "The Unemployed" but the men and women of whom this group is composed. . . .

Said the district secretary, "It was formerly the duty of a clerical worker to dismiss these cases but now I make it a point to see each man and say to him in effect, 'We cannot help you but we understand the difficulty of your position: we recognize you as a person whose integrity we do not question; we are sorry that our limitations make it impossible for us to help.'" . . .

He comes to us in a mass of "Unemployed," his self-esteem at a low ebb. Before we meet him, the competent workman has "pounded the pavements" for months. As he waits in our office he is keenly aware of the company in which he finds himself. Frequently he feels that by the nature of his appeal he is suspected of being what he has never before felt himself to be—a "bum." "Yes," said one man wearily the other day, "I know why you ask these questions; you have to know that I am honest, you have to know that I am not lying. When people ask for money you have to know that they are telling you the truth."

And many of these men we must refuse. But, concerning the manner of their refusal, a case worker recently said that if we can't investigate their story, if we can't get below the surface, can't dig in, then we do assume that the story is correct. If we are not in a position to help, we must *not* add to the burdens of an already over-burdened, needy person by taking an attitude which suggests to him that we doubt his story. Whether or not we doubt it, if we can't investigate or cannot use our resources in his behalf, we give him the benefit of the doubt. Better to permit a panhandler to think he "gets away with it" than further to humiliate an honest man by sending him away with the impression that he has been refused because we questioned his integrity.

And the man whom we see as "no good"—if we cannot take him on we do not let him know that we appraise him as an inferior person. If lack of resources makes a refusal imperative, then at least that refusal can be kindly, impersonal, giving no hint that we think little of his personality. We may not be able to meet his material needs but we can at least build up a feeling of his own worth by an attitude which suggests belief in his integrity, respect for his personality, and regret for the situation in which he finds himself.[1]

The Human Discard.—An increasing number of middle-aged unemployed men have come to realize that they will never again be reinstated in the trade at which they were at work before the

[1] ELEANOR NEUSTAEDTER, "The Social Case Worker and Industrial Depression," *The Family*, XI (January, 1931), 275–276. Reprinted by permission.

depression. "They tell me I am too old . . . I am out of practice . . . out of skill, out of joint . . . They have reorganized . . . I do not fit any more . . . My tools are out of date . . . " are typical remarks by workers who still seem to be in the prime of life, but their repeated failures to secure steady work make them permanent charges upon relief organizations. The following excerpt from a statement by a middle-aged mechanic is typical of a large group of working people who regard themselves as human discards.

I am a human being, but have been thrown on the rubbish pile like a bundle of rags. I was discarded from industry. Nobody wants me any more. "Don't need you," they shout at me and dismiss me with a wave of their hand. Are we to die like old dogs? . . . For twenty-three years I lived in this city, have grown up with it, have taken pride in its developments, and cheered its successes. I helped support charitable enterprises. I had only a remote idea of what "charity" meant. . . . Oh, it hurts to think that for the rest of my days I must do odd jobs, ring door bells to ask for a few hours' work, any kind of work. . . . What good is a trade? They take it out of your hands, and you have nothing to say, nothing to fall back on. I am licked. . . . [1]

I'm downright discouraged. I hate to admit it but I just can't see what there is ahead for me. Yesterday I went into one of the old furniture companies where the foreman knows me and my work. I asked him to keep me in mind for any opening he might have. Do you know what he told me? "Dad, I know your work is good and that you can out-work some of these young fellows we have on the bench now, but I'd lose my job if I hired you. We can't take a man over forty years old."

What am I to do? I know I'm too old for rough carpentering for I can't do the heavy lifting. All my life's savings are gone except this home and it's probably going too. Sometimes I think it would be a good plan for the government to take all men past sixty and mow them down with machine guns. It would be an act of mercy.[2]

Regarding the "upper white-collar aristocracy," Harry E. Barnes writes:

[1] Pauline V. Young, "The New Poor," *Sociology and Social Research*, XVII (January-February, 1933), 238–239. See also
"The Human Cost of Unemployment," *Sociology and Social Research*, XVII (March-April, 1933), 361–369.
[2] Reported by Evelyn Delany, Los Angeles.

There have been plenty of stories about the misery of the masses—those on the breadline, the down-and-out and the dispossessed farmers. The "neediest cases" are rather fully and quite justly publicized. But there is another group of sufferers who have been just given little attention except in a few "personal" stories of their fate since 1929. I refer to those who were formerly well-to-do—the upper white-collar aristocracy. Their plight is well described by Bishop John Paul Jones in an article on "Middle-Class Misery" in the *Survey Graphic*. He thus summarizes the nature and suffering of this class:

They are the executives, technical experts, efficiency men, promoters, lawyers, advertisers, managers and the like. Economic chaos soon sweeps them to the borderline and before long pushes them over. . . .

The kind of readjustment they are called upon to make is heroic. They undergo months of torture before they darken the door of a relief agency. . . . Viewed even from the most hopeful angle, the plight of the formerly well-to-do unemployed is tragic beyond description. Vast multitudes of them have lost financial security forever. In bewilderment and bitterness they will seek a sign of hope, and no sign will be given. Some will give up and end it all, but a great majority will go on living some kind of broken and frustrated lives.[1]

The middle class sufferers who have been broken by the depression comprise men of education and culture who have received salaries of from $5,000 to $50,000 per year. . . .

Personally I know of . . . the former manager of a large novelty manufacturing company who received a high salary, lived in a mansion on the Hudson and sent his children to expensive private schools. He has been out of work for two years and his wife now tries desperately to support the family by baking for neighbors. In another case the wife of a former real estate magnate is producing the only income for the family by going out through the city doing ordinary housework.

The developments and stages in the economic decline to psychic and material misery are fairly uniform and quite characteristic. The husband loses his job. He sets out in the near-hopeless quest for work. The children are put in public schools. The maids and other servants are dropped. The wife begins to do her own work. The reserves are used up. Sickness may wipe them out more quickly. The husband borrows on his life insurance, if there is anything left after he has used this source to meet margin calls on stock investments. The property is mortgaged, if it has not already been for market plunges. In due time the home is surrendered and the family moves into modest quarters. The wife then begins to take in work, the son sells papers and the daughter goes out to stay with neighbors' children.

[1] John Paul Jones, "Middle-class Misery," *The Survey Graphic*, LXVIII (September, 1932), 402–404.

These devices often prove inadequate and outside relief ultimately becomes necessary. This is the hardest blow of all. The unfortunates must appear before persons they may formerly have snubbed to get the mere necessities of life. And, at best, the relief given is notoriously inadequate, even for a much lowered standard of living. The situation is bad enough when everybody is sensible and makes the best of a bad set of circumstances. It is intolerable if false pride and hysteria are allowed to enter. . . . [1]

One of the outstanding characteristics of the new poor is their bewilderment, varying from fear of insecurity to indifference to the future.[2] Uprooted from the social soil which previously sustained them, they lose social balance: they plunge into moods of despair or of hyperactivity to "start life all over again,"[3] or they begin to "fight against society and the social and economic system." They are unable to define their social status. They realize they are not only workers without jobs, but human beings without the customary social environment, citizens without courage, husbands without the moral support of their wives, fathers without control over their children. They know they are men adrift. They shrink from former friends or they camouflage themselves. They do not know what to expect of old friends. They are unable to decide whether to keep up appearances and accumulate debts or to revise their whole mode of living. Frequently they resort to very ill-considered expenditures. Essential needs are confused with old wants and expensive habits. Frequently there is dissension in the home, since not all members react the same to the catastrophe. Some wish to camouflage, others insist on meeting the exigencies of the hour squarely. Prolonged unemployment and idleness, necessity of accepting relief, and the constant feeling of insecurity tend to thwart the personality and outlook of many an individual. Some become marginal men or borderline cases who fear to take

---

[1] HARRY ELMER BARNES, "The Liberal Viewpoint," *New York World-Telegram*, Quoted by GEORGE K. PRATT, *Morale: The Mental Hygiene of Unemployment*, pp. 40–41.

[2] See Oesterreichische Wirtschaftspsychologische Forschungs-stelle, *Die Arbeitslosen von Marienthal*, particularly Chap. III "Die Müde Gemeinschaft."

[3] See GRACE MARCUS, "Psychological Realities in Case Work," *The Family*, XIII (July, 1932), 147–150.

HELEN HALL, *Case Studies of Unemployment*.

their place in society as previously.   It is essential to remember Miss Richmond's warning:

Without minimizing for a moment the importance of such questions of temporary relief, permanent support, sources of support as enter into the treatment of dependency . . . I cannot agree that any of these considerations, relating to what might be called the machinery of different types of social work, are central to the task of the social case worker.   Analysis will show that they fall into second place when problems of social relationship and of personality thrust themselves forward, as they so persistently do.[1]

The interviewer is necessarily concerned with certain major interrelated problems.   The following guides may be employed in addition to those previously suggested in "The Social Case History Outline of a Family" (pp. 102–107).

The Social Case History Outline of the New Poor[2]

1. What material emergency situations are the new poor facing when all income is cut off?   Does the family need food, shelter, medical care?

2. What makeshifts has family adopted and what resources has it tapped before applying for aid?

3. How has the wage earner tried to earn a living after having lost his job?   What other occupations has he fitted himself to enter?

4. What small economies has family learned to make?

5. What social and psychological problems have arisen because of dependency and idleness and because of the necessity of adopting makeshifts?   What tensions and conflicts have they developed?

6. What alterations in personality have these people undergone in the process of adjustment to a new and unaccustomed mode of living?   Have they become embittered, or have they accepted the situation as a challenge to them?

7. How do the various members of the family define their new status? Are they identifying themselves with old friends and institutions or are they seeking new meeting grounds?   Emotional consequences?

8. To what extent does the family still hold on to old standards and customs?   Emotional consequences?

9. Does the family lack a technique of living on a new level?

10. Can the family approach the new situation rationally and sanely?

11. What habits, activities, and things has the family given up since loss of income?   Emotional consequences?

12. What changes have proven profitable or unprofitable to the various members?

13. What occupations or avocations have the members tried to follow?

14. What plans for the future did the family make for the adult members? For the children?

[1] *What Is Social Case Work?* p. 97.

[2] PAULINE V. YOUNG, "The Interviewing Approach to the New Poor," *Sociology and Social Research*, XIX (January-February, 1935), 237–238.

15. What effect does dependency and receiving aid have upon the morale of the individual members of the family and the group as a whole?

16. What philosophy of life has the family formulated as a result of new conditions faced? What philosophy of life is the family imparting to the children?

A thorough knowledge of the emotional, social, and economic circumstances of each family may not be of value in redirecting the energies of particular cases, but it is an indispensable minimum if the new poor as a whole are to be studied and understood and their situations defined or redefined to them. A lack of a thorough knowledge of what happens to families when suddenly called upon to revise their mode of living makes us incapable of knowing what the social agency can contribute outside of material relief.

These new poor often remark: "It is easier to go hungry than to be misunderstood": "Every grocery order should contain a package of quinine to get us out of the misery": "Every bit of food brings us closer to the pauperization level": "Soon we will have our sensibilities deadened and come to think that the only way to eat is through the charities."

Miss Frances Hill writes about the present emergency relief situation in terms of "disaster relief":

This facing of economic facts, without the flavor of moral judgment, gives objectivity to the inquiry and leaves the case worker free to select whatever sources will yield the desired information, making full use of the techniques of case work, but limiting, by emphasis on economic factors, the extent of both investigation and treatment.

Our staff Committee on Industrial Problems felt that we could take over the philosophy of disaster relief, adapt it to the disaster of widespread unemployment, and adjust it somewhat to cover treatment over a period of time. They drew up an outline of the kind of information that seemed to them essential and which would serve not only as a guide to inquiry but as a basis for a summarized record:

1. The father of the family (or other responsible wage earner) is:
   a. Able-bodied.
   b. Under 60.
   c. A person who has actually held a job.
   d. A man who, up until the time he was laid off, supported his family.
   e. An acceptable employee.
   f. Looking for work.
   g. A person who was working at his regular occupation when he was laid off.

2. The family is actually suffering, because of unemployment:
   a. In health.
   b. In debt.
   c. In mental attitude.
3. The normal sources have already been tapped:
   a. Savings.
   b. Insurance.
   c. Relatives.
   d. Loans on adjusted service certificates.
   e. Credit.

Negative answers to the majority of these questions are recognized as meaning that a family needs case work service rather than unemployment relief—they do not imply that the family is "unworthy."[1]

Miss Hill further remarks that it is essential to let the man

. . . know that we are taking this information not for the sake of simply filling out a form, or for checking up, but rather to help him.

Perhaps by explaining the significance of the information asked, we can enlist the cooperation of the unemployed person. Since the client can no longer work to supply his own need, he can be given some sense of security by working with the social worker to make some definite plan for his family. This is essential for two reasons: 1. The client himself will know what to expect from us, when to expect it, and what is expected of him. This will tend to give him some satisfaction for he will know that even though he can earn nothing, he is doing all he can to meet the situation. 2. It will save time for the worker for she can then make her plans to keep appointments, keep her families satisfied, and get back periodically to supervise them.[2]

As it has been remarked, it matters not so much what happens to a person but how he takes it. Some families feel themselves compromised when they are thrown out of employment. Tensions arise not so much because of loss of income but because of fear of losing status in the social group or even in one's family. The interviewer under those circumstances may explain the universality of the depression and the millions of people involved in every section of the country and abroad. Knowing that the problems are not unique to them, they do not regard themselves as outcasts. The interviewer may also find it expedient to explain that self-respect, social status in the community, and

---

[1] FRANCES L. HILL, "Disaster Philosophy and Technique in Unemployment Work," *The Family*, XII (February, 1932), 307–309. Reprinted by permission.

[2] Unpublished manuscript.

success in society no longer depend chiefly on material values and that the individual is no longer judged only by his financial success but also by his ability to weather the storm, to stand behind his children and his country and lend his support to them in the darkest hours of need.

Dr. Pratt points out that when a family is badly discouraged, when there is conflict and fear of the future, some member may express his desperation by belligerency, sarcasm, hostility. If the true motives behind these expressions are understood, the interviewer will never "respond in kind and produce a needlessly painful situation all around."[1] Frequently a family, trying to keep up appearances, will cling to some article of furniture—a piano or a refrigerator or a set of books—which might be converted into cash, because it still expresses former status and the good old times. The retention of a few bits of once fine furniture may bolster up the morale of those people who continue to live psychologically on their former level. Few interviewers at present fail to appreciate the value of those people who "refuse to cringe under distress" and who "continue to keep up a brave interest in 'cultural' and artistic things and display a non-servile manner toward those who 'investigate' them for relief."[2]

Supervisors with a full measure of current experience say that dictatorial, censorious attitudes on the part of visitors toward small indulgences by families that have hitherto made their own choices in life inevitably result in a contest of wills and wits in which the visitor, even armed with a grocery order, is the fore-ordained loser. A good worker will discuss with the family its own strategy and luck in getting these things for itself. She will not accept a permanent wave or an occasional movie spree as sufficient evidence to overturn her initial judgment on the family's need for help. If the luck seems too recurrent or the strategy a little too good to be true, a new investigation is indicated with the family told frankly why it is made.

The worker who travels along with her families treating them not with the blanket formula, 'It's against the rules,' but with the candid explanations due to reasonable people, will seldom need to resort to an ultimatum or to use the food order as a club to knock out the few remaining personal choices that unemployment has left to its victims.[3]

[1] GEORGE K. PRATT, *Morale: The Mental Hygiene of Unemployment*, p. 17.

[2] *Ibid.*, p. 50.

[3] GERTRUDE SPRINGER, "What Price the Power of the Food Order?" *The Survey*, LXIX (May, 1933), 182–193. Reprinted by permission.

Interviewers dealing with the new poor have found the following suggestions helpful in their approach:

I can generally talk them into "keeping fit" until the opportunity does arrive. Often they brace up for the sake of the morale at home, for the sake of the children who do not know what it's all about. At times, just a heart-to-heart talk will relieve tensions and buoy up an idle man. But above all, it is our attitude, our spirit and confidence which we bring into the home that counts the most. When I am tired and discouraged because "prosperity has not turned the corner" I unconsciously impart these feelings to the family. It's we, social workers, who need to hold our heads up first. . . .

I get results when I suggest that the unemployed father spend more time with his children whom he cannot enjoy when working long hours. "Play with your youngsters, take them out for a walk, teach them to be useful citizens, make up in personal relationships what they lack along material lines," I indicate to them. . . .

I have been successful in occupying the minds and the hands of the idle unemployed by suggesting tasks around the house, the yard, the neighbor's house. . . .

Often it is possible to arrange for visits to the branch libraries to read or to look at magazine pictures, or for visits to recreation centers. . . .

I think that we concentrate too much on the unemployed man and not enough on his wife who has to tolerate him all day long under her feet. I interpret the husband to the wife and vice versa and lay some foundation for new relationships.[1]

Opinion is divided among social workers whether an attempt should be made to treat the unemployment cases as if they needed social or personal service. Some workers maintain that most frequently other social and emotional problems harass the family upon the onset of unemployment, and, although emergency relief workers are able to touch these problems only superficially, they are able nevertheless to minimize in some measure the emotional tensions besetting the family. Alice Canfield, of the Los Angeles County Welfare Department, strikes a different keynote in the approach to the new poor:

[1] Statements by family welfare workers.

Frankly, I think it is a terrible thing, of far-reaching consequences, to turn jobless men and their defenseless families into public social cases; to pry into their private lives; to run their lives!

My conception of the province of the social worker is that he or she has no right to probe the spiritual, intellectual and moral problems of any individual or family, unless that individual or family has endangered public safety or public health, or plunged, *in normal times*, into chronic pauperism. I do not believe any social worker has either the right or the "omniscience" to attempt to weigh the extent to which spiritual or intellectual limitation, or moral defection, has contributed to placing an individual in the ranks of the unemployed at this time, when unemployment is an almost universal problem.

Such intimate problems of the spiritual, intellectual or moral sphere are matters upon which each individual may seek advice from religious or educational sources, if he or she so chooses, and only then. . . . She [the social worker] has no inalienable right, through talent or experience, to supervise the lives of persons whose primary problem in these baffling times is unemployment.

Such supervision is destructive of the self-respect, responsibility, morale, good citizenship and human dignity of the supervised, who become cringers, malingerers, defeatists. They may fill their stomachs from day to day but their spirits are breaking. And even their children, the citizens of the future, cannot hold their heads up, as the whole family vibrates to those mournful words, "We're on the charities now!" . . .

. . . Unemployed Americans are becoming more and more hardened, pitifully enough, to receiving official charity. Their drift is a slow, insidious, scarcely perceptible process. Without realizing it, many of our jobless and their families are being transformed into nothing more nor less than idle government serfs. Their despair has made them all too willing dependents of State, County or other political subdivision. . . .

Where unemployment is the fundamental issue . . . social case work is no longer being given. Most unemployed persons, we feel, are fine, reasonably intelligent persons who resent having their family histories explored by social workers. Those of the unemployed who maintain this decency and dignity "know they know" all about budgeting. They are not wastrels. They do not ask someone to come in and put their houses in order. They are destitute through no fault of their own. While their private lives may not be perfect, whose are? If their lives are to be subjected to the close scrutiny of social workers, for general moral improvement, why should we not also do social work on the wealthy, who probably need it more? There need be no limit at which social work should stop—until it shatters itself on some such *reductio ad absurdum*.

The matter of getting a job is a business proposition, pure and simple. When a man goes to a commercial employment agency he does not have to discuss his private troubles; but during this economic depression men have not only taken to discussing them, but to exaggerating them. To obtain charity they become more and more willing to lie pitifully, to become the most contemptible weaklings. Some men have developed physical sicknesses—mostly neuroses and psychoses—they never knew they had "in good times," in order to get out of working, especially when asked to do manual labor. They get to prefer charity—or rather, official alms-giving.[1]

Social case workers report that deprivation, coupled with continued idleness and dependency, has its demoralizing effects upon the most stable and self-respecting citizens. As time goes on they become dazed, irresponsible, and discouraged; they carry a chip on their shoulders and come to believe that the world owes them a living.

These families are bewildered, stunned, unable to reason, to comprehend, difficult to arouse from their mental coma. . . . Others are highly excitable. . . . They come to the office and yell and shake like a leaf. . . . We dare not reprimand them, for we know their plight. . . . We have brought them to such a state of affairs. . . .

These people cannot collect themselves any more. They are willing to be led, to follow any advice. . . . They are pauperized morally and mentally. . . . The customary initiative is rapidly forsaking them. They act more like children than adults. . . .

When the families first come to ask for help they are extremely sensitive, docile, pitifully embarrassed. They will not speak if the office door is slightly open. With difficulty we learn the essentials. . . . But just wait a few weeks. If the check does not arrive the day they expect it, they make a special trip to the office to learn of the delay. . . . They do not seem to be able to manage any more without our assistance. I wonder whose fault it is?[2]

Grace Marcus observes that it may be difficult to distinguish between voluntary and involuntary unemployment:

It may be difficult for the caseworker to distinguish between voluntary and involuntary unemployment. A common emotional factor in involuntary unemployment is the man's sense of inferiority and discouragement. Another factor may be his alienation from the family

[1] ALICE CANFIELD, "Are We Degrading the Unemployed?" manuscript, 1932. Reprinted by permission.

[2] CALIFORNIA STATE UNEMPLOYMENT COMMISSION, *Report and Recommendations* (November, 1932), pp. 142–143.

he is expected to support. Other difficulties may spring from his natural resistance to a humiliating fall in the economic scale, to problems of adjustment to authority rooted in his childhood experience, and to resentment of the caseworker's failure to understand his reactions. . . .

Irregular employment is destructive to steady working habits, to responsible attitudes in the wage-earner, and to practical adjustment of budget to income. Moreover, inadequate earnings may undermine the man's morale as head of the family and encourage attitudes of anxiety and resentment. Other effects of course are lowered standards of living, malnutrition, et cetera. . . . [1]

THE CHISELER

Emergency relief workers are frequently perplexed by the problem of how to distinguish the families and individuals who demand relief but who do not need it. Only thorough investigation and verification can determine a person's eligibility. Short cuts and slipshod methods only encourage chiseling. Often the chiseler withdraws before the investigation proceeds very far, since he is keenly sensitive to a thoroughgoing inquiry. Few succeed consistently and cleverly in covering up the facts from a systematic interviewer who makes a complete investigation. The problem of the chiseler then shifts to the problem of thorough investigation, which is an administrative one. However, the group of professional chiselers is relatively small and care must be taken not to have one's attitudes colored toward other clients who may be divulging information reluctantly or who may even refuse to submit to an investigation—because of emotional disturbances, because of fear of being found out by friends or relatives, or because of fear of a record at the charities.

Often people who are able to work but unwilling to accept a job when offered to them are called chiselers. In every instance it is necessary to learn why the person refuses the job offered. Some may be union members who deem it more patriotic to live on charity than to reduce the scale of wages through scab labor; some find the treatment of domestics so degrading to their self-esteem that they prefer living in a "flop" to eating in someone's kitchen alone; some have actually grown work-shy in their long period of idleness; others prefer to be supported by the large sums of money the government provides for the poor, of which they read in the newspapers. Each of these attitudes requires

[1] GRACE F. MARCUS, *Some Aspects of Relief in Family Case Work*, pp. 140; 139–140.

not only a redefinition of the situation to the real or potential chiseler but also an adjustment of the social conditions which produce such attitudes. Miss McCord says:

The very existence of a large fund of money is likely to make the individual, already conscious of his own need, feel that he should have a share in what has been provided for the aid of those in distress. Where so many thousands of dollars are available his own request seems to him proportionately insignificant and a valid claim. This feeling may exist just as truly in some people who do not happen to be eligible for assistance as in those who are eligible. . . [1]

Stories of chiselers.

I will frankly admit that I was employed more than six weeks before the worker found me out. I would not report my job to the agency because I was in debt head over heels and the friend who trusted me was a poor man. He could not get aid because of his property. Besides, we went without many things, which we consider essential, for so long that my earnings had to be spent to get some joy out of life. Say, you can't move me by this appeal that the county or the state is broke. I know it's broke, but not because of the relief to the poor, but because of the high cost of government, of the unreasonable salaries to people who have pull. If I don't get my share some "dirty politician" will, and I guess I am more entitled to it than he is. I have a family to support; I would be working regular today if I had a job. . . and look how they fight against unemployment insurance. And as for my relatives. . . you just leave them alone. Do you know anybody today in our circumstances who can support two families without breaking their neck? My father can help me with five dollars once in a great while, so can my brother, but they don't know from day to day whether they can hold on to their jobs. I have made up my mind to be as "fair and square" as all those grafters the newspapers tell us about. What's sauce for the goose is sauce for the gander. . . I know they can prosecute me for concealing my income when I had signed an affidavit and declared myself a pauper, but where is justice? That's why I will continue to chisel as long as I can get away with it. . . Yes, my conscience does bother me and that's where the rub is. . . . [2]

When will you have work for me? We need so many things. Look at this place. It is terrible. I am not complaining about what the —— has done for me, but it is not a solution. My children are not receiving the proper food. Their little bodies will suffer. They do not realize this because they are too young, but it will show in their health later, I am desperate. This can't go on much longer. It has taken me four years to come to this. My business went to pieces! My wife was sick! There

---

[1] Eliazbeth McCord, *The Emergency Worker in Unemployment Relief*, p. 11, pamphlet.

[2] Pauline V. Young, "What's on the Mind of the New Poor?" Unpublished manuscript.

were large doctor bills! What could I do? Nothing! We sold our car, my wife's jewelry, and then we sold our house. It is all gone. We have nothing! Absolutely nothing! I am ambitious. I want to work. The best years of my life are being wasted. I haven't even clothes to go out and look for work. You don't know what this means to a man. You can't understand.[1]

At times taking the chiseler into one's confidence and pointing out to him the exact number of cases needing relief each month, and the amount of money spent by the agency each month, will make it clear to him that he is depriving the widows, the sick, the destitute of their share of needed relief. Oftentimes these people are appalled upon reading in the newspapers of the large amounts of money given to charity but have little conception how that money is spent. An explanation may at times solve the problem. The following suggestions are offered by investigators as helpful in dealing with chiselers:

Make them feel that they should be congratulated when they find work and are able to aid in the support of the family when thousands of others in every community remain idle. Tell them they are hustlers and make them feel proud of their ability to work and to earn a livelihood. . . .

Make the chiseler realize that if he accepts aid those in real need must be deprived of help as the funds must be stretched too far and relief spread too thin.

Inform the individual that relief agencies are operated to some extent like banks and corporations and that the records kept indicate when he has forfeited his credit.

Appeal to his sense of fair play with his neighbor.

Make yourself a confidant whereby the individual will keep you informed of his earnings, knowing you will be more than fair in your dealings with him. Let him realize how much better it is for him to keep you posted of his earnings or income, rather than have some taxpayer report him, whereby an issue may be made of his case which may result in hardships for himself and family and at times even in imprisonment.

Treat client as a person with a problem to be worked out rather than coming to him with the attitude that he is a chiseler and is to be beaten down.

Show client a real interest so that he will not feel that you and he are at odds and that he has to conceal income, earnings, etc.[2]

[1] Reported by Miss Rhoda Julian, Los Angeles.
[2] Statements by family welfare workers.

The Short Contact Interview[1]

Bertha Reynolds[2] has recently published a monograph regarding her experiments in short contact interviewing, its nature, its problems, and methods as deduced from a variety of interviews held with applicants at a child placement agency. The following long excerpts from her study may also prove of value to interviewers in other than child placement fields:

Some Underlying Concepts and Hypotheses

What is to be called a short contact? There are obviously many varieties, from the interviews which are "single" because the two persons are to be prevented by circumstances from meeting again, and those which are "short" from pressure of a long line of waiting applicants, to those where by choice, based on some criterion found in the application itself, the case worker decides that to do what can be done immediately, without preparation for a long series of contacts, is to give the best service. Some interviews are "short contacts" for the application secretary, owing to division of labor, and not for the Society. Others are not "first contacts," but a worker filling in for an absent staff member may, with a case record to guide her if she wishes, have a fruitful single interview with no future contacts with herself to be planned for.

Whether the interview lacks a past or a future, however, it always has a present. The distinguishing feature seems to be not the length of the interview, not even whether there may be two or three of them, but the attitude of mind which one brings to an interview, knowing that opportunity for further contacts is in some way limited. This is interviewing under pressure, as it were, with no later opportunity to retrieve mistakes and with the necessity of making the most of what one has of knowledge, either of the client or his situation, at the time. There seem to be three possibilities of emphasis in the limited-contact interview:

(a) We may try, even though the material is limited to the history which can be secured in one or two contacts, to work toward the full "first interview" of *Social Diagnosis;*[3] that is, to reconstruct from the client's past how he has formerly met his life situations and to form some opinion how he can meet the present difficulty.

---

[1] See also Mary E. Richmond, *Social Diagnosis*, pp. 131–132.

[2] *An Experiment in Short Contact Interviewing* (Smith College Studies in Social Work, September, 1932).

Elizabeth McCord, "Treatment in Short-time Contacts," *The Family*, XII (October, 1931), pp. 191–193.

[3] Mary E. Richmond, *Social Diagnosis*, Chap. VI.

(*b*) We may be most interested in the way the client is expressing his personality pattern in the present situation, as revealed, for example, in his reactions to the interview itself. What does he hope to get from the agency? What are his drives and desires? History comes up to illustrate these as the client brings it up, but more reliance is placed upon observation of his behavior in the interview and upon noting the order and juxtaposition of what he says and less than in the previous method upon the content of his story.

(*c*) We may focus our interest on what the agency can do. Is this a case for us? If not, for whom? A busy intake department, where sifting must be done rapidly, is likely to have well-defined concepts of agency functions and fit the client's story into one or another of these frames. The danger is that the client may not really be seen at all in the process, and, if his problem does not clearly place him in line for the service of this agency, that he may be thought of as a discarded case rather than a person whose need should be met somewhere if possible.

Problems of "Sizing Up" the Applicant in One Interview

What can be learned in one interview about the real personality of the applicant and his situation? Perhaps we are more interested to know how anything can be learned, and what, if anything, may be "affirmed with certainty," as Miss Richmond put it. Having lost a naive confidence in our ability to size up at a glance and having swung around the circle, through the phase of belief that a multitude of witnesses establishes certainty, social workers have come again to feel that somehow . . . we must find a way of making the single interview, as far as it goes, a sound contribution to knowledge. . . .

The processes picked out for study in these applications were four: observation, use of a "sample situation," created by the worker or brought to hand by chance, use of social norms, use of psychiatric concepts—the last two being concerned with interpreting the meaning of what is perceived.

Observation is used to signify what is received by the five senses, supplementing what the applicant says to the worker as his conscious contribution to her understanding. *A sample situation* gives the applicant an opportunity to act as he feels and so perhaps to reveal something of himself when he is not consciously making an impression. When applicants brought a friend or relative into the interviewing room they sometimes acted between themselves a drama which the worker could observe with profit. *Use of social norms* does not imply the desire to apply standards of what an applicant should do or be (though some of this is inevitable in every judgment) but a conscious effort to see the person in the setting of his own group, as far as the social worker can know it, before estimating whether he will be able to fit into the Society's work. For instance, a foster mother's having done factory work would suggest a quite different social status in the colored group from that in the white, where, with a greater variety of employment open, one would not find it signifying the same degree of initiative and intelligence. *The use of psychiatric concepts* was approached in this study with caution, because speculation is both so easy and so dangerous. Psychiatric concepts did help largely, however, in the choice of what was significant to observe or to record from the applicant's story, and in reaching conclusions as to the probable assets or danger spots in a given foster home, especially concerning the presence of a dominating possessive personality or an emotionally immature one.

PROBLEMS OF DETERMINING THE CLIENT'S DESIRES AND CAPACITY FOR RESPONSIBILITY

. . . What does an applicant for service really want? Case S1 illustrates how definite a request may be, and how related to the community conception of what the Society does, yet how unrelated to what a social agency thinks is its obligation to the community and its responsibility to its contributors. Why should funds donated for social service be spent where no social service is desired? In this case, of course, there was nothing spent but a little time, for the home suggested happened not to be available for use by the Society. But the service given did fit in with the criteria of modern case work thinking; it did proceed from the supposition that the client is better able than anyone else to judge what he can use of the service, and that the more which might be pressed upon him would probably be useless until he did want it. The Society might have said, regardless of whether it had a home to suggest, that it did not believe in the client's plan and would do nothing without a full study of the situation and the drawing up of a plan which it could recommend. It does not seem likely that this client would submit to such a study. The writer's belief is that one of the important educational functions of case work was carried out when the client found a spirit of willingness to serve, a willingness to accept her own estimate of herself as a parent capable of working out her responsibility to her child as she saw fit, a confirmation of her own belief that choosing a home for a baby was an important matter.

CASE S I

2-5-23. Application and Problem. Mother came in after an appointment by telephone had been made by Miss M. of Hilbert Foundation. She came into the interviewing office stepping daintily, a slight figure with artificially gold hair in short curls around her face, delicately drawn eyebrows of darker color, straight-looking gray eyes, an engaging smile. She was becomingly dressed and was wearing a close-fitting toque and short black fur jacket with ermine collar.

Mother's Story.   As she sat down mother smiled and said, "I have the sweetest little baby in the world, and I want the best home that can be found for him, just as a temporary plan till I can have him with me.   My family do not approve of boarding him at all, but I've thought it all out and I'm sure I'm doing the best thing.   Aren't there places where trained nurses perhaps 'clique' together and have their own nursery, so as to have more freedom than private nursing allows them, the satisfaction of their own place, you know?"

Some Questions.   Worker asked, as mother paused and waited, how old the baby was.   Mother said four weeks and added how healthy and lovely he was.   Worker suggested that a nurse's place such as mother described was apt to be rather expensive but there were very good homes to be found at reasonable rates.   Mother said she could pay $10 a week.   Asked mother to tell a little more about her situation, and why her family object to boarding the baby.

More Story.   Mother said, "Well, you see, they can't understand how I feel about 'the profession.'   I was just getting started on Broadway last May when I got pregnant, and while I would not have missed having the baby for anything, I want to go on with my work.   My family just can't understand how much it means to me.   It gives me something I've always longed for and that satisfies way through.   My folks came from up in the country—they sold the land to the Morton Home and they don't see things my way."

"Is your home up country now?"

"No, my family live in Walton now."

"Are you staying with them, and is the baby, too?"

"Yes, I've been there since I came from the hospital—the baby was born at the Polyclinic, Dr. Scott—do you know him?   All my folks are crazy about the baby and can't see why I don't take him with me.   My plan is to do that in six months or so, after my husband and I have time to get settled in an apartment and get a good German maid.   Don't you think German maids are almost always reliable?   If baby is going to be away from me, now is the time while it doesn't make any difference to him as long as he is well fed and cared for, but when he begins to notice who's who, you bet I'll be right there then."

"Aren't you afraid that it may be hard for you to give up your career then?"

"I don't expect to give it up.   I shall not go on the road, but I have a good chance of getting something in Broadway productions.   I was in An American Tragedy last winter."

"Did you study for the stage?"

"Yes, but I have been interested in drama ever since I was a little girl. I studied art first and then did real estate.   I got a thrill out of that—that was when I was quite young—four or five years ago.   But there was something lacking in all those things that the stage has given me, and I don't want to lose it out of my life."

Application Blank. At this point, the lack of emphasis on husband and the general picture made worker suspect that the child was illegitimate. She was anxious to give mother the confidence to be frank, if this was so, and avoid building up a false story if possible. Leads seemed to be exhausted, so blank was resorted to, and given to mother to fill out. She made a game of it, going rather gaily to it. Mother asked questions about the blank. She filled in father's name without hesitation after stopping to ask if this meant the baby's father. Asked what alleged father meant. When worker told her that line was only used when parents were not married, "not that it makes any great difference, but we like to know," she said, "My, my, my," and passed on. Had some hesitation about address, giving her mother's home in Walton as her permanent address. Explained that she had been "in stock" before pregnancy, had had a lease of apartment up to confinement, husband was staying elsewhere and coming week-ends just now, etc. Gave husband's business as public utility and said he was continuously in New York.

When she finished blank, worker asked how baby's father feels about this boarding plan. Mother said, "He agrees with my family. He would like me to give up the stage and doesn't understand why I can't. He wants to get an apartment right away and a good maid, but he doesn't understand that a little baby cries at night some. I couldn't look after baby nights and work and neither could he stand it to lose sleep. He doesn't realize that as I do, now that I've been at home with baby two weeks."

Worker asked how mother is feeling, herself.

"Just fine. Dr. Scott said he couldn't see any reason for keeping me there two weeks. Everything was perfectly normal—no instruments needed."

"Did you nurse the baby at all?"

"He's on a bottle. I didn't breast feed him at all."

"Formula agree with him?"

"Splendidly."

Worker then asked mother to wait while she consulted the department heads. From them she got the suggestion of an excellent private home with a nurse. Worker had felt definitely that mother wanted to make her own plans and did not wish social service at all, but only advice as to finding a good home. This was confirmed by further talk with mother. Worker told her about our usual service and said she assumed mother would prefer to supervise the baby herself without his being taken into care by the Society. She said decidedly that this was so. Worker then gave her the address of Mrs. P. in Englewood, a nurse whom the Society gave up using because she wanted private work at higher rates, but can recommend for care of babies.

Reactions. Mother was very grateful for this suggestion, said this was such a "delicate matter" that she wanted to be very careful, yet had no more idea where to go to inquire than into a hardware store. Supposed Dr. Scott might know of places but hated to ask him because he would probably disapprove of the idea just as her family did. Agreed with worker that one might advertise in the paper but that it was not easy to size up a place, "You can't tell by the looks of people always."

2–10–32. Comment. Question of sifting applicants wanting or needing case work from those not wanting or needing the same. (It is perhaps too much to assume that they need case work or they would not have come, and that they should not be allowed to depart without it.)

This case looked at first like one of illegitimacy. (It may even be that it is, and thereby illustrates how a girl of high I.Q. and with some money handles her problem.) Suppose that one goes on the hypothesis that every case of illegitimacy needs social work supervision and works hard for conscience's sake to get the client to accept it. We know cases where mother and child have "gotten out from under" at the first opportunity when there was no want, *real to the mother*, which a social worker relationship would fill. (They seem to depart irrespective of whether the I.Q. is so low that colliding with some other social agency is speedily inevitable, or so high that no agency hears of them again.) If a mother is able to solve her problem, why shouldn't she? Why should anyone insist on giving her more than information service, if she does not want more, or any service at all, for that matter?[1]

There is, of course, the point of view of society, which is so concerned about the hazards of illegitimate children that in Minnesota, for example, a state supervision is maintained until majority. But why set off apart the illegitimate child? The mother is more than usually handicapped in bringing it up, it is true, but no more so than mothers with bad husbands, or deserted wives. If we are not thinking in terms of the old idea that a "fallen" girl must be a bad mother, why set off the illegitimate child for

---

[1] Miss Louise Drury of the Children's Protective Association of Los Angeles makes the following comment on Case S I, in personal communication with the author of the present volume.

"Most social workers would agree, I believe, that, although a man or woman comes to a social agency asking for some type of help, it does not necessarily mean that they need any case work service, but that they should be guided to handle their own problems in so far as possible and as soon as possible.

"However, when it comes to the placement of a child outside of his own home, no case worker, I am sure, would wish to even be a party to the placement without certain verified facts. Workers in children's agencies the country over know of many tragedies which have occurred when placements were made with inadequate information. Does the child belong to this mother? If she is married, does she have sole custody? If not, is she willing to have her husband contacted to secure his consent to the placement? If she is not married, or her husband is not the father of her child, has she given ample assurance that she can provide for her baby's board? Does she give any evidence that she intends to abandon her baby? Have we adequate information to be sure that her attitude of apparent assurance is genuine and not a defense to cover up her feeling of insecurity and inability to handle her own problem?

"When we have the answers to these questions, we may be prepared to determine whether the mother is equipped to handle her own problem or whether she needs case work service. A skilled case worker could secure this basic information even in a rather short interview."

special treatment? Why not work to protect any children from harmful conditions, and throw our resources to the aid of any parents, even fathers, who may be heavily handicapped?

CONCLUSIONS

These experiments have contributed to a conviction, expressed in the preceding discussion of theory of case work, that the most important thing in any contact, but especially in the first, is to set the keynote of the client's participation and responsibility on as high a level as he is capable of at the time. He is not allowed to dump his problem, only to be justly indignant that it is tossed back to him when he is beginning to feel relieved. He has been kept in possession of his problem all the time, and now has an understanding professional person (the Society's service to him) to counsel with him about the necessities of the case. Whether or not it proves possible for him to get, through the Society, the practical help he may have asked for, he is constantly being prepared to utilize his own resources. This, it seems to the writer, is the crucial point of case work skill.

It is undoubtedly true that some relationship between client and social worker is established in the first contact, the application interview. How can the social worker make this a relationship in which the client feels himself as much a responsible adult as he is capable of being? Probably, first of all, by believing in the possibility herself, giving the client every opportunity she can create to show how far he can decide and plan for himself and what are the fears and impediments that most handicap him. Even the filling out of an application blank can be made an opportunity. In innumerable ways, the social worker can stimulate or destroy his confidence in himself.

Does this build up a degree of rapport with the application secretary which is handicapping to later workers on the case? The social workers who subsequently had contact with the clients described in this paper say that in every instance they found them ready for a cooperative case work relationship. The ones who had talked the most freely in the application interview (S 2, for instance) went on to a most frank unburdening in the case work relationship.[1] We should expect this result if the client has had an opportunity, through the sincere interest and understanding of the application secretary, to enhance his sense of his own value and has not built up a dependence upon her. At various points he may need to express childishness, vacillation, anger, or self-distrust. The social worker does not argue with him about these moods nor, in a battle of wills, try to force him to take a stand which is beyond his strength. She takes him as he is but has some little next

---

[1] The writer did no probing on emotional issues but confined her questions to such practical matters as were directly connected with the application.

step ready whereby he can show just once more that, in spots at least, he is an adult person.

It seems that one of the indications for further experiment is found in our present inability to talk-in-action with people, thus setting up "sample situations." We put off making even the most simple suggestions through fear of doing the wrong thing before a complete diagnosis has been made. As Dr. Richard Cabot[1] pointed out, however, in his presidential address at the National Conference of Social Work in 1931, most of the medical advice given is plain common sense, and not, except in a few instances, dependent on an exact diagnosis. Fresh air, plenty of pure water, good food, and sleep can hardly hurt anyone while the doctor is finding out what else he needs. Were we equipped with resources in equally harmless and wholesome little practical things which the client might do, we might not only get much diagnostic illumination from seeing him do them, but give him an opportunity to "get the feel" or experience which we could scarcely convey in days of talking. Every application secretary needs a bag of such prescriptions, especially if these is an interval before the social worker assigned to the case can make her contact, during which time the client's sense that he is doing something on his problem needs to be kept alive.[2]

Social Background for Medical Social Service Interviewing[3]

Dr. Cabot states that there is a very close interrelation between medical work and social work since both are "branches split off from a common trunk:—the care of people in trouble," and he continues:

. . . A doctor needs to know something of social work and of the spiritual and mental life of his patients. A social worker must know something of physiology and hygiene, and all educators, whether lay or clerical, must know something both of medicine and of social work. . . .

. . . Wherever troubles are heaped up and gathered together as they are in a hospital, in a mission church, in the offices of a relief society, we find that those troubles are *assorted*. They are not neatly separated, each in its own corner. They do not heed our academic distinctions or our divisions of labor. Poverty, disease, moral shift-

[1] *Proceedings of the National Conference of Social Work*, 1931, p. 2.

[2] Bertha Capen Reynolds, *An Experiment in Short-contact Interviewing* (Smith College Studies in Social Work, September, 1932), pp. 7–8; 19–20; 56–57; 46–47; 57–60; 104–106.

[3] For content of the medical social work interview see pp. 116–117.

lessness, and spiritual torment are inextricably inter-mingled in the face and fortunes of a single sufferer. Not even the sufferer himself can tell what is root and what is branch among his troubles. . . . [1]

For lack of space we can only list in outline form Dr. Cabot's discussion of "the intermingling of afflictions of mind, body and estate" which the medical social work interviewer must consider when interviewing medical clients.

Mental or Spiritual Turmoil for Physical Reasons

1. Religious ecstasies, moral doubts, and self-condemnations are often manifestations of insanity, of hysteria, of neurasthenia, or of the stresses of adolescence with its torrential flood of developing energies. . . .

2. Excessive worry, timidity, scrupulosity is often an early symptom (though mistaken for the cause) of arteriosclerosis, of Bright's disease, anemia, or tuberculosis. . . .

3. Laziness, shiftlessness, carelessness may be only the mental manifestations of the debility of adolescence, of chorea, of cerebral disease, of malnutrition, or of any of the other diseases mentioned above. . . .

Physical complaints and even diseases may be due to mental and spiritual causes, to ignorance, mental disease, and sin. . . .

Financial dependence and want is more and more often seen to be the result of physical and mental causes. People are poor because they are sick and ignorant. . . .

Both doctor and social worker, when they have learned (each from the other) the deeper causes of their patients' ills, must go hand in hand to the educator, or at any rate must betake themselves to educational methods, when they get through with diagnosis and begin treatment. [2]

Turning his attention to the responsibilities of social workers in hospitals, particularly their watchfulness when working on cases with absent-minded physicians, Dr. Cabot says:

The philosopher, intent upon his problem, may abstractedly walk over a precipice, but I never heard of one so absent-minded as to push a young girl over a precipice as we are doing every month in our gynaecological clinics [when, preoccupied with medical problems, the medical man by his professional manner fails to mollify for the unmarried prospective mother the rigors of her future position but in effect tells her that now she will suffer breach with her family, loss of employment, social ostracism, and so on].

I say—a man who in effect gives that message to a girl and *doesn't notice that he has done so* is wonderfully absent-minded. Methodically his mind has passed on to the next case, to the sterilization of his rubber

---

[1] *Social Service and the Art of Healing*, pp. 93–94; 95–96.

[2] *Ibid.*, pp. 97–99; 101; 102; 105–106. (The last three paragraphs are in italics.)

gloves, to the record sheet on which he is writing his diagnosis and his account of the physical examination. . .

Therefore to make the doctor's work worth while to himself and to the patient, it must be done (in hospitals) in cooperation with someone who has time and ability to teach hygiene and to see that it is carried out (for instance, in tuberculosis), to study the home conditions and report upon their part in causing or prolonging disease, and to help modify those conditions, financial, mental, moral, which stand between the patient and recovery.

This "someone" is the social worker,—a man or woman trained to think of a human being as a whole just as naturally as the physician concentrates attention upon a part.

"What's missing here of the essentials of a human life?" asks the social worker. No matter whether her job is in a factory (as welfare worker or factory nurse), in an immigration station, in a court-room, in an alms-house, a schoolhouse, or a hospital,—her job is to supplement the efforts of the specialist in the interests of healthy, living character.

In a hospital-patient the missing necessities may be food and clothes, rest, work, decency, hope, self-respect, a bath, a crutch, or a confidant;— to make him wholesome the social worker looks steadfastly to the man's *whole* needs and tries to fill in wherever the need is greatest. He is *the synthesizer*, and he must stand beside the analyzing specialist always, if hospital work is to be worth the enormous sum it costs. . . .

This union the social worker can do much to promote and to develop. A patient needs (for example) to be persuaded to undergo a surgical operation. The doctor has no time to explain in detail the reason why he advises this perilous venture. It is impossible for him to blow his own trumpet and expound his own fitness to advise, his own cautious weighing of the pros and cons. But if the social worker genuinely believes in the physician with whom she works, she can speak for him and help to build up in the patient that well-deserved confidence which is half the battle in medical work.

Social workers may thus help the patient to have faith in the expert. They also help the expert to have faith in the patient. The expert naturally hesitates to explain his plans of treatment to the patient because he fears that the explanation—made hastily in a noisy room to a bewildered Jew or Italian—will convey only that scrap of knowledge which is a dangerous thing. So doctors have gone on giving bread pills (encouraging thereby the habit of depending on drugs rather than on hygiene) because there was no time or opportunity adequately to explain to patients why drugs are sometimes unnecessary, how diet, fresh air, regular habits, and clean minds may work both the cure and the prevention of disease.

But with the social worker acting now as teacher and interpreter, passing on to the patient the doctor's ideas in words of one syllable, reiterating and illustrating them, following up and correcting errors of misunderstanding, it becomes possible for the doctor to deal frankly and truthfully with his patient, sharing knowledge rather than issuing arbitrary commands. Possessing at last the *principle* of treatment, the patient can learn to apply it to himself and finally to teach others.[1]

Suggestions for Further Study

1. In what essential respects are N. S. Shaler's and R. E. Park's viewpoints regarding the alien helpful to the interviewer of social case work? What is unique about their discussion of the alien?

2. Analyze your state of mind which seems to emerge in contact with a Negro, a Mexican, a Jew, a German, a Dane, an Englishman, and point out whether this state of mind is produced by their physical characteristics, their manners, or their cultural differences.

3. How may cultural barriers between interviewer and interviewee be bridged? What are your devices in reducing or eliminating social distance?

4. Why is it necessary for the interviewer to have an appreciation of the interviewee's cultural complexes? What contribution have Park and Miller made through their book *Old World Traits Transplanted?*

5. Consult Dr. Park's outline for the social history of an immigrant (p. 138) and construct a similar one for the social history of a Jew, of a Negro, of a Chinese, of a Mexican, or any other racial group with which you may be familiar.

6. How does Dr. Park's outline differ from those prepared by Mary Richmond (*Social Diagnosis*, pp. 387–394), by E. S. Bogardus, (*The New Social Research*, pp. 149–165), from the standpoint of concepts used, the ability to penetrate into the inner life of the person and the group, and the ability to understand the cultural complexes of the group?

7. What is meant by "conflict" and "accommodation" and how are these processes related to interviewing?

8. What is meant by a philosophy of life and what bearing does a knowledge of the interviewee's as well as the interviewer's philosophy of life have upon the success of the interview?

9. How does the approach to an executive differ from that to a client? In what respects are the approaches alike?

10. What hints have you found most helpful in your interviews with executives?

11. Prepare a bibliography helpful to the interviewer coming in contact with business executives, executives in the field of social work, in journalism, in politics, in municipal government.

12. Prepare a bibliography helpful to the interviewer coming in contact with employers.

13. Discuss the viewpoints expressed by Mary Richmond, Walter V. Bingham and Bruce V. Moore, Webb and Morgan, and Beatrice Webb on the approach to the employer. Each one makes a unique contribution. Indicate suggestions you have found most helpful in your work. What policy does your agency hold regarding the approach to the employer?

[1] *Ibid.*, pp. 172–174; 177–180; 189–191.

14. Analyze the two interviews with former employers and discuss the technique used, the adequacy of the questions, and the ability to see the employer's point of view.

15. What is meant by the new poor? How does the interviewing approach to the new poor differ from that to the *nouveau riche?* to the chronic dependent?

16. What is the point to the own story of Mr. Allamy? of Mr. Mason? of the human discard? What was the interviewing approach to each of these cases? What questions were asked to receive the given replies?

17. Write a critique of Dr. Cabot's point of view as to the relationship of medical social service to social work. What is Dr. Cabot's underlying philosophy?

18. Examine the statement by Alice Canfield and point out how far her technique is applicable to the type of cases you deal with.

19. What is meant by a chiseler? What types of chiselers are there? What types have you run across in your work?

20. What is your reaction to the suggestions offered by interviewers in dealing with chiselers? How have you dealt with them?

21. What is a short contact interview? Prepare a bibliography on the subject and point out recent contributions.

22. Examine some of your cases and indicate how many and under what circumstances they could be handled by the technique described by Miss Reynolds.

23. Write a critique of the interview in the case of S I with respect to technique of interviewing, philosophy of social work, with the type of mother Mrs. S. represents.

Read Dr. Jessie Taft's book *The Dynamics of Therapy in a Controlled Relationship* and discuss Miss Reynolds' technique in view of Dr. Taft's philosophy.

24. Read, collect material, analyze cases, and prepare discussions of (1) the social situation and (2) the interviewing problem and approach to

    a. The problem boy or girl.

    b. The American youth.

    c. The immigrant youth.

    d. The second generation immigrant youth.

    e. The delinquent and criminal.

    f. The sick person.

    g. The unmarried mother.

    h. Members in family discord.

    i. The farmer, the ruralite.

    j. The socially rejected.

    k. The "charity girl."

    l. Any other type with which you make contact in your work.

Selected Bibliography

1. BINGHAM, WALTER VAN DYKE, and BRUCE VICTOR MOORE: *How to Interview*, 1931, Chap. IV, "The Employment Interview"; Chap. V, "The Industrial Relations Interview."
2. CABOT, RICHARD C., *Social Service and the Art of Healing*, 1928, Chap. I.
   Shows the close relation between social work and medicine. Discusses problems of value to the interviewer: objectives, problems of lying to patient, art of changing views.
3. PARK, ROBERT E., and H. A. MILLER: *Old World Traits Transplanted*, 1921, pp. 265–267; 273–275.
   Defines "fact," "apperception mass," "world of discourse," in relation to immigrant culture.
4. REYNOLDS, BERTHA CAPEN: *An Experiment in Short-contact Interviewing* (Smith College Studies in Social Work, 1932).
   Discusses underlying concepts, hypotheses, problems, and methods of single short-contact interviews, with several summaries of illustrative cases.
5. REYNOLDS, BERTHA CAPEN: "A Way of Understanding, An Approach to Case Work with Negro Families," *The Family*, XII (November, 1931), 203–208; (December, 1931), 240–244; (January, 1932), 267–272.
   An attempt to analyze—on the basis of problems arising with cases at the Institute of Child Guidance in New York—the psychological and social factors involved in the Negro situation arising from the culture conflict attitude, severe economic pressure, struggle for status, and maladjustment in the community.
6. SHALER, N. S.: *The Neighbor*, 1904, Chaps. VI, VII, and XI.
   A profound and stimulating discussion on the nature of and approach to "The Hebrew Problem," "The African Problem" and "The Way Out." Helpful to the interviewer in understanding what elements create and dominate neighborliness in complex modern life.
7. SMALLEY, RUTH: "The Social Worker's Use of the Interview with the Child," *The Family*, XIII (December, 1932), 266–270.
   Passivity and objectivity of the interviewer lead to the interviewee's (child's) revelation of material of real emotional significance.
8. WHITLEY, R. L.: "Interviewing the Problem Boy," *The Journal of Educational Sociology*, V (October, 1931), 89–100.
   An analysis of the wishes and attitudes problem boys have toward their problems, treatment of these problems, and of the social world in which they live. A long illustrative interview with a group of problem boys.

CHAPTER IX

ETHICAL STANDARDS IN INTERVIEWING

The Committee on Standards of the Los Angeles Chapter of the American Association of Social Workers states that "Ethics in social work is the principle of treating clients, other agencies, and the community, with the same respect, consideration, and honesty with which you would hope to be treated in your own personal relationships."[1] Miss Lula Jean Elliott has submitted an experimental draft of a code of ethics for social case workers to the American Association of Social Workers, based on the assumption that a professional code is "a conscious and rational expression of the social attitudes of the group toward the conduct of its members in the discharge of their particular service."[2]

Much of Miss Elliott's experimental draft of a code of ethics for social workers in general seems particularly applicable to social work interviewers:

I. Duties toward Clients.
  1. The social case worker's first duty is toward his clients, unless the performance of this duty jeopardizes the welfare of the community.
  2. The worker must have humanity, delicacy, and patience in dealing with clients.
  3. The sacredness of confidences imposed by clients must be inviolate.
  4. Honesty, frankness, and wisdom are three necessary attributes. Promises should be made only when there is a certainty of fulfillment.
  5. In view of the tremendous responsibility assumed in making plans with and for a family, it is necessary that the counsel given should never be casual or hurried. It should be sincere, thoughtful, and based upon an adequate knowledge of casual factors.
  6. Punctuality in keeping appointments is an obligation.
  7. The tool of encouragement should be used freely but with discrimination.
  8. An obligation of the case worker is either to render, or else to procure, the particular aid or service needed by a client when the need of such aid or service is made apparent.

[1] *A Report* of the Committee on Standards of the Los Angeles Chapter of the American Association of Social Workers.
[2] *Social Work Ethics*, p. 1.

190

9. The same intelligent and painstaking attention should be given to so-called "hopeless" cases as is given to the ones which seem more hopeful and promising.

II. Duties in Relation to Co-workers and to the Profession of Social Work.

10. The worker is under personal obligation to keep informed of current movements through study, through reading, and through alliance with organizations of social workers, city, state, and national.

11. The duty of upholding the honor of the profession is also personal in application.

12. The individual worker must have high personal standards of honor, integrity, . . . and morality.

13. The worker must avoid self-advertising.

14. No case worker, acting in his professional capacity, is privileged to do as an individual anything that he may not do as a member of the organization with which he is associated.

15. Strict adherence to the rules and regulations of the organization represented is necessary from the standpoint both of ethics and of efficiency.

16. There should be candor and courtesy in all of the interoffice relations.

17. The exposure of unprofessional conduct upon the part of a worker within an organization is the duty of his colleagues in order to maintain the integrity of the profession. . . .

III. Duties to Other Social Agencies and to Other Professions.

29. Intercourse between agencies should be direct and not through clients.

30. Frankness and honesty should characterize dealings with other agencies.

31. Promises to other social agencies should be scrupulously kept. . . .

IV. The Duty of the Social Case Worker to the Community.

35. It is the duty of the social case worker to do preventive and educational work in connection with service to individuals.

36. Social case workers should report reportable diseases or see that they are reported.

37. It is the privilege as well as the obligation of the social case worker to bear truthful witness to social needs and to social conditions needing remedy.

38. It is the professional as well as the ethical responsibility of the case worker to strive to incorporate the ideals of case work into all social relations affecting individuals.

This code is well organized, with its provisions falling into definite categories. Although it has never been officially adopted by the social work profession, it marks a distinct step in the development of a professional code and represents one of the earliest contributions of group thinking on professional ethics among social workers.[1]

[1] LULA JEAN ELLIOTT, *Social Work Ethics*, pp. 9–12.

The following are excerpts from *A Report to the Committee on Standards* of the Los Angeles Chapter of the American Association of Social Workers on ethical relations:[1]

I. Between Agency and Client.

In all relationships between an agency and its clients, the latter should be treated courteously. Workers should observe all the amenities of polite society in spite of any irritating conduct on the part of the clients. This should apply to all contacts of the agency with clients including their reception at the information desk, provision for their comfort in the waiting room, and all meetings of workers and clients.

Workers should try to avoid seeing clients when too tired or rushed to give them the benefit of their best intelligence in planning for or giving treatment. Workers are obligated to keep themselves fully informed regarding community resources and technique of modern social work.

As far as possible clients should be given an understanding of the methods used by agencies in assisting them. They should understand the reasons for investigation. They should realize that records are kept and understand their purpose and their confidential nature. If clients know there are records, they may withhold information which they do not wish to have included. They should also understand that agencies have the right of privileged communications.

No information should be secured from or regarding clients on false pretenses. Unless social treatment demands otherwise, clients should be given the whole truth regarding themselves. Promises or threats which cannot be carried out should be avoided. All this applies to competent clients but should be carried out as far as possible even in cases of incompetent clients.

All information secured from or regarding clients should be kept confidential, and used only for their benefit. Workers should respect all confidences given them and should be extremely careful with the use of record material. They should avoid passing it on to collateral sources. Record material may be given to other agencies that maintain the same ethical standards as referring agency.

No information should be given regarding clients over telephone or to inquirers in person under any guise unless the inquirer is known to the agency to be interested in behalf of the client. Special emphasis should be placed on instructions to students and volunteers regarding the confidential nature of record material. No publicity material should contain information regarding clients unless it is used following long consideration and with consent of the client.

The ethical relation of the agency to the community supersedes that of the agency to the client in certain cases. Service to the client should be given only insofar as it can be associated with the good of the group; at least, no service should be given which may prove harmful to the community.

The agency should use information regarding clients who are of extreme menace socially as one means of removing their ability to endanger the community.

[1] Mimeographed report.

II. Between Agencies.

In the relationships between agencies, reports to persons or organizations should never be falsified or colored in any way to accomplish purposes or to cover mistakes. Agencies should not criticize each other except with constructive purpose and to responsible parties. This should never happen in the presence of clients. False impressions detected in the minds of clients toward other agencies should be corrected if possible. An agency has the right to be informed of complaints made against it by clients or other persons. . . .

Social workers should feel a spirit of professional loyalty toward each other. In cooperative work in behalf of clients, when a difference of opinion exists, the matter should be settled directly with those involved. Serious disagreements should be settled by conference between supervisors.

III. Between Agency and Community. . . .

Workers and agencies should consider themselves servants of the community and should so equip themselves from a professional standpoint as to fulfill their function to the fullest extent of their ability. They should consider it their responsibility to interpret to the community necessary changes in its make-up which become apparent because of their contacts with clients. It is the responsibility of an agency to keep itself informed of needed social reform and to be prepared to support or initiate constructive social measures and to defeat harmful ones.

The following excerpts from a study of interviews with interviewers and social work executives will help to illustrate what they expect of and conceive to be the ethical code of the interviewer:

One of the most unethical procedures on the part of an investigator is to work himself into an organization by cultivating the friendship and showing favors to a member of the "rank and file" in the agency who does not know the wider aims of the agency and may disclose confidences which it guards. The interviewer should come to executives and rely on his ability to interview in getting the information desired. If the executives see fit to decline the appointment or refuse the information, the interviewer should consider this procedure the privilege of the agency.

It is unfair to an agency when an interviewer disguises himself and walks into an agency under false pretenses. It is equally unfair when he sends someone else under false pretenses to get information for him.

I detest interviewers or social research investigators who undertake to outwit an interviewee by a series of clever premeditated schemes and to confuse him to such an extent that he no longer sees the aims of the interview. This is unfair dealing and hardly becoming the dignity of a social worker. . . .

An interviewer owes it to his clients to inform himself regarding their social and cultural backgrounds so that he will be in a position to understand their points of view. . . .

The only fair method of dealing with clients is to eliminate the social distance existing between interviewer and interviewee by understanding the latter's position as to his race, nationality, social status, family problems, and so on. There is less prejudice when the interviewer seeks to understand and not to evaluate. . . .

It is hard enough to have other people pry into your business, but when this prying is done without sympathy and tact, it is nothing short of criminal. . . .

It is unfair to an interviewee when interviewers flatter him and boost his ego to the point that he loses his self-possession and discloses facts which under ordinary circumstances he would conceal. This method should be condemned as much as "third degree." . . .

An interviewer is unfair to interviewees when he expects to deal with them in a manner different from that which he expects others to deal with him. He then sets himself up as a tin god. . . .

It is unfair to interviewees when the interviewer assumes that the interview is for the purpose of giving them a patient hearing. No interviewer should set himself up as a superior tribunal and regard an interview as a hearing. Interviewers miss the whole point of their social relationship in the interview when they consider it a one-sided hearing. . . . [1]

The question is frequently asked whether or not it is fair to disclose the source of information if interviewees insist on knowing where the interviewer secured knowledge about them. The traditional practice is to shield the source of information for two major reasons: (1) some interviewees might make it unpleasant for a person or agency which revealed information told in confidence; (2) it is often best for interviewees not to know that an interviewer is in communication with outside sources of information as they might gain the feeling that he may be rendered prejudiced by someone else who did not quite understand them; they often feel that their past is trailing them wherever they go, and that they cannot make a new start in life.

If, however, the information secured about interviewees from an outside source is of the nature which is apt to help in their rehabilitation, the source might be revealed upon request, provided permission to do so has been granted by the source.

The following experience related by a social worker is in point:

Mrs. D. was told that the agency which had previously aided her was contacted in an effort to learn her background. Mrs. D. "became furious,"

[1] PAULINE V. YOUNG, unpublished manuscript.

insisting that that agency "never did understand me; never did aid me; all they wanted was to make it hard for me . . . and why is it necessary to go into the misery of the past? . . . And do you mean to say that everything I tell you now will be counted against me when I move from this district? . . . " I realized that I had made a mistake by telling her that we were in communication with the agency, but I did not want to fool her or do anything behind her back. A few weeks later Mrs. D. moved without leaving her address.[1]

Interviewers are often in a difficult position to know whether doing something behind the back of clients is fair procedure. However, the best interests of the client must always be the prime consideration.

Interviewing relatives without the knowledge of the client is another difficult ethical problem the interviewer faces. Often it is possible to secure permission from a client to see his relatives or friends who could be of service to him, but in case the policy of the agency is to interview all relatives whether the client agrees or not, the interviewer need not promise not to see them, but should explain the agency's standpoint and indicate that every precaution will be taken to safeguard all interests concerned.

Mrs. D. was cautiously informed that her wealthy sister should be contacted and requested to aid. "I don't want to have anything to do with her and you must promise me that you will not write her. . . . I'd rather starve than accept anything from her," replied Mrs. D. "Now, Mrs. D., it isn't quite fair to your sister not to give her a chance to help you. You are performing greater charity by giving her an opportunity to help than she is by helping you." "Well, that's another way of looking at it, but I know she won't take the hint. . . . However, I will write her myself and try out your method."[1]

It is obvious that the complexities of modern life make the problem of ethical professional conduct well-nigh unsolvable in many cases. No single simple principle or set of principles can be laid down from which deviations are not to be permitted. The worker is constantly called upon to decide among the equities of the client, the agency, the community, persons related to or specially interested in the client, other organizations and institutions, and his own interests and responsibilities. Errors and differences of opinions as to what is proper are therefore inevitable. Hence too inflexible attitudes on ethical questions is quite as much to be deprecated as is too much vacillation or indifference to such questions.

[1] Statement by a social worker.

Suggestions for Further Study

1. What is meant by the term professional ethics?

2. What are the essential differences in the ethical principles as formulated by the American Association of Social Workers and those presented by the Los Angeles Chapter of the Association?

3. Read Professor Cooley's discussion "The Theory of Public Opinion" in his *Social Organization* and indicate the relation of ethics to custom, to public opinion, of importance to the interviewer.

4. What is the difference between ethics and morality?

5. Read William Graham Sumner's *Folkways* and show the relation of "in-group" and "out-group" ethics which the interviewer should consider in his contacts with various nationalities.

6. Indicate what ethical principles presented by Dewey and Tufts may be of significance in social work interviewing.

7. What ethical principles do you follow in your interviewing?

8. Write your own "Ethics in Social Work."

9. What ethical problems do you face in interviewing?

10. To what extent do you modify your ethical principles in your contacts with: (a) the sick; (b) the industrial discards; (c) problem children; (d) the emotionally unstable; (e) the "gossiper"? the chiseler? the politician?

11. What professional ethics do you observe in your contacts with executives, subexecutives, employers?

Selected Bibliography

1. DEWEY, JOHN, and JAMES H. TUFTS: *Ethics*, 1908.

Standard treatise on the field of ethics, stressing the social origins and evolution of ethical principles.

2. ELLIOTT, LULA JEAN: *Social Work Ethics*, 1931.

Thoroughgoing discussion of the ethical principles involved in the contacts between case worker and client, case worker and agency, community, coworkers, etc.

3. SUMNER, WILLIAM GRAHAM: *Folkways*, 1911.

The classic work in the field of folkways, mores, tabus, ethics in their relation to societal organization.

CHAPTER X

THE ANALYSIS OF THE CASE WORK INTERVIEW

No scientific studies of the best methods of analyzing interviews or interviewing have as yet been made. Some writers stress the analysis of the technique used in interviewing and the processes taking place during the interview.[1] Other writers suggest an analysis of the data and information secured in terms of (a) social interaction between the interviewee and members of the social group; (b) their relation to the total social environment in which they live; and (c) the social attitudes and cultural patterns determining the type of interaction.[2]

J. O. Chassell is interested in tracing not only specific attitudes and experiences in the life history of a person but also the changes in attitude which might account for the behavior of an individual.[3] G. A. Lundberg stresses a summary of life histories in "some way so the uniformities in large numbers begin to stand out and group themselves into general patterns or types."[4] Cyril Burt, an English writer, advocates a study of the life histories not only of the subjects under consideration but also of a control group.[5]

There are, on the other hand, some objections raised to the logic as well as to the methods of analysis of the interview, main-

[1] AMERICAN ASSOCIATION OF SOCIAL WORKERS (Committee of the Chicago Chapter), *Interviews: A Study of the Methods of Analyzing and Recording Social Case Work Interviews.*

HELEN L. MYRICK, "Psychological Processes in Interviewing," *Interviews, Interviewers, and Interviewing in Social Case Work,* pp. 115–123.

LAURA JEAN KEISER, "Analysis of an Interview," *The Family,* VIII (March, 1927), 17–20.

HELEN L. MYRICK and ADA E. SHEFFIELD, "Reflective By-products of a Social Treatment Interview," *Journal of Social Forces,* III (May, 1925), 657–665.

[2] For the analysis of cases of domestic discord, see Harriet R. Mowrer's method quoted by E. R. Mowrer, *Domestic Discord,* Chap. VI and *passim.*

[3] *The Experience Variables, A Study of the Variable Factors in Experience Contributing to the Formation of Personality.*

[4] "Case Work and the Statistical Method," *The Journal of Social Forces,* V (September, 1926), 61–65.

[5] *The Young Delinquent,* especially Chap. I.

taining that the variables are too numerous and complex and that the results of interviews are appraised subjectively rather than measured objectively. Stuart Queen points out that "The terms used in classifying 'techniques' and 'processes' are unsatisfactory because they represent goals assumed to be clearly in the case worker's mind or results actually secured rather than characteristics of the whole process of interaction."[1] He further raises the question whether "techniques," "processes," and "purposes" are distinct phenomena and whether they can be properly designated by the interviewer.

· Several interviews and methods of analysis are here presented in detail to illustrate attempts made by social workers to interpret the interviewing situations and to give the student an opportunity to compare these techniques. The first of these is a verbatim interview reported and analyzed by the Committee of the American Association of Social Workers who stress on the one hand the analysis of the methods of approach, of establishment of *rapport*, of presentation of facts, and of stimulating the client to action and on the other hand the analysis of the processes occurring as a result of interaction between interviewer and interviewee.

The Holt Interview

Mrs. Holt. Dialogue Form by Psychiatric Social Worker with Definitive Analysis Appended

Situation. The client is a married woman 38 years of age. She was born in the United States. Her family is described as "good peasant stock," her parents coming from Alsace-Lorraine. Soon after her birth her mother suffered with a mental disease and except for a short period has been confined to a state hospital ever since.

The husband is 40 years of age. He was born in the United States and has an eighth grade education which he has supplemented by reading and taking study courses. There are two children.

There has been discord in the home ever since marriage. The husband complains that although client showed great interest in his studies before their marriage, there was a sudden change afterward and she demanded many attentions. He admits having no affection for her, and has had many "affairs" with other women. . . .

The husband has lived with his relatives since the time Mrs. H. attacked him [with a knife]. The children are with the client. The husband has supported the family, but because of his irregular employment the income has been uncertain and barely adequate for the needs. The client is working part-time as a waitress, for which she earns $10 a week.

[1] "Can Interviews be Described Objectively?" *The Journal of Social Forces*, VII (June, 1929), 530.

A month after her contact with the hospital, the client brought the 12-year-old son to the child guidance clinic, at the suggestion of her physician. The boy was doing poor school work. However, he was found to have adequate intelligence. Because of the client's condition and the boy's evident need of intelligent supervision, the psychiatrist recommended treatment through the social service department. This the client refused to consider, saying she "would have nothing like that." . . .

Purpose. (1) To convince the client that she and the husband were the real problems in the case; (2) to explain the nature of social supervision and to convince her that she needed it; (3) to convince her that the husband must be seen if their problem is to be met with understanding.

Setting. The interviewer's office. Only the interviewer and client are present.

Interview. The client is neatly dressed. She has a strained expression and clasps and unclasps her hands many times. She has brought the psychiatrist's letter which she anxiously shows to interviewer. Her eyes fill with tears almost every time she mentions the husband's name. Several times she puts her head on the desk and sobs aloud.

Throughout the interview the worker uses a firm, calm tone of voice. She is unhurried in manner. During the crying spells she quietly waits for the mother to regain her composure. Twice when the mother expresses embarrassment over her lack of self-control, she uses a reassuring tone of voice, saying, "That's all right, we'll talk when you get a grip on yourself." The worker has the impression that the mother is deriving some satisfaction from her suffering and feels that it will be possible to speak very frankly without arousing antagonism.

During the first fifteen minutes of conversation, the mother plunges into a recital of her problems, speaking very incoherently. The worker does not attempt to check the outburst. As soon as the mother reaches a lull in her emotional outlet, the worker introduces a definite conversation.

Interviewer: Tell me about your girlhood. What did you do? (Attempting to divert mother from present problem and incoherent type of thought.)

Mrs. H.: After my mother was put away, my father put me in the homes of his friends. I just went from one place to another. I helped with the housework and minded their kids. That's the reason I never got much education. (Showing self-pity.)

Interviewer: Let's see, you finished sixth grade, didn't you?

Mrs. H.: Yes.

Interviewer: I think you have quite a good vocabulary for sixth-grade education. (Appealing to pride.)

Mrs. H.: My husband is very smart. I learned some things from him. (Enjoying the praise and showing admiration for husband.)

Interviewer: When you worked in those homes, did you take part in the family life? (Continuing rapport through sympathetic inquiry.)

Mrs. H.: Sometimes, but most of the time I felt like an outsider. I never had a home until I married and that's why I'm so anxious to keep it. I want my children to have what I missed. I'd do anything for the sake of my children. (Aiming to justify her behavior in the situation.)

Interviewer: What plans have you made for helping them? (Introducing direct discussion of present problem.)

Mrs. H.: (Beginning to cry) Oh, I'm so upset all the time I can't think. I can't seem to do anything but cry, and it makes me mad with myself. I just can't live without Mr. H. When I go out on the street, I long to see him, and I'm afraid I will run into him and do something terrible. (Reverting to previous state of excitement. Disgusted with own lack of self-control.)

Interviewer: But you see that isn't getting you anywhere, and if you are crying most of the time no wonder your son, William, prefers staying out on the street. (Attempting to give her understanding of son's difficulty, and her effect upon him.)

Mrs. H.: But he was hard to manage before this ever happened. The teacher says he doesn't pay attention. (Evading responsibility.)

Interviewer: But you know we found that he is smart enough to do the work, and his interest can be appealed to. You say that he goes to the Field Museum every Saturday morning. That is very unusual for a boy of his age. I have talked to several hundred children here and I think he is the only one who goes there so regularly. You see it is not a matter of his intelligence. We think the real trouble is the kind of home life he has had. (Facing with definite facts and appealing to mother's pride.)

Mrs. H.: I know I do go to pieces now and nag him but I didn't use to and I always tried to keep him from hearing the quarrels. (Partially admitting fault but showing lack of imagination.)

Interviewer: But even if he didn't hear the actual quarrels, your expressions and your manner would affect him. Children feel those things much more keenly than grown-up people think they do. You and your husband are the real problem—William's behavior is only the result.

Mrs. H.: Well, that's a hard thing to hear! (Defensive.)

Interviewer: But isn't it true?

Mrs. H.: Yes, I suppose it is. But what can I do? Thinking about it makes me go all to pieces. I know what I ought to do but I can't control my feelings. (More reflective. Some insight but helpless.)

Interviewer: You're going around in a circle. You need someone to help you think more clearly and to plan for you until you are able to do it yourself. Right now you are spending all of your time thinking of the past and of what might have been. Your problem is to begin to plan for the future, to build up your own personality, to learn to depend upon yourself and to be a companion to the children—not a cry-baby. But I think you need help in order to do this. (Suggesting a constructive way out. Stimulating to action.)

Mrs. H.: I know there are lots of things I could do—go to lectures and read books—if I could just get hold of myself. (Responding to stimulus by show of ambition.)

Interviewer: I advise you to have the doctor refer you to our social service. I think that will help you get a grip on yourself. Would you like to know something about it? (Trying effect of direct proposition.)

Mrs. H.: Yes. (Interested.)

Interviewer: It means that your case[1] will be given to a social worker and she will help you plan your affairs.[2] You will be able to talk to her freely and "get things out of your system." I suspect that you talk to your neighbors now more than you ought to. (Indicating need of social aid by assuming facts.)

Mrs. H.: Yes, I know I do. (Embarrassed.)

Interviewer: (Laughing) Well, just remember that it will be the social worker's business to listen to you.[3] (Introducing humor to relieve embarrassment.)

Mrs. H.: It's pretty tough on her. Will the social worker be a married woman? (Responding with humor but reverting to apprehensive attitude.)

Interviewer: No, she will not.

Mrs. H.: But don't you think she could understand my problem better if she was married too?

Interviewer: It isn't possible for the social workers to have experienced personally all the problems which are presented here, and after all, is that necessary? (Meeting objections through reasoning.)[4]

Mrs. H.: But how can she feel as I do and understand my problems? (Self-centered.)

Interviewer: She will not pretend to feel as you do for that would not help you. What you need is someone who is not going to be hampered by her feelings as you are now—someone who will be able to think clearly and to help you get some of the snarls out of your own feelings. (Making use of the need for meeting client's objections by getting her to face the facts of her own problem.)

Mrs. H.: Well, perhaps you are right. (More reasonable, but hesitant.)

Interviewer: While I have advised you in this way I should explain that we can handle only a limited number of cases. It is just possible that we may be too crowded to have you referred to social service. Even if you

---

[1] [It is best to avoid the use of technical terms, such as "case," as client may misunderstand meaning. A better way perhaps is to say: "One of our workers will come out to see you and your family." P. V. Y.]

[2] [It is best not to indicate that the social worker intends "to plan affairs." A more tactful way and less likely to put client on defensive is: "The social worker will talk matters over with you," or "In my own problems (identification) I find that two heads are always better than one, and I seek suggestions from others." P. V. Y.]

[3] [Perhaps a more tactful thing to say is "When you get acquainted with the social worker, you just make her listen to you," thus heightening client's status through appeal to power. P. V. Y.] See pp. 335–336.

[4] [The above statement probably did not calm the client's fear that she will be misunderstood. A better way of approaching the subject probably is: "Well, you need not have any hesitancy, as our social workers have years of experience. They come in contact with more problems than any one family ever faces, and naturally that gives them sufficient understanding of the most difficult situations, and, of course, your situation is not very unusual. I am sure that you will think the same of our social worker when you get acquainted with her." (Laying the ground for cooperation.) P. V. Y.]

decide to ask for this help, the matter cannot be settled until I have talked with the doctor and the head of the social service.   (Utilizing a true condition to introduce an element of uncertainty.)

Mrs. H.: Do you really think it will help me?   (Somewhat less hesitant.)

Interviewer: Yes, I think so, but of course I cannot tell for a great deal will depend upon you.   (Trying to secure client's recognition of her own responsibility.)

Mrs. H.: I think I'll get you to ask the doctor to refer me.   (Accepting responsibility and making decision.)

Interviewer: Of course you understand that in asking for this help we shall expect you to do your part.   It will be necessary for the social worker to see your husband.   (Showing implications of the decision.)

Mrs. H.: But she will tell him all the things I have said about him—they are all written down—and that will get me into worse trouble with him. (Apprehensive.)

Interviewer: Everything you have told us is regarded confidentially, and wouldn't you suppose that we would have more tact than to do that?[1] The purpose of seeing him is to hear his side of the story, otherwise our treatment would be very one-sided. · What would you think if we accepted his statements about you and made no attempt to become acquainted with you?   (Appealing to reason and sense of fair play.)

Mrs. H.: Would the worker tell me when she is going to see him?   (Apprehensive.)

Interviewer: She will do nothing behind your back.   But in case she tells you, you must not telephone or write to Mr. H. trying to explain the interview for it will only make it harder for the social worker.   As soon as you can plan for yourself we shall want you to, but for a time it will be best for you to depend on our judgment and accept our plans in good faith.[2] (Anticipating probable behavior and urging her to face and accept social service methods.)

Mrs. H.: I will do anything if you can persuade Mr. H. to come back home and be congenial.   (Misunderstanding social service objective.)

Interviewer: But we do not guarantee that at all.   Congeniality isn't a thing that one can force upon another.   It may not even be wise for him to try to live with you again.   Perhaps he is as dependent upon the other woman as you are on him.   (Trying to arouse insight into husband's situation.)

Mrs. H.: I never thought of it in that light. ·I suppose you think it's awfully strange that I love him so when he has treated me in this way. (Responding to appeal.   Desiring approbation for martyr's role.)

---

[1] [The above sounds vindictive and is beside the point.   The interviewer failed to recognize that Mrs. H. had a natural reaction.   Vindictiveness on interviewer's part does not calm fears in interviewee. · The task of the former is to eliminate fears and to see that his mind meets with that of the latter.   P. V. Y.]

[2] [It is best not to indicate to client that he will have to depend on others since he might gain either a feeling of helplessness and hopelessness or of dependency.   P. V. Y.]

Interviewer: No, I don't think that. In fact, we shall simply regard it as a part of your problem. It isn't a thing we shall condemn you for or admire you for. (Impressing with objective attitude of social service.)

Mrs. H.: Did you ever have cases as hard as this one? (Self-centered.)

Interviewer: Oh, yes. This is not an unusual one at all. Perhaps you are as self-centered as you say your husband is. (Trying to secure an objective attitude toward self-pity.)

Mrs. H.: Why, I'm not. I've always tried to help other people. (Very defensive, gives several examples.)

Interviewer: (Makes no comment, wishing to secure a more reflective answer through appearing unconvinced.)

Mrs. H.: I guess you are right. I am inclined to think I'm the only person who is having a hard time. (Trying to become objective.)

Interviewer: (Bringing the interview to a close) Then you do want me to ask the doctor to refer you to social service, and you understand just what that will mean? (Making the matter definite through suggesting next step.)

Mrs. H.: Yes, when will I hear? (Accepting conditions.)

Interviewer: Within the next day or two. The social worker will telephone you and will talk with you before she makes any plans. (Reassuring client.)

Mrs. H.: And you think I'll know in a day or so? (Characteristically apprehensive.)

Interviewer: (With a tone of finality) Yes, in either case she will telephone you.

ANALYSIS OF INTERVIEW

Method	Processes
Approach.	
1. Release of emotions	1. Allowing expression with no attempt to secure coherent statements.
2. Diversion from present difficulty	2. Through reminiscences of own girlhood.
Rapport.	
3. Appeal to pride	3. Recognizing ability to express herself well.
4. Sympathy	4. Through tone of voice in inquiry concerning conditions of girlhood.
Presentation of Facts.	
5. Mother's lack of plan	5. Following cue, "I'd do anything for children" by inquiry as to specific plan.
6. Son's situation	6. Pointing out his behavior as a result of marital un-adjustment and her lack of self-control.

7. Mother's ineffectual method of meeting situation.

7. Pointing out faulty thought processes and need of assistance.

Stimulation.

8. Plan for help
9. Information

8. Suggesting aid of social service.
9. Giving details regarding social treatment.

10. Breaking down barrier

10. Meeting objections through appeals to reason.

11. Hastening decision

11. Through introducing an element of uncertainty.

12. Placing responsibility

12. Pointing out that success depends upon her cooperation.

13. Acceptance of social service methods

13. Through appeal to reason and sense of fair play.

14. Insight into husband's situation

14. Through arousing objective attitude toward him.

15. Insight into own personality

15. Through arousing objective attitude toward self.

16. Apprehension—removal

16. Through reassurance as to straightforward methods of social service.

Establishment of Confidence.

17. Acceptance of plan with no compromises

17. By maintaining throughout a calm, objective manner; meeting objections with logical statements; frankness.[1]

The Arthur Interview

In the analysis of social case work interviews Joanna Colcord stresses such terms as "conscious purposes in the mind of the case worker" and "the technical means employed" by the worker. She states further:

It was soon seen that a problem in terminology was involved and unless we could develop descriptive names for the technical processes identified in the study of case record material, we should be unable to note their recurrence or comment upon their appearance in another record. . . .

Some of the names adopted must have sounded ridiculous enough had outsiders heard the committee's earnest deliberations—whether, for instance, a certain procedure was "cards on the table," or "putting it up to you."

[1] American Association of Social Workers, *Interviews: A Study of the Methods of Analyzing and Recording Social Case Work Interviews*, pp. 47–54. Reprinted by permission.

The scientists and medical men have had the advantage of sonorous Latin and Greek in which to couch their technical vocabulary; but when their dignified terms are translated into plain English, as William Beebe is fond of doing for his readers, the names sound not unlike our own clumsy terms. If "bringing back to the main issue" is a laborious name for a process in case work, so is "side handed toothscraper" when its Latin wrappings are unwound, a clumsy name for a fish. . . . [1]

The Arthur Interview Analyzed.

The Arthur family has been known to the Family Welfare Association since February, 1922. There is unvarying history of asking for assistance, no spark of co-operation or effort to change their own very haphazard ways. Mr. A. has been a salesman during entire period of FWA contacts. Reputation with employers not very good, dishonest attitude but no actual theft and a curiously lax attitude toward him by employers, re-employing after firing, etc. Children a neglected lot, bringing themselves up as best they can—undernourishment, tardiness and absence from school. One boy, 20 years, has I.Q. 69. School teachers and principals reported noisy outbursts on Mr. A.'s part whenever he was summoned to hear some complaint or suggestions. Thirteen year old Paul in J. C. in December for petty theft (probation). Family always a matter of concern to neighbors who dislike Mr. A. but "pity" Mrs. A. and children and want relief given for their benefit. Mrs. A. a weak ineffectual creature, neglecting children to "assist" Mr. A. as in demonstration of aluminum ware, etc. All interviews with Mr. A. either dwindled away into fruitless discussions or were demands for relief, made in loud, rough tones and bullying phrases. Through the summer family usually manages but heard from at Community Fund campaign times and through the winter. Mrs. A. asks at regular intervals for "just one more help with coal and after that we can get along." In November, 1927, the oldest boy, William, was accidentally shot and killed. He had been earning regularly and was the only source of steady income.

Preceding the analyzed interview, there had been an acrimonious interview between Mr. A. and a rather inexperienced visitor, during which he made bullying demands, the interview reaching an impasse. A renewed request for relief from Mrs. A. four days later (by telephone) resulted in the District Secretary writing Mr. A. the following note:

"My dear Mr. Arthur:

Mrs. Arthur phoned our office this morning asking for coal. We are sending you a check for $3.00 for this emergency, and would like to see you at this office at twelve o'clock Friday. Please be sure to keep this appointment as further plans will be made with you then.

Yours very truly,

(Miss) GFL

District Secretary."

GFL:CN

---

[1] See WALTER BINGHAM'S statement in "Suggestions for Further Study," p. 236, No. 16.

Before the day of interview GFL thought it over, decided to try the surprise of great amiability,[1] no reference to last interview if it could be avoided, sustained calm if he roared and stick to till we got somewhere.

Processes and Techniques.

Crescendo.

1. Lessening tension

    a. Approbation

    b. Refusing to take offense

    c. Hostess

    d. Inconsequential pleasant-
        tries

2. Bringing to main issue

Mr. Arthur, a large man, well dressed, something pompous about him, arrived promptly for the interview and stood stiffly in the outer office. When GFL approached him he remarked, "My name is A. My wife said you wanted to see me." (As the note requesting interview had been sent to Mr. A. himself this seemed significant.) GFL said, "You are very prompt. I am Miss L. who wrote you the note. Will you please come into this room?" and preceded him into the interviewing room. As he entered he remarked with great sarcasm, "I suppose I can have a chair to sit on." GFL affected not to hear this remark but walked over to a window and opened it slightly making a remark something like this: "This is the kind of a room that is always too warm or too cool, but even so it is pleasanter to talk here than in the outer office." Turned from the window saying, "Won't you take off your overcoat? You will undoubtedly be too warm with it on." A slightly friendlier expression went over his face. He removed his coat and sat down. GFL made a few more inconsequential remarks about the temperature, and used this time to look him over— (thoughts—good looking enough to be conceited, easily flattered, and because he's here, going to "show" us.) Mr. A suddenly smiled and made a facetious remark about the weather outside— "Maybe spring was coming but he would have to be shown, etc."

At this point DFS entered the room. GFL remarked to Mr. A., "You know Miss S. We are all going to talk

---

[1] ["To try a surprise of great amiability" without actually feeling amiable toward Mr. A. means affectation without sincerity and the destruction of the true spirit of the interview. P. V. Y.]

a. Cards on the table

b. Anticipating client's defense

c. Specific to general

3. Keeping to main issue

a. Forestalling interruption

together.[1] He looked doubtfully at DFS and mumbled "Good morning." She seated herself, smiled at him and GFL immediately said, "Now Mr. A. we want to have a real talk about your situation. Miss S. and I can well imagine that it is just as unsatisfactory to you as it is to us and we have found that the only way to arrive anywhere in family affairs is to give them a thorough going over from both points of view." GFL then went on to outline Mr. A.'s situation from FWA point of view, i.e., a salesman on commission who could not earn enough to support a large family. FWA knew very well what it took to support eight children and knew that the income to do it satisfactorily must come in in a steady stream which a commission salesman's income would not do. The "game" interest of commission selling was certainly understandable but it was too easy to fall into the state of mind in which income looked like $300 a month when it in all probability was $300 for one month and $30 for three months following. Spoke rather rapidly in a quiet, conversational tone, (trying to avoid interruption—wanted to finish in one dose.)[2]

When the exposition of FWA point of view was finished, paused and Mr. A. responded very promptly. "Well now I can see just why you would feel that way about it, but let me tell you what splendid prospects I have with this new company. The vocophone is a music

[1] ["We are all going to talk together" sounds somewhat presumptuous. More tactful thing to say is: "If you don't mind, we should like to talk it over together." P. V. Y.]

[2] [If a man felt inclined to interrupt and was not given the opportunity to do so, it is probable that in some cases at least, the psychological process of attention was thereby made ineffective and that much of the long speech made to him fell, therefore, on deaf ears. The man should either have been given a chance to interrupt and to satisfy his queries and rationalizations or he should have been prepared for a long speech by the indication: "Now, Mr. A., there is something I have been wanting to tell you, but it will take me a little while to explain it. Let me state it first without interruption, and when I am through you may ask questions." P. V. Y.]

machine for use in restaurants and places of entertainment. It is decidedly the best thing of its kind that I have ever heard, etc., and so on." He reeled off a "sales talk," very glib and quite well phrased, once or twice fumbling on a "big" word, arriving after a bit at the statement that he had been doing "missionary work" so far because the selling field here was new and they could not expect to make sales right away. Tom So-and-So in Indianapolis made between six and seven hundred dollars in commissions last month. Interrupted him

b. Puncture

to ask whether Tom So-and-So was married and had children. He laughed and said, "No, he was a young fellow without dependents, but wasn't that a

c. Avoiding argument

good month's business?" Assured him that it was and that for Tom-So-and-So it must be very pleasant indeed, but that much as he might like to take his chance on having a $600 month sometime it was

4. Lessening tension

not possible because his situation was so different. He shook his head amiably remarking, "That's right. It sure is different to take care of eight children." Picked up his remark, replying "Yes,

a. Flattery

taking care of eight children is a man sized job. There is no doubt about that, Mr. A., and don't you agree that the

b. Following client's lead

only way really to do it is to find a job with wages attached? You see we fully understand the excitement and interest of the selling game (though I personally

c. Sharing personal experiences

could never bear its uncertainties. I like to know exactly what I am going to have and when I am going to have it.)

5. Appeal to reason

The CF agencies must ask folks like you to take the practical path in these matters. Did you ever stop to think that every man who liked commission

a. Specific to general

selling would have exactly the same right as you have to ask for assistance from FWA and that if FWA granted all these requests the CF would have to be many

b. Flattery

times as big as it is? Now as a business man you know what that would mean."

c. Yes-response

6. Keeping to main issue

   a. Forestalling interruption

   b. Rushing defenses

   c. Provocative query

7. Lessening tension

   a. Letting client talk himself out

8. Bringing back to main issue

   a. "Cornering"

   b. Closing avenues of digression

9. Breaking defense
   a. Use of acquired information

   b. Implied criticism

   c. Explaining the agency

Mr. A. paused momentarily, then shook his head and said, "No, I never did think of it that way. I guess you're right. There wouldn't be money enough to pay the bill." Assured him there would not and that CF would simply be paying to let a large group of men do what they preferred to do. Did not give him a chance to interrupt but went right on saying, "Now why don't you drop this vocophone proposition and look for a job with a salary? Perhaps you have been looking for one recently;" (implying a question). Mr. A. "bit" very promptly and said, "No, I haven't looked for a salaried job for more than twelve years. They just don't interest me. You see the wash machine game went pretty good for a while, but that is all shot now because there is so much competition. This thing is different. It is the only one of its kind and it is bound to go the minute people get on to it." He was now off at a gallop on the vocophone virtues again so let him talk himself out, both GFL and DFS sitting quietly saying nothing but looking as interested as possible.

When he paused for more words GFL said, "Have you any sales which are quite certain to be closed in the next two weeks?" He hesitated, then admitted that he had not but two or three looked very good and he wouldn't be a bit surprised if they developed. Told him this seemed entirely too uncertain to figure food and fuel on and he again nodded his head in agreement. . . .

. . . "Of course, you know people are bound to feel concerned when they think children are suffering in any way and think it's our job to look into it, and it is." Paused a moment (pumping up courage) then asked, "Mr. A., just how much do you know about the Minnesota laws for the protection of children? Did you ever hear of such a thing as the dependency of minor children?" He

d. Shock

e. Forestalling objection

f. Anticipating ultimate outcome

g. Veiled threat

10. Lessening tension

    a. Yes-response

    b. Pleasantry (smile)

    c. Following client's lead

    d. Concession-compromise

said he had not and looked rather interested. Went right on, "Since you do not know, perhaps you would be interested to know a little about them. There are, of course, many which would not affect your children in any way, but as I have been talking to you I could not help realizing that the laws covering dependency and neglect might come very near your situation and I really think you should know about them." Went on to explain dependency and neglect, making it rather technical and emphasizing the *law* phase. He seemed interested remarking, "Is that so?" "No, I didn't know that," and similar comments. Finished this explanation by saying, "Now you see if your children have to receive much more help from agencies or individuals it is going to bring them inside that dependency or neglect boundary line. Let's just assume that happens. You won't mind thinking of that unpleasant possibility just long enough for me to show you what I mean? (Large smile.) I really believe that if you had to appear in Juvenile Court for a dependency hearing the judge would say to you very much the same as I have just been saying to you. That is, that you, the father of eight children, could not manage on a commission basis and you would be ordered (whereas I can only urge you) to find a salaried job."

Surprisingly enough, Mr. A. took this calmly and even with some interest saying, "Yes, I guess that's so. I get that side of it and of course state laws go for everybody's children—mine too, I guess." Picked this up immediately, saying, "Well, if you feel that way about it now, let's work out a definite plan. You wouldn't one bit like to go Juvenile Court (laughingly) (GFL did not know at this time that Mr. A. had been to Juvenile Court in December with John) and the very best way to keep away from there is to get yourself straightened

11. Appeal to reason
   a. Balancing alternatives

   b. Putting it up to client

   c. Explaining agency

   d. General to specific

12. Helping difficult admission

   a. Sympathy

around now. We know that you can't make a change from one day to the next. Suppose we decide upon a two week period for you to turn this whole thing over in your mind[1] and do some looking around for another job. As you are entirely without money now we will help you with necessities for the two weeks. If you have not then been able to make plans to provide what the family needs, you are going to accept our suggestion and go to work on a wage basis.[2] Do you agree to that?" Mr. A. said he did. His wife was anxious to see DFS as she was entirely without groceries and "wanted to tell her about some other things too."

As the interview took place on Friday, visit could not be made until Monday, told Mr. A. an emergency check would be given him. DFS left the room to get the check. As she did so GFL remarked, "Mr. A., we would like you to know a little bit more about this organization. You may think of it only as a place to which you come when you need coal or groceries, but we want you to think of it as a place which can give you service as well as material help. Now in your family there seem to us a good many opportunities to help with service—Myron, for instance. He must be a very sad problem for you." Mr. A. admitted that he was and had not the slightest idea what to do with the boy. He never had any experience with anyone who was "not quite bright." Asked how he explained Myron's mental condition. He said in a very confidential tone, "Well, I will tell you. All the time his mother was pregnant with him she was half sick and very depressed all the time and she and I have always

---

[1] The above may be interpreted by some clients as voicing an air of superiority. It would be more effective to place the responsibility of the decision upon them by saying: "How long do you think it will take you to turn this whole thing over in your mind? Would two weeks be enough?"

[2] It would be more effective to put all these statements in the form of questions.

thought he was marked." Told him that we would be much interested in helping Myron and DFS would discuss plans for him with Mr. A.

DFS returned to the room with the check and Mr. A. immediately turned to her, saying "Before I go I want to apologize to you, Miss S. for the sarcastic way that I talked to you last Saturday. I get so nervous and upset about all these troubles that I often do things I am sorry for later. I do sincerely apologize." DFS was so overcome at this that she said nothing, though smiling amiably, so GFL rushed into the breach saying, "I am sure Miss S. is very glad indeed to accept your apology, Mr. A., and we are all going to agree now to consider your last interview a closed book. We understand how those things happen and there is nothing more to say about it." Mr. A. rose slowly, donned his overcoat, keeping up a running fire of politeness. He certainly was glad he had come to the office. Did not want FWA to think that he had purposely stayed away before or was afraid to discuss plans for his family. . . .[1]

b. Letting bygones be bygones

Stuart Queen has attempted to tabulate the physical and mental aspects of the interview, including voice, facial expression, bodily attitude, pantomimic gestures, words, and thought processes:

SOCIAL INTERACTION IN THE INTERVIEW: AN EXPERIMENT

. . . The general field of study is: the interview as a type of social interaction. The specific problem is: precisely what happens in an interview between a social worker and his client. (We would like to see similar studies of interviews between salesmen and customers, clergymen and parishioners, employers and employees, and various other combinations of persons.)

This divides naturally into a number of sub-problems such as: What part of the give-and-take is verbal? What part of it is non-verbal, i.e., tone of voice, facial expression, gesture, posture? What is the relation of the verbal and non-verbal parts of the interaction? For example, to what extent is a statement of either person conditioned by the words of the other and to

---

[1] JOANNA C. COLCORD, "A Study of the Techniques of the Social Case Work Interview, *Journal of Social Forces*, VII (June, 1929), 519–526. Reprinted by permission.

what extent by his other acts? How do these persons express various meanings verbally and otherwise? How do they interpret each other's expressions, especially when these are not put into words? In general, what correlations are there between the interview regarded as a succession of physical stimuli and responses and the interview regarded as a succession of feelings, ideas, objectives and inferences? Another group of problems involves the ways in which the nature of the interview as a whole is affected by: who takes the initiative, his general objective or purpose, the immediate setting, previous contacts or absence of the same, background of relevant experience, types of personalities represented by the parties to the interview. . . .

INTERVIEW WITH MRS. A.

Mrs. A. is old and pathetic. Of her family only a son and grandson are left. The son [Frank] is of low-grade mentality, but not insane, and has been alcoholic for years. Mrs. A. has suffered abuse beyond description at his hands, but bore with him patiently until it finally became necessary to send him to the State Hospital as a violent alcoholic. At first she was shamed and grieved to the point of being irrational. As time went on she became more reasonable and finally quite happy to know that Frank was receiving good care. He is a cleaner and presser by trade and was put in the shop at the hospital. He wrote his mother of this, also of the cheerful, clean, wholesome atmosphere. Last week Mrs. A. recognized the fact that she had reconciled herself to his absence and expressed the hope that he might remain always. The doctors had been most considerate in their communications to her. Almost immediately following her visit to the office in which she expressed greater happiness than she had known for years, she received a letter from the hospital superintendent telling her that Frank is to be paroled and that the Family Welfare Society has been notified and she must co-operate in helping Frank make his adjustment. A copy of this letter was enclosed in one sent to the Family Welfare Society.

Yesterday Mrs. A. came to the office. She has been giving practical care to a very ill client of the Family Welfare Society and has grown very fond of her patient, whom she thought improving. Mrs. A. was visibly nervous and upset. She began to cry and told of the patient's weakened condition and suffering. Sympathy was expressed and the discussion kept on the patient long enough to let her get control of herself. She also told of feeling ill and discouraged. She then introduced the topic that, no doubt, was foremost in her thoughts. . . .

The precise roles of various gestures, etc., are not yet clear to us, but we do have some clues. In case after case an excited client has become quiet in response to the social worker's slow, even, moderately pitched tone of voice. It appears that a relaxed bodily attitude contributes to the same result. In one interview, where the case worker's problem was to overcome evasion and bring the client to "face himself," part of the technic consisted in looking directly, though without tension, into the client's eyes.

In numerous instances the case worker is convinced that his inferences have been drawn from the client's physical action rather than from his words. For example, in an interview having to do with vocational guid-

(*Continued on page* 219)

SOCIAL PSYCHOLOGICAL ANALYSIS OF THE "A" INTERVIEW

Physical acts (Conversation of gestures)			Mental acts		
Non-verbal		Verbal (Dialog)	Thought processes of visitor		
Visitor	Client		Inference	Objective	Other conscious thinking
Sitting upright in chair, "poker" face, ordinary conversational tone, calm and deliberate.	Direct gaze, tears in eyes. Quick, sharp and almost shrill voice. Calm, low voice, slow and hesitant.	Mrs. A.— "Did you hear about Frank?" V.—"Yes, Mrs. A., I had a letter from Dr Parker." Mrs. A.— "He will be home in a few days. Dr. Parker told me he wrote you."	Mrs. A.'s tone and use of words implies she does not regard this as a happy event. Mrs. A. evidently has not resented content of doctor's letter.	Avoid confusion of thought. Make Mrs. A. accept as a fact and not an emotional disturbance.	Tact and kindness are going to be necessary because Mrs. A. is usually hard to deal with on this subject. Must not forget to be on guard and remember always that Mrs. A. is both a sensitive person and a "savage" one when under stress (she had recently demonstrated this).
Smile, leaning slightly forward. Smile vanishes and slight frown takes its place. Very slow voice in clear, audible tone.	Sits quietly. Tears still in eyes. Grows more tense in position.	V.—"I'm glad you have come this morning because I've wanted to talk to you ever since Dr. Parker's letter came. I answered it and asked him to keep Frank until you and I could talk things over. He told me that he felt sure Frank was cured of alcoholism, but that he could make	She wants advice, although she has not asked for it.	Assure Mrs. A. of thoughtful interest, and encourage her by building a hopeful plan.	

Physical acts (Conversation of gestures)			Mental acts		
Non-verbal			Thought processes of visitor		
Visitor	Client	Verbal (Dialog)	Inference	Objective	Other conscious thinking
		no guarantee whether he would return to the old habit. Now, I've thought and thought about it and I've decided that we will have to make a definite plan to help him. One of the things I thought of is to get him a job so he will lose no time at all when he comes."			
	Leans forward as she begins to speak, then sits very stiff and erect.	Mrs. A.— "Oh, but he can always get work. Why, there have been several men calling for him lately."	Mrs. A. is trying to protect Frank even at cost of his own good.		
Still leaning slightly forward. Smile, calm, slow but audible tone.		V.—"Yes, I'm sure he can get work, but don't you think if we had a job promised by some employer who un-			Is Mrs. A. going to relapse into the stubborn person she is capable of being without reason or intelligence?

Physical acts (Conversation of gestures)			Mental acts		
Non-verbal		Verbal (Dialog)	Thought processes of visitor		
Visitor	Client		Inference	Objective	Other conscious thinking
		derstands, it would help keep Frank away from the places where he could get liquor?"			
	Tears spring anew. Leans forward suddenly, speaks loudly and emphatically.	Mrs. A.— "But, I couldn't stand for anybody to know that he's been in the asylum."			
Calm, quiet position of comfort in chair. Hand out on desk, palm upward and open. Smile slowly comes over face. Picks up pencil and asks question in direct tone.	Tears leave eyes and perspiration forms below them. Sits quietly and seems to show some muscular relaxation.	V.—"We'll explain, Mrs. A., that he has been in the hospital and has overcome his habit ,and I'm sure if we are talking to the right man he will be glad to do anything he can to encourage Frank. Who are some of his former employers?"		Ease Mrs. A.'s mind. Calm her. Make her feel sympathy. Assume that she will respond and do away with any thought of argument.	
	Quick, low speech followed by louder and firmer tone.	Mrs. A.— "Oh, I forget, but I have some cards at home."	Mrs. A. is not convinced until she starts to answer and then she unconsciously		

Physical acts (Conversation of gestures)			Mental acts		
Non-verbal		Verbal (Dialog)	Thought processes of visitor		
Visitor	Client		Inference	Objective	Other conscious thinking
			decides to follow suggestion.		
Ordinary conversational tone.		V.—"Do you know any of them yourself? Would he be able to get drink from them?"		Don't intimate to Mrs. A. that she has done anything unusual in responding without argument.	
	Relaxed body and face muscles, calm. Deliberate ordinary conversational tone.	Mrs. A.—"I knew one place where he was paid in liquor but I think the others are all right."	Mrs. A. is interested in plan and is relieved. She has ceased to be emotional and is more rational than usual in crisis.		
Direct, louder, tone, nod of head, smile, hand out on desk again with palm open and up.		V.—"Don't *you* think it would be best to talk to his employer and be honest about things so he can help?"			Win Mrs. A. completely if possible.
	Clear voice, more emphasis of tone.	Mrs. A.— "Yes, I guess it would. Frank has always been so ashamed when he had to go to Leeds or General Hospital and never wanted his boss to know it but I would ask him	Mrs. A. has won a battle with herself. She has granted a point on intelligent reasoning and not on emotion. She is taking V. into her confidence.		

Physical acts (Conversation of gestures)			Mental acts		
Non-verbal		Verbal (Dialog)	Thought processes of visitor		
Visitor	Client		Inference	Objective	Other conscious thinking
Direct gaze, tone emphatic but not harsh.		if he wasn't more ashamed of getting drunk." V.—"Will you bring the cards over to Mrs. Wilson's tomorrow so we can get them, and call at the differ-erent places. I told Dr. Parker we would take care of it this week."		Don't give Mrs. A. a chance to change her mind.	
	Nod of head. Tone clear and full, dropping into a low, "pleading." When she leans over with new tears well-ing up in her eyes. Clasps hands together in supplication and rests them on desk while wait-ing answer.	Mrs. A.— "Yes, or I'll bring them here. But you promise don't you that you will say 'hos-pital' and not 'Insane asylum.' "	Mrs. A. is eager to help carry out plan but is suddenly confronted again by fear of Frank's displeasure.		
Open smile both with face mus-cles and eyes. Gen-tle voice but clear and loud enough to leave no possibility of misunder-standing.	Assumes natural erect position and smiles gently.	V.—"Yes, of course, be-cause it is a hospital and Frank is not insane."	Perfect understand-ing has been reached and now ready for next topic.		

ance, the bright eyes, persistent grin, rather tense bodily attitude and rapid speech of the client made the social worker believe that the boy had come for confirmation and approval rather than for suggestion and advice. In other instances it is apparent that the social worker's previous knowledge of the client is more significant than anything revealed either by word or gesture.[1]

Virginia Robinson, of the Pennsylvania School for Social and Health Work, questions whether the factors isolated and described in the above analysis are really the fundamental adequate stimuli in the interview. She also points out that the physical acts as described are not the determining factors in changing the attitudes of Mrs. A. Furthermore, it is wrong to place the emphasis on the external behavior factors, when change of attitude is the real consideration.

In the interview with Mrs. A. where so much is known of her in advance, only the worker who understands and feels with her through the whole gamut of her emotional attitude, is a safe person to interview her in this present situation where increased fear and resistance may so easily be set up; and only if the worker goes further and can feel the import of all factors in the situation for the son can she project the son's situation in such a way that Mrs. A. will build up an attitude to which he can safely return.[2]

It is of importance to note, however, that nonverbal acts and gestures have a direct bearing upon the course of the interview. External behavior is often a guide to the mental and emotional activity of both interviewer and interviewee. Moreover, communication between human beings goes on in terms of the meanings which have come to be attached to gestures—both overt physical acts and minimal incompleted movements; that is, we "understand and feel with" Mrs. A., we enter into her "emotional attitude" by means of these so-called external behavior factors. Modification of attitude is at once occasioned and revealed in the ebb and flow of physical acts of the participants.

[1] STUART A. QUEEN, "Social Interaction in the Interview: An Experiment," *Journal of Social Forces*, VI (June, 1928), 545–553. Reprinted by permission.

[2] VIRGINIA P. ROBINSON, "Some Difficulties in Analyzing Social Interaction in the Interview," *Journal of Social Forces*, VI (June, 1928), 560.

CHAPTER XI

THE ANALYSIS OF THE CASE WORK INTERVIEW

(Concluded)

SOCIOLOGICAL ANALYSIS OF THE DATA OF AN INTERVIEW

So far only the techniques and processes of interviewing have been discussed. It is important, however, that the data of the interview be subjected to an analysis since one cannot interview a person successfully without an appreciation of the significance of the material which is being secured: (1) of the social and cultural setting which conditions the life of the interviewee and his problems; (2) of his relations with other members of the groups; (3) of the causal sequences which produced the existing situations; (4) of the specific behavior patterns and attitudes of the interviewee.

An analysis of the story as it is being told helps to give direction and point to the interview. The following diagnostic interview was held at the request of the interviewee, Mrs. Pavlova. The running comments on the left side are intended to indicate the character of the scientific information which is needed in order to interview successfully such a cultural hybrid as Mrs. Pavlova.

FIRST INTERVIEW WITH MRS. PAVLOVA

Mrs. Pavlova, a young Russian woman, came to seek advice regarding constant conflict with her own parents, parents-in-law, and her husband. Life in its very essentials seemed in a constant upheaval. Tensions and unrest seemed ever present.

Mrs. Pavlova is at present under 30 years of age. She is tall, stately, good-looking, and well dressed. She seems mentally alert, frank in manner, pleasing of personality, but discouraged and dejected.

During Mrs. P.'s narratives the interviewer injected such words as "Yes?" "As for example," "I see," "Well," but assumed the attitude of a highly interested and sympathetic listener, or what Professor Lindeman calls the attitude of a "participant observer."

> **Mrs. P.:** (Ready and eager to talk) There is so much trouble at home that I just can't stand it. What am I to do about this constant turmoil?

220

(In dignified manner but tinged with emotion.)

Interviewer: What do you mean? (To draw her out.)

Mrs. P.: Well, we just seem to quarrel about everything, food, clothes, shows, friends, ideas, and everything.

Interviewer: How do you account for it?

Mrs. P. seems to have some insight into the situation and is able to analyze it herself to a certain extent.

Mrs. P.: Well, we just don't seem to get together in our thinking. My parents think I am too advanced; I think they are too old fashioned, too old-countrified. (Thoughtfully.)

Interviewer: Could you tell me something about the background of your parents, Mrs. P.? (Slowly and sympathetically.)

Conflict of cultures: It is evident that though this young woman is highly individualized, yet she cannot think of her life except in relation to that of her family and social group. However, she knows too little of their social heritage to appreciate their position or to understand their attitudes fully.

Mrs. P.: Well, there's a long story. You see, they came from the Russian Caucausus when I was about three years old. My parents, together with a number of other Russian families, came to Los Angeles to join the Colony[1] here. I don't remember much about the first few years of our life except that we were always quite poor. When I was six or seven years old we moved to Mexico, where my father took up land; but he did not make a living there and we came back to Los Angeles, where he worked for a lumber company. A short time afterward an agent came from Utah and persuaded my parents to buy some land there. He told us that many people got rich and that we had a fine chance. They worked there three years, toiling day and night, but could not make a living. Terrific sand storms covered up the fields two and three feet deep. And after a sand storm, cloudbursts soaked the fields to the point where everything rotted in the ground. They finally decided that it was

[1] For an understanding of the life of the Colony, see Pauline V. Young, *Pilgrims of Russian Town.*

desert land, that they were wasting their time, and that the sooner they got away from there the better. . . . (Pause.)

We were down and out. We had no food, no clothes, and no money. . . . My father built a wagon, in which we lived, and another wagon was built which held all of our belongings, trunks, clothes, bedding, stove—all mixed up together. We left most of our tools and equipment on the farm; there was no one to buy.

We hurried to get out of that place in our covered wagon. My father took us to a hotel for the first night. We all trailed in. My father first, my mother behind him, and then all of us kids.

Interviewer: How long did you stay there?

Mrs. P.: Oh, just overnight. And that was enough. We hurried on to Salt Lake City. We had to get work at once. I wanted to help my folks out. I was eleven years old, and very small for my age. My father looked at me and wondered if I could find work. A neighbor told me of a cookie-manufacturer not far from us who would employ me if I could give him a hard-luck story. I did not have to tell him a hard-luck story. I just told him our own, which was hard enough. I worked for him for a few weeks, for three dollars per.

Interviewer: What work did you find next?

Mrs. P.: I heard of a chocolate factory where they paid more. I wanted to appear big, so I stuffed my front out with stockings, and when the man asked how old I was, I told him I was fourteen. He looked at me so queer, but he took me. When I left his office, I could still see him gazing at me. I gave one look at myself and did not wonder any more why the man stared at

Family ties are strong and girl follows traditional lot of children in her group.

The girl welcomes new opportunities as they present themselves. Her parents act and work by habit and custom while the girl is learning to act and work "by her wits." Thus she tends to develop the Bohemian type of personality, as opposed to Philistine type of personality of her parents, who cling to social traditions.

The American-born immigrant children expect some deference to them on the part of their parents as soon as they become economically independent; the parents expect to maintain social control over them until the children establish an independent home and family.

me. One stocking had fallen down, and only one side was padded out. I blushed and felt weak on my feet. . . . I worked like a mule from seven in the morning to six in the evening. I used to get terribly worn out. I wished that the truant officer would come around and send me to school. But no such luck. When a factory inspector came, the forelady would run and tell me to hide. I hid in the washroom until he left. I worked there about a year. (With some animation.)

Interviewer: Then what?

Mrs. P.: Then we came back to Los Angeles. I started to work in a laundry—I fed the mangle. I made six dollars a week and gave the money to my mother. I changed jobs many times; and once when I was laid off, my chum and I started to look in the newspapers for work. I saw an ad for a chocolate dipper and applied. The man said that he would give me sixteen dollars a week. I was fifteen years old then. I was shocked. I never expected that much and told him that I did not have much experience, and to give me only fourteen dollars a week; but at the end of the week he gave me sixteen. I really took the job on my nerve.

Interviewer: And what is your pay now?

Mrs. P.: Oh, different. Now I make $24–$28 a week, piece work. (With some pride.)

Interviewer: That's good money these days.

Mrs. P.: Yes, I always made good money and always gave it to my parents, but we have clashes in the home nevertheless.

Interviewer: Clashes over what?

Mrs. P.: We fight about everything.

Interviewer: What is the earliest clash you can remember?

Early urbanization: The girl is aware that in the city's casual contacts judgments are based to a large extent upon personal appearance. In the primary group of her community judgment is based on personal merit.

This is a typical illustration of the need for personal guidance in problems met by younger people. It is a challenge to social agencies in softening the effect of culture conflicts upon the family.

Mrs. P.: Well, to begin with, we quarreled over my buying a hat. I wore a shawl to work as long as I could. I did not want people to think I had just come back from a parade. Once I mustered up enough courage to buy a hat for a dollar and ninety-eight cents. When my mother heard about the hat, she cried and carried on something terrible. "A hat? And what next?" To avoid trouble at home I left my hat at a girl friend's house and called for it every morning, ditching my shawl. I was determined not to go to work any more in a shawl. I continued that for six months. But my girl friend moved away. And I said to my hat: "Well, here you go home with me, and we will suffer together." When my mother saw that hat, she started to carry on again. She said she would burn it. I told her frankly that I did not mean to wear a shawl to work any more, and that if she burned that hat I would buy another. I got mad, she cried, and I felt sorry for her. I would lose my temper and fly off the handle, and I would not give in; but I got tired of so much friction. There was a fight, it seems, every time I got home.

Interviewer: What did you do about it?

Mrs. P.: Once I went to a spiritualist. I wanted to ask him just one question. I wrote on a sheet of paper: "What can I do to stop all this fighting at home?" He did not even look at my paper, and he answered my question without reading it: "Be reasonable with your parents. They are old-fashioned, they don't understand your ways, and you don't talk to them quietly and explain." Well, I thought it over and felt ashamed of myself, and decided to be calm and talk everything over with them. . . .

Once the pattern for varying behavior is set, all members of the family who find it convenient adopt such a pattern. Convenience, efficiency, and comfort are modern determinants of behavior, but are rarely criteria for personal conduct in the older group.

Further individualization of behavior occurs with the discarding of identifying marks of distinction.

Interviewer: How long did you follow his advice?

Mrs. P.: For some time, but the next fight was about my buying a new dress. I was growing up, and the comments of my girl friends made me feel ashamed of those Russian dresses my mother made at home. I wanted a simple little summer dress. I bought such a dress. My mother nearly fainted when she saw it. "Well, what next? Aren't you ashamed of yourself? How can you wear such a dress like that? That's fit for a street girl." She cried and scolded and kept on telling me that I was putting her alive into her grave. That's all I heard for days. I tried to explain: "Well, mamma, what's the difference? When we go to church I'll put on the Russian dress and shawl, but if you want me to go to work I have to look decent." "Decent? Well, only the Russian dress is decent." "Mamma, you want me to compete with the American girls and get as much money as they do. How can I when they look at me so funny and think I am so strange? We are in America now, and we have to work with Americans, and we have to dress like they do." She never saw my point. And my older sister would do everything I did. I had to fight it out for both of us. . . .

Interviewer: Just how did you fight it out?

Mrs. P.: How? I continued to wear American clothes I wanted to buy and wear. I rebelled against homemade clothes.

Interviewer: When did you start buying your own clothes?

Mrs. P.: When I started going to dances and I needed some nice evening clothes.

Interviewer: Yes?

The moral code of the immigrant youth is greatly influenced by urban standards. Ridicule is a powerful solvent of customary modes of life as the immigrant child seeks for status in the outer world.

Change in the mores: Change of dress implies only change in conventions but change in social relations among people of marriageable age strikes at the root of the mores and of family life.

Mrs. P.: I then began to resent turning over all my earnings to the folks. I gave them my whole pay envelope without even opening it. At first I felt proud that I could help out at home, but when the girls began to make fun of me and call me a "young fool," I began to think about how hard I worked and how little I was getting in return. I sure worked hard for my money. My parents allowed me fifty cents a week.

Interviewer: What was your parents' reaction to your going to dances?

Mrs. P.: The real fight started then, since I was going with an American fellow. We went out to dances together, at first without my parents' knowing it. But they nagged every time I wanted to go out in the evening, and once I said to them: "Well, you may just as well know the truth. I am going to a dance with an American fellow." My mother started with her "putting her in the grave alive"; and my father said: "You just don't have any shame at all. You have lost your soul. You have no conscience. You talk so openly and tell us so boldly that you are going with an American fellow."

Interviewer: Well, what happened then?

Mrs. P.: I was miserable. You get hell if you don't tell them the truth, and you get hell if you do. What was I to do? I told them that I did not intend to marry this fellow, that I did not care for him enough to marry him; I was just going out to have a good time. "A good time? Going to a dance? Well, that's a disgrace and a sin, and the ruination of a girl."

Interviewer: What was your reaction to that?

The girl's wish for new experience asserts itself against her parents' wish for security.

Problems of the cultural hybrid: Differences in table etiquette are apt to prove high barriers to social contacts since they frequently arouse disgust in the other group and produce great sensitiveness in the novice.

Family solidarity is still strong in the young woman, but she feels no responsibility to group mores. Her behavior is compromised for purely personal considerations for her parents, and not because of group standards.

Mrs. P.: Of course, I couldn't agree with them on that score. I had to have some fun. There were several American fellows whom I liked real well. Sometimes I sure had a wild time.

Interviewer: How did you feel in the presence of your American friends?

Mrs. P.: It wasn't all joy traveling in such high society. When I went out with American men, I did not know American table manners. At home we eat from the family dish. I was not used to several kinds of forks, knives, and spoons. Well, I watched carefully which of the implements the fellow picked up, and followed suit. But the ordering was a problem. I did not know how to order from a menu. I made a mess of it once or twice, and the next time simply asked him to order. Once I picked up a whole quarter of a pie and ate it right out of my hand. Not until my pie was all gone did I realize that I should have used a fork. . . .

Interviewer: How long did you keep company with this American fellow?

Mrs. P.: Oh, I continued to go out with him for a long time. . . . My parents became more and more anxious about my future. I wanted to marry him. My father would shake his head and look at me very sad. I had a troubled conscience. I used to say to my parents: "Now, if you will only trust me I'll never disappoint you. It's no crime to go out with an American and have a good time. If you will have faith in me, it will help me, and you will never be sorry for it. I'll try to be more like you want me to be." I would always spring such a speech on them when they were in a good humor. They disliked it, but they

Mrs. P. has divided loyalties and is unable to attain personal integration.

This is a strong evidence of the girl's emancipation from the traditional marriage norms of her group, where the child's wishes are subordinated to the will of the family and community.

Youth stresses personal distinction of individual members; the group stresses social unity and equality.

Youth generally still fears social ostracism. The individual girl is aware that she might "break her mother's heart," but if she had social backing, she could win her mother's approval later.

Loss of social control is manifested in the girl's refusal to be influenced by traditional modes of thinking and believing. She reflects upon her conduct. Modern progress is, of

could not help themselves. All Russian girls did the same, and a lot of them ran away from home and married Americans. I used to argue with my parents, and they would say: "You would not break our hearts; you would not disgrace us and marry out." Well, I just never had the heart to go against their wishes.

They trusted me, and I promised them that I would not disappoint them. But I am sorry that I lived my life for them. I am young, I am self-supporting, and I should be entitled to decide for myself and live my own life. They should never have asked me to please them alone.

Interviewer: How deeply in love were you with this man?

Mrs. P.: Well, I don't know. I believe I really loved him. I really wanted to marry an American fellow.

Interviewer: Why? (Sympathetically.)

Mrs. P.: Well, I don't know, but our men believe that they are boss, but in the American home the woman is looked up to, and naturally our girls want to get as much recognition as is due them, and prefer the American men. The trouble is that some girls don't always get the right kind of fellows, and pretty soon they are back in the mother's homes again, and are a disgrace to the family. My parents always talk about these girls. I ask them what about the Russian couples that don't get along. There we start arguing again.

Interviewer: You are pretty hard on the old folks.

Mrs. P.: Oh, well, we must argue, otherwise they will never change. They have come a long way since I started arguing with them. Why, there will never be progress in

course, a foreign idea to the older Russian peasant.

"Barriers of language put a curious limitation upon the sympathies." (N. S. Shaler, *The Neighbor*, p. 37.)

Social distance between parents and children widens as differences of age, of experience, of urban contacts widen. But accommodation occurs as youth approaches maturity.

Russian Town if the younger ones don't make the older ones change their notions.

Interviewer: How much influence do the children have upon their parents?

Mrs. P.: You should see how my kid brothers treat the old folks. They just don't have any respect for them. They don't even take the trouble to argue with them. They rule the folks. My father and mother have been in this country twenty-five years, and they cannot speak English. My father is in business [truck-driver] and of course has picked up some English—just enough to get by; but my mother just can't get along at all. My little brother comes home from school and starts telling her something of what had happened during the day. She listens to him, but cannot make out what he is saying, and he repeats to her, but she says: "Well, what are you talking about? I can't understand you." And he gets impatient: "Well, I am trying to tell you. Why can't you understand?" And both of them get mad. He runs out on the street and tells the boys all about it, and she never does know what happened. You see, they just don't speak the same language. The older children learned Russian, and they speak half English and half Russian to their parents, but they get along.

We always used to say to our parents, when they did not understand us, that they were old-fashioned; and when we were very mad, we would call them "ignorant." Now these little kids just tell them very plainly that they are stupid. My mother always tells us how she had to mind her parents. There never was any back-talk to her parents. When her father told her to do something, there was no "maybe" about it. My mother tells us that she, too, liked dancing. She says that when she was a child she danced in the woods on a floor of pine needles. But when she became of age, she put away all such childish things. . . . It's getting late, I must be going. . . .

SECOND INTERVIEW WITH MRS. PAVLOVA

(After greetings were exchanged, Mrs. P. at once resumed the conversation and appeared eager to talk.)

Mrs. P. shows insight into the problems of her group.

Mrs. P.: I have been thinking a lot of what we talked about last week. I really feel sorry for my parents. They are trying to do the best they know how. They are used to the Russian ways, and you can't change them in a few years. They have suffered so much in America, and they have seen such wickedness here, that they'd rather hold on to what they are accustomed to than to try to change and take on new ways. The children know that outsiders make fun of their parents, and sometimes they do not know who is right. They are just half-way between the American and the Russian ways.

Interviewer: When do you choose the Russian ways and when the American?

Emancipation from the group control is fairly complete when Mrs. P. fails to be influenced by the marriage ceremony—one of the most crucial moments of her life.

Loss of social control by the group over the young is also fairly advanced when the elder finds no method for dealing with "rebels." In the true primary group there is little which the individual can call his own private life.

Mrs. P.: Well, I married a Russian man, that ought to tell you. (Pause.) But even at the wedding I was still at the cross-roads. Something happened at my wedding I will never forget. During the confession the elder asked if I have ever drank, smoked, danced, or played cards. I sure did feel funny, as I was guilty of all four things he asked. He looked so steadily into my face, and I looked back at him; I don't know what struck me, for I said quite positively, "No, I never have." He sure did look queer at me. I know he did not believe me, but I was not going to tell him about my private affairs, and that sure is private, and he would not understand anyway.

Interviewer: Has the elder ever spoken to you since then?

Mrs. P. is still sensitive to gossip, and, therefore, is still in a measure controlled by her community.

Mrs. P.: No, I kept out of his road. I hardly ever go to church now. I have two Russian dresses and a shawl, and I dress up during some big doin's—the first day of a big holiday, or a feast, or a funeral, or a wedding. I never work on the first day of any holiday, but I don't like to go to *sobranie* because some women look down on me. They say I am too Americanized. . . .

Interviewer: How long have you been married now?

Indifference or hostility to the mores of the group and indifference to the highest social value—human life—is a significant indication of the extent of personal demoralization.

Mrs. P.: I have been married over two years. . . . My sister has been married seven years, and neither of us wants any children.

Interviewer: Would it be too personal to ask you why you don't have any children?

Mrs. P.: Nothing is too personal. . . . Well, we had enough of them at home. And then I figure, John and I don't get along. Why tie myself down to a family? It isn't fair to a baby. . . .

My mother and I never talk about sex life, but once she said it was a sin to be married and not bear children. I flared up and said: "Sin nothing! It's a sin to raise children as you did. We never had any shoes, and no education." Of course, she was deeply hurt, and said: "That's the thanks we get for suffering for you and raising you according to God's will. If the children did not have any education, they would feel happier and make their husbands happier." Sometimes I really think she

Mrs. P. as a cultural hybrid frequently oscillates from one set of standards to another, unable to strike a middle ground; this produces many tensions and much unrest.

is right. I wish I did not have an idea in my head.

Interviewer: How do you get along with your parents when you are in such a mood?

Mrs. P.: My parents think it's terrible the way we live. We fuss and quarrel. My mother is typical of the older generation. She is very religious and hard-working. She never puts herself first. She wants me to live like that. Well, why should I? Conditions have changed. I know many things my mother does not know. Why should I go back to the olden days and even olden ways? Why should I?

Interviewer: It's a question of what is best to do for everybody concerned.

Mrs. P.: It sure is strange. I don't like to live like my mother does, but I can't live like the Americans. Sometimes I think I am "advanced," as my parents say; but sometimes I just don't fit in anywhere. (Pause.) Now we are back to where we started. What am I to do? What could I do?

Interviewer: Do you belong to any of the Russian young people's organizations?

Mrs. P.: No. You see, that's like church. When I was much younger I took religion to heart, but not any longer. . . . I'll never forget when once some American girls played a trick on me. They gave me a pork sandwich and told me it was lamb. When I found out that it was pork, I fasted twenty-four hours. I did not tell my parents about it. They would have worried too much. But I sure have changed. And they have too. They have to change; they can't go on like they did in Russia. They say they change because they have to make a living. I say to them, "What do you care about a

Reflective thinking: The girl's application of hard logic to the rationalizations of the parents frequently embarrasses them. They cannot out-reason her, and she is aware of it.

Mrs. P's modes of behavior and thinking are typical of those of the cultural hybrid. Her loyalties are

living? You have to do as your religion orders you." Oh, sometimes they get a little mad and say, "Oh, you're too smart." They don't like an argument, they say, but they sure do argue. . . .

Interviewer: How does your husband react to such arguments?

Mrs. P.: Well, here we are. I have avoided talking about him. He is so uninteresting and I don't care much at times what he thinks. If I had to do it all over again, I would choose for myself—I want a companion and not only a man to live with.

Interviewer: He loves you.

Mrs. P.: I know he loves me, but he has very little to give me, and he approves of so few things in which I am interested that we have very little in common. When we are at home and I read a book, he says I love a book more than anything else in the world. I look at him and say to myself, "Oh, well, there is no use. We can't understand each other," and I go on thinking my own thoughts.

I feel sorry for him. I married him, and he loves me, and I have ruined his life as well as mine. I am just waiting every day for something to happen. I don't know what that something might be, but I am waiting. I have not the heart to leave him, because he would be disgraced. With the Russians, when a couple separate, there is a lot of gossip, and it's a disgrace to live apart. And I am sure that my parents would feel heartbroken. And here I am, living my life for my folks again. I married for them and continue to live with a man against my will—for them too. I don't know what is holding me to them.

Interviewer: You are very loyal to your parents.

frequently divided and she is unable to attain integration either in her own group or in that of the larger community. At times she becomes irritated at the decisions she makes in favor of her home, and considers the life of the sectarian group too burdensome. To compensate for this feeling she plunges into the "wild life" of the city with new vigor, but the obligations of her home and parents continue to reassert themselves.

Cultural barriers are hard to cross. Few people with immigrant backgrounds who continue to live in the area of first settlement have shown complete adaptation to outside or secondary social groups. Young people strive to approximate American social standards, but they find they lack that versatility and ingenuity which prolonged education supplies. They struggle with incompatible attitudes of two groups having irreconcilable social experiences.

Mrs. P.: Yes, I guess I must be. Otherwise I would have forsaken them long ago.

Interviewer: In which group do you feel most at ease?

Mrs. P.: I must admit that I feel most at ease in my own Russian community. I can't even get away for a few days without being lonely. . . . Perhaps I miss the arguments. (Jokingly.) But it sure is strange, the Americans feel cold, distant, unfriendly. . . . We all live together and stick together.

Interviewer: In view of what you say in which group do you believe you would be happier?

Mrs. P.: I don't believe I could give up my parents. I would have to be near them, but the whole colony is too much for me. . . .

Sociological Analysis of the Process of Interviewing Mrs. Pavlova

I. Establishment of *Rapport.*
   1. Assumption of role of sympathetic listener and "participant observer."
   2. Placing importance on own story, on inner life.
   3. Guiding the interview along lines of concern to interviewee and from her point of view.
   4. Assumption of objective attitude (though highly friendly) and refraining from passing judgments regarding interviewee's conduct.
   5. Refraining from invading interviewee's personality.
   6. Avoiding irrelevant questions or comments.
   7. Heightening social status (by allowing considerable time for interview, by assuming an attitude of reverence toward all accounts, by imparting belief that interviewee understands own situation and can master own problems).

[1] Pauline V. Young, "The Problems of a Cultural Hybrid," manuscript. This material appears in summary form in Pauline V. Young, *Pilgrims of Russian Town,* pp. 161–174.

II. Method of Approach to Understanding Situation.

   8. Provision of opportunity to reveal own experiences, dynamic propelling attitudes, and own reality.

   9. Provision of opportunity to explain own situation, from own point of view.

  10. Provision of opportunity to explain how own present reality relates to the reality of those around her.

III. Tracing Development of Behavior Patterns.

  11. Securing meaning of and reactions to earliest experiences to interviewee.

  12. Securing data regarding her relations with members of her group, with members of outside groups.

  13. Attempts to learn personality problems, conflicts, accommodations, range of attitudes, of sympathies.

  14. Attempts to see life as a natural sequence of events, in a definite social setting rather than as isolated experiences unrelated to social forces operative within the social environment.

IV. Attempts to Understand Social and Cultural Setting of Interviewee.

  15. Securing meaning of family organization, of family ties, and of family control to interviewee.

  16. Securing meaning of communal organization, of communal ties, of *mores*, and of social controls to interviewee.

  17. Securing meaning and interpretation of the life of outer groups by interviewee (from the standpoint of a cultural hybrid).

V. Attempts to Understand Personal and Social Philosophy of Interviewee.

  18. Securing meanings of the problems of cultural hybridism and of tensions assumed by interviewee.

  19. Securing meaning of group relations maintained by interviewee.

  20. Learning outlook on life of interviewee.

  21. Learning of plans for the future, of wishes and of hopes of interviewee.

VI. Laying Tentatively the Groundwork for Social Therapy.

  22. Attempts to orient interviewee to her life problems and bring her to a realization of the problems and issues a cultural hybrid faces in own group as well as in the larger community.

  23. Attempts to bring interviewee to a realization that her choice must be made on the basis of the extent of the satisfactions she achieves in either group and on the strength of ties and attachments she maintains in these groups.

Suggestions for Further Study

1. Review carefully E. R. Mowrer's analysis of the interview in *Domestic Discord* and show to what extent his method is applicable to the analysis of the interviews with which you are familiar. What is the advantage to the social worker of Mowrer's sociological analysis? What distinction does he make between diagnosis and analysis?

2. Compare critically Lundberg's methods of analysis with those of Mowrer. It is remarked that "By the statistical methods we would secure the central type and then study other cases in terms of their deviations

from this central type." Explain. Discuss the relative advantages and disadvantages of such procedure in social case work.

3. What does J. O. Chassell mean by the "experience variable"? How does his method of analysis of life histories differ from that of Mowrer's and Lundberg's? (See page 197, footnote 3.)

4. Analyze the Holt interview in terms of Mowrer's, of Lundberg's, and of Chassell's methods.

5. What are your reactions to the expressed purpose of the Holt interview? Formulate your statement of the purpose of this interview.

6. Comment on the interviewer's approach to the case.

7. What is your reaction to interviewer's statement beginning with "You are going around in circles. . . . " What might have been the reaction of the client? What else might have the interviewer said to the client?

8. What is your reaction to the interviewer's statement beginning with "She will not pretend to feel as you do. . . "? How would you have replied to the client?

9. What is the form of social interaction taking place between interviewer and Mrs. H.?

10. Using the client's statements as a starting point, formulate the replies which you would give if you were interviewing Mrs. H.

11. Review the methods and processes under the analysis of the interview and point out where they best fit the interview as recorded.

12. Write out the Arthur interview in dialogue form, using the clues as reported in the case.

13. Comment critically upon the interviewer's approach to Mr. Arthur.

14. Indicate where the minds of the interviewer and interviewee succeeded or failed in meeting.

15. Analyze the Arthur interview in terms of the concepts used in the Holt interview; in terms of the concepts used by Stuart Queen in the interview with Mrs. A.

16. Walter Bingham observes that it matters little whether the technical labels used in the analysis of interviews are "common phrases, slang terms, algebraic symbols, or derivatives from the Greek," as long as these terms are defined accurately and precisely.[1] What are your reactions?

17. Comment on the objections raised to the analysis of the interview on the basis that interviews cannot be analyzed since "the variables are too numerous and complex," or because the "results have been appraised subjectively" instead of being "objectively measured." How valid are these objections in your opinion? How can the handicaps mentioned be overcome? Should we discard the analysis of the interview altogether because of these handicaps?

18. What is the relation between the verbal and nonverbal parts of the A. interview?

19. To what extent is Mrs. A. conditioned by the interviewer's questions and comments?

[1] "The Personal Interview Studied by Means of Analysis and Experiment," *Journal of Social Forces*, VII (June, 1929), 530–553.

20. Does the reported analysis of this interview indicate such conditioning?

21. How does Mrs. A. interpret the interviewer's statements?   Do their minds meet?

22. Analyze the A. interview in terms of the stimulus-response pattern.

23. Indicate when Mrs. A. takes the initiative and how the interviewer's reply is affected and vice versa.

24. Analyze one of your own interviews according to Professor Queen's method.   What is the advantage of such an analysis?

25. Do you make the same inferences as stated in the analysis?

26. What are the objectives of the A. interview as you see them?

27. What does Professor Queen mean by "other conscious thinking"? Do you agree with the logic of this reported thinking?   What other thoughts suggest themselves to you?

28. Interchange analysis of the techniques and processes between the Arthur, the Holt, and the A. interviews and discuss the results obtained.

29. On the basis of the reported analyses of the above interviews, write out a plan of treatment (as far as possible with the information at hand).

30. The above three interviews are analyzed in terms of techniques and processes.   Write an analytical statement of the information obtained in these interviews.

31. How does the analysis of the Pavlova interview differ from that of those reported above?   What are the relative advantages and disadvantages of this form of analysis?

32. Is this form of analyzing the data of the interview separately and the technique of interviewing separately applicable to cases with which your agency deals?

33. Apply this form of analysis to the Holt and Arthur cases as far as the situations permit.

34. Outline a plan of treatment on the basis of the facts given by Mrs. Pavlova.

35. Outline a plan of treatment keeping in mind both the facts stated by Mrs. Pavlova and the analysis of the data.

36. Formulate your own analysis of the interview with Mrs. Pavlova.

37. Secure an interview with a cultural hybrid of a different social group and work out a method of analyzing the data; the method of interviewing.

Selected Bibliography

1. AMERICAN ASSOCIATION OF SOCIAL WORKERS: *Interviews: A Study of the Methods of Analyzing and Recording Social Case Work Interviews*, 1928.
   Many verbatim interviews and analyses in terms of techniques and processes involved in interviewing.

2. BOGARDUS, E. S.: *Sociology*, 1934.
   Gives clear and concise explanation of sociological terms essential in sociological analysis.

3. COLCORD, JOANNA C.: "A Study of the Techniques of the Social Case Work Interview, with Discussions," *Journal of Social Forces*, VII (June, 1929), 519–527.

A sample interview is reproduced verbatim, and the techniques and processes analyzed in terms of "conscious purposes," "tensions," "social processes," etc.

4. LUNDBERG, GEORGE A.: "Case Work and the Statistical Method," *Journal of Social Forces*, V (September, 1926), 61–65.

   Points out that the case method is the initial step in scientific method. Interviews need to be analyzed and subjected to statistical treatment.

5. MOWRER, E. R.: *Domestic Discord*, 1928.

   Chapter VI, "The Process of Diagnosis," differentiates between diagnostic and analytical factors; discusses the data required for analysis; presents and analyzes case of domestic discord in terms of "family organization," "cultural pattern," "social interaction," "factors in conflict and adjustment," and "rationalizations."

6. MYRICK, HELEN L.: "Psychological Processes in Interviewing," *The Family*, VII (March, 1926), 25–29.

   Many psychological factors—emotions, attitudes, prejudices of interviewer and interviewee—affect the course and nature of the interview. Presents outline for analyzing and recording interviews; presents case, analyzes it and discusses technique.

7. MYRICK, HELEN L.: "The Non-verbal Elements in the Interview," *Journal of Social Forces*, VI (June, 1928), 561–564.

   Study by Chicago Chapter of American Association of Social Workers emphasizes psychological concepts in dealing with relation of psychological to physical activities in the social interview.

8. MYRICK, HELEN L., and ADA E. SHEFFIELD: "Reflective By-products of a Social Treatment Interview," *Journal of Social Forces*, III (May, 1925), 657–665.

   A report of an interview by the first author and an analysis by the second.

9. PARK, ROBERT E., and E. W. BURGESS: *An Introduction to the Science of Sociology*, 1921.

   Supplies definitions of sociological concepts essential to an understanding of a sociological analysis of interviewing.

10. QUEEN, STUART A., "Social Interaction in the Interview: An Experiment," *Journal of Social Forces*, VI (June, 1928), 545–558.

    Several verbatim interviews presented and analyzed in terms of what goes on in an interview due to gestures, tone of voice, facial expression— as distinct from inferences and thought processes of visitor.

CHAPTER XII

PERSONALITY PROBLEMS IN INTERVIEWING

Scientific Viewpoints on Personality[1]

In daily practice the interviewer may be quite unaware that any theory of personality enters into his interviewing. Indeed he may be wholly innocent of any consciously accepted formal theory, yet his judgments of and reactions to the interviewee indicate by implication his conception of personality and its springs to action.

Scientific professional work assumes that one utilize as far as possible the available scientific theories in daily practice. Judgments of personalities and personality traits are inherent in almost all interviews.[2] The interviewer attempts to estimate the interviewee's intelligence, or cooperativeness, or sociality, or reliability; and the interviewee searches for a sympathetic attitude, or a domineering attitude, or cordiality, or craftiness, or generosity. Adjustment in the interview is constantly made on the basis of interpretations of each other's traits.

A vast amount of data regarding personality and its traits has been accumulated in scientific fields by research conducted from various points of view. There is no agreement, however, among the scientists as to nature, evolution, development, or changes of personality under given social conditions. M. A. May observes that the interpretation of personality is closely linked with the particular science which studies it:

A group of psychologists, psychiatrists, neurologists and physiologists, who by training and temperament have become interested in inner

---

[1] An adequate discussion of personality would require a separate volume. The present brief review is intended only to stimulate the student to read further and to acquaint himself with some of the sources. The serious student owes it to himself to read widely in this field. One of the crucial tests of professional competency is the adequacy of the student's theory of personality and the skill with which he utilizes it in practical work.

[2] For a discussion of the dangers involved in "character analysis" see K. Dunlap, "The Reading of Character from External Signs," *Scientific Monthly*, XV (1922), 153–165.

mechanisms, and their biological antecedents, believe that the foundation stones are in the shape of reflexes, habit patterns, muscle tensions, tissue wants, metabolism, or else in the shape of instincts, impulses, urges, drives, complexes, motives, and the like. Another group of psychologists, psychiatrists, sociologists, and cultural anthropologists, who by their training and temperament have become interested in the social environment and its cultural antecedents, find the foundations of personality in group codes, social standards, family adjustments, living conditions, economic standards, or else in culture patterns, such as customs, mores, types of language, beliefs, superstitions and other manifestations of social traditions.[1]

A rapid review of numerous modern points of view may accomplish at least two purposes for the interviewer. First, such a review will acquaint him sufficiently with the current theories of personality to enable him to recognize a particular theory held by the scientists and specialists whose help or advice he seeks in working out a case work problem. It is of importance that the interviewer understand to what extent the psychologist, for instance, who examines a client relies on the native instinct theory of personality, or to what extent he believes personality is a product of the social environment; it is important to know what is involved when a psychiatrist proposes alteration of personality by means of social reconditioning or by means of glandular treatment. The interviewer must be keenly aware of the theories of the specialists he meets in order not only to follow their discussion intelligently, but to be able to adopt, modify, or reject their recommendations and to follow adequately a consistent plan of treatment.

Secondly, the interviewer needs a review of the current theories of personality to provide him with some basis for independent judgment. He may not be able to construct a theory of personality of his own, but yet by comparison of various theories he learns to analyze social situations from various angles and points of views.

Furthermore, a study of personality is of vital importance to the interviewer, as it will supply him with some knowledge as to how to approach interviewees with different personality traits and will lead him to appreciate better the interaction of his own personality with that of the interviewee. Successful intercourse,

[1] M. A. MAY, "Foundations of Personality," in *Psychology at Work* (edited by P. S. Achilles), p. 99.

motivation, satisfaction of the wishes, elimination of conflict, and so on obviously depend to a large degree upon knowledge of the nature of personality and of personality traits.

The Genetic Theory of Personality.[1]—The scientist is rare today who still wholly relies for an explanation of the nature of personality on native instincts, original nature, hereditary equipment. But there is a group of modern psychologists[2] who point out that there is a tendency—of various degrees and strengths—for individual temperaments to be predetermined and to grow and develop according to genetic types. There is another group who recognize the presence of certain original tendencies at birth and the social conditioning of these tendencies before birth sets in, but limited by "the inner metes and bounds to the area of conditioning."[3]

To the extent that personality is specifically predetermined by genetic factors the case worker is debarred from developing or reconditioning the personality of the interviewee and will be compelled to achieve social adjustments by reorganization of communal factors. There is always a subtle danger in dealing with difficult personalities that the worker will consciously or unconsciously jump to the conclusion that the failure of the client to respond to treatment is due to constitutional limitations. Such a diagnosis tends to put a check upon further efforts to adjust the client by direct methods. The worker at this point is only too apt to fall into ready rationalizations for failure to secure adjustment.

Personality from the Standpoint of the Behaviorist.[4]—The behaviorist tries to understand life and human personality through observation of biophysical and biosocial stimuli and responses.

To the behaviorist sensory-motor function is the element of human as well as of animal behavior, the element in a process by which an individual becomes a part of society. This conception of a "reflex psychology" grew out of the work of a physiologist, Pavlov.

[1] E. Kretschmer, *Physique and Character* (translated by W. H. J. Spratt).
  C. R. Stockard, *The Physical Basis of Personality.*
[2] Helen T. Wooley, *A Handbook of Child Psychology.*
  R. W. Washburn, *Genetic Psychological Monograph*, VI (1929), 397–537.
[3] A. G. Gesell, *The Guidance of Mental Growth in Infant and Child.*
[4] John B. Watson, *Psychology from the Standpoint of a Behaviorist.*
  M. C. Jones, *A Handbook of Child Psychology.*
  I. P. Pavlov, *Conditioned Reflexes.*

Pavlov, a Russian, was accustomed to start the flow of saliva in his experimental dogs by the stimulus "food." He soon noticed, however, that the animals began to salivate before the food was in their mouths; often the mere sight of the food, or rattle of the pan—even the sound of the keeper's footsteps—would be sufficient to stimulate a secretion. This second hand type of stimulation seemed so significant to Pavlov that he concentrated his attention upon it—named it "conditioned stimulation," and the reflex (salivary secretion) which followed "a conditioned reflex." He experimented with these conditioned reflexes under many different controls, noting that he could condition the dog's behavior almost any way he cared to.

If, for instance, for a few occasions he offered food and sounded a bell at the same time, later the mere sound of the bell would produce the flow of saliva. Again if he struck a tuning fork of high pitch while offering food, and at other times struck a low note, offering no food, the dog would salivate for the high note, but not for the low note. The dog "learned" *without the intervention of consciousness,* to expect food with one note and not with the other.

Pavlov found also that he could "uncondition" a reflex by training. For example, after frequent association of bell and food had accustomed the dog to expect food, frequent stimulation of the bell alone caused him in time to cease salivating.

It is in this way, by associating stimuli with response, that reflexes are built up—simple and complex, and highly involved integrations of reflexes. The actual application of this theory to human behavior was carried out by other Russian investigators—Bekhterev and Krasnogorski—and in America the experimental work was headed by J. B. Watson.[1]

Watson has strongly stressed environmental conditioning as the essential basis of emotional life and has to a large degree succeeded in shaking the traditional point of view of hereditary predeterminism of personality. He says:

Let us mean by the term personality an individual's total assets (actual and potential) and liabilities (actual and potential) on the reaction side. By assets we mean first the total mass of organized habits; the socialized and regulated instincts; the socialized and tempered emotions; and the combinations and interrelations among these; and secondly, high coefficients both of plasticity (capability of new habit formation or altering of old) and of retention (readiness of implanted habits to function after disuse). Looked at in another way, assets are

---

[1] GLADYS C. SCHWESINGER, *Heredity and Environment* (edited by Frederick Osborn), pp. 387–388. Reprinted by permission of The Macmillan Company.

that part of the individual's equipment which make for his adjustment and balance in his present environment and for readjustment if the environment changes.

By liabilities we mean similarity of that part of the individual's equipment which does not work in the present environment and the potential or possible factors which would prevent his rising to meet a changed environment.[1]

This conception of personality provides clarity of approach, but it does not provide a basis for understanding how personality reveals its modes of responding to social, psychical, and physical stimuli. Furthermore, it is pointed out that the behaviorists in general ignore the inner experiences of a person, do not concern themselves with how he feels and thinks, and "find it unnecessary to postulate an 'experiencing individual' (consciousness) as a reference point to which behavior is to be attached."[2]

Despite this shortcoming, the interviewer who can achieve the objectivity urged by the behaviorist and who cultivates the habit of noting carefully the overt behavior of the interviewee during the interviewing process will inevitably improve in interviewing technique. That is, social work can make considerable use of behavioristic methods in the development of its techniques without committing itself to the theories of behaviorism.

Personality from the Standpoint of the Gestalt Psychologist.[3]— The Gestalt psychologist, on the other hand, stresses inner experience of an individual and does not think of behavior apart from the experiencing individual.[4] Miss Schwesinger summarizes the Gestaltist's viewpoint as follows:

There is something over and above summation of parts which makes up a whole; there is the attachment and integration of parts one with another. By breaking a thing up into elements, one destroys the concept one is trying to explain. Elements must be held together by something; it is this assumption of a "tying-togetherness" which, in itself, cannot be explained; which, in essence, distorts the interpretation of a

---

[1] J. B. WATSON, *Psychology from the Standpoint of a Behaviorist*, p. 394.

[2] GLADYS C. SCHWESINGER, *Heredity and Environment*, p. 393.

[3] W. KÖHLER, *Gestalt Psychology*.

K. KOFFKA, *The Growth of the Mind*.

GLADYS C. SCHWESINGER, *op. cit.*, pp. 393–402.

W. I. THOMAS, "The Configurations of Personality," in *The Unconscious —A Symposium*.

[4] For a contrasting point of view read Nels Anderson and Eduard C. Lindeman, "Urban Personality," *Urban Sociology*, Chap. XI.

"whole being made up of the sum of its parts." Gestalt, whether of physical or psychological data, implies an inherent interrelation or wholeness of structure and function. Gestalt psychologists refer to the work of earlier "associationist" schools as a "brick and mortar psychology," with emphasis on the bricks, but no light on the mortar. . . .

Gestalt psychology holds that personality is not a mere sum of separate traits (however accurately these may be measured!), but an organized whole, which includes the relation of one trait to all the others, and of the organism to its environment. Personality is an "historical and experiential" continuum—a Gestalt.[1]

This conception of personality stresses the importance of knowing as much as possible about a person and the dangers involved when one tries to interpret behavior in the light of bits of information. The interviewer learns that since life is woven into an inseparable whole, interpretation of a single activity or an isolated experience becomes very inadequate. This point of view is widespread in social work and grew up independently of psychological sanctions. For example, juvenile court procedure has abandoned the older criminal law method of dealing with the isolated criminal act as such and now attempts to deal with the total personality of the child, interpreting the delinquent act with reference to the entire life situation of the child.

The interviewer soon discovers in practical work that it is exceedingly dangerous to accept responses and bits of behavior at face value. The social matrix in which the response has its roots must be known if it is to be correctly interpreted. That is, while the worker's observational technique is greatly benefited by use of behavioristic methods, the interpretation of the social data so acquired can be interpreted by use of the Gestaltist's method of analysis. Social work deals not simply with overt acts but with social meanings.

Personality from the Standpoint of the Modern Psychiatrist.[2]— The modern psychiatrist has enlarged Pavlov's conception of conditioned reflexes and has included a whole series of integrated reflexes, emotional responses and mental reactions. The psychia-

---

[1] GLADYS C. SCHWESINGER, *op. cit.*, pp. 393–396.

[2] ADOLF MEYER, *A Psychiatric Milestone.* See also the work of the *National Committee for Mental Hygiene* (especially since 1921).

WILLIAM A. WHITE, *Forty Years of Psychiatry.*

EMIL KRAEPELIN, *Psychiatrie.*

A. J. ROSANOFF (Editor), *Manual of Psychiatry* (6th ed.).

trist studies personality expressions and problems in their relation to the emotional life and neurosis. Dr. Rosanoff writes of the relation of the traits of the normal and abnormal personality:

Among the traits *qualitatively* distinguishing normal personality are to be mentioned inhibition, emotional control, a superior durability of mind, rational balance, and nervous stability. The result of the lack of these traits is psychopathic individuals, and only secondarily direct observations of them have enabled us to preserve and evaluate them in normal individuals.

Normal persons are not free in most cases from selfish motivations and anti-social or violent or destructive impulses, but are distinguished mainly by ability to inhibit them; they are of course not free from emotion but seem to possess a controlling mechanism whereby they are protected from excessive emotional manifestations, i.e., at least to the extent of preventing interference with steady and purposeful activity.
. . .

Turning our attention to *quantitative* contrasts between abnormal and normal types of personality, we find, as the most significant fact of experience, that either between the different abnormal types or between them and normal types sharp lines of demarcation cannot be drawn: mixed types are the rule, pure types the exception.[1]

The psychiatrist, like the social worker, deals with pathological situations and has many points of common contact. His types are, therefore, apt to lean heavily to clinical varieties and less to processual conceptions. Though the social worker may not be able or be ready to follow the psychiatrist in his attempt to develop a theory of personality, yet the experiences of the psychiatrist in dealing with diseased minds is invaluable to the social worker. The psychiatric examination includes an effort to penetrate into the inner recesses of the mental processes of the patient. The diseased and the healthy mind do not meet, hence the psychiatrist is forced to employ highly developed interviewing methods if he is to get at the mental content and thought processes of his patient.

Since the psychiatrist is a medical man by training, biological factors weigh heavily in his analysis of personality. He minimizes the role of social factors as thus his theories tend to restrict the field of operation of the case worker to manipulation of the

---

[1] A. J. ROSANOFF, "A Theory of Personality Based Mainly on Psychiatric Experience," *Psychological Bulletin*, Vol. XVII, No. 9 (September, 1920), 287–288.

communal resources.　The recent development of social psychiatry is a strong countermovement which emphasizes social experience and functional relations rather than genetic and organic factors.　This movement is an aspect of a larger movement which had its origin in the psychiatric field—the psychoanalytic movement.

Personality from the Standpoint of the Psychoanalyst.[1]—There is considerable dissension among psychologists, sociologists, and psychiatrists as to the nature of personality, but it is possible to present their views in more or less general terms.　The psychoanalytic viewpoints, on the other hand, are so divergent that each school must be presented separately.

Personality, from the standpoint of Freudian psychoanalysts, develops because an individual's opposing, expressive, resisting tendencies create tensions in an attempt to meet the counterdemands put upon him.　Freud's theory is based chiefly on the conceptions of (1) infantile sexuality as motivated in behavior; (2) the unconscious, including forbidden, feared, repressed wishes which are powerful and strongly emotionally toned, but unrecognized by the individual laboring under them.　Many of these personal wishes conflict with group custom, particularly those associated with sex life and, therefore, tensions develop; (3) polarity and dualism of ego and libido (that force by which the sexual instinct is represented in the mind), of ego-ideal (identified as conscience); (4) mechanisms of adjustment, such as repression, conversion, rationalization, daydreaming, etc., which the individual develops in his attempts to harmonize his own desires with the established practices of those of his social group.

The task of the psychoanalytic interviewer, therefore, is to guide and cause the patient to relive earlier experiences which have contributed to emotional conflict and to discover those defense mechanisms which are designed to drain off tensions but

[1] For a comprehensive summary of the major concepts of this field see
WILLIAM HEALY, AUGUSTA BRONNER, and ANNA M. BOWERS, *The Structure and Meaning of Psychoanalysis.*

GLADYS C. SCHWESINGER, *Heredity and Environment*, pp. 417–445.
For a discussion of Neo-Freudians see
J. JASTROW, *The House that Freud Built.*
S. ALEXANDER, *Psychoanalysis of the Total Personality.*
OTTO RANK, *Technik der Psychoanalyse.*
S. FREUD, *Psychopathology of Everyday Life: Group Psychology and the Analysis of the Ego.*
See "Psychoanalytic Interviewing," Chap. I, pp. 16–18.

which in reality are only a compromise between fears, urges, and group controls.

Alfred Adler,[1] a disciple of Freud, maintains that personality problems and neuroses are due primarily to feelings of inferiority created because of physical, social, and intellectual defect or weakness—which bring in their wake frustration and maladjustment. A frustrated wish to power drives an individual to pretend success, or to invent excuses or to make arrangements with himself, and in short to create a style of life which will enable him to hide his weakness or defect. Adler differs greatly from Freud on the matter of sex. Adler says:

Sexual components cannot even be correctly estimated except in relation to the individual's style of life. The erotic phases are functions of this individual life-style, and we can gain insight into the erotic life with all its waywardness, hesitation and elusive subtleties, only so far as we grasp the individual's style in the prototype. By the prototype I mean the original form of an individual's adaptation to life. The psychic prototype is a finished being by the time the child is four years old.[2]

The interviewer gains from Adler's writings the importance of establishing self-confidence and a feeling of security and of providing a wider range of activity so the person who undervalues himself and his achievements may find self-expression in other fields.

Jung, also a disowned disciple of the Freudian school of psychoanalysis, postulates a libido, or an urge to life, as the motive force in activity, but a libido more inclusive than sexuality described by Freud, since according to Jung the libido contains within it affects other than those arising from sexual drives— artistic, religious, moral drives.[3] Jung's study of personality types has been particularly helpful to the interviewer: the introvert and the extrovert, which are not mutually exclusive. The extrovert is aggressive, interested in others, absorbed in the social environment, and finds expression through overt action and feeling. The introvert is deliberate in his actions, holds himself aloof, expresses himself through reflection, and creates a rich inner life.

[1] *The Problems of Neurosis.*
[2] *Ibid.*, p. 93.
[3] C. G. JUNG, *Collected Papers on Analytical Psychology.*

Psychoanalytic theory has stimulated far-reaching researches in the field of personality. Though there is little general acceptance of any of the varied points of view in this field, yet the concepts have gained wide currency and are very useful in practical social diagnosis. The interaction processes in interviewing are readily analyzable in psychoanalytic terms.

Personality from the Standpoint of the Mental Hygienist.[1]— Proponents of mental hygiene and of institutes of child guidance have carried Gestalt psychology into the clinical laboratory and have concentrated on the structure of personality as the "product of all that has gone before, including not only original constitution but the modifying influences of the development of life itself."

The only safe method for the interviewer is to explore as completely as possible the individual's background, early experiences, his own reactions to them, and to study not only overt behavior, but the emotional complexes and inner life. The overemphasis of intellectual factors in the approach of many psychologists to the problems of personality and the overemphasis of biological, genetic, and pathological factors of the psychiatrists have been considerably modified in the work of the mental hygienist.

Personality from the Standpoint of the Social Psychologist.— Floyd Allport contends that although the physiological basis of personality traits lies wholly in the individual, these traits are, nevertheless, evoked only through the social environment or the social group:

A man's self-assertion, submission, quickness of temper, suspicion, pride and inferiority are all dependent upon the existence of other human beings toward whom these attitudes may be displayed. His refinement, tact, and morality could not have come into existence without social instruction and control. The hermit exhibits little personality, except in the sphere of pure intelligence. The social side of his nature, while latent as a physiological possibility, remains unexpressed because his solitary environment contains no stimuli adequate for evoking it. With the exception of a few traits, personality may be defined as the individual's characteristic reactions to social stimuli, and the quality of his adaptation to the social features of his environment.

In its genetic development, also, personality is dependent upon social contacts. Only recently have we realized the importance of the early

[1] L. G. LOWREY (Editor), *Institute for Child Guidance Studies.*

L. G. LOWREY, "Environmental Influences in the Evolution of Personality and Behavior," *Bulletin, New York Academy of Medicine* (second series), IV (1928), 871–880.

influences of parents and other relatives in the formation of lifelong attitudes toward self and society. Personality is therefore a result of social behavior.[1]

In the physical basis of personality Allport includes the following personality elements:

. . . qualities of nervous tissue underlying intelligence, physiological characteristics as exemplified by speed of function in nerve and muscle, levels of visceral and glandular response, and finally such simple anatomical aspects as stature, beauty, deformity, and the like. While some of these qualities may be influenced by environmental conditions (use, accident, disease, etc.), they are for the most part ascribable directly to the native constitution of the individual and the laws of growth.[2]

In the second group of personality-forming elements Allport includes the systems of habits developed in the process of the individual's adjustment to the particular social environment:

. . . An intimate connection between native endowment and habit formation probably exists in the developmental trends of every personality. Level of native capacity may determine whether one shall learn a profession or a skilled trade. Visceral factors may direct a lifelong interest in art or other emotional pursuits. Special bodily defects frequently give rise to strong habit trends in the direction of overcoming them or compensating in other ways. Height and strength may contribute decisively to traits of leadership, while submissive habits commonly attend an inferior physique. Unconsciously Nature affirms in each personality her adaptive principle of making the most of what the organism has.[3]

Allport groups personality traits into five broad categories (with a number of subdivisions): (1) intelligence (capacity for solving the problems of life); (2) mobility (motor characteristics, such as speed, impulsiveness, control, skill); (3) temperament (feeling and emotion); (4) self-expression (drive, compensation, insight, expansion); (5) sociality (susceptibility of the individual to the influences of society).[4]

Much use of personality traits has been made by social workers. The observation of the traits displayed by an interviewee are

[1] FLOYD HENRY ALLPORT, *Social Psychology*, p. 101. Reprinted by permission of Houghton Mifflin Company.

[2] *Ibid.*, pp. 101–102.

[3] *Ibid.*, p. 102.

[4] *Ibid.*, pp. 104–125.

commonly entered in the case history, frequently under the heading "worker's impression." The difficulty in their use has been twofold: (1) the necessity for inferring the presence or absence of the trait from the actual behavior which, as observed, is a physical matter; and (2) the fact that traits are so closely related to the situation that the generalization of the trait is a matter of uncertainty. One is intelligent, honest, truthful, energetic, and so on under certain conditions and it is important to know the conditions which call forth the trait. Failure to state these conditions may lead to erroneous judgments of the behavior of the individual. It is for this reason that many of the pencil-and-paper personality tests do not reveal the traits of the subject.

Personality from the Standpoint of the Sociologist.[1]—The sociologist approaches the study of personality from the standpoint of the meaning of the role or roles an individual assumes in a social group or groups. "By usage," say Park and Burgess, "personality carries the implication of the social expression of behavior. Personality may then be defined as the sum and organization of the traits which determine the role of the individual in the group."[2]

Park and Burgess list the following characteristics of the person which have an effect upon his social position and efficiency as a member of the social group:

a. Physical traits, as physique, physiognomy, etc.

b. Temperament.

c. Character.

d. Social expression, as by facial expression, gesture, manner, speech, writing, etc.

e. Prestige, as by birth, past success, status, etc.

f. The individual's conception of his role.[3]

These traits are of importance to the interviewer in so far as they enter into the role or dominate the life of the interviewee. Furthermore, it is of primary consideration to understand the role the individual conceives himself to play in relation to his fellows. The interviewer must ascertain, for instance, whether a given child conceives his role as that of a gang leader, of a truant,

---

[1] E. W. BURGESS (Editor), *Personality and the Social Group.*

[2] ROBERT E. PARK and E. W. BURGESS, *An Introduction to the Science of Sociology,* p. 70.

[3] *Ibid.,* p. 70.

or of a loyal devotee to home and school, or whether a given man plays the role of a nobleman, an urbanite, an invalid, a patriarchal father, etc. Little can be accomplished either in diagnosis or treatment until a thorough knowledge of the conception of the role that the interviewee assumes is gained.

Professor Cooley further develops the significance of the individual's conception of his role, in terms of the reflected self:

In a very large and interesting class of cases the social reference takes the form of a somewhat definite imagination of how one's self—that is any idea he appropriates—appears in a particular mind, and the kind of self-feeling one has is determined by the attitude toward this attributed to that other mind. A social self of this sort might be called the reflected or looking-glass self:

> "Each to each a looking-glass
> Reflects the other that doth pass."

As we see our face, figure, and dress in the glass, and are interested in them because they are ours, and pleased or otherwise with them according as they do or do not answer to what we should like them to be; so in imagination we perceive in another's mind some thought of our appearance, manners, aims, deeds, character, friends, and so on, and are variously affected by it.

A self-idea of this sort seems to have three principal elements: the imagination of our appearance to the other person; the imagination of his judgment of that appearance, and some sort of self-feeling, such as pride or mortification. The comparison with a looking-glass hardly suggests the second element, the imagined judgment, which is quite essential. The thing that moves us to pride or shame is not the mere mechanical reflection of ourselves, but an imputed sentiment, the imagined effect of this reflection upon another's mind. This is evident from the fact that the character and weight of that other, in whose mind we see ourselves, makes all the difference with our feelings. We are ashamed to seem evasive in the presence of a straightforward man, cowardly in the presence of a brave one, gross in the eyes of a refined one, and so on. We always imagine, and in imagining share, the judgments of the other mind. A man will boast to one person of an action—say some sharp transaction in trade—which he would be ashamed to own to another.[1]

This conception of personality in terms of the reflected self suggests that an interviewer, for instance, might easily influence

[1] Charles H. Cooley, *Human Nature and the Social Order*, pp. 183–185. Reprinted by permission of Charles Scribner's Sons.

or guide his clients' self-feelings, reflections, sentiments, judgments, and actions. The interviewer must then ascertain not only the clients' conceptions of their own role, but also what they understand the interviewer's role to be in relation to themselves.

Stuart Rice, in his discussion of the studies of personality made by Thomas and Znaniecki, summarizes the essentials as follows:

As Thomas and Znaniecki conceive personality, it is not something that can be described in static terms. It is not an action pattern or a system of habits merely. Personality is in constant evolution. It evolves, however, not merely under the influence of an environment which exists external to it, but more especially under the influence of an environment which it selects and defines and in a sense creates. In short, a man—and this distinguishes him from the lower animals—may be said to have a career.

A child comes into the world not merely without a character, but without personality. It is at the outset a mere bundle of reflexes. Its instincts, whatever they may be, are, in the language of Thomas and Znaniecki, temperament attitudes. Gradually, by a process that has been described elsewhere as conditioning, the child's impulses are integrated, and instincts are converted into habits. In the natural course, and under the influence of associations with other individuals, the child develops self-consciousness and a conception of himself. At the same time, and in the same natural way, he defines his role in a social group; he may define it in several social groups. In so doing, however, he gains a control over himself which he did not possess so long as his life was a mere series of more or less automatic responses to stimuli. In becoming self-conscious the child makes himself not merely an object, but he makes his life, as he projects it ahead of him in imagination, a project. Eventually he formulates principles of action and organizes his life in ways which seem likely to further his life aim. This conception of himself, and the codes and rules by which the individual seeks to maintain this conception and this project in a changing world, is what the authors mean by a life-organization.

With this conception of personality as growing up in response to the changing social situations, the authors have described three different types of personality with reference to their ability to adjust themselves to a changing moral world: the philistine, the bohemian, and the creative personality.

The philistine is the individual who conceives himself in the conventional social pattern; whose life-organization is taken over from, and stabilized in, the patterns which he finds in the society about him. The philistine achieves a consistent life and a stable character, but on such terms as "practically [to] exclude development of any new attitude in the given conditions of life."

Opposed to the philistine is the bohemian, "whose possibilities are not closed simply because his character remains unformed." The philistine is always a conformist, always "accepting social tradition in its most stable elements." The bohemian, on the other hand, is likely to be a radical, responding to every new program or project as it presents itself, but never able to achieve a stable character or make a career. In any case, "Inconsistency is the essential feature of his activity."

In contrast with the philistine and the bohemian is the creative personality. He is one who is able to maintain a consistent life-organization in a changing world; a man who, in order to widen his control over his environment and himself, learns "to adopt his purpose to the continually increasing sphere of social reality." . . .

Personalities, in short, may be distinguished with reference to their tendencies to grow. The philistine, with his tendency to develop a stark, fixed character, constitutes the solid structure of society. The more mobile bohemian, disposed as he is to reflect the changing aspects of social life, becomes a medium for communicating them. The creative personality makes the original contribution to culture.

Personalities may be further characterized by the degree to which they are predisposed by temperament or experience to respond to (1) the desire for new experience, (2) the need for security, (3) the desire for recognition, and (4) the desire for response.[1]

The person is an individual who has status. We come into the world as individuals. We acquire status, and become persons. Status means position in society. The individual inevitably has some status in every social group of which he is a member. In a given group the status of every member is determined by his relation to every other member of that group. Every smaller group, likewise, has a status in some larger group of which it is a part and this is determined by its relation to all the other members of the larger group.

The individual's self-consciousness—his conception of his role in society, his "self," in short—while not identical with his personality is an essential element in it. The individual's conception of himself, however, is based on his status in the social group or groups of which he is a member. The individual whose conception of himself does not conform to his status is an isolated individual. The completely isolated individual, whose conception of himself is in no sense an adequate reflection of his status, is probably insane.

It follows from what is said that an individual may have many "selves" according to the groups to which he belongs and the extent to which each of these groups is isolated from the others. It is true,

[1] STUART A. RICE (Editor), *Methods in Social Science*, pp. 170–172. Reprinted by permission of the University of Chicago Press. See also
W. I. THOMAS and F. ZNANIECKI, *The Polish Peasant in Europe and America*, pp. 1853–1863.
For a discussion of the four wishes see Chap. XVII, pp. 345–354.

also, that the individual is influenced in differing degrees and in a specific manner, by the different types of groups of which he is a member. This indicates the manner in which the personality of the individual may be studied sociologically.[1]

An understanding of the nature and development of personality helps to visualize the mental experiences the interviewee and the interviewer are undergoing when confronted by each other. The former in particular constantly defines his role in terms of what the latter may approve or sanction. The interviewer's task is to penetrate beyond the assumed role and discover the inner life and the real attitudes and values created by the interviewee in the process of his social becoming. If the interviewer is careful not to attack the status of the interviewee and not to put him on the defensive, he may succeed in learning the inside truths of the personality of the interviewee, his hopes, fears, plans, and the story of his private life. This is far more important than mere biographical sketches of the heads of the house and of their children, says Mary Richmond: "Families have their own plans, and their own ideals—more definite ones than the social worker realizes. These must be understood and taken into account from the beginning. All our plans otherwise will surely come to grief."[2]

Porter Lee summarizes the current social work conceptions of personality:

Personality is conceived as the combined functioning of the physical, intellectual, and emotional parts of the human organism.

For the social worker the conception of personality includes a conception of potential self-control with respect to the interests and relationships of the individual.

From one point of view the human personality is the highest product of evolution.

From another point of view it is a divine implantation.

From another point of view it is the seat of all which distinguishes significantly the human species from other species.

From another point of view it is the emanation of certain physical processes largely chemical in their nature.

Social case work seems to have been motivated by the point of view that handicapped and undeveloped individuals share the effort of the race to achieve satisfaction and are entitled, therefore, to a reasonably

---

[1] ROBERT E. PARK and E. W. BURGESS, *op. cit.*, p. 55.

E. W. BURGESS, "The Study of the Delinquent as a Person," *The American Journal of Sociology*, XXVIII (May, 1923), 657–680.

[2] *Social Diagnosis*, p. 126.

fair opportunity to participate in this general effort.   If this is so, then, to the social case worker, personality has a high value in itself.

The obligation of the social case worker with respect to the personality of his client would seem to be, first, to conceive of the client as having a dignity, a status, and a right to the control of his own affairs different in no particular from the dignity, status, and right to self-maintenance of any other human being.

When there is a conflict over the right of a personality to develop at the expense of others, the social worker may have to decide where his influence in the matter shall be thrown, and his decision must be guided not only by his respect for personality as such but by his consideration of factors which may not be apparent to those directly concerned.[1]

PERSONALITY TRAITS OF INTERVIEWERS

Successful interviewers have found the following social and personal traits of help in interviewing: Ability to attract people, which depends essentially on the ability to be interested in their experiences, interests, problems, and desires.   Ability to respond to their moods and thoughts.   Mental alertness in noting all turns in the story, in adapting oneself from moment to moment to the changing situation.   Ability to deal with unusual or unsavory social situations dispassionately.   Ability to sense and appreciate the dominant spirit of home, neighborhood, sect, gang, and ability to place individual or group in appropriate social setting.   (The individual cannot be understood apart from the social habitat which conditions his attitudes and social values.) Ability to carry on teamwork; to plan together with interviewee. Ability to be a good loser, when the other party is obstinate, belligerent, challenging, contrary, or when demanding a course of action which is not in accord with that the interviewer wishes taken.   Cordiality.   Respect for attitudes of interviewee and his social group, particularly of those interviewees who are not of the same race, or culture, or social class, or economic level.

E. W. Burgess says that the primary requisite of the social investigator is:

. . . a sense for the dramatic in all human life, a sympathy broad enough to encompass the manifold diverse manifestations of human nature, even those that are commonly regarded as shocking or even outrageous.[2]

---

[1] Quoted from the statements by Porter R. Lee by Mary A. Cannon and Philip Klein, *Social Case Work, An Outline for Teaching*, pp. 41–42.

[2] "Statistics and Case Studies as Methods of Sociological Research," *Sociology and Social Research*, XII (November-December, 1927), 118.

. . . Some persons are too rigid, too compulsive, and too impatient to make such investigations. Many attempts to secure "inside" information . . . are futile simply because the person doing the work has no flair for the proper manner of approach.[1]

Dr. Van Waters shows how personality traits enter into social work situations:

The adjusted personality, with the life of impulse, and life of reason in adequate balance has attained a position from which flows tolerance and understanding. The selfishness of the personality with inferior inhibition makes it difficult for him to appreciate struggles of others. Inhibition gives a tremendous driving force to personality and is perhaps the secret source of that superior durability which is the distinguishing characteristic of the normal person. . . .

"The normal personality has rational control." Applied to social workers the life of reason is seen in following a guiding-line, or clear idea, as over against the welter of everyday experience. . . . Ability to maintain against the confusion of our modern world, a clear concept of our place in nature, and our goal as social workers is to attain rational balance. . . .

The especial malady of social workers who deal with disordered human beings is a mood that fluctuates between enthusiasm and despair. . . .

Only steady, warm, continuous interest in human beings, ability to bring to each day's work fresh insight into manifold capacities of human nature to recuperate, can successfully combat unrest and delinquency. Perhaps that is the secret of influence of some fortunate personalities; they produce tranquillity because their emotional energy is flowing in a steady current that is not subject to sudden droughts or torrents. They are adjusted to life; they possess what Adolf Meyer calls *constructive composure*. . . .

The social worker's own emotional balance must be so steady that irritation, disappointment, petty set-backs from superiors, or co-workers have no power to alter the feeling-tone and need no outlet in displays of resentment, or distrust of the client. That the social worker . . . should be himself contented and secure in his personal and professional life needs no demonstration. Anything which unduly hampers him in the community, such as an impossible political situation, will make for insecurity, but the only force which can permanently destroy his work will be inner disharmony which expresses itself in lack of faith.

The mainspring of the social worker's influence over individual . . . is an absorbing interest in human experience. To the virile personality

[1] STUART A. RICE, *Methods in Social Science: A Case Book*, p. 521.

everything is an adventure, a test of strength; to the defeated, everything is dull. Children respond almost immediately to one who is filled with vital interests, that is to say, one whose emotional attitude toward life is sound. Affection flows toward the adult who can unlock the doors which hold the child a prisoner within himself. For example, no demonstration of affection on the part of Miss Sullivan, teacher of Helen Keller, had power to win the child, or to awaken interest until the child discovered that through her teacher she was in possession of new power to explore the world.[1] If the social worker is mature emotionally, it will be *expressed* in ability to nourish, rather than to absorb, life in others.[2]

Ruth S. Cavan has compiled opinions of 38 investigators as to the qualities and attitudes of a successful interviewer. She reports as follows:

	No. of Times Mentioned
Expert knowledge in the field of investigation	5
Broad general knowledge	2
Previous knowledge of the interviewee	1
Poise, interviewer should be organized emotionally, should understand himself	5
Prestige in the eyes of the interviewee	5
Good personal appearance, pleasant manner, well-dressed	5

Attitude toward interviewee:

Respect interviewee, understand his point of view, do not ridicule or talk down to him	19
Helpfulness, "here is a friend"	13
Non-moralistic or non-critical attitude, without emphasis on misdeeds of interviewee	13
Impersonal, detached, unsentimental, unsympathetic	11
Sympathetic	10
Unemotional, never feel surprise or shock	8
Responsiveness to interviewee, never bored	6
Impartial, unprejudiced	5
Be a good listener, give interviewee complete attention	4

General qualities, mentioned by only one or two persons:

Health, drive, perseverance, humor, patience, jollying, cheerfulness, punctuality, courage, business-likeness, ease in talking.[3]

---

[1] HELEN KELLER, *Story of My Life.*

[2] MIRIAM VAN WATERS, *Youth in Conflict*, pp. 247–252. Reprinted by permission of New Republic Inc.

[3] RUTH S. CAVAN, "Interviewing for Life-history Material," *The American Journal of Sociology*, XXXV (July, 1929), 104.

The following types of social workers—also applicable to interviewers—are based chiefly upon (1) the role which they conceive themselves to play and (2) their dominant personality traits.

1. The *salesman or missionary type of interviewer*, who thoroughly believes in an idea he has formulated and plans to "sell" to his interviewees. He is so strongly convinced of the integrity of his idea that he feels himself justified in using any device or sales talk which will break down resistance and override objections of interviewees or clients. This type of interviewer has great difficulty in appreciating the problems of his clients and in seeing those problems from their particular point of view. When he does see their problems he feels an urge to solve them without taking the client's point of view fully into consideration.

2. The *routine type of interviewer*, or the detailist, is generally concerned with performing certain routine operations, observing minute technicalities, such as filling out face-sheets, in a meticulous manner. He has little imagination or incentive and is apt to reduce social situations and relations to paper-and-pencil work. He goes through many motions but mistakes these motions for the thing itself. He does not see his clients as persons and rarely, if ever, gets acquainted with them. The job stands between them. He is overly conscientious on the one hand, but is apt to be a clock-watcher on the other hand. He rarely takes adequate stock of himself or carefully questions the product of his work.

3. The *research type of interviewer* is apt to regard all material obtained as equally relevant. He does not sort it out in terms of relative values. He tends to pursue bypaths at the expense of discovering the immediate problems confronting his interviewees or his agency. Often he is very shrewd and skillful as an observer but he is apt to fill his record with what interested him from a research point of view. He plays an important role in collecting and analyzing data but he should not be made responsible for diagnosis or treatment of cases. He is an abstract thinker and sees social situations in general—as a scientist—and neglects the specific immediate problems essential in the art of social work treatment.

4. The *therapeutic-nihilist type of worker* is generally on the lookout for pathological situations and social disease processes. He has research interests but in his approach he is primarily a clinician. He is inclined to allow pathological situations to run their whole course with little or no interference. He does not appreciate the practical objectives of case work. His energy is absorbed in diagnosis and not in therapy.

5. The *scatterbrain type of interviewer* stands in sharp contrast to the research type or the clinician. The former is talkative, cannot keep

the purposes or objectives of the interview in mind. His mind is undisciplined and his thoughts are unorganized to such an extent that he finds it difficult to get a well-rounded story from his interviewee or to plan with him in a consistent manner.

6. The *domineering type of interviewer* takes the lead too frequently and does not give his interviewees an opportunity to react to his proposals or plans. He often suffers from an inferiority complex which is hidden behind a superiority complex. He has little patience with poor, weak human nature. He is also apt to be brutally frank and to meet resistance in interviewees head-on and to trample rough-shod over their ideas and proposals. The domineering type of interviewer often puts leading questions into the mind of his interviewees and believes himself to be able to read their motives and desires from some casual remarks they are able to make or even by the look in their eyes.

7. The *moralistic type of interviewer* is usually intolerant toward the set convictions with reference to right and wrong to which his interviewees may happen to cling. He often openly clashes with his interviewees particularly if they are of different cultural, religious, or social groups. The moralistic type is apt to be mentally inflexible and is given to categorizing his clients in terms of "worthless," "irresponsible," "undeserving," "ne'er-do-wells," and so on.

8. The *"Paul Pry" type of interviewer* has a distorted set of social values and interests and "noses around" to discover things which the more wholesome person is frequently embarrassed to take note of. Frequently this type of worker has serious unsolved personal problems and he is not capable of developing and of carrying on satisfactory personal relations with his clients. Persons with such perverted interests seldom attain to full professional status.

9. The *sentimental type of interviewer* has little control over the emotions aroused in interviewing situations. He weeps with his clients or goes into ecstasy and sentimentalities over their situations. He identifies himself too easily and generally on the wrong basis with his interviewees.

10. The *give-and-take type of interviewer* sees situations from the clients' point of view and is able to accord them proper recognition of social and personal status. He is tolerant of divergent views and practices and is able to interact wholesomely with his interviewees. He plans with them and not for them and has genuine sympathetic insight into their problems.[1]

---

[1] Adapted from lecture notes by Erle F. Young, Professor of Sociology, University of Southern California. See also

Erle F. YOUNG, "What Type of Personality Should be the Goal of Social Case Work?" *Sociology and Social Research*, XVIII (November–December, 1933), 123–130.

The above is a rough classification by dominant traits of many interviewers. While it is clear that there are many undesirable types and few desirable ones, it must be remembered, however, that there may be social situations which occasionally require some one of the above types of interviewer. The administrative problem remains, however, of restricting their activities to those situations in which their traits may be used to best advantage.

Personality Traits of Interviewees

William C. Robinson and Richard Harris have analyzed the problem types found among witnesses in legal proceedings— largely based on temperamental traits—but these types are also found among the interviewees social workers meet in their daily practice.

The Rambling Witness: His Treatment. . . . In many individuals there apparently exists no power of fixing the attention on a single object and persistently pursuing its consideration, and from such an individual it is useless to expect any exhaustive and coherent statement of the facts within his knowledge. Any idea which suddenly arises in his mind, during the course of his narration, diverts his thought into another channel; he loses sight of many details which he should remember, and continues his relation without consciousness of the omission. If he endeavors to express this new idea, his effort to explain it leads him still further from his proper subject, and when he returns to it, if ever, it is at a point different from that at which it was abandoned, while the intermediate ideas, however necessary to the comprehension of the whole, are left unuttered. The examination of a witness of this defective mental character should be close and catechetical. The questions of the advocate should lead him step by step through the entire subject of his testimony, in logical order and without omissions. If he persists in rambling and irrelevant replies, he should not be rudely interrupted, for any mental shock or moral perturbation will increase his difficulties, but when he has finished what he wishes to relate, the question from whose true reply he has departed should be patiently repeated, and the examination pass from this point to the next only when the proper answer is obtained.

The Dull and Stupid Witness: His Treatment.—The same obstacles are encountered in eliciting the evidence of a dull and stupid witness. His perceptions are cloudy and indefinite. His processes of recollection and reflection are slow and disconnected . . . patience of the advocate in this examination must be inexhaustible. To take the witness again and again over his story in order to recall to him some event or fact

which seems to elude every effort of his memory, to construct questions
which contain some word or phrase suggestive of the missing thought,
to contrive methods of explanation or illustration which enable him to
make himself clearly understood by the jury, to afford him opportunities
for reconciling inconsistencies into which his misapprehension of the
questions or the inaccuracy of his replies has led him, taxes the ingenuity
and perseverance of the most adroit and indefatigable lawyers. . . .

The Timid and Self-conscious Witness: His Treatment.— . . . His attention is divided between the ideas which he is requested to present, and
the effect that he supposes is to be produced by their disclosure on
himself or on the cause. His apprehensions and conjectures often
work through his imagination on his memory, until without intending
falsehood he omits or colors facts to a degree irreconcilable with truth.
No sooner are his ideas uttered, however, than he becomes conscious
of their error. . . . Thus, with the best intentions at the outset, and
knowing matters of importance to the cause, a nervous, apprehensive
witness may finally retire suspected of the grossest perjury, and without
having related a single matter as it actually occurred. No witness who
is liable to this infirmity should be permitted to narrate material facts
until his embarrassment and fear are overcome. By simple questions
in reference to his occupation, residence, or relation to the parties of
the cause, eliciting replies in which mistake will be impossible, he should
be gradually assured that he is capable of understanding, and of properly
responding to, the inquiries which are to be proposed to him, and his
entire attention fixed on the proceeding in which he is now engaged.
When at last fully at his ease, the more material portions of his evidence
should be approached, the questions made, if possible, even more
simple and direct, and limiting the answer to the point required. . . .

The Bold and Zealous Witness: His Treatment.—The moral weakness
of a bold and zealous witness creates almost equal difficulties. He
also is self-conscious, but in him self-consciousness is manifested by
a high opinion of his discernment of the real requirements of the cause,
and of the importance and conclusiveness of his own evidence concerning it. . . . This witness requires the most prudent and at the same
time the most inflexible control. While he should not be irritated by
sensible restrictions, he must still be kept within the narrowest limits,
and his evidence confined in matter and expression to the precise truth
which it is necessary for him to disclose. . . . The entire examination
of this witness should be conducted with a view to the dangers which
will attend his cross-examination. Exaggerations in his evidence,
which are likely then to be exposed, should be corrected as soon as
made, by questions bringing him to some known standard and furnishing
a measure of his actual meaning. If he endeavors to conceal unfavorable facts which are certain sometime to appear, such inquiries should be
propounded as will now elicit them in the least unfavorable form. . . .

The Hostile Witness: His Treatment.—Incompleteness or obscurity in the testimony of a hostile witness is caused by difficulties of an entirely different character. The obstacles encountered in the examination of the rambling, the self-conscious, or the stupid witness arise from intellectual or emotional defects, and can be overcome by enlightening the mind of the witness, or by assisting him to bring his impulses under control. The obstacle encountered in an adverse witness, however, is an antagonistic will. He labors usually under no mental or emotional embarrassments. He knows clearly and precisely the facts which ought to form his evidence. He is able to narrate them positively and coherently, if he so chooses. But, actuated by interest, or partiality, or more secret impulses, he is determined to withhold the knowledge he possesses, or, if, compelled to yield it, to communicate it in language which will make it as valueless as possible. Where such a witness is the sole repository of ideas which are essential to the cause, the advocate has no other course than to produce him, and render him as useful as he may. Otherwise, he should avoid him altogether. For it is seldom that the benefit to be derived from such a witness is equal to the injury which his reluctance to assist and his perversion of the facts inflict. When, however, it becomes necessary to improve him, the advocate must first discover the cause and character of his hostility. If it be partial only, manifesting itself toward a single person or a single feature of the cause, it may be possible during the whole examination to ignore the objectionable individuals or issues, and to approach the witness solely upon matter concerning which he will freely testify. . . . Once in a good humor with himself and with the advocate, his motive for concealment or perversion of the truth exercises less influence upon his mind, and he replies with little hesitation to cautious inquiries which do not directly touch his prejudices, or present anew to him the exciting cause of his antagonism.[1]

The Flippant Witness.—When a witness comes into the box with what is commonly called a "knowing" look, and with a determined pose of the head, as though he would say, "Now, then, Mr. Counselor, I'm your man, tackle me," you may be sure you have a Flippant and masterful being to deal with. He has come determined to answer concisely and sharply; means to say "no" and "yes," and no more; always to be accompanied with a lateral nod, as much as to say, "take that" . . . .

In dealing with this witness an advocate should carefully abstain from administering rebukes, or attempting "to put the witness down." His object should be to keep her up as much as possible, to encourage that fine frenzied exuberance, which by and by will most surely damage the case she has come to serve. . . .

[1] WILLIAM C. ROBINSON, *Forensic Oratory: a Manual for Advocates* (1893), p. 126. Quoted by WIGMORE, *The Principles of Judicial Proof*, pp. 526–529.

The Dogged Witness.—The dogged witness is the exact opposite of the one I have just been dealing with. He will shake his head rather than say no. As much as to say: "You don't catch me. . . . " He seems always to have the fear of perjury before his eyes, and to know that if he keeps to a nod or a shake of the head, he is safe. He is under the impression that damage the case he must, whatever he says. "A still tongue makes a wise head," has always been his maxim.

How are you to deal with him? . . . Insinuation will help you with this witness. But carefully avoid asking for too much at the time. *Get little answers to little questions*, and you will find as a rule that answers are strung together like a row of beads within the man. . . .

The Hesitating Witness.—A hesitating witness may be a very cautious and truthful witness, or a very great liar. You will find this out before you begin to cross-examine. In most cases the hesitating man is wondering what effect the answer will have upon the case, and not what the proper answer is. By no means hurry this individual. Let him consider well the weight of his intended answer, and the scale into which it should go, and in all probability he will put it into the wrong one after all. If he should, *leave it there by all means*. I advise this, because I have so often seen young advocates carefully take it out again and put it into the other. Besides, your giving him plenty of time will tend to confuse him—as confused he should be if he is not honest. He can't go on weighing and balancing answers without becoming bewildered as to their probable results. . . . Very often he will repeat the question to gain time. Sometimes he pretends not to hear, sometimes not to know; all this time he is adjusting his weights, and in all probability some of them are false. . . .

Hesitation, however, may result from a desire to be scrupulously accurate, in which case you must be careful that the mere strictness of language does not convey a false impression. The letter sometimes, even in advocacy, kills, where the spirit would make alive.

The Nervous Witness.—A nervous witness is one of the most difficult to deal with. The answers either do not come at all or they tumble out two or three at a time; and then they often come with opposites in close companionship; a "Yes" and a "No" together, while "I don't know" comes close behind. . . . You must deal gently with this curious specimen of human nature. He is to be encouraged. . . .

The Cunning Witness.—The cunning witness must be dealt with cunningly. Humor would be mere pastime, and straightforward questioning out of character with him. . . .

The Witness Partly True and Partly False.—The witness who is partly true and partly false, without hypocrisy, knowing that he is giving color to some facts, suppressing others, and adding little ones to make good measure for his party, is the most difficult of all to deal with. The process of separating the true from the false requires skill as well as ingenuity and patience. You must have a delicacy of touch in manipulating evidence of this kind that comes only by actual practice. . . . You must watch carefully to find out if there be a want of assimilation in the parts of the story; if there be a disagreement between some of the false parts and some of the true, you must ascertain whether the alleged facts can exist together and in connection with one another, and must cross-examine for causes and effects; you will then determine whether they agree with the facts stated by other witnesses. Men do not gather "figs off thistles," and if you find the same cause producing opposite effects, there is falsehood somewhere. . . .

The Positive Witness.—There is another class of witness which may be mentioned, and that is the positive witness (generally a female or of female tendencies). It is usually very difficult to make the witness unsay anything she has said, however mistaken she may be; but you may sometimes lead her by small degrees to modify her statement, or induce her to say a great deal more in her positive way; and the great deal more may be capable of contradiction, or may itself contradict what has been said before by the same witness. . . .

She would unhesitatingly have sworn that Abel struck the first blow if she had been called on the side of Cain. She always stands up for what she calls "her own side." Beware how you try to convince her that she must be wrong. Such questions as "How can that be?" will only draw the answer, "I don't know how it can be, but I know that it *is.*" You might just as well try to convince a street mongrel that barking is done away with, as to attempt to persuade her that she ought not to be quite so positive.[1]

There are no studies available which would indicate how far the above traits of the witness are part and parcel of his general personality and temperamental make-up and how far they are simply manifestations of reaction responses to the cross-examiner in the circular response series.

Webb and Morgan, offering aids in estimating people's traits, stress the following points to be considered:

Has he the habit of compensating for a sense of inferiority—By rising to a dare? By strutting: is he a peacock—vain about almost everything? By boasting? By putting up a false front of confidence? By being haughty and superior or quarrelsome? By responding unfavorably to suggestions: Is he "negativistic"?

Or is he really a big man who welcomes suggestions, criticisms? Has he a pet vanity? If so, what is it? If he has a swelled head, is he, as usual, covering up a sense of inferiority? Or is he that rare type, the

---

[1] RICHARD HARRIS, *Hints on Advocacy* (Amer. ed., 1892), pp. 65, 107. Quoted by J. H. WIGMORE, *The Principles of Judicial Proof*, pp. 530–534.

grown-up spoiled child, with a genuine superiority feeling, who must at times be handled roughly, and whom it is dangerous to praise? Does he shirk responsibility or does he seek it? Is he clever or stupid? . . .

When we discover what holds a man's attention and what he neglects, what makes him angry or glad or sorry, what frightens him, what rouses his pride or tickles his humor, we begin to see him as he is. We find out what we really want to know: how he is probably going to feel and act under certain circumstances.

If Smith gets himself into trouble, will his fears master him? Will he try to shift the blame to us and lie out of it? Or will his sense of honor cause him to shoulder the blame and to shield others?

There can be no certainty of what Smith will do. But we find a *clue*, at least in what he has felt and done in the past under similar conditions.

Like all of us, Smith has formed habits of feeling and acting which largely control him. These habits of his we call traits of character. And they are revealing themselves constantly: in all his actions, in his posture, in the *changing* expression of his face, in the things he says, in his tone of voice.

Even when people take no apparent action, they usually betray their real feelings in some way. . . .

In dealing with people whom you wish to control or influence, consider all the points of difference that set them apart from others: the traits of their characters, their capacity, their special problems, wants and interests. Plan to treat each person differently in the light of his own nature and viewpoint.

Be on the lookout for clues that reveal traits of character and ability. Be on the alert for tell-tale trifles. Try to understand what trait lies back of actions that are unusual, even if they seem trivial. And above all, be sure to make use of every bit of information about people which you already possess.

Remember that the only safe clues to character are things people do or have done when they are off their guard. Watch their actions and the changing expression of their faces. . . . [1]

Suggestions for Further Study

1. How do you account for the variety of current theories of personality?

2. List several reasons, exclusive of those suggested in text, why a social work interviewer should be concerned with theories of personality? With general studies of personality?

3. State in your own terms the genetic theory of personality.

4. What does Kretschmer mean by "character"? What does W. I. Thomas mean by "character"?

[1] E. T. WEBB and J. B. MORGAN, *Strategy in Handling People*, pp. 140; 143; 154. (Most of the material is in italics.)

5. What dangers does an interviewer encounter when he relies wholly on the genetic theory of personality?

6. What advantages can he derive from such a theory once he is aware of its limitations?

7. What is meant by "behaviorism"?   How do W. I. Thomas and D. S. Thomas treat behaviorism?   (See *The Child in America.*)

8. What common points do you observe in the theory of personality held by the geneticist and the behaviorist?

9. Of what value is Pavlov's experiment on conditioned reflex to the social worker who deals with personality problems?

10. What reflexes have you observed some of your clients to have acquired without the intervention of consciousness?

11. State the advantages and disadvantages of Watson's definition of personality.

12. To what extent can the criticism directed against the behavioristic theory of personality be justified?

13. To what extent can the social worker make use of the methods of the behaviorists without adopting their theory of behaviorism?

14. What is meant by a Gestalt?   List several Gestalt psychologists who have contributed to a theory of personality.

15. Of what value are these to the interviewer?

16. The Gestaltist regards personality as unified or integrated.   Can personality be unified or integrated under urban conditions of life?   What is meant by "segments of personality"?

17. Read Nels Anderson and Eduard C. Lindeman's "The Urban Personality" in their book *Urban Sociology* and point out the common meeting grounds and point of view between the above authors and the Gestaltists.

18. What does the modern psychiatrist contribute to the social worker's understanding of personality?

19. List several psychiatrists who in your opinion have developed a satisfactory theory of personality.

20. What are the differences in the method of study of the psychiatrist and the psychoanalyst?

21. Which of the several psychoanalytic schools do you favor?   Why?

22. List ten major concepts Freud uses in his study of personality and show their relation to the problem of interviewing.

23. Define ego, libido, id, ego ideal, mechanisms of adjustment, and show their relation to the problem of interviewing.

24. In what respect do Freud and Adler differ so far as their theories of personality are concerned?

25. What does Adler contribute to the social worker's understanding of personality?

26. Define ten major concepts Adler uses in his study of personality and show their relation to the problem of interviewing.

27. Explain Jung's theory of personality.   How does he differ from Adler and Freud?

28. To what extent can you make use of Allport's study of personality traits in your analysis of the traits of social work clients?

29. Which of the several sociological theories of personality do you find most useful?

30. Analyze the definition of personality advanced by Park and Burgess and show its value to the interviewer.

31. What does Cooley mean by the "reflected self"? Of what value is this concept to the interviewer?

32. How does the sociological theory of personality differ from the psychological and psychoanalytic?

33. Using the three different types of personality discussed by Thomas and Znaniecki, classify Mr. Walker, the various members of the Greek family interviewed by Shaw, and Stephen S. (See pp. 324–327.) Are these types of personality useful in the analysis of your clients?

34. List types of interviewers you have observed in your work. How closely do they approximate those described by Professor Young?

35. What are the major difficulties of such a classification?

36. On the basis of the social and personal traits described above, list additional types of interviewers.

37. Describe types of interviewers you have met in your own work.

38. To what extent are the types of witnesses described by Robinson and Harris applicable to the types of people whom social workers contact?

39. What can the social worker profit from the above classification of witnesses and their treatment?

40. What are the dangers involved in drawing such analogies?

41. To what extent do the classifications of types of witnesses listed by Robinson and Harris overlap?

42. Which types would you include in your list of types of interviewees in social work?

43. Analyze the types of interviewers and interviewees discussed in the text in terms of Floyd Allport's discussion of personality traits.

Selected Bibliography

1. ALLPORT, FLOYD HENRY: *Social Psychology*, 1924.
   Chapter V, "Personality—The Social Man," points to the fact that personality is largely a product of the social environment; discusses the foundations of personality, the selection of personality traits.
2. BURGESS, E. W. (Editor): *Personality and the Social Group*, 1929.
   A collection of papers designed to give a scientific background for the understanding of the nature, development, and the various types of personality in relation to the social setting.
3. DUNLAP, K.: "The Reading of Character from External Signs," *Scientific Monthly*, XV (1922), 153–165.
   "An evaluation of various methods of character analysis. In many cases, the conclusions from character analyses are not valid, but are only rationalizations."
4. HARRIS, RICHARD: *Hints on Advocacy* (Amer. ed., 1892). Quoted by J. H. WIGMORE, *The Principles of Judicial Proof*, pp. 530–534.
   An analysis of the problem types of witnesses and their treatment.
5. ROBINSON, WILLIAM C.: *Forensic Oratory; a Manual for Advocates*, 1893. Quoted by J. H. WIGMORE, *The Principles of Judicial Proof*, pp. 526–529.
   A brief discussion of the problem types of witnesses.

6. SCHWESINGER, GLADYS C.: *Heredity and Environment*, 1933.

Chapter V, "Viewpoints on Personality," is an excellent brief objective "account of the points of view held by the leading schools of psychology and psychiatry on the development of personality." Provides an extensive bibliography on the subject.

7. THOMAS, W. I., and F. ZNANIECKI: *The Polish Peasant in Europe and America* (2 vol. ed.), Vol. II, pp. 1831–1914.

An excellent discussion of the evolution of human personality in relation to social status, life organization of individual and group, social wishes; distinguishes between personality and temperament; discusses Bohemian, Philistine, and Creative types of personality in relation to their wishes and social setting.

8. YOUNG, Erle F.: "What Type of Personality Should be the Goal of Social Case Work?" *Sociology and Social Research*, XVIII (November-December, 1933), 123–130.

Points out that the city requires a special type of personality—the accommodated personality.

CHAPTER XIII

PSYCHOLOGICAL PROBLEMS IN INTERVIEWING

Psychologists have been experimenting with controlled types of interviewing problems but have described chiefly the characteristic forms which testimony and reporting take. Errors are known to arise from bias, illusion, delusion, faults of memory, and so on. Acquaintance with the psychology of interviewing enables the interviewer to make suitable allowance for the distortion of data which occurs when the subject seeks to recall and report an experience.

Interviewing is, however, a form of social contact and social interaction carried on by means of language. It is, therefore, a social as well as a psychological process. So far as it has to do with the social attitudes and values of the interviewer and his relations with other persons, its subject matter is sociological. Only the major problems in the psychology of interviewing can be undertaken in the following brief treatment.

Psychological Factors in Interviewing

Illusions of the Interviewee.—Professor Hugo Münsterberg, who for many years carried on experiments relative to illusions, tricks of memory, emotional coloring, and untrue confessions of witnesses, maintains that these phenomena belong in the realm of the normal, healthy, intelligent persons and belong to the domain of study of the psychologist. The alienist, on the other hand, studies amnesia, hallucinations, fixed ideas, and so on.[1]

There had been an automobile accident. Before the court one of the witnesses, who had sworn to tell "the whole truth, and nothing but the truth," declared that the entire road was dry and dusty; the other swore that it had rained and the road was muddy. The one said that the automobile was running very slowly; the other, that he had never seen an automobile rushing more rapidly. The first swore that there were only two or three people on the village road; the other,

---

[1] *On the Witness Stand*, Chaps. I–III.

that a large number of men, women, and children were passing by. Both witnesses were highly respectable gentlemen, neither of whom had the slightest interest in changing the facts as he remembered them. . . .

Again, there was a case where it was essential to find out whether at a certain riot the number of guests in the hall was larger than the forty who had been invited to attend. There were witnesses who insisted that there could not have been more than twenty persons present, and others who were sure that they saw more than one hundred. In a case of poisoning, some members of the family testified that the beverage had a disagreeable, sour taste, others, that it was tasteless, and others, that it was sweet. . . .

There is no need of heaping up such illustrations from actual cases, as everyone who remembers the last half-dozen murder trials of his city knows with what regularity these differences in reports of witnesses occur. . . .

To make memory responsible is indeed the routine way. It is generally taken for granted that we all perceive our surroundings uniformly. In case there were only twenty men in the hall, no one could have seen one hundred. In case the road was muddy, no one can have seen it dusty. . . . If there is still disagreement, it must have crept in through the trickery of memory. The perception must be correct; its later reproduction may be false. But do we really all perceive the same thing, and does it have the same meaning to us in our immediate absorption of the surrounding world? Is the court sufficiently aware of the great differences between men's perceptions, and does the court take sufficient trouble to examine the capacities and habits with which the witness moves through the world which he believes he observes? . . . Legal theorists have even proudly boasted of the fact that the judges always found their way without psychological advice, and yet the records of such cases, for instance, in railroad damages, quickly show that the psychological inspirations of the bench are often directly the opposite of demonstrable facts. . . .

The study of these powers no longer lies outside of the realm of science. The progress of experimental psychology makes it an absurd incongruity that the State should devote its fullest energy to the clearing up of all the physical happenings, but should never ask the psychological expert to determine the value of that factor which becomes most influential—the mind of the witness. The demand that the memory of the witness should be tested with the methods of modern psychology has been raised sometimes, but it seems necessary to add that the study of his perceptive judgment will have to find its way into the court-room, too.[1]

---

[1] HUGO MÜNSTERBERG, *On the Witness Stand*, pp. 15–20. Reprinted by permission of Clark Boardman Company.

The Memory of the Interviewee.[1]—In spite of best intentions, in spite of good memory and calm mood, a whole series of confusions, of forgetting, or wrong conclusions may upset the interviewer, and the interviewee may give untrue accounts. Professor Münsterberg writes:

The sources of error begin, of course, before the recollection sets in. The observation itself may be defective and illusory; wrong associations may make it imperfect; judgments may misinterpret the experience; and suggestive influences may falsify the data of the senses. Everyone knows the almost unlimited individual differences in the power of correct observation and judgment. Everyone knows that there are persons who, under favourable conditions, see what they are expected to see. . . .

Any imaginative thought may slip into our consciousness and may carry with it in the same way that curious feeling that it is merely the repetition of something we have experienced before. . . .

We must always keep in mind that a content of consciousness is in itself independent of its relation to the past and has thus in itself no mark which can indicate whether it was experienced once before or not. The feeling of belonging to our past life may associate itself thus just as well with a perfectly new idea of our imagination as with a real reproduction of an earlier state of mind. As a matter of course, the opposite can thus happen, too; that is, an earlier experience may come to our memory stripped of every reference to the past, standing before our mind like a completely new product of imagination. . . . Yes, we fill the blanks of our perceptions constantly with bits of reproduced memory material and take those reproductions for immediate impressions. In short, we never know from the material itself whether we remember, perceive, or imagine, and in the borderland regions there must result plenty of confusion which cannot always remain without dangerous consequences. . . . [2]

Relative to the psychological processes Miss Richmond observes:

The Attention of the Interviewee: The closeness of attention on the part of any witness to an incident in his own or another's situation[3]

[1] See J. H. WIGMORE, *The Principles of Judicial Proof,* "Interpretation of Specific Testimony to Establish the Extent and Sources of Error."

E. H. MOORE, "How Accurate Are Case Records?" *Proceedings of the American Sociological Society,* XXVIII (May, 1934), 45–54.

[2] HUGO MÜNSTERBERG, *On the Witness Stand,* pp. 56–61.

[3] In one of the short, unpublished papers referred to in the Preface, Mr. Julian Codman, writing on "Evidence in its Relation to Social Service," gives the following instance of inattention.

"One day Mr. P, a lifelong resident of Nahant, a man of high cultivation and exceptional ability, and an enthusiastic golfer, came to the chairman

depends upon the importance which at the time he attaches to it, or, it may be, upon the existence of a similarity between some part of that incident and something which he has experienced before—upon his *"funded thought."* This "funded thought" is his material for thinking, the sum total of ideas which his traditions, education, and experience have made an integral part of his mind. New experience which is entirely strange, which he can relate to nothing in his past thinking, he will not heed.

A woman whose husband showed signs of mental disturbance consented to his being observed with a view to commitment for hospital care. She did this, however, merely because she was desperate at what she considered his incorrigible laziness, and because she knew she would be better off without him. The social worker interested could neither make her see that he was other than normal mentally, nor give her a conception of what it meant to be insane without violent mania. His occasional abuse of his wife, his desire to keep her in the house so that she should not talk with neighbors, his ungrounded suspicions of her fidelity and of his son's honesty, she apparently took for granted as "crankiness—the way he was made." His incompetence even in the least skilled work she of course accounted for as wilful indolence.

This woman was familiar with the idea of the unreasonable and lazy husband, and totally unfamiliar with the idea of an early stage of insanity. This last idea therefore could not command her attention and credence as an explanation of her troubles. A case worker who wants to get evidence throwing light on mental abnormalities from uneducated people is likely to have better success by leading them to

---

of the green committee of the Golf Club and told him that he thought part of the course was unsafe for passers-by. This was a place where the country road crossed the course. He said that he thought a notice should be put up warning all players to look and see that the road was clear of foot-passengers and carriages before playing a ball from the teeing ground. The chairman suggested a notice as follows, and asked if that would be sufficient:

"'DANGER: All persons before driving from this tee are cautioned to see that no one is passing in the road.'

"Mr. P said that he thought such a sign would be just the thing.

"'Well,' said the chairman, 'a sign in exactly those words in letters three inches long in black paint on a white ground has been in front of your eyes every time you have driven off that tee during the last six years.'

"Have you any doubt that, if Mr. P had been called on the witness-stand to testify as to the presence or absence of a sign in that particular tee, he would have taken his oath that no such sign existed? And he would have so sworn with the utmost confidence in his correctness. (The explanation for this gentleman's apparent inattention may have been that for six years he had heeded the warning given by the sign board automatically, and that therefore its importance for himself had long disappeared.)"

talk not about "peculiarities" but about temper, laziness, etc.—familiar domestic phenomena. The social worker, then, in weighing evidence, must take account of differences in the funded thought of witnesses, in so far as this is likely to affect the objects or incidents to which a particular witness will give attention. . . .

Suggestibility: . . . affects a person's competence as a witness . . . By that we mean an over-readiness to yield assent to and to reproduce the assertions of other people. A witness may confuse observations made by others with his own; he may give a facile acceptance to what he reads as well as to what he hears. . . .

The case worker must bear in mind that suggestibility may influence not only the client's conduct, but also his thinking and his standards. . . . A kindly bias common to social workers leads them, in the case of any client who interests them, especially a young one, to try to get at those traits that give most promise of amended conduct. Roused by this bias, the girl's suggestibility, taken together with her desire to please, may make her not only seem but be so different a person while in the presence of the social worker that the latter forms a mistaken estimate of her character as a whole. What is true of such a girl as the one referred to, is true to a lesser extent of the man who was influenced by the probation officer.

Suggestibility may even reach the extent of leading to mistaken confessions. . . .

Leading Questions: Closely related to the suggestibility of witnesses is the response which they may make to "leading questions." The social case worker must be on guard against getting back as alleged fact some mere conjecture of his own which he has implicitly expressed by his wording, or by the inflection of his voice. A case worker with little faith may ask, "You have no relatives who would take in the baby while you go to the hospital, have you?"; whereas the worker who gets results would put the question, "Which of your sisters could best take the baby?" . . .

It cannot be claimed that framing such questions as will elicit the truth is always easy, nor will there be unanimity of opinion as to what is and what is not permissible on ethical grounds. Take, for illustration, a statement in Mrs. Solenberger's book on homeless men.[1] To a homeless man of over thirty, applying for relief and guidance, she was accustomed to say in her first interview not "Are you married?" but "Where is your wife?"; not "Have you a family?" but "How much of a family have you?" Some students of social work have objected to this as a form of deception, advocating "Are you married?" as the more honest question. Experience has shown, however, that "Are you

[1] ALICE WILLARD SOLENBERGER, *One Thousand Homeless Men: A Study of Original Records*, p. 22.

married?" usually leads to the answer "No," while "Where is your wife?" usually reveals the existence of a wife.[1]

James Ram in his discussion *On Facts as Subjects of Inquiry by a Jury* points out the advantages of leading questions:

A witness about to narrate facts may be left to tell his story in his own way, or it may be drawn from him by questions put to him.

The former method of telling the story is open to these objections: The witness may not think enough to call to mind all he can relate; from carelessness or oversight he may omit to mention some circumstances; he may think or fancy the circumstances he withholds are not material to a proper understanding of his story; indeed, he may think or fancy that his story will be best understood, if it be not loaded with matters which he views as redundant, but which nevertheless are essential to see the facts in their proper proportions and color. . . .

There are two ways of questioning: one where the words made use of in the question suggest or prompt a particular answer, and which is called a *leading* question; the other, where the question does not so lead, but is put in general terms, without at all pointing to a particular reply. This may be called an *open* question; it is open to any answer. . . .

Each kind of question has, however, its advantages and disadvantages. If the witness be dishonest, and there be connivance between him and his interrogator; or supposing the former honest, and the latter not to be so; it is plain that a leading question may tend to bring out the answer which the interrogator desires. And assuming that both the witness and the interrogator are honest, both wishing the truth to be spoken; here, if the witness remembers little or nothing, or if he be dull, or heedless, or be confused, or embarrassed by timidity or any other cause, there is danger that, if he is addressed by a leading question, he may, without thought or consideration, echo in his reply the words put in the question, and so fail to speak the truth.

An open question imposes on an honest witness the necessity of thought, a consideration of both the question and reply. It forces him to resort to, and, if need be, to ransack his memory, and obliges him to utter only what he remembers. On the other hand, it is very possible, in many cases probable, that from sickness, old age, or other cause, his memory may be so infirm that he cannot be brought to a correct answer, except by a leading question. All open questions, every question short of a leading one, may fail to quicken his memory, and bring him to express the fact of which he has knowledge. Nothing, for instance, is more common, than to forget a person's name, and,

---

[1] MARY E. RICHMOND, *Social Diagnosis*, pp. 66–73. Reprinted by permission of Russell Sage Foundation.

without hearing it again, to be quite unable to call it to mind. We constantly hear people say, "If I heard his name, I should know it directly." If the name be pronounced, the hearing of it refreshes the power of recollection, and the name is instantly remembered.[1]

Pathological Lying.—The average interviewer learns to discern between fact and fancy and to recognize that falsehoods are of many origins and forms. "Classed by their underlying causes," says Cyril Burt, "we may recognize at least six or seven varieties of lies, all broadly distinguishable, yet running imperceptibly the one into the other."[2] The approach to each type of lie depends largely upon its origin. There is the playful liar or the make-believe and "let's pretend." There is the lie of confusion, the lie of vanity, the lie of revenge, the lie of loyalty and convention, and the pathological lie.[3]

At times interviewers will spend considerable time in checking and verifying information, or in attempts to change an interviewee's attitude, in having him follow a particular course of action only to discover that they have been deceived at each step. While persistent and pathological liars are comparatively rare, the perplexing problems which they present justify a discussion of the subject.

There is little that the average interviewer can do with pathological liars. They are subjects for psychiatrists and psychologists. However, the interviewer must be able to recognize the pathological liar and not waste time or delay getting the patient in competent medical hands. Dr. William Healy writes:

Definition: Pathological lying is falsification entirely disproportionate to any discernible end in view, engaged in by a person who, at the time of observation, cannot definitely be declared insane, feeble-minded, or epileptic. Such lying rarely, if ever, centers about a single event; although exhibited in very occasional cases for a short time, it manifests itself most frequently by far over a period of years, or even a life time. It represents a trait rather than an episode. . . .

It is false accusation indulged in apart from any obvious purpose. Like the swindling of pathological liars, it appears objectively more pernicious than the lying, but it is an expression of the same tendency. The most striking form of this type of conduct is, of course, self-accusa-

---

[1] JAMES RAM, *On Facts as Subjects of Inquiry by a Jury.* Quoted by J. H. WIGMORE, *The Principles of Judicial Proof,* pp. 508–510.

[2] *The Young Delinquent,* p. 361.

[3] *Ibid.,* pp. 362–366.

tion. Mendacious self-impeachment seems especially convincing of abnormality. Such falsification not infrequently is episodic.

The inclusion of swindling in our discussion is due to the natural evolution of this type of conduct from pathological lying. Swindling itself could hardly be called a pathological phenomenon, since it is readily explicable by the fact that it is entered into for reasons of tangible gain, but when it is the product of the traits shown by a pathological liar it, just as the lying itself, is a part of the pathological picture. It is the most concrete expression of the individual's tendencies. This has been agreed to by several writers, for all have found it easy to trace the development of one form of behavior into the other. . . .

The only method by which good understanding may be obtained of the types of personality and mentality involved in pathological lying, accusation, and swindling, as well as of the genetics of these tendencies, is by the detailed reading of typical case histories. . . . Appreciation of the nature of the phenomena can only be obtained through acquaintance with an entire career. Any of us may be confronted by fabrications so consistent as to leave at one or several interviews the impression of truth. . . .

A short career of extensive lying, not unfrequently met with in work for juvenile courts and other social agencies, seems, judging from our material, to be always so mixed up with other delinquencies or unfortunate sex experiences that the lying, after all, cannot be regarded as purposeless. It is indulged in most often in an attempt to disguise undesirable truths. . . .

A fair question to ask at this point is whether pathological lying is ever found to be the only delinquency of the given individual. We should hesitate to deny the possibility of its being the sole offense, but in our study of a long list of cases, and after review of those reported by other authors, it seems practically impossible to find a case of this. The tendencies soon carry the person over to the production of other delinquencies, and if these do not come in the category of punishable offenses, at least, through the trouble and suffering caused others, they are to be regarded essentially as misconduct.

The reverse of the above question deserves a word or two of attention; are there marked cases of delinquency which do not show lying? . . . we have been profoundly astonished to discover that a considerable percentage of the cases we have studied, even of repeated offenders, have proved notably truthful. Occasionally the very person who will engage in a major form of delinquency will hesitate to lie. Our experience shows this to be less true, however, of sex delinquency than perhaps of any other. This statement is based on general observations; the accurate correlations have not been worked up. Occasionally the professional criminal of many misdeeds is proud of his uprightness in other spheres of behavior, including veracity. But even here one would have to classify carefully, for it is obvious that the typical swindler would find lying his best cloak of disguise. On the other hand, a bold safe-blower may look down with scorn upon a form of criminality which demands constant mendacity. . . .

Hazel M. at 16 years of age created a mild sensation by a story of woe which brought immediate offers of aid for the alleged distress. One morning she appeared at a social center and stated she had come from a hospital where her brother, a young army man, had just died. She gave a remarkably correct, detailed, medical account of his suffering and death. In response to inquiry she told of a year's training as a nurse; that was how she knew about such subjects. In company with a social worker she went directly back to the hospital to make arrangements for what she requested, namely, a proper burial. At the hospital office it was said that no such person had died there, and after she had for a time insisted on it she finally said she must have been dreaming. Although she had wept on the shoulder of a listener as she first told her story, she now gave it up without any show of emotion. . . .

The next day Hazel started in by saying, "It's enough to convince anybody that I was not in the hospital when Mrs. B. and I went there and found out that they said I had not been there. Truthfully I don't know where I was. If I was not there I must have been some place or I must have been in a trance." . . .

Hazel's stories were successfully maintained for several days until a shrewd detective, who got her to tell some street numbers in Chicago, ferreted out her family. She had persistently denied the existence of any of them in Chicago, and, indeed, stated that her father and mother had died years previously. One of the most convincing things about her was her poise; she displayed an attitude of sincerity combined with a show of deep surprise when her word was questioned. For example, the moment before her mother was brought in to see her, she was asked what she would say if anyone asserted that her mother was in the next room. Her instantaneous, emphatic response was, "She would have to rise out of her grave to be there."

We soon learned that not a single detail the girl had given about her family was true. She was born and brought up in Chicago and had never been outside of the city. She had never studied nursing nor had she ever nursed anybody. In public school she had reached eighth grade.

Hazel came of an intelligent family and we were able to get a good account of the family and developmental history. Heredity seems completely negative as far as any nervous or mental abnormalities are concerned. . . .

We are at once forced to agree with previous writers that an unusual number of the pathological liar group show great aptitude for language.

This is shown by their general conversational ability and by the fact that many of them have found out themselves that they had capacity, for instance, for writing compositions. . . . A considerable number of our group were characterized as great talkers, and several as romantic, dramatic, fantastic, etc., even by ordinary observers. All this goes to show clearly that the native traits making for verbal fluency are strongly correlated with pathological lying. . . .

The general mental and moral weakness of the constitutional inferior very naturally leads him to become a pathological liar; he follows, by virtue of his make-up, the path of immediate least resistance—lying. . . .

A characteristic of pathological liars is undoubtedly a deep-set egocentrism, as Risch states. If one goes over our cases it may be seen that there is exhibited frequently in the individual an undue amount of self-assertion. There is very little sympathy for the concern of others, and, indeed, remarkably little apperception of the opinions of others.[1]

Stereotypes.—"Case," "budget," "client," "pauper," "indigent," "relief," are pictures in the heads of social workers which habituate their minds to a universe in which these pictures are the values. Social workers, like all those who follow a certain occupation, play out the roles which go with it rather consistently. And at the same time there are people who come to think of these roles as characterizing the occupation, and when they think of one they think of the other.[2]

Professor Waller observes:

. . . Experience of persons playing those roles leaves residua in the form of imagined constructs relating to the appearance or behavior of persons falling within certain occupational categories. These imagined constructs are *stereotypes*. When a stereotype has been organized out of the community experience of persons belonging to certain occupational groups and consistently playing out certain roles that go with it, the members of the community tend to organize all experience of the persons in such an occupation in terms of the existent stereotype; they have a low perceptual threshold for behavior conforming to the stereotype, and a high threshold for facts which argue against the correctness of the stereotype. A stereotype, once established, reenforces itself; it proves its own correctness by arguing in a perfect

[1] WILLIAM HEALY, *Pathological Lying, Accusation, and Swindling*, pp. 1–4; 9–10; 43–45; 250–253. Reprinted by permission of Little, Brown & Company.

[2] WILLARD WALLER, *The Sociology of Teaching*, p. 415.

circle. When a stereotype has once become current, it may be passed from one individual to another by social contagion, and it tends to distort the first naive experience of new members with persons belonging to the group included in the stereotype. Stereotypes are predominantly visual. Lippmann has aptly called them "pictures in our heads." Some stereotypes have the form of very definite visual images; others merely represent types which we can recognize but not reproduce.

Much of social interaction rests upon stereotypes. The interaction of intimates largely escapes the influence of the stereotype, and so does naive experience for which no model exists in one's social world. But a very wide range of social interchange is affected by the presence of more or less definite stereotypes, sometimes stereotypes which have currency in an entire group (this is the best use of the term) and sometimes constructs of our own relating to particular persons or classes of persons. This is possible because in many kinds of relations we do not respond to another person directly, but always to a more or less veracious construct of him in our own minds. Certain consequences follow; one of the more important is that an individual's behavior in our presence is no criterion of his behavior in the presence of others, no matter how stabilized his behavior in our presence (unless we have experienced him fully and with no intervening stereotype, and he has presented to us an equally unbiased segment of himself). The error of generalizing an individual's behavior toward us, limited by the possibilities of behavior which we, reacting to our own imagined construct of him, have offered to him, accounts for many of the surprises of social life and for some of the unexpectedness of human nature. The young man's fiancee, worshipped and idealized by him, is seduced by another in an evening. A gruff employer is rendered human by an unusual approach. Disraeli won over Queen Victoria by treating her as a human being. It seems that people gain who treat others as human beings, neglecting as far as possible the conventional restrictions or stereotyped ideas as to how they ought to be treated. In inferiority-superiority relationships the influence of the stereotype is particularly vicious, for the parties involved almost invariably conclude that because the relationship is stereotyped the person is but an enlargement of the stereotyped relation.[1]

Waller points out also that there are two different stereotypes of the teacher, and enumerates certain traits characterizing each type. Applying the same traits to the social worker—resulting from a hostile reworking of the residua of community experience —we see one stereotype as caricature, "hard-boiled," given to "red tape," and the other that of self-sacrificing, gentle, kindly, self-effacing creature, overworked and underpaid, but always

[1] *Ibid.*, pp. 415–416. Reprinted by permission of John Wiley & Sons, Inc.

ready to help the "down-and-outer." This is the resultant of a friendly reworking of experience; it is an idealization of the social worker. Our concern here is not only with the stereotype but also with its effect upon the social worker and the consequent social contacts he makes with his clients and the community. Some social workers tend to conform to what is expected of them; others attempt to escape from the occupational role, to pierce through the wall which imprisons them within the stereotype, and to affect others as a distinct individual rather than as a stereotyped social worker. The attitudes of social workers toward their profession are very important determinants of the effect which their profession has upon them.

Conversely, trained social case workers no longer see their clients as stereotypes—worthy, deserving, pauper, unwilling to work, of no account—but have learned to take into consideration also the unique elements of personality by which each is differentiated from the other. This is the greatest single step forward in modern social work.

Suggestions for Further Study

1. What are the essential differences between the sociology and the psychology of interviewing?

2. Indicate what a complete treatise of the psychology of interviewing might include?

3. List some of the illusions which you have observed in your interviews. How did they arise?

4. List some of the tricks of memory you have observed in your interviewees. How do you account for them? How might they be overcome?

5. List the social and psychological conditions under which you have been able to secure attention of the interviewees, the conditions under which they have been able to concentrate, and the conditions under which the reverse is true.

6. What is meant by suggestibility? What is the relation of suggestibility to illusion and to attention?

7. What is the relation of suggestibility to freedom of choice? to true confession?

8. What are leading questions? Pick out leading questions in any interview presented in the text? What is their relation to the reply?

9. What is the difference between lying and pathological lying?

10. Who is a playful liar? What are his motives? How may he be recognized? How may he be dealt with?

11. What is a lie of confusion, of vanity, of revenge? What technique may be employed in overcoming these?

12. What is the relation between lying and defense mechanism?

13. What is the cause of emotional coloring? What precautions should the interviewer observe to avoid it? in the interviewee, in himself?

14. What is the relation between emotional coloring and invasion of personality?

15. Read Walter Lippman's discussion of stereotypes in his volume *Public Opinion* and indicate its relation to interviewing.

16. In what respects are the teacher stereotypes and social work stereotypes similar?

17. What stereotypes do you carry of clients? of other social workers? of school teachers?

18. Compile a comprehensive bibliography on the psychology of interviewing.

19. Formulate suggestions for further study in the field of psychology of interviewing.

20. Secure illustrative cases which will aid in better understanding of the topics listed in this chapter.

Selected Bibliography

1. HEALY, WILLIAM: *Pathological Lying, Accusation, and Swindling*, 1926.
   A study of the nature and traits of pathological liars and their methods of treatment.
2. JASTROW, JOSEPH: *The Psychology of Conviction: A Study of Beliefs and Attitudes*, 1918.
3. JELLIFFE, S. E.: *The Technique of Psychoanalysis*, 1920.
   Psychoanalysis is described as a method for securing data; discusses methods of securing "transference," of combating "resistance," of avoiding "leading questions" and distractions.
4. MÜNSTERBERG, HUGO: *On the Witness Stand*, 1925.
   A lucid discussion of the various psychological factors—illusions, tricks of memory, suggestibility—which affect the reliability of evidence.
5. WALLER, WILLARD: *The Sociology of Teaching*, 1932. Chap. XXIII.
   Discusses role of stereotypes in relation to teachers and teaching; has many applications to social work situations.
6. WHIPPLE, G. M.: "The Obtaining of Information: Psychology of Observation and Report," *Psychological Bulletin*, XV (July, 1918), 217–248.
   Presents numerous principles to be observed in obtaining information.
7. WOODWORTH, R. S.: "Psychological Experience with the Interview," *Journal of Personnel Research*, IV (1925), 162–165.
   Good brief statement of psychological factors—variable error, constant error, preconceptions, mind set, rationalization, and self-concern—affecting the reliability of the interview.

CHAPTER XIV

SOCIOLOGICAL PROBLEMS IN INTERVIEWING

The present treatment presupposes many limitations to the interview.[1] The most vigorous objections made are based on its lack of reliability because the interviewer often secures rationalizations, insecure opinions, prejudices, and not genuine attitudes. Following Read Bain's discussion "The Validity of Life Histories and Diaries," we may imply that the problems of the interview are complicated both by the interviewee and interviewer and by the nature of the task: (1) the interviewee may tell only what he thinks the investigator wants; (2) the interviewee may be more self-justificatory than factual; (3) the interviewee may have a story complex, and the interview may result in romantic over- and under-statement; (4) the investigator tends to see what he is looking for, or, as it has been cited, Freud, for example, always sees his subject as a bundle of "sex complexes and repressed *libido*"; Adler sees "organ inferiority," while Jung sees "introversion or extroversion and racial archetypes"; (5) the "case situations are seldom comparable . . . in a pluralistic universe of variables" and thus it is impossible to establish norms, to formulate objectives or to gain vision as to what the next step should be.[2]

SOCIOLOGICAL FACTORS IN INTERVIEWING

Professor Rice's analysis of two thousand records of interviews with homeless men held by twelve different skilled interviewers shows that a contagious transfer of each investigator's individual bias alters and often distorts replies to questions asked. Interviewers who are strong prohibitionists extracted information from

---

[1] See WALTER V. BINGHAM and BRUCE V. MOORE, *op. cit.*, Chap. I, "Some Doubts about Interviewing," and Chap. XII, "General Studies of the Interview and Related Techniques."

G. A. BOWERS, "Issues in Research Method," *Journal of Personnel Research*, IV (1925), 155–161.

[2] READ BAIN, "The Validity of Life Histories and Diaries," *The Journal of Educational Sociology*, III (November, 1929), 156–159.

about two-thirds of these homeless men that their downfall was due chiefly to liquor, while the interviewers who had socialistic tendencies secured industrial explanations of their misfortunes most frequently.[1]

The limitations of the personal interview are further complicated by the fact that life, particularly in urban communities, is becoming more and more formalized and conventionalized, and the experiences of men are becoming more and more varied.

The impersonal and anonymous aspects of life grow in spite of the rapid increase in the number and frequency of social contacts, owing in part to the development of transportation and the high degree of cooperation and of economic interdependence. Individuals tend to come into a condition of social isolation and to develop unique social worlds of their own. They resort to wearing masks; their minds fail to meet; they lack a common definition of the social situation and develop wide differences in their social philosophies. Hiding behind a mask, particularly in the vast tide of modern cosmopolitan life, has become almost a daily practice. Dr. Park says:

The mask represents the conception we formed of ourselves—the rôle we are striving to live up to—this mask is our truer self, the self we would like to be. In the end, our conception of our rôle becomes second nature and an integral part of our personality. . . . Our faces are living masks which reflect, to be sure, the changing emotions of our inner lives, but tend more and more to conform to the type we are seeking to impersonate. Not only every race, but every nationality has its characteristic "face."[2]

Dr. Louis Petroff points out that the mask is a protective device against intruders:

In any group a large part of the total human being is hidden from those about him. He talks with more or less intimate associates in various groups, exchanges ideas, plays his role, but he is an independent unit, a sort of closed system. How little of what he *is* is exhibited to the group! Indeed, he may do much acting and talking; but his acts and words do not express his totality. He is hiding, not always consciously, behind a mask. The human being, more than any other creature, puts on all sorts of externalities, such as dress,

[1] STUART A. RICE, "Contagious Bias in the Interview," *American Journal of Sociology*, XXXV (November, 1929), 420–423.

[2] ROBERT E. PARK, "Behind Our Masks," *The Survey Graphic*, LXI (May, 1926), 136–137.

make-up, and manners to hide his real self. Says Emerson, "One protects himself by solitude, and one by courtesy, and one by an acid worldly manner,—each concealing how he can the thinness of his skin, and his incapacity for strict association. . . . But how insular and pathetically solitary are the people we know! Nor dare they tell what they think of each other when they meet in the street. We have a fine right, to be sure, to taunt men of the world with superficial and treacherous courtesies. . . . "[1]

When X meets Y, does X see through the mask of Y, or Y through that of X? The Autocrat of the Breakfast-Table[2] says that when X and Y meet there are six different persons: X as he sees himself, X as Y sees him, and X as he really is; Y as he sees himself, Y as X sees him, and Y as he really is. Eubank asks the question, but "*who* and what are X and Y as they 'really' are?"[3] We ask the same question, but do not attempt to answer it fully. We suggest, however, that the isolation between X and Y consists chiefly in the secrecy of what X knows about himself but does not communicate to Y, and of what Y knows about himself but keeps secret from X. A synthesis of what X and Y know about themselves and about each other would be perhaps near the "real" X and the "real" Y.

From the standpoint of masked isolation, the often quoted saying, "If one could only see himself as others see him" is not complete; it should be supplemented with another just as meaningful or even more so, "And if others could but see him as he sees himself." If these conditions were achieved, then the minimum possible degree of sociopsychological isolation might be reached. We say *might* be reached, because it might or might not.[4] For another factor must be taken into account, namely, "intimacy breeds contempt." Man feels uneasy when his inner life, the man under the mask, is known even by his most intimate friends; nor does the ordinary friend consider his friend's unmasked-self attractive. Furthermore, the masked-man usually resents criticism, in spite of the fact that in his masked-manner he might say that he welcomes it. Know your friend intimately and criticize him frankly and unsparingly, though constructively and with good intentions, and the chances are that you would lose an intimate friend. He will close his door on you, he will put on his mask again. Frankness is a dangerous weapon; it hurts not only the man who is struck with it, but also the one who strikes with it. "Give every man thine ear, but few thy voice." Polonius might have added: but *not all* your voice even to the few. It will be observed, however, that the masks men wear are not air-tight or water-proof. In ordinary social

[1] RALPH W. EMERSON, *Society and Solitude*, pp. 7–9.
[2] See OLIVER W. HOLMES, *The Autocrat of the Breakfast-table*, pp. 54 *ff*.
[3] E. E. EUBANK, *Concepts of Sociology*, p. 103.
[4] OLIVER W. HOLMES, *op. cit.*, p. 56.

contact the observer, especially the keen one, can often feel or hear or see the man behind the mask. And in the process of gleaning something from the other fellow, the observer also reveals glimpses from behind his own mask.[1]

Men Are Strikingly Individual Beings.—By virtue of differences in personal, social, and group experiences, in culture complexes, in mental and emotional make-ups men are often separated from their fellows by gulfs that are hard to bridge. They may exchange greetings, they may try to bring their parted natures in closer contact, they may try to convey a sense of themselves to each other, but across the gulf that parts them there is no bridge by which they can wholly enter into one another's life.[2] Professor Shaler observes:

Whenever we behold the life of creatures allied to ourselves, the mammals and birds, we find them continually engaged in an effort to come to an understanding with the neighbors of their kind by means of sympathetic calls, gestures, or fondlings; they, too are trying to escape from the loneliness which is the sore burden of individuality. They probably succeed far better, relatively, than man, for the reason that they have little save a narrow range of emotions to exchange; the needed sympathy can be aroused by mere sounds or gestures; the signals of kinship can be sent back to them by the same simple means. With man it is different; not only is the scope of his emotional life really far greater than in the lower species, but there is an indefinitely wide range of ideas, more or less mingled with emotions, which demand expression as a means of inducing that sympathetic motive which he would arouse in the kinsman.

To set forth his state of mind to the neighbor, man is engaged in ceaseless endeavors. He has invented thousands of languages and words innumerable for no other purpose save to bridge the gulf between these fearfully remote neighbors. He contrives dances and pageants, creates sculpture and painting, makes endless plays and stories, all in the ancient effort to come near to his kind.[3]

Complete exploration of the other's personality is probably never effected, since this would mean knowledge of his every particular thought and feeling. We can only "form conceptions of a personal unity out of the fragments of another person in which he alone is accessible to us," and "the unity so formed

[1] Louis Petroff, *Solitaries and Solitarization* (Doctoral Dissertation, University of Southern California, 1934).

[2] N. S. Shaler, *The Neighbor*, p. 204.

[3] *Ibid.*, pp. 105–106.

necessarily depends on that portion of the other which our standpoint of the other permits us to see."[1]   However, as Simmel remarks elsewhere:

All relationships of people to each other rest, as a matter of course, upon the precondition that they know something about each other. . . . Within each social stratum the individual knows approximately what measure of culture he has to presuppose in each other individual.   In all relations of a personally differentiated sort there develop, as we may affirm with obvious reservations, intensity and shading in the degree in which each unit reveals himself to the other through work and deed . . . each knows the other with whom he has to do, in a rough and ready way, to the degree necessary in order that the needed kinds of intercourse may proceed.[2]

Men Live in Different Worlds of Discourse.—Differences in experience result in differences in the universe of discourse.   An attitude may be wholly foreign to the persons questioned, and their minds may never meet that of the interviewer on the subject.   Under such circumstances the questions asked seem out of place and the replies given prove, quite beside the mark. As Hans Gross comments in speaking of witnesses:

It may be said, indeed, that so long as two people converse unaware of each other's "funded thought" they speak different languages. Some of the most striking misunderstandings come from just this reason.   It is not alone a matter of verbal values, leading to incompatible inferences; actually the whole of a man's mind is involved.   It is generally supposed to be enough to know the meaning of the words necessary for telling a story.   But such knowledge leads only to external and very superficial comprehension; *real clearness can be attained only by knowing the witness' habits of thought in regard to all the circumstances of the case.*   I remember vividly a case of jealous murder in which the most important witness was the victim's brother, an honest, simple woodsman, brought up in the wilderness, and in every sense far removed from idiocy.   His testimony was brief, decided and intelligent.   When the motive for the murder—in this case most important—came under discussion, he shrugged his shoulders and answered my question— whether it was not committed on account of a girl—with, "Yes, so they say."   On further examination I reached the astonishing discovery that not only the word "jealousy," but the very notion and compre-

[1] GEORG SIMMEL, "Sociology of Secrecy and Secret Societies," *American Journal of Sociology*, XI (January, 1906), 442. (Translated from the German by Albion W. Small.)
[2] *Ibid.*, p. 444.

hension were totally foreign to the man. The single girl he at one time thought of was won away from him without making him quarrelsome, nobody had ever told him of the pangs and passions of other people, he had had no occasion to consider the theoretic possibility of such a thing, and so "jealousy" remained utterly foreign to him.[1]

Walter Bingham and Bruce Moore found that the word "arbitration," though properly defined, had come to mean to some textile workers on strike "surrender." While the question asked was: "Are you in favor of arbitration?" it was actually interpreted to mean "Are you in favor of surrendering?"[2]

Lack of Common Definition of Situation.—Ideals, concepts, activities, sentiments, traditions, and all our "spiritual private property" which do not lie within the culture of the interviewee may be misconstrued, and thus incongruous results occur. Knud Rasmussen, in interviewing Eskimos whose language and customs were familiar to him, relates the following experience:

I tried to explain to him [a native Eskimo] in the first instance, that I was interviewing him on behalf of a daily newspaper; that all that passed between us would be made known to many people through the medium of "talk-marks" such as he had seen me making in my notebook, printed on sheets of fine "skin" for men to learn what is happening each day.

But this in itself he regarded as a witticism, a humorous exaggeration; the world of the white men was big, no doubt, yet it could not after all be bigger than that a man might learn all the news there was by enquiring at the nearest tent. . . . [3]

Marriage to the old Russian Molokans, a peasant sectarian group, is a strictly religious, and not a legal matter.

. . . "God alone can sanctify a holy marriage." In Russia the elders performed the ceremony, and the couple were thereby united in the holy bonds of matrimony. The marriage license had no place in the customs of the brother-hood. They were greatly shocked to learn that in the eyes of the American law, unions without licenses were illegitimate:

Can the court be better than God? Can man-made laws be more important than divine law? We were told that children by such unions were illegitimate. . . . [4]

---

[1] HANS GROSS, *Criminal Psychology*, pp. 21–22.
[2] *How to Interview*, p. 5.
[3] KNUD RASMUSSEN, *Across Arctic America*, p. 194.
[4] PAULINE V. YOUNG, *The Pilgrims of Russian Town*, pp. 144–145.

It is frequently said that sympathy—ability to feel with the interviewee—may bridge the gap even when interviewer and interviewee are not in the same world of discourse. But sympathy presupposes actual or vicarious experience as well as intellectual appreciation of the experiences revealed by others. An interviewee may deeply appreciate the problem of parents whose children refuse to attend church, but the limits of his sympathy may be reached when the church in question proves to be that of the Holy Jumpers.

Often also mere intellectual appreciation of problems of the Negroes, or the Orientals, or the Jews, for instance, or even of those problems confronted by members of the same race but of different economic or cultural status does not insure ability to win confidence or ability to get along with them. Many social reformers who work in behalf of oppressed groups or persons are not able to make even a satisfactory approach to them in face-to-face associations. Certain mannerisms may be annoying; the biological characteristics irritating; the modes of thinking provoking, and so on.

Differences in Social Philosophy.—Differences in social philosophy in the accustomed forms of thinking are difficult to bridge. Attempts to overcome such differences belong in the field of social and group treatment. Such conflicts radically alter the exploration type of interview. When the inquirer makes his interviewee conscious of such differences, the answer may frequently take the form of rationalization. This problem is illustrated by an experience of Rasmussen's among the Eskimos, and may be frequently duplicated in the field of social case work and social research:

I had frequently brought the conversation round the subject of tabu with a view to ascertaining the purpose of these highly complicated and apparently meaningless observances; this thing insisted on and that strictly forbidden. But here lay the difficulty. Everyone knew and all were unanimously agreed, as to what must be done or avoided in any given situation, but as to the why and wherefore, none could advance any explanation whatever. They seemed, indeed, to regard it as unreasonable on my part to demand, not only a statement, but a justification, of their religious rites and ceremonies. Aua was as usual the one I mainly questioned, and one evening when I had been endeavoring to extract some more positive information on this head, he suddenly rose to his feet and invited me to step outside.

It was twilight, the brief day was almost at an end, but the moon was up, and one could see the stormriven clouds racing over the sky;

every now and then a gust of snow came whirling down. Aua pointed out over the ice, where the snow swept this way and that in whirling clouds. "Look," he said impressively, "snow and storm; ill weather for hunting. And yet we must hunt for our daily food; *why?* Why must there be storms to hinder us when we are seeking meat for ourselves and those we love?"

Why?

. . . I could make no answer. And Aua took me to a little hut apart, where his aged sister, Natseq, who was ill, lay alone. She looked thin and worn, and too weak even to brighten up at our coming. For days past she had suffered from a painful cough that seemed to come from deep down in the lungs; it was evident she had not long to live.

And for the third time Aua looked me straight in the face and said: "Why should it be so? Why should we human beings suffer pain and sickness? All fear it, all would avoid it if they could. Here is this old sister of mine, she has done no wrong that we can see, but lived her many years and given birth to good, strong children, yet now she must suffer pain at the ending of her days?"

Why? Why?

After this striking object lesson, we returned to the hut, and renewed our interrupted conversation with the others.

"You see," observed Aua, "even you cannot answer when we ask why life is as it is. And so it must be. Our customs all come from life and are directed towards life; we cannot explain, we do not believe in this or that; but the answer lies in what I have just shown you.

"*We fear!*

"We fear the elements with which we have to fight in their fury to wrest out food from land and sea.

"We fear cold and famine in our snow huts.

"We fear the sickness that is daily to be seen among us. Not death but the suffering.

"We fear the souls of the dead, of human and animal alike.

"We fear the spirits of earth and air.

"And therefore our fathers, taught by their fathers before them, guarded themselves about with all these old rules and customs, which are built upon the experience and knowledge for generations. We know not how or why, but we obey them that we may be suffered to live in peace. . . . "

Aua's explanation was reasonable enough from his point of view. There was no more to be said.[1]

Even scientifically minded investigators often have difficulty in appreciating the role which magic and fear of the supernatural

[1] KNUD RASMUSSEN, *Across Arctic America*, pp. 128–131. Reprinted by permission of G. P. Putnam's Sons.

play in the conduct of people and are, therefore, often unable to bridge the gap in their social and moral philosophies. When the Eskimo explained his conduct on the basis of fear there was no more to be said between him and the investigator.

Clashes of Interests Not Always on the Surface.—It is difficult to discover hidden fears early, so that interests of the interviewee will not be jeopardized and his confidence lost.

I was interviewing a long line of transient, homeless men with a view to ascertaining how long they have been homeless and how far they have traveled. I made my aims clear at the outset to the group as a whole, and to each man as he came to be interviewed. Almost at the end of the line was an aged man, a local resident, who gave his replies willingly enough to conceal a hesitating and faltering manner. Not until the man was ready to leave did I notice much relief from subdued tension. I invited him to sit down once more and reviewed my purpose in interviewing him, in an earnest but friendly manner. "Lady, what I just told you is all wrong," was his reply. "I see now that you are sincere and don't mean to fool me and send me back to the Poor Farm."[1]

At times, in spite of all precautions taken to make the purpose of the interview clear, the interviewee may gain wrong notions of what is expected or he may not understand the questions because of his experiences and cultural background. "Why anyone would be bothered with such stuff. . . . What difference does it make anyway?"

Frequently the interests of the interviewee and the interviewer are the same but they are not seen in the same light. Both worker and mother have the best interests of the child at heart but each has a different conception of how to attain them. The worker may be thinking in terms of the health clinic, the parent in terms of ritualistic remedies, home cures, or patent medicines.

The above and other limitations to the personal interview are recognized by all those who have used it either as a tool in diagnosis or for purposes of social therapy. But since the interview cannot be dispensed with and since we cannot confine the study of human beings to records or mere observations or limit the adjustment of personality problems and attitudes to the improvement of social conditions, our task is not only to recount the weaknesses of the interview but to discover ways and means by which they might be overcome. "Forewarned, the inter-

[1] PAULINE V. YOUNG, "The Transient Problem in California," manuscript.

viewer can avoid or at least minimize the dangers. He can school himself to identify, analyze and set aside his own pre-dilections, opinions and prejudices."[1] After all, the reliability of the interview depends to a large extent upon the quality of the investigation and the training and experience of the investiga-tor. In social research the persons to be interviewed can often be chosen carefully, and in social welfare work the interviewer needs to determine the competence of the persons interviewed. It must also be remembered that self-justifications, story com-plexes, romatic over- and under-statements in the interviewee are perhaps just as important clues to the understanding of his personality and his problems as an accurate and painstaking account of his measurable and verifiable problems. Self-justifica-tion, prejudices, romantic fabrication, and so on, when a part of an interviewee's life, must be recognized as an element to be considered in social therapy, and a skilled interviewer will be quick to sense them and to understand how and why they exist and to what degree they dominate the attitudes of the interviewee and how they effect the interview.

The sociological problems of the interview—lack of common definition of the social situation, due to differences in personal and group experience, differences in the social philosophy, and the presence of social distance—are also surmountable to a large degree in the case of a skillful, trained investigator who knows how to bring people into a common world of discourse, how to redefine the social philosophies so that both interviewer and interviewee have at least some common denominators, and how to reduce social distance. In one sense, the entire discussion on the technique of the interview deals with just such problems. Mary Van Kleeck suggests also that when the rules of evidence are kept in mind, when they are verified and checked against other sources of information, and when the interview is written up immediately after it took place, the validity of the interview can be greatly increased.[2]

Suggestions for Further Study

1. Search in the literature on interviewing for a comprehensive discussion of the problems of the interview and of the validity of the interview.

2. How may the skillful interviewer overcome the objections to the inter-view raised by Read Bain, by Stuart Rice?

[1] WALTER V. BINGHAM and BRUCE V. MOORE, *op. cit.*, p. 200.

[2] "The Interview as a Method of Research," *Bulletin* of the Taylor Society, XI (1926), 268–274.

3. Read Bingham and Moore's discussion of the "Doubts of Interviewing" and indicate to what extent these doubts are justified.

4. What is meant by the sociology of secrecy? How does secrecy affect the validity of the interview? Outline Simmel's discussion "Sociology of Secrecy and Secret Societies" and indicate its importance to the interviewer.

5. Why do people hide behind masks? How far do they succeed in hiding true facts about themselves?

6. What is Dr. Petroff's contribution to the study of the problems of the interview in his discussion *Solitaries and Solitarization?*

7. What is meant by a "contagious transfer" in the interview? How may it be overcome?

8. Why are men strikingly individual beings? How can they be strikingly different when it is maintained that human nature is always and everywhere the same?

9. Read N. S. Shaler's book, *The Neighbor,* and show its significance to the interviewer.

10. In what respects are Park's and Shaler's philosophies as expressed in this chapter similar? What is their significance to the problem of interviewing? Illustrate.

11. What is meant by "a world of discourse"? How do different worlds of discourse arise? How do these problems affect the interview? Illustrate.

12. What is meant by "funded thought"? by "meeting of minds"? How do these processes affect the interview? Illustrate.

13. What is meant by "a common definition of the situation"? How do you arrive at a common definition of the situation? Illustrate.

14. What is meant by "differences in social philosophy"? How do you arrive at a common social philosophy? Illustrate.

15. Why cannot the interview be dispensed with?

16. What methods may be employed to increase the validity of personal interviews?

17. What does the validity of the interview depend upon?

18. To what extent are the sources of error, opinions, rationalizations of the interviewee as important to an understanding of his personality as true attitudes?

Selected Bibliography

1. BINGHAM, WALTER V., and BRUCE V. MOORE: *How to Interview,* 1931.
   Chap. I, "Some Doubts about Interviewing."
   Chap. XII, "General Studies of the Interview and Related Techniques."
2. PARK, ROBERT E.: "Behind Our Masks," *The Survey Graphic,* LXI, (May, 1926), 135–139.
   An analysis of personality in terms of interaction patterns. Differentiates between the public and private or inner life of the person. A good interpretation of the unique behavior of the Oriental.
3. RICE, STUART A.: "Contagious Bias in the Interview," *The American Journal of Sociology,* XXXV (November, 1929), 420–423.
   Reports various interpretations and individual bias of several interviewers when interviewing a group of homeless men.

4. SIMMEL, GEORG: "Sociology of Secrecy and Secret Societies," *The American Journal of Sociology*, XI (January, 1906), 441–498. (Translated from the German by Albion W. Small.)

Discusses the problems involved in penetrating the inner sanctum and the spiritual private property which individuals seek to conceal for various reasons.

5. VAN KLEECK, MARY: "The Interview as a Method of Research," *Bulletin* of the Taylor Society, XI (1926), 268–274.

An analysis of the interview as a tool in research. Points out the following problems affecting the reliability of the interview which need scientific study: definition of the investigation; purpose of the investigation; units of measurement; sources of information; methods and processes studied; verification.

CHAPTER XV

DYNAMICS OF THE THERAPEUTIC INTERVIEW

The subject of social therapy in social case work is a new and uncharted field. Little scientific research has been done on the therapeutic processes in case work, particularly upon the therapeutic aspects of the personal interview, which might help to determine goals, methods, and philosophy of procedure.[1] If we have succeeded in learning that certain methods work in certain cases, we rarely know why they work in these cases and fail in others. Often we do not even know what worked and whether adjustment was secured because of the use of certain techniques or in spite of them. Within the last three or four years social case workers had started to analyze their interviewing techniques and to reflect upon their role in social therapy[2] but to some extent had to abandon this new professional interest for the time being and turn their attention to the problems of disaster relief created by the economic depression of 1930.

The therapeutic interview—whether in standard case work or emergency relief—is only one method of social case work therapy, that is, it is that phase of the whole adjustment process in which verbalization and face-to-face relations are the chief means by which therapy is accomplished. However, the two other major phases: the use of services and of material things—provision, for instance, of medical care, employment, recreation, or groceries, rent, clothing, etc.—also depend to a large degree upon the use of personal interviews and personal relations. The interview is not only the medium by which these services are provided but "it also has a bearing on the effort which the client will put forth on

[1] See AMERICAN ASSOCIATION OF SOCIAL WORKERS, *Interviews: A Study of the Methods of Analyzing and Recording Social Case Work Interviews.*
KARL DE SCHWEINITZ, *The Art of Helping People out of Trouble.*
WILLIAM HEALY. For a list of major publications consult bibliography.
MARY B. SAYLES, *The Problem Child at Home; The Problem Child at School; Three Problem Children.*
[2] See VIRGINIA P. ROBINSON, *A Changing Psychology in Social Case Work.*

his own behalf and the value which he will place on the contribution of time, of effort, of relief."[1]

The philosophy of the case worker is predicated on the belief that it is easier to reconstruct human personality than to change or rebuild a social and economic order.   It is of interest that many of the activities in present-day Russia are based on this belief, according to Maurice Hindus.   In their great offensive "for a new world along two vast all-embracing fronts—that of economics with the aim of creating a new economic order, and of sociology with the aim of creating a new human personality"—they have suffered many rebuffs on the economic front, but "within short space of sixteen years [they have] so 'reboiled' or 'reforged,' the human being in Russia that he is a new personage on earth, with a body of new aims, attitudes and responses."[2]

On What Is Social Therapy Based?

Social therapy, in order to be rational and consistent, must be based on: (1) a knowledge of existing social problems, attitudes, wants, and hopes of those people who are unable to cope with their environment; (2) a complete understanding of the causes of these problems, attitudes, and the bases of the hopes and ambitions.   The interviewer needs to know, for instance, whether domestic discord is due to sex incompatibility, to financial straits, to interference of relatives, conflict of cultures, etc., or to what combination of these conditions.   Obviously, the interviewer in domestic discord cases where the cause is sex maladjustment needs to use a different approach than in one where the difficulty arises out of interference of relatives or financial straits.   It is frequently remarked that "Once the cause is determined the rest is easy" or "Understanding the problem is more than half the cure"; (3) a knowledge of the personalities of these people who are unable to find their way through the complexities of their surroundings.   The truism that "It matters little what happens to a person, but it matters much how he takes it" is of special significance to the case worker.   This was clearly demonstrated to the American Red Cross, for instance, during the World War:

[1] ELEANOR NEUSTAEDTER, "The Role of the Case Worker in Treatment," *The Family*, XIII (July, 1932), 151.

[2] *The Great Offensive*, p. viii.

Two men walk into the office at the same time: both have lost their right arms on the battle field. One is cynical and dejected and "the world has nothing to offer him" except a living. "The loss of my arm is the unmaking of me." The other accepts his loss as a challenge to his ability: "never before have I had to apply myself to any work as I do now; in a way it is the making of me."[1]

Outwardly both men face one and the same problem, but a mere artificial substitute for the lost arm is not enough. Both men must be helped to make the moral adjustment, to redefine their ambitions and hopes and to conceive themselves as totally different persons from what they had been—persons with very different habits, associations, and ideals[2]—but in their reeducation each man must be approached differently—one must be aroused to self-help; the other must be watched so that he does not overtax himself.

(4) Therapy must be based on a knowledge of the social world and the social forces to which the person in question is responsive. Mrs. Sheffield says:

Since all of any given person's significant habits form themselves within relationships between himself and environing persons, institutions, and ideas, his personality is a web-like creation of a self interacting with other selves in a succession of situations. As this idea gains ground we shall talk less of the individual as a solid and self-contained unit, moving and acting in an environment of other solid and self-contained units, all mutually distinct and external. We shall talk more of defining relationships, of motivations among lives that interpenetrate. . . .

The "Social point of view . . . " differs from that of most medical men, psychiatrists included, and from that of most practicing psychologists—those who examine people for their intelligence levels. These specialists from the very nature of their training and their daily work, tend to take an atomic view of the individual, to think of him more as a self-sufficient unit impinged upon by environmental forces than as an integral part of his social setting. This fundamental difference of conception often prevents these members of the more established field of study from getting as much as they might from social work.[3]

MECHANISMS OF SOCIAL THERAPY

There are many mechanisms by which social therapy may be accomplished through the personal interview, but within the

[1] Statement by a Red Cross worker.

[2] ROBERT E. PARK, "The Significance of Social Research in Social Service," *Journal of Applied Sociology*, VIII (May-June, 1924), 263–267.

[3] ADA E. SHEFFIELD, *Case-study Possibilities: A Forecast*, pp. 10–12.

limited scope of the present treatise only certain major methods can receive attention. Furthermore, these methods are not presented in the spirit of charting a new course in social therapy but as illustrations of how some typical interviewing situations were met. It must be remembered that rarely, if ever, are these mechanisms mutually exclusive, that is, that only one mechanism may be employed to the exclusion of all others. Frequently several mechanisms are employed to bring about desired results. In the interview with Mrs. Parker, for instance, the interviewer induced mental catharsis, redefined the social situation, provided for the satisfaction of the wish for response and recognition, etc.

Sympathetic Insight.—Sympathetic insight is fundamentally the ability of a person to enter imaginatively and reflectively into the life of another, based on an intellectual and rational awareness of his attitudes and values. Furthermore, it implies feeling with another and a certain congruence of the emotional states of the observer and the observed. Interviewees are quick to discern when the interviewer has passed the gulf which separates man from man and when he becomes *we* in another form. All the devices of personal communication often fail to win across the void and to bring the two beings closer together but the interviewer "with a step of sympathetic spirit passes the gulf."[1] Professor C. H. Cooley observes that only through sympathetic insight can we influence others.

Sympathy is a requisite to social power. Only in so far as a man understands people and thus enters into the life around him has he any effective existence; the less he has [of sympathy] the more he is a mere animal, not truly in contact with human life. And if he is not in contact with it he can of course have no power over it. This is a principle of familiar application, and yet one which is often overlooked, practical men having, perhaps, a better grasp of it than theorists. It is well understood by men of the world that effectiveness depends at least as much upon address, *savoir-faire*, tact, and the like, involving sympathetic insight into the minds of other people, as upon any more practical faculties. There is nothing more practical than social imagination; to lack it is to lack everything. All classes of persons need it— the mechanic, the farmer, and the tradesman, as well as the lawyer, the clergyman, the railway president, the politician, the philanthropist, and the poet. . . .

A person of definite character and purpose who comprehends our way of thought is sure to exert power over us. He cannot altogether be

[1] N. S. SHALER, *The Neighbor*, p. 227.

resisted; because, if he understands us, he can make us understand him, through the word, the look, or other symbol, which both of us connect with the common sentiment or idea; and thus by communicating an impulse he can move the will. Sympathetic influence enters into our system of thought as a matter of course, and affects our conduct as surely as water affects the growth of a plant. The kindred spirit can turn on a system of lights, to recur to the image of the last chapter, and so transform the mental illumination. This is the nature of all authority and leadership. . . . [1]

Professor E. W. Burgess, in his discussion of Clifford Shaw's technique in dealing with problem boys, goes a step further by maintaining that:

The first step in the course of treatment is the approach to the boy, not by sympathy, but by empathy. Through his life-history his counselor is enabled to see his life as the boy conceived it rather than as an adult might imagine it. Empathy means entering into the experience of another person by the human and democratic method of sharing experiences. In this and other ways rapport is established. Sympathy is the attempt through imagination to put one's self in another person's place with all the fallacies which are almost necessarily involved. . . .
Mr. Shaw does not use the methods of the psychoanalyst, he is not dealing with the materials of the unconscious, but with the memories, wishes, plans, and ambitions of the conscious mind. Working with these, he devises an experimental plan of treatment that attempts to take into account the personality pattern, the attitudes, interests, talents, and plans of the boy himself. [2]

It is not sufficient merely to know the needs of those we interview; it is necessary to appreciate their entire mental and emotional complex by fashioning our thought and emotions out of the material from our own lives under similar circumstances.

The most significant thing about any experience is having it, and the next most significant thing is being able to reflect upon it. In an immediate sense the social worker lives his way into his thinking. He does not experiment upon people, but he shares a certain experience with people. The ability of human beings to interpenetrate and yet maintain awareness is the germ of the matter. [3]

[1] CHARLES H. COOLEY, *Human Nature and the Social Order*, pp. 140–142. Reprinted by permission of Charles Scribner's Sons.
[2] E. W. BURGESS, "Discussion," in CLIFFORD R. SHAW, *The Jack Roller*, pp. 194–195.
[3] GORDON HAMILTON, "Sharing Experience," *The Survey Graphic*, LIX (December 1, 1927), 317.

Sympathy presupposes that the interviewer has had actual or vicarious experiences analogous to those of the interviewee, that he can enter imaginatively into his mental life. Going along with the interviewee, however, is not so much a matter of emotional reaction as it is of intellectual appreciation of the significance of the story and unfailing interest in it as it unfolds. That is, the process of *rapprochement* does not necessarily run counter to the processes of impersonalization or objectification. The participants grow closer to each other, as it were, as they come to look less and less at each other's face, observe less each other's reactions to the story, and turn their gaze upon that third person—the detached self of the interviewee. It is for this reason that the story told as both look into the retreating distances at night from the rear platform of an observation car, or sit side by side gazing into the fire, or merely sit side by side in any suitable place, is more apt to plumb the depths of personality than one told when the participants sit facing each other across a table or an intervening space.

The following excerpts from interviews aid in understanding how sympathetic insight is used as a method in therapy:

(Mrs. Martin had long resisted the proposed placement of her twelve-year-old daughter in a foster home where she would not witness "the drunken orgies of her stepfather.")

They all tell me I am selfish, that I haven't the girl's welfare at heart, but I am afraid to trust them when they can't read a mother's heart better than that. . . . The visitor sold me the idea of sending Mary away from home when she said to me: "Mrs. Martin, I know what it means to have a drunken husband; I know how lonely you think you will be when your only child is away from home; I know what it means to part with a child. I don't blame you for clinging to Mary; every loving mother would, and just because you love her so much you must protect her."

She said to me: "Do you realize what living in constant fear does to a child? She may never be able to get over her fears. And while Mary is away you can use your influence on your husband. There is a cure for him. . . . " She didn't argue with me, and as she talked I knew she *understood*, and I trusted her. I can still hear her say these things to me.[1]

Many factors enter into the above situation, but we note that the interviewer not only had sympathetic insight into the case

---

[1] Statement by a client of a child placement agency.

but also developed in the mother sympathetic insight into the case of her daughter. Undoubtedly the mother had considerable sympathy for the child, that is, she felt with her, shared her pains and joys, but did so perhaps with little conception of the inner and true nature of the child's behavior and possible conflicts. The interviewer supplied her with insight, that is, with an inner view of the girl's feelings and attitudes and attempted to develop an ability at their rational evaluation.

The blind sailor (see pages 324–327, interview with Mr. Stephen S.) had strenuously objected to his many contacts with "those sighted folks who had no conception of how a blind man feels, what he should do, and how he should act," but he unhesitatingly submitted to a plan of procedure which members of the Club for the Blind outlined for him, which procedure differed little from the one proposed in the first instance by "the sighted folks."

The immigrant father who attempts to beat his children into good behavior according to traditional old-world methods is not to be persuaded to abandon his technique of chastisement by threatening him with the law, nor by moral arguments, but by providing him with sympathetic insight into the new social and economic urban forces to which his children are responding. The interviewer likewise must have insight into the father's cultural background and understand the group's means of social control.

When a family refuses to move into more desirable quarters in a superior neighborhood, the interviewer needs to ascertain the motives prompting the refusal. Is the family emotionally attached to the old shanty or to certain friends or native organizations in the neighborhood? Are some members of the family of the Philistine type of personality who do not welcome change? Is the new neighborhood approved by their social group, and so on and on.

As early as 1910 Miss Mary Richmond wrote:

Friendly visiting means intimate and continuous knowledge of and sympathy with a . . . family's joys, sorrows, opinions, feelings and the entire outlook upon life. The visitor that has this is unlikely to blunder either about relief or any other detail; without it he is almost certain, in any charitable relations with members of the family, to blunder seriously.[1]

---

[1] *Friendly Visiting among the Poor*, p. 180.

Behavior cannot be influenced without an understanding of motives.[1] The prime problem of the interviewer is to understand these motives and later to orient the interviewee to his own problems and to unravel, so to speak, his state of mind to him. To provide the individual with insight is perhaps the most difficult problem the interviewer faces. He is limited not only by his own range of sympathy, but also by the client's ability, customary reactions, deep-seated habits, personality traits. However, patient and tolerant redefinition of the social situation on a level comprehensible to the interviewee will ultimately gain results. "It is not so much the client's stupidity which fails to make the needed adjustment," says a social work executive of wide experience, "as the interviewer's impatience and the lack of ability to put himself across to clients with limited ability. After all, every man's mind can be reached."

Identification.—Identification, or the ability to exchange experiences, is closely related to the problem of sympathetic insight. Elizabeth Dexter's discussion of the social case worker's attitudes and problems as they affect her work throws further light on social therapy:

The worker who feels little identification with her clients and is unable to bridge the gulf between herself and them is likely to have a feeling of superiority and look upon them as a different order of being. She regards their problems as peculiar to their social setting, or she is inclined to minimize their difficulties by converting them into humorous anecdotes. . . .

Human relationships depend upon our ability to identify ourselves with one another. This is the only basis for understanding. We cannot all be delinquent girls nor deserting fathers, but by understanding their motives and recognizing the same motives in ourselves, we can appreciate their problems and understand their behavior. Without identification the case worker cannot get the emotional significance of her client's experiences or reach any real understanding of his problem.

---

[1] Professor Lindeman's discussion of the participant observer is particularly pertinent in this connection. He maintains that information sought in the study of human behavior should be classified from the point of view of (1) what is the person or group doing (observation from the outside); (2) what does the group think it is doing (observation from the inside). The information secured under the second category involves cooperation and participation in the activities, interests, and attitudes of others. The participant observer becomes a part of these individuals or groups. (See Eduard C. Lindeman, *Social Discovery*, pp. 190–200.)

Personal prejudices are the usual barrier to identification. If the worker has religious bias or racial prejudice she will be confused in her handling of cases involving these issues, for in reacting to her prejudice she will lose sight of the client as a unique individual and not understand the painful situation that confronts him. If she has been brought up with narrow ideas on sex, she will find it difficult to accept the sex irregularities that crop up in her cases. . . .

Since identification is at the basis of case work, as of all human relationships, it is essential for the case worker to recognize it as a mechanism that must be controlled. Otherwise it operates unconsciously and she is unaware of the need to guard against the prejudiced view it may give her. Her control will depend upon her objective attitudes and her ability to distinguish for her clients and for herself the reality issues otherwise obscured by subjective factors. The worker who allows herself to become entirely absorbed in her work is motivated by complete identification with her clients. She lives their lives, suffers their pain, is concerned with every detail of their existence. She becomes her client, and by this move loses the most valuable contribution she has to give, namely, her objective attitude toward his problem. She sees the problem only through his eyes, overestimating his justifications and overlooking his bias; or, as the situation unfolds, she identifies herself first with one member of the family and then another, mistaking these shifts for impartiality. Her perspective on the case is distorted to the degree to which she remains identified with any part of the situation, for she will be as blind as is her client to the reality issues, and unable effectively to help him work out of his entanglement because she has allowed herself to become entangled too. She has gone over to his subjective position instead of withdrawing to a vantage point where she would have the perspective of which he is at present incapable. She must be able to see beyond him and understand him as part of the whole situation if she is to succeed in giving him that objectivity which will enable him to manage himself more successfully.[1]

Mental Catharsis.—Men have perhaps a natural impulse to communicate their inward feelings and sensations, particularly when under tension. "The desire to 'tell about it' produces intense satisfaction of the emotions. Suppression involves tensions, and a general uneasiness."[2] Frequently active, extroverted people or those under tension seek out a person to

[1] ELIZABETH H. DEXTER, "The Social Case Worker's Attitudes and Problems as They Affect her Work," *Proceedings* of the National Conference of Social Work (1926), 438–439.

[2] ANNA ROBESON BURR, *Religious Confessions and Confessants*, p. 40.

whom they can unburden, confess, or talk at length to find relief as they "get it off their chest." This process of release from tension is also called mental catharsis. "When it occurs the effect is a pouring out of the mental jam by which the person has become disorganized,"[1] at least for the time being.

Catharsis is impatient of fulfilment. The release is usually very rapid and followed by the lassitude usually attendant upon strong emotional reaction. Few persons can prolong catharsis longer than a day or two. Confession at its best is hot and eruptive. It breaks out with the force of molten lava after a period of inner convulsions which may be thought of as a process of mounting tensions which . . . breaks over into a final discharge.[2]

On the other hand, it should not be supposed that the secrets of the mind are exposed for the mere asking. The methods of suppression, inhibition, and hiding behind a mask are primitive means by which the self seeks protection (Franz Alexander). However, social work interviewers do not often deal with people who require secrecy. Generally these people, when under tension, arrive at a critical point beyond which it is painful for them to remain silent. Then it is necessary, in Macbeth's words, "to cleanse the stuff'd bosom of that perilous stuff which weighs upon the heart." Secret knowledge isolates us; confession reassimilates us into the group. So dependent are we upon interaction with our fellows that no punishment is harder to bear than solitary confinement or being "sent to Coventry."

Daniel Webster vividly describes the behavior of a man who cannot keep his undetected guilt secret:

Meantime the guilty soul cannot keep its secret. It is false to itself; or rather it feels an irresistible impulse of conscience to be true to itself. It labors under its guilty possession and knows not what to do with it. The human heart was not made for the residence of such an inhabitant. It finds itself preyed on by a torment, which it dares not to acknowledge to God or man. A vulture is devouring it, and it can ask no sympathy or assistance either from heaven or earth. The secret which the murderer possesses soon comes to possess him; and like the evil spirits of which we read, it overcomes him, and leads him

[1] E. T. KRUEGER, "The Value of Life History Documents for Social Research," *Journal of Applied Sociology*, IX (January–February, 1925), 198.

[2] E. T. KRUEGER, "The Technique of Securing Life History Documents," *ibid.* (March–April, 1925), 291–292.

whithersoever it will. He feels it beating at his heart, rising to his throat, and *demanding* disclosure. He thinks the whole world sees it in his face, reads it in his eyes, and almost hears its workings in the very silence of his thoughts. It has become his master. It betrays his discretion, it breaks down his courage, it conquers his prudence. When suspicions from without begin to embarrass him, and the net of circumstances to entangle him the fatal secret struggles with still greater violence to burst forth. It *must* be confessed, it WILL be confessed. There is no refuge from confession, but suicide,—and suicide is confession.[1]

The ease with which mental catharsis is secured depends to a large extent on: (1) The degree of *rapport* established between interviewer and interviewee.[2] (2) The delicacy of the subject matter to be discussed. Sex problems and tensions are generally more difficult to talk about than those arising because of financial difficulties or even those due to conflict with one's children or one's mate. (3) The language at the interviewee's command which will express his problems in a conventional manner. The interviewer must often supply the terminology descriptive of sex tabus, mental disturbances, religious ecstasy, etc. (4) The extent to which the whole conflict is at the level of consciousness. Often the interviewee is not aware of what is involved in the conflict producing the tensions and the situation is not sharply defined to him. When he is able to grasp a definition of the social situation and secure insight into his own problems, he is eager to talk them over.

Mechanisms of Mental Catharsis.—The techniques by which mental catharsis is secured vary from mere listening to prolonged and painstaking psychoanalysis. There are no specific questions or behavior patterns on the part of the interviewer which will initiate mental catharsis. Most individuals in whom inhibitions are not pathological will unburden to sympathetic listeners, under conditions which do not compromise their status and assure privacy and confidence. Bogardus says:

In securing mental release there are certain mechanisms which may be "touched off" as it were. The principle of mechanical discharge may

---

[1] Quoted by J. H. WIGMORE, *Principles of Judicial Proof*, p. 540, from *Great Speeches and Orations of Daniel Webster*, p. 192.

[2] For a discussion of to whom confessions are most easily made, see Read Bain, "The Impersonal Confession and Social Research," *Journal of Applied Sociology*, IX (May-June, 1925), 356–361.

be illustrated in five ways. First, there is the *naive* type of habit mechanism. Every person at times speaks naively and simply. What he is stimulated to say seems entirely natural and normal, and so he speaks frankly without being aware of it. As informal and as natural a conversation in every particular as possible is ideal. . . .

Second, there is an *egotistical* type of mechanism, which, when released, will open the flood-gates of experience. Nearly everyone feels pleasant when his ego is appealed to, and falls before an increasing sense of personal importance. . . .

Third, there is the *confessional* type of mechanism, whose release brings "relief." The desire "to tell someone," whether an intimate friend or a "stranger" who probably will never cross one's path again, is often strong. . . .

Fourth, there is the purely *scientific* type of mechanism indicating the willingness to tell all for the sake of truth and science by one who takes an objective viewpoint concerning himself, who scorns much of the conventional snap judgments of "right" and "wrong," and who is willing to sacrifice "himself" for the sake of science. . . .

Fifth, there is a *sophisticated* type of mechanism whose release is the most difficult of all to secure. Some persons are "hard-boiled" as far as being interviewed is concerned. . . .

In other words, there are some people who are always on their guard —until you get them clear away from all the stimuli of their daily environment.[1]

Therapeutic Values of Mental Catharsis.—The mere process of talking over one's problems or confessing one's innermost thoughts and difficulties to a sympathetic listener often tends to relieve tensions. Though not a permanent or very effective treatment, it helps, and its very simplicity commends it. Karl Menninger's experience is undoubtedly duplicated manifold in the work of most interviewers:

. . . Often it suffices for the psychotherapist to be a sympathetic, uncritical listener. I have a very intelligent patient, with a very bitter cross to bear, who comes to see me periodically, pours out a great burden of woe about which I can do absolutely nothing (as she well knows), and then pays her bill and takes her departure declaring that she feels much better.[2]

It should also be remembered that often while the telling of one's story releases tensions it may set up new tensions, particu-

[1] E. S. Bogardus, *The New Social Research*, pp. 110–115. Reprinted by permission.

[2] Karl Menninger, *The Human Mind*, p. 380.

larly if the listener is discovered or imagined to be the wrong one, or when the looked-for response is not forthcoming, or when the explanation of the social situation is unsatisfactory.

> I had lots on my mind and heart. I had to talk. I told the visitor that she had to listen to me. It relieved me greatly to unburden, I felt like a new person who could start life all over again. . . . When I was all through I suddenly realized that the visitor did not understand me, that perhaps I had made a fool of myself, that it would have been better to let well enough alone, and I felt a sharp pain, but the story was out. . . . But that did not last long, I was permanently relieved of my burden and I felt better than I had in years. I knew that even with the new misgivings I could go on lighthearted.[1]

Perhaps one of the chief values derived from a confession is the fact that in relating one's experiences a person may gain an objective view of himself. Self-revelation goes on best as the individual separates himself farther and farther from the story he is telling of himself. When he can treat his own self as the object of dispassionate observation, the conditioning complexes will exert only a minimum effect on the telling of the story, however large a part they may have played in the story itself. The introverted person is much less able to detach himself from the stream of events than the extroverted person; the hypochondriac is probably never able to make the separation. The following quotations illustrate the effect of mental catharsis:

> The very act of pouring out one's experiences not only has a cathartic effect, particularly where tensions and inhibitions are released, but also gives the subject perspective upon his life. This gaining of perspective upon one's experience is the chief way in which persons achieve control over their impulses and motives and work out their destiny toward some challenging goal.[2]

The psychology of confession is well understood and has long held a prominent place in social theory and practice. Confession is one of the cornerstones of the Catholic Church polity; . . . the Methodist testimonial meeting and all prayers are largely confessional; psychoanalysis is based upon it. . . .

Confession is based on the social nature of man and his instinctive desire to "tell." It is only by "telling" in some form that we can objectify our experiences. In the case of "evil," we triumph over it

---

[1] Statement by an interviewee.

[2] E. W. BURGESS, "Discussion," in CLIFFORD R. SHAW, *The Jack Roller*, p. 195.

by confessing it. Insofar as we gain sympathy, we feel justified in our own eyes, i.e., in the eyes of others. In any event, we are likely to get advice. . . . Every confession is thus more or less an art product, a species of sublimation, . . . [1]

In opening ourselves to another we are impelled to imagine how our conduct appears to him; we take an outside view of ourselves. It makes a great difference to whom we confess: the higher the character of the person whose mind we imagine, the more enlightening and elevating is the view of ourselves that we get. Even to write our thoughts in a diary, and so to confess, not to a particular person, but to that vague image of an interlocutor that connects itself with all articulate expression, makes things look different.

It is, perhaps, much the same with prayer. To pray, in a higher sense, is to confront our moral perplexities with the highest personal ideal we can form, and so to be unconsciously integrating the two, straightening out the one in accordance with the other. . . .

Whatever publishes our conduct introduces new and strong factors into conscience; but whether this publicity is wholesome or otherwise depends upon the character of the public; or, more definitely, upon whether the idea of ourselves that we impute to this public is edifying or degrading. [2]

The following interview illustrates under what conditions mental catharsis may be secured from an interviewee under tension who faces serious social problems: [3]

Interview with Mrs. Parker.

(Woman in office asking for an emergency grocery order . . . Family consists of American widow and two children. Son, John, age 21, daughter, Amelia, age 18.)

Mrs. Parker: Oh, isn't this awful, I just can't control myself. Every time I have to come into a County office to ask for anything I go all to pieces. I can't help it. It all seems so dreadful that I have to ask for even the bread that goes into my children's mouths. Poor Daddy tried so hard to provide for us all and it all went for nothing, everything he tried to do has been wasted. Well. . . I can't beg for bread like I had to do last year. I won't do it!

Interviewer: Won't you sit down, Mrs. Parker. Just rest awhile. It will take a few moments to have your grocery order written.

Mrs. Parker: Oh—can you get me a grocery order? I need it so badly. They told me they couldn't help me until I got my release from the Unem-

---

[1] READ BAIN, "The Impersonal Confession and Social Research," *Journal of Applied Sociology*, IX (May-June, 1925), 356–357.

[2] CHARLES H. COOLEY, *Human Nature and the Social Order*, pp. 386–387. Reprinted by permission of Charles Scribner's Sons.

[3] Interview held and recorded by Mrs. Dorothy Krise, Los Angeles.

ployed Cooperative Unit. I've been down there three times and they tell me that I don't need a release because I'm only registered on the inactive list. I waited as long as I could but I finally just had to come down.

Interviewer: We won't worry about that release, Mrs. Parker. We can arrange to get it for you. I'm afraid the managers of the units don't quite understand what we need. And now if you will excuse me for a moment I will have your order prepared. (Pause to allow woman to gain composure).

Interviewer: (Returning with a glass of water) Isn't it warm today, Mrs. Parker? Won't you have a glass of water?

Mrs. Parker: Thank you. I didn't expect anyone to trouble about me in a County office. After the experiences I've had. Oh, I could tell you how I've been treated. If I let myself think about it I should go mad. And I'm so worried about my son. He gets so desperate I'm afraid he'll do something dreadful some day.

Interviewer: How old is your son, Mrs. Parker?

Mrs. Parker: Twenty-one. Too young to have seen so much trouble.

Interviewer: All young people are facing a hard situation at present, Mrs. Parker, and they need all of the help and cooperation we can possibly give them.

Mrs. Parker: My son won't take my advice any more. He says: "You and Dad have lived the most decent hardworking lives of any people I know, and what have you got to show for it? Honesty and decency don't pay. If anybody deserved a break you and Dad did. And now you have to beg for every mouthful of food we eat."

Interviewer: You won't have to beg here, Mrs. Parker. This office is run with money from the Federal Government, as well as from the State and County, to help people who are unemployed until they can find work. Money which you and your husband helped to supply during the years you paid taxes on your property. In a way it's just coming back to you, you see. Does your son have a trade?

Mrs. Parker: Oh, no. He had to leave High School to look for a job. He was so upset about it. You know he was a fine football player. We hoped he'd get a scholarship to a university. He's interested in aviation.

Interviewer: That's splendid. My brother is a little younger than your son, and he is anxious to become a pilot. Perhaps we can find him a job as apprentice at some airfield, or he might join the Army aviation service; they have a fine training school there.

Mrs. Parker: (Bitterly) He'd never do that. He's had enough of military training to last him a lifetime. . . . And then he has these wild notions in his head about the Government. Sometimes he scares me. But I can't say I blame him. I used to be proud to be an American citizen but now I hate the very sight of the flag (clenching her fist and pounding on the table) and when the time comes to fight for our rights I'm willing! I'd pick up a knife and run into the streets and kill and kill until we rid the world of these unspeakable creatures who make us crawl on our knees before they'll give us a piece of bread. Poor Daddy asked and asked for work and do you think they'd give it to him? I should say not. But they had work to give to those dirty foreigners who have children like animals. But how about the reasonable people who use self-control and only bring children into the world when they can take care of them? We always tried to bring ours up to be true to Christian ideals and respect law and order but what can you tell them when they look around and see a hideous world that's all wrong? They are helpless in a situation they had no hand in making.

Interviewer: Young people have a hard time seeing beyond their own troubles, Mrs. Parker. They don't realize that their misfortunes are not reaped upon them by an avenging hand but are the product of a situation that can be remedied and will be if we have faith that the ideals on which our country was founded are not at fault and work with every ounce of strength in us to prove it. You know as well as I do, Mrs. Parker, that you are not sorry that you have brought your children up to be honorable, industrious, and ambitious. In great crises a country must always depend upon such people to pull it through and how much help are the young people going to be if we let them quit, give up, lie down, and cry "the world's all wrong," and do nothing about it. We have a president who knows all about "the little fellow." The CCC camps and the CWA have proved life-savers to thousands of families. We are not living under the heel of a tyrant. We will have to help your son to bring his thinking up to date. He's way behind the times.

Mrs. Parker: If only I could have some work. I feel so helpless with nothing to do. I know that everything you say is true and I do carry on and say things I don't really mean, but you don't know the real circumstances. (Beginning to cry again) Oh, how can I tell you? It was such a dreadful thing!

Interviewer: I know you have had much greater misfortune than unemployment and poverty, Mrs. Parker, because I can see that a woman of your character and ideals could stand hard times and come through them splendidly. If you think I can help you in any way and want to tell me what is on your mind, please do so. It will help me to understand your situation better.

Mrs. Parker: You have helped me and I do want to tell you. Last year we applied for help to the County. Daddy had been unemployed for so long. Our home was clear but we had to borrow on it. Then we couldn't even pay the interest on the loans. We lost our home. We borrowed on our insurance and our car and lost them both. Daddy had been suffering so with his teeth that he couldn't sleep nights, he was in such pain. My married daughter, Louise, was very good to us. She just did everything for us. I was so ashamed to have to have help from her husband, and they couldn't really afford it. Her husband had his time cut down so they just couldn't help us any more. We applied to the County but they said something about not being able to give aid to unemployment cases or something; anyway they wouldn't help us. We got some groceries from an agency when we got right down to nothing and they finally sent us back to the County. The visitor came out and talked to us. She seemed real nice and left us an order for food and said she would try to get Daddy some work. His teeth got so bad the visitor told him to go to the County Hospital to have them out. He did but then he couldn't eat anything his gums were so sore, and he was worried about John who was getting so restless. Well, John got into trouble; he was arrested for trying to hold up a gas station with some other boys and was sent to a reformatory for a year. I was almost glad because then I didn't have to worry about his being tempted and staying out on the streets late at night, and he was trying to get Amelia to go out and "enjoy life," as he called it. She is such a good girl I didn't want her spoiled. The visitor offered me some housework jobs but I didn't want to leave Amelia, she was such a comfort to me. Daddy got worse and worse. No work, not able to eat anything, and John on his mind. He couldn't stand it. He shot himself (laying her head on the desk and sobbing). One morning we woke up and he was gone——

Interviewer: (Very quietly) I should like to know Amelia. It must make her very happy to know that she is the one person you can depend on and confide in. It is a heavy burden for a little girl to bear but I know you don't want to overburden her. When you are cheerful and able to forget I imagine that is her greatest happiness.

Mrs. Parker: That's right. She is always trying to make me cheer up. She is such a good girl.

Interviewer: (Gently) Then you have a great deal to live for, haven't you, Mrs. Parker? You have the biggest job in the world to accomplish. You have two fine youngsters to keep steady during these hard times. Their lives are just beginning. It really rests with you whether these experiences that they are going through will warp their viewpoints and make them unhappy or whether they are going to say, "With Mother going ahead starting life all over again after all she has been through, how can we quit?"

Mrs. Parker: I think I have been expecting too much from the children. (Apologetically) I'm not very cheerful to live with since—But there is so little to do—(Pause) Thank you so much. Oh, I do feel better. You are a good Christian girl.

Interviewer: I should like so much to meet your son. Would he care to come in to see me?

Mrs. Parker: I don't know if he'll come. He's always afraid they'll make him sign papers. But I'll tell him he has nothing to be afraid of. (Standing up ready to go.)

Interviewer: Good-bye Mrs. Parker. Oh, wait a moment—Don't forget your grocery order.

Mrs. Parker: Oh yes—Thank you very much. Good-bye. (Woman left the office, smiling.)

The interviewer imparted a contagious composure and an attitude of confidence. She listened with sympathetic insight and respect and thus assured her client that she (the interviewer) was participating in a difficult situation in which Mrs. Parker is evidently active but, as far as can be judged from one interview, not resourceful. She must be steadied and reassured before she can go forward. The interviewer broke down negativism and resistance by showing good will; she still has to arouse imagination and initiative and create possibilities for growth not only in Mrs. Parker, but, to all present indications, in her son John.

Perhaps the greatest contribution the interviewer made in dealing with Mrs. Parker was the recognition of the client's rage and hysterical condition as an outward symptom of deep-seated emotional problems. The interviewer says that she was "ready to listen, first of all to understand the woman's predicament and secondly to bring about mental catharsis." However, emotional problems of a client cannot be solved by hearing a tirade, but an attempt can be made to secure "recovery of his responsible identity through the discharge of resentment upon a case worker who need not punish him for it."[1]

Angry and shouting interviewees should not be shut off or ushered out of the office, or threatened with a policeman or with discontinuance of relief. They should be given an opportunity to air their grievances, to discharge their emotions and pent-up energies. Threatening a client or throwing him out of the office means running away from the problem which does not disappear but becomes augmented through the persecution complex; the individual thus treated only seeks an outlet in a more violent manner than originally displayed. Shouting clients who jeopardize the order of the office and the peace of other waiting clients might be subdued by asking them specific questions in a low and calm manner: "Have you ever talked with me?" "What is it that is disturbing you?" "What plan would you care to offer?" Frequently as their energies are drained off into mental processes, their emotional outbursts cease.

A few excerpts from "Only a Conversation" by Viola Paradise illustrate how to induce the release of tensions and the value of such a release to the interviewee:

. . . The government lady was in the door . . . "Good afternoon, Mrs. Kazalski. I'm Miss Edgmont of the Children's Bureau. May I come in?"

"Sit down," she said, in a dull voice . . . she looked at the short, slight, brown clad figure, the pointed piquant face under the close fitting little brown hat. . . .

"Did you ever hear of the Children's Bureau," began Miss Edgmont. And when Mrs. Kazalski had said, "No'm," she continued, "Well, it's a part of the government that is trying to find out how children and mothers are getting along, and what they do, in order to learn what things are best for them. Now we are visiting all mothers with children in these small canning camps. How many children have you?" . . .

[1] GRACE MARCUS, "Psychological Realities in Case Work," *The Family*, XIII (July, 1932), 149.

Despite her resolution to be circumspect in her dealings with this intruder, Mrs. Kazalski scarcely listened to what she was saying, so preoccupied was she in her personality. . . .

"You 'Merican lady?" she asked.

"Yes," said Miss Edgmont, "but my grandparents came from the old country. How long have *you* been in America?"

"Nine year. How old are you, lady?"

If Miss Edgmont was surprised, she did not show it. "Thirty-two," she replied. "And you?"

Mrs. Kazalski's eyes opened wide. Thirty-two! Why, she herself was only thirty. She would have guessed Miss Edgmont fully ten years younger. . . .

"I'd like to know," Miss Edgmont went on, in her soft, even voice, "about the work you and the children do in the cannery—just what you do, and how much you earn, and what time you go to work, and some other things. But first, are you sure you understand just why I'm asking these questions? Sometimes people are suspicious, can't understand why the government far off in Washington, should send someone way down here to ask questions. Maybe you'd like to ask me some questions before you answer mine?"

"Mrs. Oshinsky says you come to collect fines."

"Fines?"

"Twenty-five dollars for people, if their children work. You inspector?"

"No," said Miss Edgmont simply and it surprised Mrs. Kazalski that the accusation did not embarrass her. "There are inspectors," Miss Edgmont continued, "and there are fines for employing children; but the bosses, not the workers, pay the fines. Only, my work has nothing to do with fines. The government is making a study of what's good for children and what's bad for children. You see, children are the most valuable things in the world; but it is only lately people have learned that, in order to make them healthier and happier, we have to study them, and see how things affect them. The Children's Bureau is finding out how work affects them—how it affects their health and their chances of growing up strong and healthy and happy. What do you think about it? How do you feel about the work your children do, and the other children?" . . .

But now, here was a new thing. Her opinion was being asked. She shrugged her shoulders. What had she to do with these things? . . .

"I think it is too bad for children to work; but what you can do? It's better to work and live than to starve and die. What would poor people do without husband, if the children don't work? Without the children, I no could make half to live on. Even with the children, I got a debt of eighteen dollars at the store. And you—the government—it don't give money, no? No, just questions it gives. How can help us—questions? The row-boss says you get money for questions, that's why things cost too much for tax. You say it's good for children—questions. Will it help my children?"

This was a long speech for Mrs. Kazalski. She was breathing hard and perspiring with the effort of it.

Miss Edgmont's face was thoughtful. "I'm not absolutely sure it will help your children." She spoke slowly, experienced in making simple people understand new things. "I'm not sure the results of a study like this will come soon enough, so they may come in time to help the younger ones. Do you know," she went on, "that some states give money to widows, so that their children can go to school? . . .

"You, when you tell me about your children's work and about your work, are helping the government to make things better for children, even though the changes may not come tomorrow or for several years. I believe they will come in your children's life time. Don't you want to help make things better for children?"

Mrs. Kazalski felt strangely moved. . . . To think, for the first time in one's life, of anything outside the range of one's experience and observation, is a profound experience. . . .

And when Miss Edgmont took up her questioning, again, with "How did you happen to leave Baltimore, to come down here?" Mrs. Kazalski found herself wanting to tell the whole story of her hardships. It would be a blessed relief to talk about her troubles, to put them into words. . . . Yet there was nothing in her voice, no moisture in her eyes, to tell Miss Edgmont, who was listening with understanding, of her emotion. She had sent the children out of doors, and in a low voice—that her neighbors might not hear—she had begun:—

"Things were enough good with us, till the accident. After five months sick, my man died; and was left in the house only five dollar thirty-eight cents. Katie coughed bad. That night come the row-boss——"

She told of Mike Salinsky's visit, of her trip down, of her disappointment; of the draughty coldness of the canning shed in bad wet weather; how the roof of her house "leaked like a basket" when it rained; how she lay awake at night too tired to sleep, worrying, waiting for the siren, yet dreading it; waiting and dreading the watchman's pounding on the door, which never failed to fill her with anger; hating to force the children from their beds at four or five or six o'clock in the morning—according to the size of the catch; how fast the shucking-gloves wore out—"one glove a day, and cut our hands yet"; how much worse picking shrimps than shucking oysters, because of the acid in the head of the shrimp: "After two days at shrimps my hands looked like butcher-shops, that's the only one thing to make think there is in the world meat! And the stink! You smelt it once? So!"

But, the worst of all was the worry about Katie's cough. That kept recurring again and again in her outpouring. She talked with the simple vividness of a person unused to fluent speech. "I no would care about work, I would no care about nothing, if Katie would get well. When I go away from Baltimore, I say, charity the Kazalskis no take. But now I think foolish to be more proud than to care of your children's health. It ain't proud, having them work over mud and wet, in clothes soaked and torn like noodles. And I think maybe oysters no good for cough."

"Did you ask the boss if he would send you back, instead of waiting till the end?"

Mrs. Kazalski laughed bitterly. "He give me a mouthful," she said.

"Excuse me, I tell you all this," she went on, "but you want to know why children got to work. That's why, but if Katie would get well, I'd give—I'd give—well, I ain't got nothing to give. Excuse me, miss, your face looks very sorry. But you ask—and now you know. . . .

"Well," she said, bringing her eyes back to Mrs. Kazalski, "you had a hard time. . . About the debt, I should not worry too much. Are you the only person there with a debt at the store?" . . .

"Well, surely the company won't want to keep all you here, for your debt. . . And thank you very much for giving me this information. Would you mind if I look over this card to see that I haven't forgotten to ask anything? I am supposed to have an answer for every question . . . "

Miss Edgmont stayed a few minutes longer to get in detail the earnings of each member of the family since their coming and the hours of work. Presently she left, hoping things would go better, hoping Katie would improve, suggesting a Baltimore clinic. . . .

That night she [Mrs. Kazalski] went to bed with a new feeling. . .

Yet she told herself, nothing had happened, really. A woman had come, had asked questions, had gone away. She had answered questions, had stated her situation. "Yet nothing has *happened*," she repeated to herself in Polish, "only a conversation. Talk, only . . . " Why then this new courage, this strange warm feeling, which reached out, even beyond this roomful of her own family—which included even more than the whole camp? Was this, she asked, what they meant by *patriotism*?[1]

[1] Viola I. Paradise, "Only a Conversation," *The Atlantic Monthly*, CXXXI (January, 1923), 89–93. Reprinted by permission.

CHAPTER XVI

DYNAMICS OF THE THERAPEUTIC INTERVIEW

(Continued)

Definition and Redefinition of the Social Situation.—A clear statement of what is involved in defining or redefining a social situation to a person or group is given by Park and Burgess:

Actually common participation in common activities implies a common "definition of the situation." In fact, every single act, and eventually all moral life, is dependent upon the definition of the situation. A definition of the situation precedes and limits any possible action, and a redefinition of the situation changes the character of the action. An abusive person, for example, provokes anger and possibly violence, but if we realize that the man is insane this redefinition of the situation results in totally different behavior.

Every social group develops systematic and unsystematic means of defining the situation for its members. Among these means are the "don'ts" of the mother, the gossip of the community, epithets ("liar," "traitor," "scab"), the sneer, the shrug, the newspaper, the theater, the school, libraries, the law, and the gospel. Education in the widest sense—intellectual, moral, aesthetic—is the process of defining the situation. It is the process by which the definitions of an older generation are transmitted to a younger. In the case of the immigrant it is the process by which the definitions of one cultural group are transmitted to another.

Differences in meanings and values, referred to above in terms of the "apperception mass," grow out of the fact that different individuals and different peoples have defined the situation in different ways. When we speak of the different "heritages" or "traditions" which our different immigrant groups bring, it means that, owing to different historical circumstances, they have defined the situation differently. Certain prominent personalities, schools of thought, bodies of doctrine, historical events, have contributed in defining the situation and determining the attitudes and values of our various immigrant groups in characteristic ways in their home countries. To the Sicilian, for example, marital infidelity means the stiletto; to the American, the divorce court. And even when the immigrant thinks that he understands us, he nevertheless does not do this completely.

At the best he interprets our cultural traditions in terms of his own. Actually the situation is progressively redefined by the consequences of the actions, provoked by the previous definitions, and a prison experience is designed to provide a datum toward the redefinition of the situation.[1]

One of the commonest and perhaps one of the crudest methods attempting to define a social situation is by means of prohibitions and commands. An interviewee is told, advised, persuaded, and at times even ordered or commanded to do or not to do thus and so.

I know that much of this sounds theoretical to you, Mrs. M., (mother of two very bright but problem children) and for that reason I have made a short list of definite things for you to do and remember in training and directing John and Annie. As we go along we will add things to this list of suggestions. Now you can see that the house is neat and the children's meals always regular.[2]

The above is what W. I. Thomas calls the "ordering-and-forbidding technique" but scarcely a method of defining social situations to be commended to social case workers.

The oldest but most persistent form of social technique is that of "ordering-and-forbidding"—that is, meeting a crisis by an arbitrary act of will decreeing the disappearance of the undesirable or the appearance of the desirable phenomena, and using arbitrary physical action to enforce the decree. This method corresponds exactly to the magical phase of natural technique. In both, the essential means of bringing a determined effect is more or less consciously thought to reside in the act of will itself by which the effect is decreed as desirable and of which the action is merely an indispensable vehicle or instrument; in both, the process by which the cause (act of will and physical action) is supposed to bring its effect to realization remains out of reach of investigation; in both, finally, if the result is not attained, some new act of will with new material accessories is introduced, instead of trying to find and remove the perturbing causes. A good instance of this in the social field is the typical legislative procedure of today.

It frequently happens both in magic and in the ordering-and-forbidding technique that the means by which the act of will is helped are really effective, and thus the result is attained, but, as the process of causation, being unknown, cannot be controlled, the success is

---

[1] ROBERT E. PARK and E. W. BURGESS, *Introduction to the Science of Sociology*, pp. 764–765. Reprinted by permission of the University of Chicago Press.

[2] Statement by family welfare worker.

always more or less accidental and dependent upon the stability of general conditions; when these are changed, the intended effect fails to appear, the subject is unable to account for the reasons of the failure and can only try by guesswork some other means. And even more frequent than this accidental success is the result that the action brings some effect, but not the desired one.[1]

Instead of explaining a client's situation to him an interviewer at times tells him: "Quit worrying," or "Forget it, there is nothing wrong with you." To tell a patient "If you would stop thinking about yourself you would be all right," is "very weak and sloppy re-education," says Karl Menninger. "It is exactly this transfer of interest which the patient cannot make and which he must be educated to make."[2]

Social work executives maintain that those visitors who take pains to explain to their clients why certain information must be procured, or how an agency administers relief, why some clients receive groceries and some cash, or why their applications are rejected or their budget reduced, rarely have difficulty in securing the desired information or in following a certain plan of therapy. Unless the situation is clearly defined to the interviewees, they may see neither rhyme nor reason as to why they are expected to behave in the prescribed manner.

"I don't see why I should have my business broadcasted to former landlords and to prospective employers. . . . I don't see why I should answer questions about my past when all I ask is a grocery order?" angrily demanded an interviewee. I took time to explain that we did not doubt her integrity, that our information is confidential, but since we deal with 145,000 cases at any one time we must secure certain identifying information which is not much more than a private physician, or a credit manager, or an attorney would ask if she turned to them for advice or help. Such clients generally answer: "Yes, I see now," "I understand."[3]

Almo is an American Oriental boy eighteen years of age who steadily secludes himself because of a strong feeling that his friends and classmates are prejudiced against his "racial uniform" and background. He is very unhappy in his isolation and has developed a decided self-pity. Assuming that Almo is actually the subject of prejudice I tried to redefine the situation to him in several different ways: (1) the prejudice

---

[1] W. I. THOMAS and F. ZNANIECKI, *The Polish Peasant in Europe and America*, p. 3.

[2] *The Human Mind*, p. 389.

[3] Statement by an emergency relief interviewer.

was not directed against him personally but against an undefinable "something" in the whole race; (2) he could to some extent minimize race-prejudice by avoiding conflicts and attention; (3) that he was just as intolerant toward others in his bitterness and isolation as they were toward him; (4) that he had a "mission in life" if he could overcome prejudice by displaying good will. The boy is intelligent and gradually accepted the new situation as a challenge to him. He thus acquired a new outlook on life.[1]

The following interview with Mr. Anderson[2] illustrates how an interviewer redefined a difficult situation to a desperate and discouraged man:

(Man in office asking for aid. He had been employed as bank teller and accountant for 13 years, and was let out about six months ago due to a reduction in the personnel. He was fifty years old, had a wife and three children, ten, thirteen, and sixteen years old.

Visitor called at the home; the house seemed deserted, and although it was a very warm day the door was closed, the windows down, and the shades drawn. After repeated knocks and ringing of door bell, which was in service as visitor could faintly hear the jingle, the door finally opened and a man in shirt sleeves, no tie, neckband opened, hair a bit ruffled, appeared like a man in a daze.)

Interview with Mr. Anderson.

Interviewer: Good afternoon. Are you Mr. Anderson?

Mr. Anderson: Yes. (In a rather loud and gruff voice.)

Interviewer: I am Mr. Miller of the County Welfare—office. Are you the Mr. Anderson who was in our office a few days ago?

Mr. Anderson: Won't you come in? I am rather hard of hearing and I don't want the neighbors to hear of my condition.

(After entering, the man closed the door, and raising a few window shades, said:)

Your office advised me that you would try to be here tomorrow, as they said you were very busy.

Interviewer: I noticed that your call was promised for tomorrow, but whenever it is humanly possible I try to make my visit ahead of time.

Mr. Anderson: Probably it was a good thing in this case, as tomorrow I would not be here to be interviewed.

Interviewer: Why, were you going out?

Mr. Anderson: Oh, no. I was going to end it all this afternoon (nodding to an automatic lying on the desk).

Interviewer: Well, this is quite a coincidence, because I had a similar thought about a year ago, and although I had a wife to leave behind to face the hardships. You, I understand, have a wife and three very fine children. By the way, where are they?

Mr. Anderson: Oh, the children are at school, and the wife left this morning shortly after they did. She thought she might find something to do.

[1] Pauline V. Young, "Problems of Cultural Hybrids," unpublished manuscript.

[2] Interview held and recorded by Lee Miller, Los Angeles.

Interviewer: You certainly must have a wonderful wife, and it looks to me that you have many things to live for and I am sure you would not like to pass out of this life and go into the next, carrying with you all the horrible dreams which you have been thinking of this afternoon. I think you have been very fortunate during all this depression. I understand that you held your position until about six months ago. Well, I was out of work for three years, and I would not take a small fortune for the experience and knowledge gained, which I could never have attained if good times had continued.

Mr. Anderson: Well, I am handicapped on account of my hearing.

Interviewer: In one sense that may be true, although looking at it from another angle I would say it was a blessing in disguise because in this age of speed and whirl the noise at times drives many of us almost out of our minds, and you are blessed by not having to go through this. I understand you are an accountant and bank teller.

Mr. Anderson: Yes, that is true. Most of my work is accounting.

Interviewer: Well, that means to me continual concentration, and you know that you can do this far better when all is quiet, and I feel you can do better work in less time than we who hear perfectly, because we are continually being distracted by the foreign noises about us.

Mr. Anderson: I never looked at it that way. Possibly you are right. Nevertheless, I have been so discouraged as I have trod the streets making applications here and there for the past six months to no avail.

Interviewer: I am glad to hear this because it has kept you occupied, and you were probably tired at night and slept well.

Mr. Anderson: I did until a few weeks ago when my savings ran out, and I was worried about the family, as we had been living on reduced rations, and you know how growing children can eat.

Interviewer: Gee, Mr. Anderson, it is just too bad you were not with me on my last three calls. If you had been there you would feel like a king sitting on top of the world.

Mr. Anderson: I imagine you do run across some pitiful cases.

Interviewer: Yes, and it would do you a world of good to see and hear some of the pathetic cases.

Mr. Anderson: Yes, I suppose, but, with me I am at a loss which way to turn. My friends have helped and I just cannot ask them any more. The only living relation I have is my brother in Chicago who is married and out of work, so I cannot expect help from him.

Interviewer: How about your wife's family?

Mr. Anderson: She was an orphan, and does not have anyone to turn to. All I want is work.

Interviewer: Well, Mr. Anderson, I feel sure that there is a place for you. In the meantime the County and Government will help you.

Mr. Anderson: I certainly will need it very soon as I have but one dollar left.

Interviewer: Will this carry you for a few days? Our store in this district is not open today, but I can bring you an order which includes practically everything you will need.

Mr. Anderson: Yes, we can manage. . . .

Interviewer: In the meantime would you do two things for me? Will you promise to do it with the best of your ability?

Mr. Anderson: I will do it if it is possible.   What are they?

Interviewer: First, allow us to assume the responsibility for this month of taking care of your family needs.   I mean by this, food and utilities. Second, will you continue during this month's time to keep contacting as many companies as you possibly can, and making applications for work?

Has the thought ever come to you that since liquor and the state sales tax have been in effect, there are thousands of small store-keepers who have in the past kept accounts in a helter-skelter method.   And now are forced by law to keep an accurate account of their business.   You know that 90% of these smaller business men do not have the knowledge to do this, and their business does not warrant paying for a bookkeeper by the week, but, could pay $10.00 or $15.00 a month to have their accounts kept, by someone who could spend a night or two a week doing it. . . .

Mr. Anderson: Well, I certainly could handle that type of work all right, and I promise you I will start out tomorrow morning.   I guess you are right. I never looked at the small business man that way.

Interviewer: I am very glad that I came and I will be back soon.   In the meantime, keep your chin up and don't forget your promise.

(Within ten days the following letter was received from Mr. Anderson:)

I desire to inform you that I have at last secured employment and I will not need further aid except for the check this month.   I will not receive any pay until the first of the month, and if you can send me a check as soon as possible, I can get along.   I am badly in need of funds to pay carfare to and from work, and water, light and gas bills.

Many, many thanks for the assistance you have rendered me during those dark days that I hope have passed forever, and if in the future, I can be of any assistance to you, I hope you will not hesitate to call on me.

Very sincerely
(Signed)

Conditioning and Reconditioning of Attitudes.—The behavioristic school of psychology, particularly John B. Watson, I. P. Pavlov, and N. I. Krasnogorski, have carried on considerable experimental research in the field of "conditioned reflexes," conditioning, unconditioning, and reconditioning of attitude patterns, habits, and emotions.[1]   They maintain that in order to accomplish these changes it is necessary to change the environment in such a way that new adaptations and habits are called for.   Watson even "foresees a time when we shall have special institutions devoted to the problem of reshaping psychological characteristics just as today we have plastic and other surgeons

[1] See I. P. Pavlov, *Conditioned Reflexes.*

N. I. Krasnogorski, "The Conditioned Reflexes and Children's Neuroses," *American Journal of Diseases of Children*, XXX (1925), 756–769.

John B. Watson, *Psychology from the Standpoint of a Behaviorist.*

W. I. Thomas and Dorothy S. Thomas, *The Child in America*, Chap. XII.

who change physical characteristics."[1] This belief, though it excludes the notion that individuals can take their "internal environment with them in the shape of words and word substitutes," implies that the internal environment may be influenced by such forces as friends, teachers, movies, etc.[2]

The sociologist may accept the behavioristic conceptions as far as they go and then add to this theory of change of attitudes and personality all those inner forces of thought, feeling, and experience which undergo modification under the influence of interaction with persons or social groups. Thus, it may be assumed that from the standpoint of external forces the individual's environment is changed either by removing him directly from the social and physical forces which exercise influence over him and by transplanting him into a new, more satisfactory milieu, or by altering the forces in the old environment by means of the slower changes in public opinion, in the folkways, mores, and social institutions. This manipulation of the social situation of which the individual is a part may result in molding and remolding personality and social attitudes from without. Interviewers dealing with urgent personal or family problems often resort to influencing persons directly, through the personal interview, and try to bring about a change of attitudes from within. The method and philosophy by which the modification of attitude from within is accomplished have undergone considerable change in recent years. The interviewee is no longer regarded as something to be made over or somebody to persuade even by means of gentle pressure. Miss Neustaedter's words are significant:

The worker perceives the impossibility of accomplishing these objectives and the destructiveness of attempting them. She respects the personality of the individual, seeing him not as someone to be manipulated but as a human being with possibilities for growth. She recognizes that she cannot change the attitudes of another, that people themselves change when they have the feeling that another type of behavior or activity will be more satisfying. What he may become she does not know but she gives him the spur of awareness that in his relationship to her he, the client, is a free man. . . .

Is there a better method of arousing self-esteem than by respectful consideration of the problem of another? The manner in which an

[1] GLADYS SCHWESINGER, *Heredity and Environment*, pp. 392; see also 387–393.

[2] JOHN B. WATSON, *Behaviorism*, p. 302.

application is received carries conviction to the client as to his standing
with the worker. To listen, to assume that the ideas of the applicant
about his own situation are of primary importance, to accept the
client's statement without cross questioning is to treat. For by this
method the worker conveys the impression that the one who appeals
to her for help is a person whose opinion she values and whose reticence
she respects. . . . [1]

Dr. Taft's conceptions of the dynamics of therapy in a controlled relationship stress the importance of avoiding any
attempt to "conquer the subject." She advocates the relationship therapy which provides an opportunity "to experience more
completely than is ordinarily possible the direction, depth, and
ambivalence of the impulses which relate the self to others, to
outer reality, and to discover at first hand the possibility of
organization into an autonomous creative will."[2] An additional
illustration of how the internal environment may be modified by a
personal relation is supplied by Dr. Taft's studies of transference:

A girl of seventeen was reported from the high school because of the
poor work she had been doing during the last term, whereas her work
had hitherto been satisfactory, and because she seemed to be brooding
over an unfortunate experience which had taken place about ten
months before when she was seized by two men, forced into an automobile but rescued from an actual sex assault by the appearance of
police officers. From that time on the girl had seemed to become more
and more timid and could not be induced to go out alone or leave
her home even for a vacation. In her interview with the psychologist
the girl, although self-conscious, was unusually frank and outgoing
in her attitude. There was no difficulty in getting her to talk. She
was an attractive, likable youngster, who appealed to the psychologist,
and a comfortable *rapport* was established at once. . . .

The mother had given no sex information until forced to when Anna
at fifteen worked in a mill and heard things from the other girls which
made her ask questions. What she knew about sex, she knew only
from her experience of assault and the unlovely picture given by her
mother.

The psychologist, using sex instruction as a vehicle, tried to get
over to Anna a sense of the value of sex and of her own normal but
repressed interest in it. Anna had denied erotic day-dreams, all
interest in boys, as well as interest in the love part of love stories.

[1] ELEANOR NEUSTAEDTER, "The Rôle of the Case Worker in Treatment,"
The Family, XIII (July, 1932), 155.
[2] *Op. cit.*, p. 288.

Everything on the sex side seemed quite sincerely to be a blank except the fact that she was always thinking about the abduction. . . .

During the interview, from time to time the psychologist kept the girl from feeling herself criticized or shut out, by recalling attitudes and experiences of her own youth similar to those now making life difficult for Anna and carefully refrained from anything which might be interpreted as disapproval of the mother herself, although her point of view toward men and sex had to be opposed. . . .

When Anna left at the end of the interview, there was an atmosphere of warm, friendly feeling and a sense of comfort and relief which was unmistakable.

What has happened in this interview? Nothing permanent, probably, unless the mother can be reached, but within the narrow boundaries of the office, on this single occasion, a very shy, inhibited child who has had a violent sex experience, accepted by herself and her family and acquaintances as horrible and revolting, has suddenly been enabled to drop all her conventional standards and habitual sex repression, and see, however temporarily, with genuine insight and without fear her own underlying interest in the whole affair.

Anna also accepted the psychologist's assertion that too much of her emotional life was being centered in her mother, that it should be going into the interest in boys and the friendships with girls which were normal for girls of her age. . . .

The interview was able to relieve her conflict, not because it presented ideas but because an adult, who for the time being stood to her in the place of a mother, gave her freedom from the repression of the real mother's standards and made her needs not only articulate but legitimate and approved. There must be first the existence of a need for which the idea may become the tool and second the reassuring and uncritical emotional medium which makes it possible for that need to become conscious. . . .

Here the emotional *rapport* gives an ideal basis for an educational or re-educational process. The ideas and interests to which the client is introduced during this period become dynamic through their identification with the person who suggests them, and become in time natural channels for draining off a large part of the emotion which has been going into the transfer. . . .

There is no need to argue about the value of the ideational elements in case work treatment. The case plan, the new point of view, the releasing idea, are accepted without reservation. The purpose of this paper is to call to your attention the nature of the underlying forces used consciously by the analyst and unconsciously by the case worker to vitalize ideas and—plans. The emotional going over of the client to the case worker breaks down old fears and inhibitions and provides a safe medium in which the growth of new thoughts, feelings and habits becomes possible.[1]

The following interview with Mr. S. illustrates a method of remolding attitudes from without and a process of reeducation which became possible only after his attitudes were changed:[2]

Interview with Mr. Stephen S.

(Visited Mr. Stephen S., a blind sailor who lost vision in both eyes in an explosion in a battleship. He is of Bohemian descent. He and his partially paralyzed mother occupy two small, half-dark basement rooms. The floor was littered with cigarette butts; a pail of beer stood on the table at his elbow. He appeared very "sour," caustic and cynical; he swore several times during the interview.)

Interviewer: Mr. S., I am Miss V. from the American Red Cross. . . .

Mr. S.: Now, hold on. Who sent for you? I have no desire to talk with anyone from the Red Cross. I suppose you're another one of them damn social workers who try to control other people's business. The sooner you (social workers) leave me alone the better for both of us. Remember, I did not ask you to come.

Interviewer: Why, Mr. S., you just take my breath away. You did not send for me, that's true. I should be sorry that I came. (Pause due to uneasiness of Mr. S.) If I were not a social worker, just a young lady who came to talk in Bohemian to your mother and you about your experiences (Identification), would you drive me out the house too?

Mr. S.: I didn't drive you out the house, just asked you to leave.

Interviewer: Well, that's not so bad. You really want me to leave? Somehow, I flatter myself that you don't any more. Do you speak Bohemian? Perhaps I can express myself better, when I don't have to speak English. It's still a little awkward. (Identification and distraction from present difficulty.)

Mr. S.: The old lady understands nothing but Bohemian. You will have to speak English with me. How long have you been in this country?

Interviewer: A little over three years.

Mr. S.: You speak English pretty well.

Interviewer: Thank you. I had to learn in a hurry. Life is pretty hard for an immigrant girl in America without the language. (Identification.)

Mr. S.: The old woman has been here 18 years and speaks no English.

Interviewer: Well, you see, I came here as a young girl.

Mr. S.: How old are you?

Interviewer: Now, now, you are getting a bit personal. You know, a young lady's age is a great secret. I don't mind telling you my age if you

[1] JESSIE TAFT, "The Use of the Transfer Within the Limits of the Office Interview," *The Family*, V (October, 1924), 143–146. Reprinted by permission.

[2] Interview held and recorded by Pauline Vislick (Young) while in service for the American Red Cross, Chicago Chapter, Home Service Division. This interview appears in summary form in Pauline V. Young and Erle F. Young, "Mutation of Personality," *Journal of Applied Sociology*, IX (July–August, 1925), 442–449.

tell me something about yourself. I am . . . (Identification.) Now, how old are *you?*

Mr. S.: I am 27 years old, and have been blind for over two years. How big are you?

Interviewer: Not very big, but just big enough. I really don't know exactly.

Mr. S.: Would you mind if I felt how tall you are? I can tell by putting my hand on your head. . . . Well, you're real tiny.

Interviewer: Yes, I am, and you're big, so you have to be good to me. (Laughing; an attempt to lessen tensions.)

Mr. S.: I have a Victrola here. If I turned on a record would you dance with me just one dance?

Interviewer: Well, I really never danced with anyone whom I did not know well, because I dance so poorly and step on their toes. Let's get acquainted better. . . . We sighted folks know nothing about the problems of the blind folks. Tell me, how do you manage? (Attempt to create similar worlds of discourse.)

Mr. S.: Manage? I don't manage! I live on a miserable government pension. I was a fool to accept it because I had to promise that I would not go begging. But let me tell you I can beat that. In New York I had a good corner and a good sign. I used to make good money—sometimes $50 a week. Never saved a nickel. The saloon at the Bowery got it all. There were a good many fakers there and they took advantage of a blind man, but they helped me forget my misery. I would have gone crazy without them. Well, that's what I am doing now. Just going crazy. A pail of rotten beer don't make you forget. No place to go and nothing to do. Just sit and think about your misery. (Signs of mental catharsis.)

Interviewer: Mr. S., would you be interested in going with me to a club meeting of blind folks only? (An attempt to incorporate him into a social world.)

Mr. S.: Blind folks only? What you know about it?

Interviewer: You see, I have a friend, a physician, who was born blind. He is the president of this club for the blind. As a matter of fact I have already spoken to him about you and he invited both you and me to a meeting tomorrow night. I am very anxious to go but I will not be admitted unless a blind person takes me there, and that person can't be an officer in the club. They have a regular meeting, then music and dancing, they tell me. We can dance there, if you like. (An attempt to assimilate him into a primary group based on a common trait, blindness, which isolates them individually.)

Mr. S.: Are you sure that all the members are blind folks?

Interviewer: That's what the doctor tells me. He is very anxious to meet you.

Mr. S.: If it is a club of sighted folks, I don't want nothing to do with them. They try to learn you to weave baskets and other kindergarten stuff. They tell you to learn to read. What do they know how to teach blind folks and how blind folks learn? None of them systems is any good. They expect you to work. How can a fellow work without any eyes? I've done my duty by the country. (Mental catharsis.)

Interviewer: There is a good deal in what you say, but of course, some of those folks have specialized in the art of teaching the blind. At any rate, you will have an opportunity to hear what other blind men have to say. . . . (Attempt to break social isolation.)   I am not very well acquainted in the city, and besides I have a date with another man. You see, I am a pretty fast worker, I date up two men for the same evening. Now, may he and I come here tomorrow so we can all go together to the club. (Attempt to bring situation into conformity with social convention.)

Mr. S.: Well, have it your way. I'll take you.

Interviewer: Thanks, much. See you tomorrow.

(The trip downtown lasted a full hour.   Mr. S. talked freely and behaved in a characteristic manner.)

Mr. S.: Never mind helping me over the curbs. I'm not so far gone as that. Say in New York I could get through the busiest streets, go any place I wanted. But those damn Elevated platforms get me. A man could walk right off of them and never know what happened to him. Sorry we can't take the surface cars tonight. Of course, the downtown cops all knew me in New York. I had a good corner there and a good sign. Used to make good money—$35 to $50 a week. . . .

Well, none of that now. Oh, I go over to the corner saloon for a pail now and then but it's pretty quiet for me here. No place to go and nothing to do. . . . [And he went off into a detailed sarcastic description of the defects of three or four of the "systems" he knew of.] Why don't they figure out a decent method? . . .

As to working, I can't understand how you expect a fellow to do any work without any eyes. I've done my duty by the world. . . .

You social workers are all alike. Don't know a damn thing about being blind, but you know how a blind man ought to think, ought to feel, and just what he should do. I know! I lived in one of those famous institutions for the blind run by sighted folks. Enough to drive a man crazy. I beat it out of there just as soon as I could. Never again! I'm my own boss, and you [string of lurid adjectives] social workers can tell it to the marines!

(The club staged a program by their own members after a brief business meeting. Readings and musical numbers alternated. Several of the numbers were quite creditable. More notable, however, was the spirit of camaraderie, the evident pride in accomplishment, and the freedom from a sense of defeat and failure in life. . . . They were confident, sincere, square-fighting people who accepted their handicap as a challenge to endeavor.

So stimulating was this atmosphere that Mr. S. was at first unconvinced. "Was the secretary who read the minutes blind? Was the president blind? Could not the pianist see? And the musical quartette?" . . . Just before adjournment the president asked whether the ex-service boy had come. After vigorous nudging, Mr. S. answered haltingly, "Here." "Very well, I want everyone to meet him before leaving. Make yourselves known."

And everybody met him. Soon he was the center of a small group all trying to catch his ear. A stream of questions began. Could he read Braille? If not, would he not like someone to come and teach him? There was a probability that a Braille typewriter could be secured. Could he dance? The club held dances occasionally and one of the young ladies would be glad to teach him. Another offered to teach him basketry. Mr. S. was embarrassed but delighted by so much attention. He tried to answer all his questioners at once and ended by agreeing to all proposals.)

(On the way home he said:)

Well, well, the blind give dances. Did they really mean it? How do they do it?

Interviewer: Well, we'll see. They said they will come to invite you.

Mr. S.: I heard of one of the Braille typewriters but never expected to operate one. And did you hear that they would teach me to read newspapers? Do you think they'll come?

Interviewer: Well, I am positive they will. You know, Mr. S., the finest thing about these people is the fact that they all earn their living. Not a single one of them begs. You can't be a member of the club unless you work for your living. They want to be as self-respecting as the sighted folks. They have all demonstrated that it can be done. You will find them excellent company. You won't ever have to sit around doing nothing.

Mr. S.: Well, we'll see, but they got me all right.

Subsequent interviews with Mr. S. revealed that he diligently set himself to learn Braille and the weaving of various articles. In fact, he proved such an apt pupil that arrangements were made for a special course of study in New York City, where he spent eighteen months. During this period reports were received from the agency in charge that Mr. S. had given up begging and drinking and that he was gradually becoming adjusted and personally organized.

Mutation, a rapid and sudden change of attitude, was accomplished in this case through (1) provision for active interests and for participation in a social world which does not penalize for defect, (2) breaking up of social isolation, (3) indicating methods for compensating for physical defects and avoiding exploitation, as through begging. It must be noted that Mr. S.'s desires for new experience, for response and recognition,[1] were satisfied by above means.

Both the interviewer and Mr. S. set out upon a mutual exploration of the situation, but the burden of interpretation and of accepting the situation fell directly upon Mr. S. Thus we eliminate the dangers inherent in openly forcing him into a plan of action which he is neither emotionally nor mentally ready to accept and to follow.

Professor Dewey's discussion of the relation of habit and attitudes to conduct and to will clarifies the fact that reconditioning occurs through a series of intermediate outward acts:

. . . habits are arts. They involve skill of sensory and motor organs, cunning or craft, and objective materials. They assimilate objective

[1] See pp. 345–354.

energies, and eventuate in command of environment. They require order, discipline, and manifest technique. They have a beginning, middle and end. . . .

Honesty, chastity, malice, peevishness, courage, triviality, industry, irresponsibility are not private possessions of a person. They are working adaptations of personal capacities with environing forces. All virtues and vices are habits which incorporate objective forces. They are interactions of elements contributed by the make-up of an individual with elements supplied by the out-door world. . . .

A bad habit suggests an inherent tendency to action and also a hold, command over us. It makes us do things we are ashamed of, things which we tell ourselves we prefer not to do. It overrides our formal resolutions, our conscious decisions. When we are honest with ourselves we acknowledge that a habit has this power because it is so intimately a part of ourselves. It has a hold upon us because we *are* the habit. . . .

We feed our conceit by recalling that the habit was not deliberately formed; we never intended to become idlers or gamblers or roués. And how can anything be deeply ourselves which developed accidentally, without set intention? These traits of a bad habit are precisely the things which are most instructive about all habits and about ourselves. They teach us that all habits are affections, that all have projectile power, and that a predisposition formed by a number of specific acts is an immensely more intimate and fundamental part of ourselves than are vague, general, conscious choices. All habits are demands for certain kinds of activity; and they constitute the self. In any intelligible sense of the word will, they *are* will. They form our effective desires and they furnish us with our working capacities. They rule our thoughts, determining which shall appear and be strong and which shall pass from light into obscurity. . . .

Recently a friend remarked to me that there was one superstition current among even cultivated persons. They suppose that if one is told what to do, if the right *end* is pointed to them, all that is required in order to bring about the right act is will or wish on the part of the one who is to act. He used as an illustration the matter of physical posture; the assumption is that if a man is told to stand up straight, all that is further needed is wish and effort on his part, and the deed is done. He pointed out that this belief is on a par with primitive magic in its neglect of attention to the means which are involved in reaching an end . . . [1]

To *reach* an end we must take our mind off from it and attend to the act which is next to be performed. We must make that the end. . . .

[1] JOHN DEWEY, *Human Nature and Conduct*, pp. 15–28. Reprinted by permission of Henry Holt & Company.

The only way of accomplishing this discovery is through a flank move-ment. We must stop even thinking of standing up straight. To think of it is fatal, for it commits us to the operation of an established habit of standing wrong. We must find an act within our power which is disconnected from any thought about standing. We must start to do another thing which on one side inhibits our falling into the custom-ary bad position and on the other side is the beginning of a series of acts which may lead into the correct posture.[1] The hard drinker who keeps thinking of not drinking is doing what he can to initiate the acts which lead to drinking. He is starting with the stimulus to his habit. To succeed he must find some positive interest or line of action which will inhibit the drinking series and which by instituting another course of action will bring him to his desired end. In short, the man's true aim is to discover some course of action, having nothing to do with the habit of drink or standing erect, which will take him where he wants to go. The discovery of this other series is at once his means and his end. Until one takes intermediate acts seriously enough to treat them as ends, one wastes one's time in any effort at change of habits. Of the intermediate acts, the most important is the *next* one. The first or earliest means is the most important *end* to discover.[2]

The speed with which reconditioning of attitudes occurs varies widely from slow change to sudden mutation. Generally, recon-ditioning through the interview is a process of summation, that is, each succeeding stage gives rise to the next while the ultimate response is not foreshadowed in the original or in the earlier preceding stimuli. One thing gradually leads to another often so imperceptibly that the interviewee may arrive at the goal without conscious effort and without violence to his organization of life.

The other day I was told that it fell to my lot to interview a couple and to tell them that they were destined for the Poor Farm. The wife had been ill in a sanitorium for some time and her husband was keeping house for himself. I approached the subject by explaining how much better it would be if they could be together. Then I related to them the experiences of some couples in "homes" who prefer the companionship of each other to the privacy and loneliness of their separate existence. Later I proposed that they think over a possible plan for entering a cottage at the Farm and finally suggested that

---

[1] The technique of this process is stated in the book of Mr. Alexander already referred to, and the theoretical statement given is borrowed from Mr. Alexander's analysis. [M. Alexander, *Man's Supreme Inheritance*.]

[2] JOHN DEWEY, *Human Nature and Conduct*, pp. 34–35.

they allow me to take them out to look the cottage over.[1] It was a hard struggle for them to decide to enter the Farm. Every time I came to see them I slowly introduced a new element into the situation and they gradually started to associate my visits with the Poor Farm, and slowly came to see the advantages of the Farm for them.[2]

Motivation.—The process of motivation is a very difficult one since we know very little as yet as to what motivates human beings, particularly those who are unable to cope with their environment because of economic, social, health, religious, or personality problems. We know that people respond to certain personal and social influences and that they are sensitive to certain social pressures. In many instances it may be necessary to know the whole life history of a person before it can be discovered to what stimuli he will respond. It is evident, however, that few persons can be motivated by commanding them to follow a certain course of activity. One must personally want to follow such a course and it must also be satisfying to him. No permanent constructive results can be expected from a high-pressure technique, "third degree" methods, or control mechanisms which the person does not understand and accept. He needs to build out of his own experience and strive toward a self-determined goal. Miss Reynolds says:

How is one to hand out vision and motive power? There is the mainspring of the whole problem. We have tried to give vision and motive power as a "hand out," and we have failed. We talk to a boy of ten in a child guidance clinic about his behavior. He sits on the edge of a chair while we enlarge upon making the most of his school opportunities or being nicer to his devoted mother (who, incidentally, makes a fool of him before the boys). He goes out with a sigh of relief and plunges into play to forget the disagreeable incident. We spend an hour telling a mother that the organization of her household is all wrong, and that is why Dorothy acts like one possessed. She

---

[1] Karl De Schweinitz's comment in this connection is of interest: "Often that which prevents people from entering institutions is the fear of the unknown. One way of overcoming such a difficulty is to suggest a visit to the hospital or the home in question. Seeing the place gives it a concreteness and definiteness that clears away the disturbing element of vagueness and uncertainty. Its inherent attractiveness both allays fear and provides an additional reason for seeking admission." (*The Art of Helping People out of Trouble*, p. 199.)

[2] Statement by a student visitor.

says "yes" respectfully, and goes home having gained the impression that those people would know more if they had children of their own. When the social worker calls to ask how Dorothy is doing, it is easier to say, "Oh, ever so much better!" than to listen to another lecture. That counts as a success till Dorothy runs away and the sad story of home misunderstanding opens out again.

It looks as if we have to give vision plus, vision close to, and even through, experience, and sometimes after experience has given the *feel* of what success would be like. . . .

Some people need stimulation; some, of limited capacities, need regulated amounts of direction; some need the lashing of reproof as the worker allies her power of personality with that of the patient's weaker better self to fight against his worse. Whatever is done, reproof, comfort, cheer—opportunities all to get new motive powers into operation—all should be given as social prescriptions adequately thought out, never as outlets for the worker's own sentimentality or lack of self-control. Then, too, why do we not take the trouble to find out what people want for themselves and why? We force a child of muscular peasant build, craving the out-of-doors, into an education fitting him for a highly artificial career in finance. Business concerns give rest- and clubrooms when the workers want fair treatment and independence. We accuse our clients of ingratitude when we have only offered them what we think they should want. . . .

The social worker of today, then, has the challenge of limitless discovery in methods of educating people through their own experiences —interpreting those past and helping to use those in the present and find better in the future. We know almost nothing about such interpretation in terms of speech—speech that really conveys ideas that mean action, that reaches the real self underneath superficial words. One thing we do know—that we are far too technical and didactic. We might learn a great deal by study of the speech and thought of our clients themselves. . . .

I know that I shall be charged with being visionary in describing a race of social workers with a genius for getting other people, the misfits of the earth, to choose and hold to courses which will make them no longer social liabilities. How are such social workers to be recruited and trained? How do we become such? I think our practical problem is one of our own attitude toward our work. If we cannot help the Jones family to turn its adversities into occasions for the development of what strength there is in them, the Joneses might just as well receive the minimum allowance for subsistence from an automatic machine and fight it out alone. Why spend millions for social work, for services, as say, if that service is merely the imposition of a dogmatism based on privilege. If we aim, not at being little dictators, but leaders and educators in the best sense, humbly learning with our families the ways of turning experience to good account for them, we shall find ways to reach our goal.[1]

Interviewers able to motivate their clients are artists in human relations, particularly if motivation becomes a quickening of the desire for successful living with one's fellows with emphasis on beauty, restoration of health, regularization of life, challenge to one's activities, or family pride.[2]   In times of financial emergencies it is particularly difficult to motivate those people who "live only where they are told to live, in houses not of their own choosing, are clothed with hand-me-downs that violate self-respect, are compelled to eat what is given them and in many instances are moved from place to place without having a voice in their own disposition. . . . "[3]   Such a situation violates our common accepted standards of what constitutes proper conduct in a democratic society.   Case workers might well regard with concern those persons who would submit unresistingly to arbitrary domination, suffer no pangs upon surrender of standards of living, loss of self-respect, or right of self-determination.   Such persons would, indeed, need the services of a case worker.

Karl De Schweinitz discusses the problem of motivation in a wide variety of social work situations helpful to the interviewer. In all of his illustrations one senses his deep sympathy with the struggle of the human personality and the universal searchings for happiness.   His philosophy is that successful living grows out of stable family life, protection of children, respect for the rights of neighborhood and society, the control of the environment of individuals to "accomplishments which they would never have dreamed themselves to be equal."[4]

A certain elderly gentleman was discovered by his relatives to be living a hermit's life on the top floor of a cheap and wretched rooming

[1] BERTHA C. REYNOLDS, "Treatment Processes as Developed by the Social Worker," *Proceedings of the National Conference of Social Work* (May 26–June 2, 1926), 403–406.

[2] See KARL DE SCHWEINITZ, *The Art of Helping People out of Trouble*, Chap. XII.

[3] GERTRUDE SPRINGER, "Partners in a New Social Order," *The Survey*, LXIX (July, 1933), 244.

[4] These are, no doubt, acceptable modes of life in our American milieu since they are in line with our social tradition and current ideology.   However, successful living might be differently defined in other culture groups or periods.   The interviewer must beware of accepting them as having ultimate social validity.   [P. V. Y.]

house. He was a university graduate, a person of taste and refinement, who had traveled widely and had been accustomed to wealth. Domestic troubles had left him without a home and he had drifted hither and thither as circumstance directed, until at last he had reached his present miserable quarters. . . .

A social worker was asked to help him move to an environment where he would be comfortable and where he would find friends, but when it came to the point, the old gentleman could not make up his mind to go. He was well acquainted with the facts of his situation. He knew what it would mean to pass another winter in unheated rooms. He was miserable in his loneliness and in the barrenness and the inconvenience of his quarters. He had none of the attachment for them that age frequently has for its home. He wanted to escape from the wretchedness of his present condition, but his desire to move was not strong enough to decide him in favor of a change.

It was to the quickening of his desire that the social worker addressed himself. Having discovered a possible boarding-house, he suggested that the old man go with him to inspect it, for there is nothing more effective in bringing an individual to a decision than the presentation of a concrete proposition which must be either accepted or refused.

The social worker set forth the arguments in favor of the new living place . . . described how worried about him his niece was, and how happy it would make her to know that he was comfortable and well. The man's eyes filled with tears, but he looked at the furniture about the room and felt that he could not move. What was he to do with it all? It was like a rope around his neck.

The social worker promised to undertake the moving. He would bring an assistant and the old gentleman could sit in a chair and watch while they disposed of things as he desired. What he did not want to keep could be sold. He could move to his new home without any of the worry that having these possessions gave him.

And what a terrible thing it was for a man of his tastes and his education to be living in this way. He should be in the sort of surroundings to which he had been accustomed, not in these dismal quarters.

Such were the suggestions which the social worker advanced to develop within the old gentleman the desire to move to a better environment. Back and forth over this ground the conversation went, the suggestions being introduced from different angles. Finally, after a discussion of more than two hours, the man promised to think it over by himself that night. The next day he called at the office of the social worker and said that he had decided to move. . . . [1]

Pride, and its corollary *shame*, are among the strongest motives to which one can appeal.

[1] Karl De Schweinitz, *op. cit.*, pp. 179–183.

"Why, you're a slacker, aren't you?" said a social case worker to a boy as he entered her office one morning during the war, coughing heavily.

The boy straightened up and took a step forward almost as if he were about to strike her.

"What do you mean?" he asked.

"If you let that cough run on, the army won't accept you when your turn comes," was the reply.

"When can I go to the doctor?" was the boy's almost instant response. He stopped smoking, and recovered from his cough. The boy had wanted to be rid of his cough, but not until his pride had been touched at its most sensitive point, his courage, and at a time when courage was at a premium, was he willing to make the sacrifice upon which his recovery was contingent.

"Don't let the neighbors see you move anything into the house that isn't in first-class condition," urged the social worker upon Mrs. Dorello when at last another home had been found. "You are going into a new neighborhood. Don't let them think that you own anything that is dirty."

Mr. and Mrs. Dorello rose immediately to this suggestion. They washed the beds and painted them; they gilded the frames of their pictures; repaired furniture; scoured the pots and pans; and disposed of all the odds and ends that were not worth saving; and thus were able to make a fresh start in keeping house.

A similar appeal to pride and shame was that made to a man who, while his wife was ill in a hospital, asked:

"What about my wife? Must I still stay with that woman?"

"Would you go and leave her now that she is sick?" said the social worker.

"I don't like her and I don't want to stay with her."

"Does it mean nothing to you that she is the mother of all your children?" was the reply. "Think what she has endured to bring them into the world and what it has meant to her to take care of them. You wouldn't want people to say, 'There goes Hansen. Look at the kind of man he is. He just walked off and left his wife and family.'"

A simple appeal of this sort to a man's pride is obviously not alone enough to solve a problem of maladjustment between husband and wife. There were many other things that needed to be done, but the use of this motive was not without its effect, as was also a reference to the welfare of his children. . . . [1]

[1] *Ibid.*, pp. 191–193.

As a positive stimulus fear is one of the strongest of motives. It is responsible for many successful careers, careers that have found their genesis in the very fear that they would not be successful. The fear of what people might say, the fear of consequences has been a stabilizing force in countless lives and many a boy and girl brought up in country, village, or town has learned the beginnings of foresight and thrift through the haunting fear of the poorhouse.

Powerful though this motive is the use of it is the least desirable of all the ways of influencing individuals. Back of an appeal to it usually is the implication of force, and to apply force . . . is generally to confess a lack of skill and understanding. The use of all other motives partakes in a greater or less degree of the nature of inspiration. To arouse fear is to command. The appeal to most motives leaves a man free to choose. It is a form of leadership. Fear drives.

Reward is a far sounder method of reinforcing an individual's desires. Lacking the same compulsory element, it can be used with greater justification. Obviously, opportunity for increased income is a more satisfactory way of developing a man's industrial efficiency than the threat of the loss of his job. Interesting the individual in the task itself, work for the sake of work, would be still more constructive.[1]

Many stories circulate as to how General Wood disciplined and built soldiers out of raw recruits and ignorant "rookies" who never before were subjected to systematic training and discipline. He is reported to have used the following strategy with a soldier who—in company with his girl—seeing the general approaching stooped to tie his shoestring.

"You saw me, didn't you?"
The man shuffled about uneasily. "Yes, sir," he said.
"But in order to avoid saluting me," the general went on, "you pretended to tie your shoe string. . . . Reluctantly the man admitted that was it.
"Now, I'll tell you what I would have done if I'd been in your place," the General remarked. "I'd have said to my girl, 'Now watch me make the old man take my salute!' Get the point?"
The soldier saluted. "Yes, sir," he said grinning. The General answered the salute with marked precision and drove on. . . .
"Why are the men so fond of Wood? one of the staff officers was asked.

[1] *Ibid.*, pp. 200–201. Reprinted by permission of Houghton Mifflin Company.

"I'll tell you why," was the answer. "Because Bill Smith in the rear rank thinks that as far as the general is concerned he is the whole Division."[1]

By raising the status of his men and by making them feel that they and their jobs are important a successful leader wins their devotion and cooperation. It is pointed out that Daniel Guggenheim, the copper magnate, imparted even to his office boys a sense of dignity and importance. "'Boys must be treated with just as much consideration, as anyone else in the whole organization. If a boy comes with a message from others, or on any other duty, he must not be kept waiting, for his time is just as valuable to him as mine is to me.'"[2]

One emergency relief interviewer remarks that she has little difficulty in having her clients look for work and accept jobs "much beneath them and their training" because she compliments them highly on their initiative, resourcefulness, and ability to meet hard times with a determination characteristic of true manhood. "When a man makes a few dollars a week I praise him for his ability to hustle and find work when hundreds in his community sit idle." Such visitors are generally the first ones to be informed when their clients find work. Case work supervisors generally agree that those interviewers who make their clients sign affidavits that they will be informed when there is an income in the family accumulate many chiselers in their files. Here is a case in point:

Ada White, a colored lady, refused to accept a job as a domestic for $30.00 a month. "Why, Ada, what's the matter with you, preferring to live on charity than to earn your own bread in a self-respecting manner?" asked the astonished interviewer. To which Ada replied: "Self-respect? Not much of it left when you, young Miss, call a woman long ago old enough to be your mother by her first name." A new visitor was assigned to the case shortly afterwards who treated Mrs. White with deference and respect for her ability as a housekeeper and for her spirit of independence. The first suitable job assigned Mrs. White was thankfully accepted by her.[3]

The following interview with Mr. Norris illustrates how an interviewer induced a man who was ready to desert his family to change his mind.

[1] HERMANN HAGEDORN, *That Human Being—Leonard Wood*, pp. 90–94.
[2] B. C. FORBES, *Men Who Are Making America*, p. 180.
[3] Statement by a family welfare worker.

Interview with Mr. Norris.

(Mr. Norris, a very quiet and noncommittal man, and very attentive, stated that he had just taken his wife, a woman of a different race and culture, to the County Hospital: "And now since she is there they can keep her there. I am through. . . . Had enough of her," he added in a determined voice.)

Interviewer: Won't you sit down, Mr. Norris, there are some things I would like to talk over with you. (Seated in quiet room.) Mr. Norris, I believe I understand what prompts you to say that. Of course, you think Mrs. Norris is an unsatisfactory housekeeper, that you are no longer sexually compatible, that she is nervous, irritable, quarrelsome. But she is your wife and you are a man of honor. (According man social status.) You know she has had a hard life. You know what made her irritable. Don't you think you have a responsibility toward her? (Appealing to a desire to help others.) (No answer.)

But let's look at the situation from another angle. I know you love your twins. Would you like to go through life alone, childless? Or do you think you can begin all over again at the age of forty-five? It has been done, it is possible, but you may find it very difficult. (Pointing out the uncertainties of the future.) You know, of course, that Mrs. Norris will not give up the children and the court would never give you custody if you walk out on them, and at a time when your wife is at the hospital. (Providing insight into the facts of the situation.) In such matters we have to take a long look into the future. In desertion cases a man's past record is looked up and the whole story unwinds in court. (Appeal to fear of consequences as a stabilizing force.) (No answer.)

But there is still another side to this situation. I know you regret the fact that you did not have the care and comfort of a home when you were a child. Do you remember your own childhood? (Pause.) And what you are trying to do now to your own sons is to repeat in their lives what you have resented in your own throughout all these years. I know, you don't mean to do that deliberately but that's what it amounts to. (Appeal to strong love toward his small sons.)

I know it's hard for you to live as you are; a man has just so much patience and no more. We all arrive at times at our wits end and believe we can go no further. You always provided for them. (Leaving an opportunity for face saving.)

Mr. Norris: I love Mrs. Norris and the boys and have always loved them, but it burns me up when she puts on the dog. I must admit I am jealous of her. She still thinks of a man she wanted to marry but didn't. Why should she still think of him? She even used to talk about him to me but I told her she must quit. She had to shut up.

Interviewer: O, well, don't you believe that her thinking about him is harmless enough? She doesn't even know whether he is dead or alive or where he is. Has she tried to see him?

Mr. Norris: No, she hasn't. . . . Well! I guess, we are strange beings. It does make a man jealous to have his wife think of another man. If I ever meet him, he better look out. You know there is lots of fight in me.

Interviewer: I sure would like to see you two together. Please send me an S. O. S. when you meet him face to face. I want to be a mouse in the closet. (Attempt to release tension.) Well, it's almost time for my next appointment, and I must be there in a few minutes. Tell me, Mr. Norris, when are you going to see Mrs. Norris?

Mr. Norris: Don't you worry, I will see her Saturday.

Interviewer: That's fine. I knew you would. Let me know how she is getting along.[1]

The situation was critical. Previous appeals to maintain family ties have failed. There was no intention of threatening with the law, only of making the man consider what would face him did he fail in his duty as father and husband at a time of most urgent need.

Persuasion.—Miss Jean Lucas in replying to those who inquire "how are people *made* to do these things" writes:

We are patient with such ignorance. To conceive of coercion in this age of individualism is preposterous. Yet must we not confess that most of us are guilty of "bossing" now and then? We are all loud in our condemnation of the dictatorial manner, or withholding a necessity until the wisdom of our decisions is acknowledged. But how many of us have been flattered to be told that no one else could have persuaded Mrs. A. to go back to her husband? Did she return with a full realization of all the difficulties and with new wisdom and courage, or was it because Miss B. was so lovely she did not want to disappoint her? How many of us have had a secret satisfaction in the suspicion that our successor will not be able to maintain a certain confidential relation? Was it a relation more founded on admiration on one side and by pity on the other than by a mutual understanding of problems and solution?

Mr. Lee has recently used the words "executive" and "leadership" in the description of certain phases of treatment; but practically there are very few forms of treatment which permit executive impulse without unlimited leadership preceding, a leadership based on mutual purposes, established by confidence. We are all familiar with histories which record a series of memoranda, sending a man to a clinic or escorting a child to a dentist. One feels that some unseen power commands but the rationale is concealed from client and worker and is still less comprehensible to the onlooker. We know the worker who descends without notice upon a Slavish woman speaking little English, to tell her that her eight-year-old boy is to be examined within half an hour by a famous psychologist. The child, dirty and rebellious, is dragged from under a table, kicking and striking his mother, to be escorted in this defiant mood to the doctor. Of what practical value is such an examination? To be sure, it has been accomplished and can be checked on a card as a task done, but what is learned? What barriers

---

[1] Interview held and recorded by a student visitor.

have been built up between that child and the visitor? How inexplicable are her actions to the mother? If she had known that the doctor might help to explain why Albert found school so hard and was so difficult to discipline, would she not have been glad to have had him ready? If Albert had known that the doctor was interested in games that he might play with, how cheerfully he would have gone—and who can deny that his I.Q. would have been higher? Such treatment can be compared to a cyclone. Things happen without reason. People are seized and, after whirling about, are dropped in bewilderment if not in actual fright. More and more we realize that acts which are unrelated in the client's mind, no matter how vital and apparent to the worker, will cause ultimate defeat in treatment. These unrelated episodes become meaningful when they are seen as definite steps toward a plan evolved by the experience and imagination of the worker, modified by the desires and deep purposes of the client. . . .

To be brief, persuasion is dependent on an appreciation of the power of personal desires and of purposes which control the direction of every act. Persuasion is possible when the distasteful and alienated things of life are consciously related to our interests. It is as if one connected the small silent wheel of an idle machine with the belt that brings power to the whole plant. The wheel moves as if by magic.

But how can we know where power lies? By thoughtful consideration of the story made up of the spoken explanations adorned by the brief glimpses of hidden purposes and interests. Often these moments of self-revealing occur during conversation, but sometimes they stand out in the process of investigation. We have an apologetic attitude toward this process. But though some of the creed may be outworn, we must not turn aside. Let us breathe new life into routine. Let us cease to be satisfied with facts and follow the footsteps of purpose into a living reconstruction of the past. A past, so revealed, illuminates the present. With such knowledge one may attempt persuasion, if it be conceived as the leading of thought to a vision of life as a whole. With such vision the immediate obstacle obscuring the horizon is easily surmounted.[1]

Dr. Rosanoff's discussion of the relation of suggestion and motivation to psychotherapy indirectly contributes helpful hints to interviewing therapy.

An essential element of psychotherapy is suggestion. Its successful practice is dependent on the nature of the disorder, the attitude of the patient, and the personality of the physician. . . .

[1] JEAN M. LUCAS, "The Interview of Persuasion," *Interviews, Interviewers and Interviewing in Social Case Work*, pp. 26–27; 33. Reprinted by permission of the Family Welfare Association of America.

The patient must have full confidence in the physician and in his methods. "The nervous patient is on the path to recovery as soon as he has the conviction that he is going to be cured; he is cured on the day when he believes himself to be cured."*

It follows that the physician must be able to inspire respect and trust. According to Griesinger he must have "a kind disposition, great patience, self-possession, particular freedom from prejudice, an understanding of human nature resulting from an abundant knowledge of the world, adroitness in conversation, and a special love of his calling."

As to the manner of employing suggestion the indications must be sought in the individual case. In some cases, the patient's faith being strong, a mere statement that the symptoms are quickly disappearing may be sufficient. In other cases "rational" suggestion with an explanation of the cause of the symptoms and of the best means of combating them is more effective. "There is a great difference in mentality between the man who is content with a statement, who allows himself to be under the influence of the personality of a healer, and the man who acquires confidence by the clear exposition of the reasons to believe."† In still other cases hypnotic suggestion affords good results.[1]

Thus we see that in order to motivate others the interviewer may resort to several techniques: (1) Arouse enthusiasm and a sense of pride in their work, possessions, responsibilities. (2) Respect their ability and show genuine sympathy for their problems. (3) Display a wholehearted interest in their point of view. (4) Show that their welfare is placed above the immediate needs of the agency. (5) Reinforce a desire with other desires to strengthen the influence of one motive by appealing to supporting motives (as in the case of the elderly gentleman motivated to give up his hermit-like life). (6) Instill a spirit of competition, especially competition with oneself. (7) Remove opposition. (8) Appeal to the desire for the welfare of others (one's children, relations, friends).

* PAUL DUBOIS, *The Psychic Treatment of Nervous Disorders* (translated by Jelliffe and White), p. 210.

† PAUL DUBOIS, *op. cit.*, p. 227.

[1] A. J. ROSANOFF (Editor), *Manual of Psychiatry*, pp. 389–390. Reprinted by permission of author.

CHAPTER XVII

DYNAMICS OF THE THERAPEUTIC INTERVIEW

(*Concluded*)

Mutual Planning.—Social case work interviewers know that there is hardly any phase of treatment that "is more delicate or that cuts closer to the roots of one's philosophy than that which has to do with the development of the plans by which an individual makes his way out of a difficulty."[1] Yet there is often the tendency on the part of the interviewer to take the matter into his own hands and guide, suggest, at times even urge and insist on a definite and prescribed course of action. The sound techniques of social therapy, as already indicated, stress the necessity of a client's self-expression, of "living his own life."

. . . everybody wants to govern his own life and to make his own decisions. Puzzled, bewildered, and buffeted though a man may be he never loses the urge to self expression. No matter how submissive he may have become to another's suggestions, no matter how prone he may be to turn to some one else for the solution of his problems, when he reaches that which to him is vital he wants to be the arbiter of his own desires.

How can he enter enthusiastically into a plan that is wholly the creation of some one else? He must have had at least a part in its conception. He must feel a sense of ownership in it. Without this there is little hope that the plan will be successfully executed or have anything of permanence about it.[2]

Interviewers frequently ask what to do when their clients are unable to devise ways and means of overcoming their difficulty. The first essential is to learn why they are unable to do so. If they do not understand their problem, then before any planning can be undertaken, the problem needs to be explained to them and they need to be supplied with insight into their own situation. Frequently, once they discover what is involved in the problem, they also discover a plan of meeting it. Under these circum-

[1] KARL DE SCHWEINITZ, *op. cit.*, p. 139.
[2] *Ibid.*, pp. 139–140.

stances the interviewer becomes the interpreter of the situation but not the arbitrary manipulator of the subject. At times, however, the problem is fully interpreted but the clients, though intelligent, do not have enough resourcefulness to plan. Even in these cases the interviewer cannot be oversolicitous or make the decisions for them, for if the person lacks resourcefulness essential in arriving at a decision, he will also lack it in consistently following a prescribed plan. These people must be guided, to be sure, but only in stimulating them to follow a course suitable to them and one which they have helped in charting. When it is necessary to suggest a plan of action, it is well to watch the interviewee's reactions and to ask him to modify it: "What do you think about it? How will it work in your situation?"

The other day I interviewed a woman whom you could call plainly "stupid" without any insult to her intelligence, but I recognized in her a strong desire to be credited with whatever changes were made in her behalf. I said: "Do you think you could persuade your mother to keep your boy while you are away at work? . . . I know you would rather have him with her than on the street. I could speak to your mother if you want me to, but I am sure you can manage it better by yourself." And of course, she could. I motivated her to act for herself, to assume her own responsibility but, I had to suggest, though I did not advise, the initial step.[1]

More often, however, interviewers assume the responsibility not only for suggesting a plan but also for carrying it out: "I know you will agree with me, Mrs. O., that the children need a change of school. Therefore, I have arranged to have them transferred to another district." Whether Mrs. O "agreed" or not, she felt completely left out of a situation in which she should have had the privilege and responsibility not only of deciding but also of executing the decision. The worker later complained that Mrs. O. was uncooperative. Obviously lack of cooperation on the part of the worker will induce similar behavior in the client. It would, perhaps, have been better to lead Mrs. O. to the conclusion that a change of school was necessary and have her arrange for the transfer.

Another case in point. Mr. Nathan's wife was expected to be paroled from the insane asylum, and the social worker, visiting the family to ascertain the home conditions, sensed the presence of considerable conflict in the home. Addressing herself to

[1] Statement by a student visitor.

Mr. Nathan and his children, she said: "When Mrs. Nathan comes home you must provide her with rest, relief from worries, nourishing food, and a quiet congenial home. . . . You must recognize that your mother will still show some peculiarities and make suitable allowances for them."

The family agreed but had only a vague notion of what was expected of them. The surer way of approaching this family would have been to ask each member how he in his own way expected to prepare for the mother's return, picturing the needs of the patient just returning from the hospital; to allow each child to propose in what way he is to provide for the mother's rest and relief from worries.

An ingenious interviewer can tie up mere tasks with something that really grips people and makes tasks interesting, satisfying, and, therefore, wanted. Unless a plan is satisfying and wanted it will be evaded and defeated. As with children, one may make a game of a task as the easiest way of accomplishing it. "Only too often a sanguine enthusiastic personality will embark a man upon plans in which he has no fundamental interest, mistaking his acquiescence for a positive desire. Once the buoyancy and optimism of the helper is removed, the individual slackens his efforts because he has never really made the plan his own."[1] Frequently also a person resents advice and by many devious methods will seek to defeat it. Only when advice is sought and specifically solicited has it any place in the relations between therapist and client. Even then the facts in the situation can be discussed in general terms while the client is allowed to relate them specifically to his own situation.

The other day a client asked me if I did not think it best for her to leave the husband who "has been abusing her for many years" and who had a "vicious influence upon the children." I related to her what had happened to families under similar circumstances that I knew or had read about. I discussed the children's angle, her angle and the man's angle and left her to decide for herself.[2]

Professor Dewey says:

There is a sense in which to set up social welfare as an end of action only promotes an offensive condescension, a harsh interference, or an oleaginous display of complacent kindliness. It always tends in this

---

[1] KARL DE SCHWEINITZ, *op. cit.*, p. 149.
[2] Statement by a student visitor.

direction when it is aimed at giving happiness to others directly, that is, as we can hand a physical thing to another. To foster conditions that widen the horizon of others and give them command of their own powers, so that they can find their own happiness in their own fashion, is the way of "social" action. Otherwise the prayer of a freeman would be to be left alone, and to be delivered, above all, from "reformers" and "kind" people.[1]

Frequently clients come to case workers with a plan which is unsatisfactory and inadequate from all standpoints and no single phase can be indorsed or recommended. The client should be complimented for the creation of a plan whether it has a chance of success or not. Stimulating him to take pride in the production of a plan he may be induced to work out one which will "do him more justice."

Mrs. B., a widow past forty, came to me proposing that I close her case since she had found "a way out" for herself. She accepted a job as "housekeeper" for a middle-aged bachelor. "I am not fooling myself," she said, "I know that he expects me to be much more than a 'housekeeper' to him, but it's a way out and I am going to do it. He also promised to marry me." I complimented Mrs. B. for her independence of spirit and grit, but pointed out to her that she was reducing her chances of marriage. "Why should he marry you when you give him all he wants without marriage?" I asked her. She then began to regard her plan from another angle.[2]

Certain clients, however, have developed mental habits of submission to the point that they prefer to be told what to do. Prolonged subordination to a dominating spouse or parent may make the necessity for individual action and independent judgment a difficult if not painful matter. Parental fixations and personal attachments may, in fact, in extreme cases amount to a pathological condition analogous to *folie à deux* in which two minds have so far merged that they have lost their separate identities. The social worker may, therefore, be called upon to play the role of the dominating personality for such a person.

Our present therapeutic goals insist upon the client's achieving a considerable measure of independence. Subordinated personalities, however, will resist the effort to make them "stand on their own feet" and they will prefer to "lean on the worker." Direct command is

[1] JOHN DEWEY, "The Good of Activity," *Human Nature and Conduct*, p. 294.

[2] Statement by an interviewer.

necessary in such cases until a degree of independence can be won by the client.

The more frequent situation is, of course, that in which a client who has a considerable degree of independence and initiative is little by little brought into a state of dependence upon the worker through the worker's too ready use of direct commands in dealing with the client. That is the surest and quickest road to pauperization.[1]

The more one works with people the more one realizes that the way of freedom is the only sure road to success, maintains Karl De Schweinitz.

The plan that carries through is the plan that is a man's own. Suggest it to him, perhaps, but only as a thought for him to digest and to make a part of himself. Offer him the stimulation that comes from a meeting of minds, from the action and reaction of ideas, from the thinking out aloud with some one who understands; edit, perhaps criticize, but let authorship remain with him. It is both his right and the way of his salvation.[2]

Satisfaction of the Wishes.[3]—Whatever forms of social therapy the interviewer adopts—sympathetic insight, mental catharsis, reconditioning of attitudes, motivation, mutual planning, or some other form of therapy—he succeeds only in so far as he is able to satisfy the fundamental wishes of the individual or the group he interviews. No appeal to reason is effective without an accompanying satisfaction of the basic social cravings of men for (1) new experience, (2) security, (3) recognition, and (4) response.

The desire for new experience manifests itself in man's craving for new sensations, change, motion, adventure, travel, learning. He wants to grow and develop and create. He seeks to relieve everyday monotony by new stimulations. The desire for new experience "ranges in moral quality from the pursuit of game and the pursuit of pleasure to the pursuit of knowledge and the pursuit of ideals."[4] This desire implies originality and creativeness and is particularly strong in youth, but it dominates adults

---

[1] From a statement by Erle F. Young.

[2] *The Art of Helping People out of Trouble*, pp. 154–155.

[3] For a systematic discussion of the social wishes see W. I. Thomas, *The Unadjusted Girl*, Chaps. I and II.

[4] ROBERT E. PARK, "The Sociological Method of William I. Thomas and William Graham Sumner," in STUART A. RICE (Editor), *Methods in Social Science: A Case Book*, p. 174.

as well; it "is found equally in the vagabond and in the scientific explorer."[1]   When the drive for new experience is very strong and no wholesome outlet is provided for its expression, it may result in personal instability, social irresponsibility, or disregard for the prevailing standards and interests of the group.

An interviewer can aid only indirectly in the satisfaction of the wish for new experience by indicating ways and means for recreation, association, reading, improvement on the job, associations with friends, social institutions, clubs.   "When we stimulate people to join church activities, evening school classes, settlement affairs, or their own communal organizations, we enlarge their social world and bring them out of the rut. . . . "   "There is always something new going on in the community and we need to bring our clients in contact with the communal resources," say social work interviewers.

In the interview with Mr. S., the blind sailor, the interviewer sought to satisfy his craving for new experience by proposing that he join the Club for the Blind, a very active and energetic group.   Mr. S. was provided with an opportunity to learn to read Braille, to weave baskets, even to dance.   Thus the basis for his complaint that life was stale and monotonous and that "There is nothin' to do except sit around and do nothin' and think about your misery," was removed.

The desire for security, being almost directly opposed to the desire for adventure, though it may manifest itself at the same time in the same individual, implies avoidance of risk and danger, of mobility and stimulation.   It enforces conservatism, traditional methods of behavior, and a desire to be incorporated in a family group, a neighborhood, or a larger community.   With the loss of economic security and in many instances with social security threatened or seriously undermined, the individual becomes confused and bewildered, and his basic cravings are thwarted.   Nothing can supply that sense of security which comes to a man who earns his daily bread.   But the interviewer can often allay fears and strengthen his client's religious beliefs, his confidence in American democratic principles, through giving him a sense of belonging even in case he is an industrial discard.

This was the guiding principle in the interviews with Mrs. Parker and Mr. Anderson.   The interviewers sought to create a feeling of worth on the part of the clients and to build up their

[1] *Ibid.*, p. 174.

sense of security by displaying an attitude which showed belief in their integrity and respect for their ability and personality.

The following brief interview with Henry shows how a feeling of belonging is instilled in a child, which provides him with a sense of security in the social group.

Interview with Henry.

(Interviewer was advised by the school board even before the term opened that they "had enough of Henry to put him in a school of correction." Interviewer asked that the boy be given "a chance," but it was understood that the "sacrifice" could not interfere with the best interests of the school or of an individual.

Henry was eleven years old, large for his age, sullen, uncommunicative, and unhappy. . . . He was molesting the smaller children on the playground and on the way to and from school. The community was beginning to feel "things had gone far enough" and were insisting that steps be taken "to place him in a school of correction.")

Henry: I hate school. I hate teachers. I am going to quit and run away.

Interviewer: I am sorry to hear that, Henry, because I am in trouble and I thought you might help me.

(Henry looked rather surprised that anyone but himself could ever be in trouble.)

Henry: (Sarcastically) What's the matter with you?

Interviewer: Well, there are so many of the children getting hurt on the school ground and I am rather puzzled as to just what to do.

Henry: (Sarcastically) What am I to do about that?

Interviewer: I was thinking about it last night and I was wondering if perhaps one of our larger boys could be a "big brother" and supervise during intermissions. I find my work so heavy that I do not have the time to be constantly on the playground.

Henry: Who would want a "sissy" job like that?

Interviewer: I thought it was quite a task. You know they never put women or weak men on a police force.

Henry: Well, what do you want me to do about it?

Interviewer: I was hoping you would be that "big brother" and I am sorry to learn you are going away. Could you suggest anyone to take that responsibility?

Henry: The kids wouldn't let me take care of them, they don't like me.

Interviewer: Let us forget about likes and dislikes. After all there is work to do and this "big brother" is only to be concerned with the safety of the smaller children on the playground.

Henry: Do you really think they would let me do it?

(Henry's facial expression was still somewhat sullen, there was an expression in his eyes similar to that of an abused or hunted animal.)

Interviewer: Kindness will do a great deal for any of us. I have often noticed your dog Jinx, you must have been very kind to him, Henry, to make him love you so much.

Henry: (As though turning the matter over in his own mind) Do you really think I could do it?

Interviewer: I never would have asked you, Henry, if I did not believe you could.

(The boy was near tears at this point of the interview. However, he soon became master of the situation and blurted out—)

Henry: Well, when do you want me to start?

Interviewer: Right away. With both of us working together, I am sure that our playground troubles will soon be over.

(There were many "ups and downs" before things were finally adjusted, but the above interview seemed to have been the turning point in Henry's attitude toward teachers and school life. . . . The community was touched by his protective attitude toward the other children and they soon ceased to speak of him in terms of "a bad boy." When Henry moved from the school to another district, he asked for a letter to his new teacher explaining his work as a "big brother" and perhaps she would let him carry on this work in his new school.)[1]

Henry's wish for recognition and response was also satisfied, but his social status in the group and the response he received from the teacher and the children assured his security and the sense of belonging.

The wish for recognition manifests itself in various devices for attaining distinction and status in the eyes of our fellow-men. Every person craves status in some society, in some group in which he is somebody, "somewhere or other, in short he must be a person rather than a mere cog in the economic or social machine."[2] Park and Burgess observe that when we are born we are *individuals,* but as we acquire status we become *persons.*[3] Under these circumstances there is little wonder that the struggle for status or position in lesser or greater degrees is ever present in young and old alike.

. . . A list of the different modes of seeking recognition would be very long. It would include courageous behavior, showing off through ornament and dress, the pomp of kings, the display of opinions and knowledge, the possession of special attainments—in the arts, for example. It is expressed alike in arrogance and in humility, even in martyrdom. Certain modes of seeking recognition we define as "vanity," others as "ambition." The "Will to power" belongs here. Perhaps there has been no spur to human activity so keen and no motive so naively avowed as the desire for "undying fame," and it would be

[1] Interview held and recorded by Miss Della Forney, Long Beach, California.

[2] ROBERT E. PARK, "The Significance of Social Research in Social Service," *The Journal of Applied Sociology,* VIII (May-June, 1924), p. 265.

[3] *An Introduction to the Science of Sociology,* p. 55.

difficult to estimate the role the desire for recognition has played in the creation of social values.[1]

It has been advocated as advisable to raise or inflate a person's ego when it is necessary to draw him out, to handle him, or to control him. From the point of view of the competent interviewer such procedure is neither ethical, constructive, nor expedient. He should not be engaged in drawing out interviewees by increasing their ego, but rather in turning their attention away from themselves to their social situation and in creating a wider social world and perspective for them. Neither is he interested in handling or controlling people. A person's self-esteem is best enhanced when he knows that he can guide his own life destiny and that he is thereby accepted by his fellow-men.

Nothing will arouse initiative in a client as rapidly as a feeling of social recognition, is a general belief of social workers. The best way to motivate them to action is to accord them social status by showing respect for their judgment and their personality, by consulting them on matters which they know have significance to us, by assigning them tasks they can perform well, by making them feel at home in our presence, and by assuring them that they have a definite role to play in life and in their own group.

The challenge of the economic depression has given case workers a sharpened realization of the capacities and judgments of the new poor. Clients who were regarded as demanding, irresponsible, nagging, and who were supposed to be able to speak of nothing but their gas bills were discovered able to discuss policies, work projects, self-help enterprises with clarity and objectivity.[2] They gain in self-confidence as their social status is justifiably heightened.

Interviewers cannot always provide possibilities whereby a client's social status will be heightened, but they can take care not to wound his pride or injure his ego—practices leading to further struggles for status, to rationalizations, to defense mechanisms, and even to falsification. An experience of Beatrice Webb in the company of Charles Booth illustrates the point:

[1] Adapted from ROBERT E. PARK, "The Sociological Methods of William Graham Sumner and William I. Thomas and Florian Znaniecki," in STUART A. RICE (Editor), *Methods in Social Science: A Case Book*, 174–175.

[2] ELIZABETH DUTCHER, "When Clients Participate," *The Survey*, LXX (February, 1934), 42.

Amusing interview with L., factory inspector (at) Home Office. . . .
He welcomed me with a funny self-important air; he was "delighted
to see me in connection with a subject that had occupied so much
of his thought." He knew that my object was to do good, etc., etc.
That had been *his* object, and he had labored night and day to accomplish it. And then he opened out in a burst of indignation against
the Board of Trade and Burnett's Report. He thought it disgraceful,
stealing men's brains; that is what Burnett had done. He had come
to him, and cross-examined him and put all he said, without acknowl-
edgment, into this report (Burnett had told me that L. had refused
to give him any information) . . . Charlie (Booth) became very
impatient with this tirade and cut it short by asking for special and
definite information. L. then gave us the usual hackneyed account of
"Sweating," a great deal of which we recognized as inexact and absurdly
sensational. Then Charlie, rather unwisely, asked him bolt out: would
he give him list of names and addresses of "sweaters"? "No," said L.,
somewhat testily, "I can't do that." And then as Charlie explained
his object, Mr. L. smiled at him with conscious superiority, as much
as to say, "You all of you are amateurs, and think you know a great
deal; but your ideas are impracticable." All this was simply the
result of the lack of sympathy Charlie had shown to the man's wounded
vanity. Altogether, I was sorry I had not been alone with him; I
should have managed him better, with softer and less direct treatment.
As it was, we got nothing out of him, except the picture of a man
smarting under the consciousness of another man reaping the fruits
of what he considered he had sown.[1]

Webb and Morgan observe:

The small man often lets his hearers feel that he is clever and that
they are dumb—but not the real leader who sweeps people off their
feet. His strategy is to make his *listeners* feel clever.

Take care to safeguard the self-esteem of all people with whom you
wish to maintain friendly relations. Protect them from your own
desire to feel superior and important. Remember that this desire is
always at work within yourself, whether you realize it or not.[2]

The wish for response manifests itself in a craving for personal
relations, attachments, and affection. The human is a social
animal, and he seeks not only companionship and associations
with his own kind, but intimate appreciation by individuals.
The wish for response expresses itself in love, family affection,
friendship, or kinship.

[1] BEATRICE WEBB, *My Apprenticeship*, pp. 316–317.
[2] *Op. cit.*, pp. 114–115. (The last paragraph is in italics.)

The interviewer attempted to appeal to the desire for response when interviewing Mrs. Parker[1] and pointed out the daughter's love and attachment to her. Similarly the interviewer appealed to the old gentleman who lived a hermit-like existence that it would please his niece to know that he had moved to more comfortable quarters.[2] The interviewer relied on Mr. Norris'[3] love for his children in reawakening a sense of responsibility in him toward their mother. Furthermore, the interviewer's friendly and sympathetic contacts with the interviewee oftentimes satisfy the wish for response.

Case work interviewers, consciously or unconsciously, have generally attempted to satisfy this wish for response in their clients. Miss Robinson describes the process as follows:

In early days the relationship between the client and the worker was accepted by the worker as a matter of simple, natural, human friendliness. "To be really interested, to be able to convey this fact without protestations, to be sincere and direct and open-minded—these are the best keys to fruitful intercourse," says Miss Richmond.[4]

Dr. Southard writing in the *Kingdom of Evils* in 1922 describes the relationship as a mixture of authority and friendship in which the worker must contrive to be at the same time a personal friend and an impersonal adviser.[5] In a friendly contact the worker could express her own natural, spontaneous, best self, she could make use of her own personality, interests, and even her own problems to win the confidence of the client as she would with a friend. Miss Kempton illustrates this approach in an article in *The Family* in 1926[6] where she quotes an episode in which the worker finding her client antagonistic and reticent introduced into the conversation a personal problem of her own and thereby won the client's sympathy to a point where it was possible to have a three-hour conversation with her. This concept of a friendly contact in which the worker uses her own natural equipment spontaneously has been hard to resign. This the worker understands from her own experience. Perhaps in her experience the word friendship defines the most complete relationship possible. But the client frequently requires of the case worker far more understanding and patience and

---

[1] See Interview with Mrs. Parker, pp. 307–310.
[2] See pp. 332–333.
[3] See Interview with Mr. Norris, pp. 336–338.
[4] *Social Diagnosis*, p. 200.
[5] Pp. 547–548.
[6] "How Do We Effect Leadership?" *The Family*, VI (February, 1926), 290–293.

self-discipline than one is ever called upon to exercise in the relationship of a friend.

Gradually more technical words, usually borrowed from psychoanalytic literature, are substituting for "friendly" in the case worker's vocabulary, "transfer," "rapport," "identification." Their usage indicates an increasing and more objective concern with the meaning of relationship to the client and the worker's responsibility in this experience. They are still vague and confused in meaning and reacted to by some workers as to something unknown, fearful, and uncontrollable. The first frank use of the word "transfer" as far as I can discover was in a paper read before the National Conference at Toronto by Dr. Jessie Taft called "The Use of the Transfer in the Office Interview."[1] The transfer was described as the emotional relationship in which the client gained sufficient security to release impulses to which fear and guilt were attached and secondly, through identification with the worker, took over the ideas and interests "which during this period become dynamic through their identification with the person who suggests them, and become in time natural channels for draining off a large part of the emotion which has been going into the transfer.[2]

Some interviewers fear any personal relations with their clients on the ground that they will get themselves involved in some responsibility. Clearly they become involved or assume responsibility when they attempt to disentangle domestic discords, child problems, financial and vocational difficulties. Personal problems need to be adjusted in an objective and scientific manner, that is, the interviewer must show no partiality to one client over against another, he must keep cool-headed and not be swayed by displays of emotion, he must be systematic and consistent in his attack upon the problem, but the influence which he exerts over another human being cannot by virtue of its very nature be anything but personal.

The interviewer may not always be able to satisfy the social wishes of his interviewee, but he can at least avoid thwarting them. At times, an interviewer is elated that he has succeeded in conquering stubborn or willful clients, that he made them "come across," that he got them to do what they were asked to do. This is a very shortsighted success. Such an interviewer may gain victory temporarily, but he neither builds constructively nor provides for the satisfaction of the wishes. Every

[1] *The Family*, V, (October, 1924), 145.

[2] VIRGINIA P. ROBINSON, *A Changing Psychology in Social Case Work*, pp. 128–129. Reprinted by permission of the University of North Carolina Press.

time someone wins, someone else loses and no one relishes being the loser. Skillful interviewers must also be good losers, must be able to give up cheerfully, for in the long run, paradoxically enough, they may win by losing. It is poor strategy to satisfy one's own wishes by subjecting another to the pressure of one powerful will against another no matter how benevolent the purpose, since only negativism can result. With profound reverence for the will of clients the interviewer needs to utilize the forces already within them and center everything upon them and even to orient himself with regard to them.[1]

A good many people, case workers, teachers and even some psychiatrists dislike very much the thought of an emotional relationship to the client, student or patient. They often think of this as a sentimental appeal, a use of one's personality to induce the individual to do something which he would naturally evade or resist, an encouragement of crushes, a personal desire for admiration or adulation. People who have this strong aversion to emotional responses in themselves or their clients like to believe that treatment, successful readjustment of families and individuals comes from practical use of resources and the education of the individuals concerned through ideas and rational appeals.

While I sympathize with the objection which such people feel for the unprofessional attitude and lack of insight which often characterizes the personal contacts of the untrained or unadjusted person who bungles on the job because he does not understand himself or the methods he is unconsciously using, I do not think that the existence of bunglers should prevent us from recognizing that the basis of all case work therapy is primarily emotional, not rational or intellectual, and that we who deal with people are responsible for accepting and understanding technically the tools which we have been using more or less consciously and skillfully.[2]

Whether this process is designated as friendliness, *rapport*, identification, transfer, relation, sympathetic insight, or empathy, it aims to establish a bridge across which an interviewer and interviewee can convey a sense of their mental and emotional natures to each other, whereby they can become "we" in another form, winning across the void which separates man from man and gaining a feeling of kinship.

[1] JESSIE TAFT, *The Dynamics of Therapy in a Controlled Relationship*, 100 *ff*.

[2] JESSIE TAFT, "The Use of the Transfer within the Limits of the Office Interview," *The Family*, V (October, 1924), 143.

No social therapy is complete, in short, whatever mechanisms we use to accomplish it, until the interviewer has been able to stimulate the interviewee to plan for himself, to think for himself, to act by himself within the accepted standards of his group, and to guide his own life destinies and satisfy his social wishes in conformity with prevailing group standards and on occasion, perhaps, to contribute something toward the improvement of group standards and collective life.

Suggestions for Further Study

1. What is the distinction between "social treatment" and "social therapy" as discussed by Jessie Taft in her book *The Dynamics of Therapy in a Controlled Relationship?*

2. Read Virginia P. Robinson's book, *A Changing Psychology in Social Case Work*, and trace the development of the techniques in social therapy.

3. What do the above writers mean by "relationship therapy"? What is meant by the statement "not alms but a friend"? (Octavia Hill)

4. How does relation therapy differ from the executive phase of treatment and the leadership phase of treatment discussed by Porter Lee. See pp. 338–339.

5. Why is the subject of social therapy a new and uncharted field?

6. How does social case work therapy differ from interviewing therapy? How are they related?

7. What is the relation of one's social case work philosophy to his interviewing therapy?

8. What is meant by a consistent and rational plan of social therapy?

9. What are the bases of a plan of social therapy?

10. Elaborate on Mrs. Sheffield's discussion of the social point of view as opposed to the psychiatric point of view.

11. Compile a bibliography on the recent studies of social treatment or on research in the field of social treatment.

12. What are the methods by which social therapy may be effected? Define, illustrate, and analyze these methods.

13. Read two or three interviews in *Interviews*, by the American Association of Social Workers, and analyze their methods of therapy in the light of De Schweinitz's discussion of motivation and mutual planning; of Thomas' discussion of the satisfaction of the social wishes; of Burgess' discussion of empathy; of Cooley's discussion of sympathetic insight.

14. What is the role of persuasion, suggestion, urging, advice in social therapy? Illustrate.

15. What does Gordon Hamilton mean by "sharing experience"? See *Survey Graphic*, LIX (December, 1927), 317.

16. In view of the highly individualized nature of the modern urbanite, how is it possible for one person to enter into the inner life of another?

17. What are the dangers of the method of sympathetic insight as used in interviewing? What are the advantages? Illustrate.

18. Can people of different races and cultures gain sympathetic insight into their respective problems?

19. Which of the interviews cited in previous chapters used the method of sympathetic insight? Show results obtained.

20. What are the essential differences in the methods of identification and of sympathetic insight?

21. What is meant by "mental catharsis"? How may it be brought about? What ethical problems are involved? What dangers?

22. Do social workers receive confessions from interviewees?

23. What is the psychology of the confessional?

24. Write a critique of Dorothy Krise's interview with Mrs. Parker indicating the method of approach, the interviewing technique, the social work philosophy held by Mrs. Krise (see p. 307).

25. Under what circumstances is mental catharsis inhibited? Induced?

26. Under what circumstances did the interviewer induce mental catharsis in Mrs. Parker? in Mrs. Kazalski?

27. What are the aftereffects of mental catharsis? How should they be dealt with?

28. How may tensions be lessened? What varieties of tensions are there? How do you lessen tensions in your interviewees? How were the tensions lessened in Mrs. Parker? in Mrs. Kazalski? in the blind sailor?

29. What is meant by a definition of the social situation? a redefinition? What is their role in social therapy?

30. What is meant by the ordering-and-forbidding technique? What bearing does this technique have on motivation? When do you employ the ordering-and-forbidding technique? What results do you obtain?

31. How was the social situation redefined to Almo? to Mrs. Parker? to Mrs. Kazalski? to the blind sailor? to Mr. Anderson?

32. What other interviews in this text illustrate redefinition of the social situation?

33. What is the difference between reconditioning of attitudes and redefining the social situation? Illustrate.

34. Read Dr. Healy's writings and indicate the philosophy underlying his attempts at reconditioning of attitudes. (Consult bibliography.)

35. What are the essential differences between the philosophy of Dr. Healy, Dr. Taft, Dr. Burgess as illustrated by their writings on the subject of reconditioning attitudes? (Consult bibliography.)

36. Analyze the interview with the blind sailor and show how mutation of attitude was accomplished.

37. What is the relation of habit to reconditioning of attitudes? What are the bases for reconditioning of attitudes?

38. What role do the social wishes play in the process of reconditioning of attitudes?

39. What is meant by motivation? How are persons motivated? What social and personal situations should be taken into consideration? Illustrate.

40. Under what conditions are persons best motivated? least motivated?

41. What type of interviewer can best motivate interviewees? adults? children? the sick? the unemployed?

42. Analyze the quotation from Karl De Schweinitz and indicate how the interviewer motivated the elderly gentleman.

43. What is meant by mutual planning? With what type of clients can you mutually plan? Why? Illustrate.

44. When do you plan with your clients and when for them?

45. What is the test of a good plan?

46. Under what circumstances are clients pauperized?

47. Indicate how the satisfaction of the wishes was attained in the interviews cited in the text.

48. How do you bring about satisfaction of the wishes in the lives of your clients? Illustrate.

49. Write a critical review of W. I. Thomas' discussion of the satisfaction of the wishes, with particular reference to the values the interviewer can derive from such a discussion. See *The Unadjusted Girl.*

50. What are the tests of a successful therapeutic interview?

Selected Bibliography

1. BURGESS, E. W.: "Discussion," in CLIFFORD R. SHAW, *The Jack Roller,* 1930, pp. 184–197.
   Discussion of sympathy and empathy as methods in social treatment.

2. BURGESS, E. W.: "The Study of the Delinquent as a Person," *The American Journal of Sociology,* XXVIII (May, 1923), 657–680.
   A problem personality is best understood when studied in the light of the role he conceives himself to play, in the light of dominant wishes and relation to other members of the social group.

3. DE SCHWEINITZ, KARL: *The Art of Helping People out of Trouble,* 1924, Chap. X, "Planning"; Chap. XI, "The Cultivation of Responsibility"; Chap. XII, "Motivation."

4. DEWEY, JOHN: *Human Nature and Conduct,* 1922.
   Read particularly chapters entitled "Habit and the Will," "Changing Human Nature," "The Good of Activity."

5. FRANK, LAWRENCE K.: "The Management of Tensions," *The American Journal of Sociology,* XXXIII (March, 1928), 705–736.
   "The development of personality may be studied from the point of view of the individual's learning to manage his physiological tensions. Tensions are more acute when a substitution of a new for an old stimulus occurs. As a result of shock physiological tensions arise. Childhood and youth are periods which should be occupied with learning to sustain and diffuse tensions and to achieve ever more tensional releases according to the demands of social life."

6. LEE, PORTER R.: "A Study of Social Treatment," *The Family,* IV (December, 1923), 191–199.
   Discusses the task of social treatment; the executive and leadership aspects of treatment.

7. LINDEMAN, EDUARD C.: *Social Discovery,* 1924.
   An attempt to present definition and techniques for scientific study of social problems. Chapter III discusses methods of observation, questioning, function of the "participant observer."

8. NEUSTAEDTER, ELEANOR: "The Rôle of Case Worker in Treatment," *The Family,* XIII (July, 1932), 151–156.

9. ROBINSON, VIRGINIA P.: *A Changing Psychology in Social Case Work,* 1930.
   Chapter X, "Treatment in Social Case Work," Chap. XI, "The Problem of Relationship."
10. ROSANOFF, A. J. (Editor): *Manual of Psychiatry,* 1927.
   Helpful suggestions for dealing with difficult cases. See particularly
   "Psychiatric Therapeutics."
11. SALSBERRY, PEARL: "Techniques in Case Work," *The Family,* VIII (July, 1927), 153–157.
   Offers practical suggestions for the management and lessening of tensions, making interviewees articulate, overcoming fear and negation.
12. TAFT, JESSIE: "The Use of Transfer Within the Limits of the Office Interview," *The Family,* V (October, 1924), 143–146.
   Cites cases wherein emotional interests were transferred to interviewer-psychologist and when adjustment was attained to the ideals which the psychologist desired to inculcate in interviewee, the former withdrew.
13. TAFT, JESSIE: *The Dynamics of Therapy in a Controlled Relationship,* 1933.
   A detailed record of prolonged personal contacts with two young problem children and a theoretical statement of the concepts and methods of therapy.
14. THOMAS, W. I.: *The Unadjusted Girl,* 1924.
   See particularly Chaps. I and II for the analysis of the social wishes in problematic behavior. Illustrated by many life histories.

APPENDIX A

INTERVIEWS PRESENTED FOR STUDY AND ANALYSIS

Social Treatment from the Standpoint of a Client[1]

. . . In the following account of the interview there has been some re-arrangement and condensation of the material, but as often as possible the mother's statements are quoted verbatim. Such an article as this should not be considered in any sense as a rounded discussion in whole or in part, nor as an attempt to discuss case work methods as such, but merely to present one client's attitude toward a few of them. Whether or not these attitudes are a comment upon human nature, itself, rather than social case work methods, whether or not they reflect upon social case work methods of today are questions which this paper does not try to answer.

Q. Did you know anything about social agencies in the old country?

A. They haven't got them there. In a nationality like ours they make their own living before they take charity—struggle through somehow. . . . .

Q. Did you have any dealings with a social agency before your marriage?

A. I didn't know anything about them until the year my husband died. Before that we struggled along. I worked. He stayed home and watched the kids.

Q. What was your feeling about the questions you were asked at first?

A. I didn't like their questions at all. They asked too many when they didn't understand themselves. They usually think you have more than you tell them you have. That's what hurts us. It's really the opposite— you don't like to tell them you have so little.

Q. You mean you want to keep up a front?

A. Yes.

Q. Did you feel that they were trying to pry into your affairs?

A. Yes. One came and said, "Let me see your pantry if you got something in it." She would not sit down and be friendly with you. She sat in the chair—spinster-looking like this (demonstrating) and looking around.

Q. That made you feel uncomfortable?

A. Yeh. Sometime you feel like asking them, "Where do you think you sit?"

Q. Did you get over that feeling about her?

A. Yes. Later on she was very nice to me and gave me my share. She found out I had no mattresses and bought some and sent them. I told her I couldn't be handled like that—it hurts. She wanted to know why I had five children, too. She thought I was not very wise—broadminded—to have so many children and a sick husband. In one way she was right, but I said I lived the life, not her. . . .

[1] Claudia Wannamaker, *The Family*, VI (April, 1925), 31–36. Reprinted by permission.

She had told me she would bring some clothes for the baby but she didn't. My husband was laying on his deathbed at the time and I couldn't hear anything about him.   I found out afterwards the neighbors came to see me but they wouldn't let them in—only nearest relatives can get in a hospital.

Q. Did you ever tell the social worker about the strain you had been under?

A. No, I never had a chance. She went away and dropped the trouble and another one came. Had one right after the other then. I never got very friendly with any one of them.

Q. Do you like being changed from one to another?

A. No, you like one because they find out more. You are always on guard with a new one and can't be natural. If you know she's good to you you lose yourself and say nothing.

Q. Did you ever get acquainted with a social worker right away—felt at ease at first, or do you have to go through a certain period?

A. Never right away. You never know which way they are coming. They keep things to themselves and you don't know whether they are trying to take off from you or give you.

Q. What is it that makes you feel most on your guard?

A. Most of them look down on you and that hurts you so you don't want to say any more. They think you are green—immigrant you know. When you tell them you are different you get in wrong. You're always glad when they are gone. You know everybody has a feeling and if your feeling is hurt—! . . .

The minute they begin asking, I'm on my guard because I don't know which way she is going. If they ask me how my children are, if they are well and going to school I know then she is interested in me and the kids. But if she begins, "How do they help you?" and comes to find out what I'm getting and what I'm making and what's left, then I feel like keeping things to myself.   I found out if you tell them it can't be any worse than it is, they are satisfied. . . .

TWO CONSECUTIVE INTERVIEWS WITH MRS. SALTERS[1]
Family Set-up.

                    M   53 years;   W   35 years
Children.

Joe	18 years
Stanley	17
John	14
Mary	11
Henry	9
James	6

W complains that M nags incessantly, has deserted frequently, never worked much, frequently threatened suicide and was causing a great deal of nervousness in the children. Since last year she has been coming to the conclusion, slowly, with vacillations, to separate from him. She herself

[1] Interviews held and recorded by members of a family case work agency in Cleveland.

attempted suicide a few years ago and is quite unstable now. However, she has considerable intelligence and insight into human behavior and through the year of contact a strong relationship has been built between her and worker. Many long and fairly intimate interviews have taken place with W in which worker has taken the role mostly of listener. In psychiatric seminar it was criticized as giving too much sympathy to W, so in the following interviews an attempt was made to help W face the situation better. A few months ago she tried to have M probated, but since his psychoneuroticism was not extreme enough, he was allowed free again. Following that she decided to divorce him, but ambivalent drives were evident in her vacillation between attitudes toward M.

The family, chiefly W, was involved in a case of larceny this winter of which the facts seemed to point out her innocence, but still her extreme emotion led one to suspect otherwise. It is still unknown what the degree of guilt was.

M, Joe and W have all been seen by the psychiatrist. M for diagnostic purposes and Joe for interpretive purposes. W saw him only once and this was when she was upset over the larceny episode. A divorce was recommended by the psychiatrist. In the meantime W felt more and more that she could not stand to have M around.

First Interview.—W at the office during office hours. Instead of her usual smiling greeting W presented a serious countenance. As soon as she had sat down she exclaimed with all the vehemence of pent-up emotion:

Mrs. Salters: Have you heard anything about a room? I *can't* stand it any longer!

Interviewer: (Remaining motionless, asked in an even tone) Why can't you?

(This brought a torrent of tears and exclamations, although the room had a number of people in it. This was the first time W had shown emotion before others besides worker.)

Mrs. Salters: I've tried and tried and it can't go on any longer. Either he or I will have to go. It's driving me insane. It would be better if I left and then they would have to place the children. They'd live a happier life, wouldn't they?

(Interviewer remarked quietly that the children needed her.)

Mrs. Salters: Yes, but it seems to me it would be better if I stopped trying and just walked out. It must be better for them in a Home than it is now. I tell you I can't stand it! (A gesture of despair and more tears followed.)

Interviewer: What does he do that gets you so upset?

Mrs. Salters: Oh, it's just words, words! If only he'd beat me. It wouldn't be so bad. But words just kill me. He's tricky. Now he stays at home. He used to be away during the daytime but now when the children are all at school he starts in. He knows it's harder for me then. When the children are there I can sort of control myself, but when they're gone, I—I— oh! (Words evidently could not express the extent of her emotion.)

Interviewer: Why do you let it bother you? You know how to take it.

Mrs. Salters: I don't know why. I can't help it. The next minute he's all different. After the worst quarrel he can seem as if it never happened.

Interviewer: He evidently doesn't consider his words to be very important.

Mrs. Salters: No, but I'm not like that.   (She again exclaimed that it was impossible to live with him.)

Interviewer: Have you ever thought of leaving the house for a short while when it's so unbearable, just to take a walk?

Mrs. Salters: No.   Where would I go?

Interviewer: How about some of your friends, for instance the G——?

Mrs. Salters: (Impatiently) Oh, I don't go to see my friends any more!

Interviewer: Why not?   It would help you, I think.

Mrs. Salters: Yes, I know it would, but I've just lost interest in everything.

W was obviously calmer by now; worker attempted to telephone the other office where efforts were being made to find a room for M, but the line was busy.   Returning, worker asked if W were interested in having a garden. W's face lit up immediately and she said that she had read the notice in the paper and had wished that she lived in a house where there was space for a garden.   Worker explained the project to find garden space for those who had none.   W seemed unusually interested and explained that everyone in the family would enjoy working in it.   By this time she had lost all her emotionalism.

Worker again tried to telephone, was successful and learned that a room had been found for M.   W was given the address where she was sure M would go.   She smiled a good deal but said little.   As she left she remarked with feeling,

Mrs. Salters: I'm glad I came down.   I was wondering whether to come or not and I feel better.   (From the way she spoke, it seemed that she was not referring just to the success in finding a room for M, but also for being helped in getting a new lease on life.)

Following this interview there was a short call in the home when W related the difficulty she had had in persuading M to leave and had been forced to threaten that if he did not go before morning, she would.   M finally left but returned to report that he could not bear the room.   W repeated her urging and M departed; but W did not know where he was staying.   She planned to file the papers for the divorce the following day.   Called at L.A.S. and learned from the lawyer handling the case that W had said she and M were not married because M did not know whether his wife in N. Y. had obtained the divorce which she planned to do.   Mr. A. did not think there would be difficulty in proving it a common law marriage.   Wrote W a note suggesting that she call at the office the following afternoon to discuss the possibility of getting $10 for filing the petition, which Mr. A. had mentioned.

Second Interview.—W at the office.   She was early for the appointment. There was a noticeable change in spirit about her, a buoyancy observed only once before when M had previously left.   She was neatly and attractively dressed and smiled as she entered the room.   The first few minutes were spent in reviewing the possibility of W's different relatives helping with the money.   W showed special resentment against her sister for refusing to help.   The conversation naturally drifted to M's departure and whereabouts.   W knew that he was not at the room which A.C. had found for him because M had said he was with friends, although he would give no address.

There were several pauses in the conversation when worker hoped W would enter the subject of their marriage, but when W said nothing about it, worker broached the matter, remembering that before, it had proved helpful when worker introduced subjects.

Interviewer: (Quietly and casually) Mr. A. said something to me about your not being married.[1] Do you want to tell me about it? (Gives woman a loophole of escape.)

Mrs. Salters: (Laughing with embarrassment and turning her head away) No, I don't.

Interviewer: (In understanding tone) Why not?

Mrs. Salters: Because—you are so young. You haven't lived long enough to understand some things. I told him not to tell, but then I thought he would. (This, with no resentful tone, but falteringly.)

Interviewer: But when we have been in this work for some time we have had so much experience that it's as if we were fifty.

Mrs. Salters: (Her intelligence coming to the rescue) Yes, yes, of course. It must be so.

Interviewer: However, it doesn't matter if you would rather not. Only you know, don't you, that what we care about is the people's happiness whom we are working with. We are not setting ourselves up as moral judges.

Mrs. Salters: Well, as far as that's concerned, I didn't mean no wrong. But that's why his nagging and calling me names bothers me so. Now, I know that it don't mean nothing for a husband or wife to call names. Everybody does it. But it bothered me because it was just true enough to mean something. Oh, I met him in a perfectly respectable way! At the G. Club through friends. (W was fairly launched and all worker did for some time was to listen attentively and nod, murmuring "yes" once in a while. W started out with a little embarrassment, but soon lost it and proceeded as if it were an interesting story. Worker asked questions only after a pause.)

He seemed wonderful to me then and everything he said was right. (She smiled at herself.) He hadn't been in C. long but he had a few friends already and one of them told me to be careful because he had a wife in N. Y. I asked him (M) about it and he said, "No." Naturally I took his word for it. He was perfect. (She smiled knowingly again.) And I was pretty ignorant about the world then—only sixteen.

So we kept on going together and I told him to get a marriage license. But he always had some excuse. He didn't have time that day, or he left the papers somewhere, or something. I began to be afraid and kept telling him, and when I knew that I was pregnant, I was frantic.

Then he came out and told me he couldn't. Imagine how I felt! I was going to leave him, I was. Only he made me think my parents was coming.

Interviewer: How did he explain things?

Mrs. Salters: He showed me a letter from his family. He had the letter all the time but never showed me until I was pregnant. His family wrote that his wife in N. Y. wrote to them that she was going to get a divorce.

[1] Better to say: "I understand you were not married," which does not involve Mr. A.

Interviewer: Did she get one?

Mrs. Salters: I don't know anything about it. He said something about his being sick in a hospital and her trying to get a divorce. How do I know whether he was really married or not? He's like that, but I didn't know it then. Just like when he scared me saying my mother and father was coming over here. He said he'd told them we was married. (W expressed this with a gesture of despair.) Oh, then of course I had to stick it out. Then I found out they wasn't coming after all, so I was trapped again. Just before Joe was born they suddenly decided to come because the War broke out, and in a week they was on the boat ready to sail.

They come over here and right afterward John (M) left me and I went to my mother's. I never would have gone back to him if mother would have taken care of Joe, but she said, "Place him" and I couldn't do that. Of course, I don't blame her for not wanting to take care of him because he was only 4 pounds and had to have a bottle. But that's the reason I went back to him. He (M) was in Pittsburgh at that time, you know.

Oh, it bothered me, not being married. It just ate at my heart. You know, at first it wasn't no long time that we wasn't going to be married. I thought only a year or so. And when the second one came, and the third one, I worried a lot, but after a while it didn't bother me much, only sometimes. But it still bothers me that I can't never have a wedding. I'm a sentimental person. (Smiling at herself.)

Interviewer: Does your family know?

Mrs. Salters: (Nodding significantly) Yes. They knew his people over there and they told my people he was married, so my people wondered if we was married. They don't say nothing. But, when the third one was born I was back in Cleveland and they was here, too, you know. I wanted John to be baptized and to test me they sent my younger brother over to tell me I had to show my marriage license at the baptism. That got me all frantic and I told him.

Interviewer: What did he say?

Mrs. Salters: Oh, he was a little kid then and he didn't say nothing.

Interviewer: How did you happen to tell him?

Mrs. Salters: Oh, I couldn't stand keeping it to myself any more. I had to tell someone.

Interviewer: Did he tell the others?

Mrs. Salters: (Smiling with more amusement than resentment) That was a secret between him and me, but he told them—but I guess I would, too, I can't keep secrets. I don't have many but—(Her train of thought was interrupted by a noise in the room.)

Interviewer: (Finishing) But you aren't able to keep the few you have?

Mrs. Salters: (Laughing) Yes, but that was what I was going to say. (Pause.)

Interviewer: Did your family mention it to you?

Mrs. Salters: No, they never did. Only once mother got mad at me. She does get mad like that and then she doesn't care what she says. There was a neighbor in the house, too. When mother walked out she said, "Well, you'd better get straightened out and get married before you do anything else." (W seemed not especially angry at this.)

Interviewer: How about your sister?

Mrs. Salters: Oh, she! (Vindictively) She's told me that she doesn't want to have an unmarried person in her home. But that's all. Nobody else said anything—Well, I know I done wrong and if I could do it over again I would certainly do it different. (With conviction.)

Interviewer: How would you have done it?

Mrs. Salters: Oh—different. (Looking away.)

Interviewer: Well, what?

Mrs. Salters: (Turning suddenly as if there were no use in avoiding it longer) Well, in the first place I should have waited until we was married.

Interviewer: Did you understand the physiology of it?

Mrs. Salters: Oh, I understood enough. I was ignorant, but I knew enough. (She looked straight at worker as much as to say, "Now we have reached the root of it.")

(Worker merely nodded. Pause.)

Mrs. Salters: It took me a long time to decided to tell Mr. A. but I figured that it would have to come out anyway and if it came out in court it would look still worse, wouldn't it? Wouldn't they go to look it up in the records to see if we was married?

Interviewer: Probably.

Mrs. Salters: There, I thought so. When I went down to see him I made up my mind I was going to tell him. It was hard, but everything always comes out some time, doesn't it?

Interviewer: Generally, it does. How did you feel afterwards?

Mrs. Salters: (Face lighting up) Oh, you have no idea how much lighter and younger I felt. It was a big load off my shoulders.

Interviewer: It does help to tell things, doesn't it? You are facing things much better than you did.

Mrs. Salters: I don't know that it's facing them. I don't care no more.

Interviewer: Has this anything to do with your fear of courts?

Mrs. Salters: (Matter of fact) Oh no, everybody from Europe has that feeling. Of course, I wondered if it would come out when it was in court and I had a notion to tell her [probation officer] about it but I figured it wasn't quite the place for it.

(Pause.)

Interviewer: How about the children?

Mrs. Salters: (Slowly) I thought maybe they didn't need to know. Do they have to go to court?

Interviewer: Oh, no.

Mrs. Salters: Of course, they always heard the filthy names he calls me and even though we quarrel in German I know the older ones know what we are saying. You remember I told you Joe said to me, "Mother, no matter what you were before you were married we love you just the same." He (M) always throws it up to me and says, if he hadn't got me someone else would have. He rescued me! Now it is true that I done wrong, yes I done wrong, but I met him in a perfectly proper way.

Interviewer: Is there a possibility of the children thinking it happened differently from the way it did?

Mrs. Salters: (Thoughtfully) Maybe, with all the things he's said against me.

Interviewer: Had you thought of telling them how it did happen?

Mrs. Salters: Yes, I did think I would do it once. I don't know what to do. Maybe I will.

Interviewer: Sometimes it's better to know the whole truth rather than parts of it.

Mrs. Salters: (Thoughtfully and slowly) Yes, maybe they would hear from someone their mother did this and that. Maybe they would be grown up and have children and someone would tell them. They would feel bad, then—I think I will tell them. (Resignedly.)

It's so peaceful at home now. Of course, he comes, but he don't beg to come back like he did before. He used to say, "We'll get married and then we'll be happy" but I told him it wasn't for that I was getting a divorce. If he starts in bothering me again I'll get a court restraint. Do you think I should get one now?

Interviewer: What would be best?

Mrs. Salters: (Quickly) Of course, if he wanted to kill us, a court restraint wouldn't do no good, but I don't think he would. He's not that kind. Then, too, if I do get the restraint it might make him mad. I don't think I will unless it's absolutely necessary.

Interviewer: I think you are wise.

FIVE CONSECUTIVE OFFICE INTERVIEWS WITH MRS. HAYNES[1]

First Interview.

Interviewer: The doctor was here this morning to examine the children.

Mrs. Haynes: Was John all right? He has been quite cross lately.

Interviewer: The doctor said his tonsils were very much enlarged and no doubt were keeping him from gaining normally. Have you ever thought of having them out?

Mrs. Haynes: My doctor said once before they should be removed but I'm afraid of operations and hate to think of having it done. Where could I go? You know I couldn't pay much. I'm only earning $13 a week now.

Interviewer: Some of the mothers go to the Children's Hospital. Just now they have a long waiting list. It would probably take five or six months to get in. However, the Eye, Ear, Nose and Throat Clinic take the day nursery cases for $5 and can operate within a week or two.

Mrs. Haynes: Could you people make the arrangements for me because I work all day?

Interviewer: Yes, we will be glad to make the appointment and one of the teachers will take John down in her car if you will arrange about the fee and sign the permission slips.

(The mother took the slip home and said she would return it with the fee, and the school should go ahead and make the appointment. John's appointment was made. The mother said she was still a little afraid, but would bring him so that he could go with the rest. The child did not come, however, and the next day the mother came to the office.)

Mrs. Haynes: I guess you think I'm a dandy but when I went home and talked to my mother she said not to risk it. One of my married sisters who has children said I was foolish not to have it done when the school would

[1] Interviews held and recorded by Miss Arilita H. Roberts, Los Angeles.

help so much and my other sister said it was too dangerous. So I didn't know what to do.

Interviewer: Of course, you are certain to take a chance if you leave them in. He is cross and listless now and not gaining weight as he should. The doctor thinks the bad tonsils cause this condition.

Mrs. Haynes: Yes, I know, but it's hard to get the money together too. Well, I'll tell you the thing I'm really afraid of is—you know the children's father is in the state insane asylum. He had an operation during his sickness and afterward was crazy and I'm afraid John might not be all right after the operation.

Interviewer: But wasn't that a blood clot on your husband's brain that they tried to remove?

Mrs. Haynes: Yes, it wasn't the same kind of operation as this would be.

Interviewer: The condition that made the blood clot brought about the insanity. The operation was just a chance that they could cure it. Of all the many children I have ever known who had a tonsil operation none of them has suffered unfavorable results afterward and in almost every case they have eaten better and gained weight quickly.

Mrs. Haynes: I guess maybe you are right. One's reasoning gets twisted sometimes about things. I've been sort of afraid of doctors and hospitals since Richard was put in the asylum. If I do get up courage later would you take him after my backing out this time?

Interviewer: Yes, surely, you think about it and later if you wish to have it done you come and tell me and we will make another appointment.

(The next week she came in to say that the child had been very "sick with his vaccination.")

Second Interview.

Interviewer: Good-morning, Mrs. Haynes. We have been wondering if John was going to start to the nursery this week since you decided to postpone the operation?

Mrs. Haynes: Oh, honey, I've had just a hard time. He got awful sick from his vaccination. And do you know that the doctor charged me $25 to examine him and give him the vaccination. Now, you know, me working the way I do I can't afford that expense. But then I want the best for my baby. Nothing is too good for him.

Interviewer: That was too bad. That was an exorbitant rate for a nursery mother. Perhaps we can arrange to have the diphtheria shots at one of the city clinics. Would you like to have me take him some time later?

Mrs. Haynes: All right if you would, honey. Just don't tell me when you do it because I suffer so for him. He screamed and screamed when the doctor examined him. I'll sign the card and you just take him.

Interviewer: Has John ever had any unhappy experience with doctors or barbers before his examination?

Mrs. Haynes: No, nothing that I know about and he has always been well cared for in my own home. But, golly, he sure is afraid of them; we both had to hold him while the doctor worked. He just kicks and yells.

Interviewer: Well, we will try to help him get pleasant associations with our clinic and nurse here at school and perhaps gradually we can help him get over some of these fears. Most of our boys and girls here coax to go along when a group go to the clinics or the dentist. Even the littlest ones say, "Me too, I want to go, I'll be big."

Mrs. Haynes: I don't know though. I'm afraid of doctors myself and can't stand pain so I suppose maybe he inherits it, don't you think?

Interviewer: Usually we find that little children take the emotional attitudes of the adults they live with rather than inheriting them. If mother shows she is afraid of dogs, or storms, or doctors the chances are the little boy or girl will be too, because mother has set the example. Something that SHE should be afraid of is pretty terrifying. The very fact that she is frightened takes away his sense of security.

Mrs. Haynes: Well, maybe you are right. I never thought of that before. You've had lots of children in your teaching haven't you? Did any of the others act like this?

Interviewer: Yes, I've perhaps worked with five or six hundred nursery age youngsters and many of them have had such fears and we have been able to help them and their parents.

Mrs. Haynes: Imagine that. I really don't know anything about children. I had only my other one that died, you know, and this one. (*Smiling.*) But I just love children. I would just love to work in a place like this. But, then, I wouldn't have the patience. I guess it takes a lot of patience doesn't it?

Interviewer: Yes, indeed, it does to be a mother too, doesn't it?

Mrs. Haynes: I guess it does but I don't have much. I'll be so glad, honey, when he is well enough to come in and be getting the right care. Can I bring him just as soon as he is well?

Interviewer: That will be fine. We will expect him some time next week.

Third Interview.

(The following week the child entered the nursery. He was thin and underweight with a sallow complexion, much taller than the average three-and one-half year old but extremely thin. He wore layers of clothing, long woolen underwear, a woolen suit and sweater and an overcoat and cap. His black stockings came to his knees, and the shoes—heavy and high. The hair stuck out shaggily from beneath his cap. His brown eyes were dull and lifeless. His whole body gave the impression of utter listlessness. Hanging head, dangling arms, stooped shoulder position while standing.)

Interviewer: Good-morning, Mrs. Haynes, and this is John? Good-morning, John. (John turned his head away from the worker and looked dully off into space.)

Mrs. Haynes: (Sternly, with impatience) Say "good-morning," John, say "good-morning" to the lady. He is very bright but a little shy of strangers. Aren't you ashamed not to talk?

Interviewer: Never mind, we will get acquainted by and by. (Smiling at John.) Now we will show you where Miss Brown is. She is the nurse who helps us all keep well at the nursery. All of the boys and girls go to see her when they first come in the morning. This is her room here. (Introductions and John began to scream when he saw the white uniform.)

I wonder, Mrs. Haynes, if John isn't dressed a little too warm for a heated building in California. You see the other children just have wash-cotton things and no stockings.

Mrs. Haynes: Oh, no, he must be dressed like that or he will take cold. I have such a time with him keeping him from having a cold. I can't risk his getting pneumonia. No, honey, he must wear those things. That's the doctor's orders.

Interviewer: Shall we see how it works and talk again about it later? He has had colds, hasn't he?

Mrs. Haynes: Yes. Oh, he always takes cold. The least thing will give him a cold.

Interviewer: Now, John may have this locker to put his things in during the day. John, would you like to say good-bye to mother and we will go down to the play room with the other children?

(The mother descended upon him and removed the coat and sweater putting them and the cap in the locker and closing the door. The child didn't make the slightest effort to help himself. The mother gave him a peck of a kiss on the cheek and pushed him toward the worker. He made no response to her slight show of affection.

During the day it was discovered that the child did not know how to do anything for himself. He stumbled when he walked and had to be helped up and down the stairs. He stood in helpless dejection before a button. Apparently he had had no bathroom training but had to have his clothing changed several times during the day. He had no words with which to talk and made grunting noises when he wished to attract attention. For the most part, however, he ignored both the children and the teachers. He made no response when spoken to other than deliberately turning his head to the side away from the speaker and avoiding their eyes. When given food he refused to feed himself and swallowed it all whole, apparently not knowing how to chew. When he went into a new room instead of investigating as an ordinary child would he either stood with head and arms hanging or crawled under a table or into a cupboard. On the playground he made no effort to play with any of the toys or equipment.)

Fourth Interview.

(During the week the contacts with the mother were made by the teachers and nurse and the fourth interview with the worker took place on Friday evening of the first week. The teachers reported that the child had to have individual attention, his clothes were changed on the average of three times a day and he did absolutely nothing for himself. He was perspiring excessively most of the time because of the heavy clothing.)

(Mrs. Haynes came to the worker crying hysterically.)

Mrs. Haynes: Oh, I don't know what to do. He'll get sick being exposed that way.

Interviewer: Why, what is the matter with John?

Mrs. Haynes: Just look at him. He soiled all of his other suits I brought and look what the teacher put on him, underwear with no legs or sleeves.

Interviewer: He does have his long stockings and his woolen suit on top though.

Mrs. Haynes: That isn't enough; he must have the woolen underwear with long legs and arms.

Interviewer: Mrs. Haynes, I'm sorry to be arbitrary about this but I'm afraid I must ask you to dress John in lighter clothes if he is going to come to the nursery.   You see I have 74 other little children to consider too. The building is warm enough for them and far too hot for your boy.   He perspires and then gets chilled and is perfectly miserable physically most of the time.   Our doctor feels that children are less likely to take colds if they are exposed to more sunshine.   When they are playing in the sun their arms and legs ought to be bare with a warm sweater to put on when it gets chilly.   Through all of that clothing the sun never touches John's body. You say he has had colds using your method, why not try ours?   You see all of the other children are well.

Mrs. Haynes: Oh, I'm afraid he will get sick.   He's all I've got in the world.   I don't know what I would do if anything happened to him.

Interviewer: I wanted to talk to you a bit about his bathroom training. Hasn't he been used to going to the bathroom at home?

Mrs. Haynes: Well, I'll tell you, honey.   That woman didn't train him. Sometimes I would have six diapers a day for that boy and he makes me so mad because he is big enough to know better.   But he will get it quick here because the teachers will train him.

Interviewer: You knew the rule of the nursery was that children are not admitted until they are trained that way.

Mrs. Haynes: Yes, but he will learn quickly because he is bright.

Interviewer: He doesn't seem to be able to do anything for himself, Mrs. Haynes.   And he is not responding to the training the teachers are trying to give him the way children usually do and I'm not sure—

Mrs. Haynes: (Interrupting angrily) He is perfectly all right.   He is absolutely normal.   I've had him examined and tested and he has a fine mind.   He isn't feeble-minded, I've got the records to prove it.

Interviewer: Yes, I believe he is normal and this dullness of response is the result of lack of training at the proper time.   But, whatever the cause, unless some sort of development or adjustment is shown within a few weeks I will not be justified in keeping him in the nursery.   Our children are being neglected now while the teachers are giving time to John.   We are glad to do that at first if it is just temporary but we cannot keep him indefinitely if we have to care for him like a baby.   We will try until the end of the month.

Mrs. Haynes: Oh, honey, I'm afraid he isn't just right.   If you could just teach him I'll do anything you tell me to and I don't know what to do for him.   (Tears.)

Interviewer: We will do the very best we can for him, Mrs. Haynes, and will you send him tomorrow with the thinner underwear?

Mrs. Haynes: Yes, I'll do that if you think it will be all right.

(Next morning Mrs. Haynes brought a little plant for the children's patio. John had his woolen underwear on but she had taken a huge tuck around the waist making three layers there but nothing on his legs and big rolls on his upper arms.)

Fifth Interview.

(By the end of the month, with careful training, the child was beginning to make shy advances to the other children, he would go to the bathroom when necessary although he still needed help.   He knew where his locker was, came when called and made feeble attempts to help dress himself.   He learned to use his spoon at the table and gradually learned to chew hard foods. He played on the slide in the yard. When he began to learn to talk he developed echolalia. He simply repeated everything that was said to him but made no response of his own. When someone said, "Good-morning, John," he repeated, "Good-morning John." "What is this?" only elicited "What is this?"

The teachers had reported that the mother pounced upon him at night straightening his suit and hair and generally arranging him, putting on the sweater and cap, closing his locker and hurrying him out of the door. All the time keeping up a steady flow of rapid talking.)

Interviewer: Mrs. Haynes, you know we have found here at school that John doesn't like to be touched very much and we are trying to let him learn to do just as much as he can for himself. Have you seen him put on his sweater?

Mrs. Haynes: Say, honey, maybe that's why he had a temper tantrum the other night when I tried to put it on? He's got an awful temper.

Interviewer: What do you do when he has a temper at home?

Mrs. Haynes: Well, I lick him but it doesn't do any good. The other night I whipped him until I was exhausted and he just got worse. Say, maybe I touch him too much. Maybe he wanted to open the door himself the other night.

Interviewer: Whipping doesn't help when a child already has a tantrum. You probably got cross yourself too, didn't you?

Mrs. Haynes: Oh, he just makes me mad he gets so stubborn. And I will have a child that minds.

Interviewer: Usually when a child shows temper it means that he is either tired or not well. Putting him in a room quietly alone for a few minutes we find usually works. We have discovered that it is better not to try to do anything with a child while we are angry ourselves.

Mrs. Haynes: I always feel terribly about it afterward and we both cry and I try to make up to him by buying him candy or a toy next day. But he acts sometimes as though he is afraid of me. He's all I've got in the world but I won't let him grow up spoiled. I don't know much about children. My father was always strict with us. Once I was naughty when I was a little girl and he got so mad he threw me out of the second story window after he whipped me. Maybe whippin' isn't so much good. It always made me mad but I didn't know what else to do to John when he is bad. You teachers here talk so soft to him and he does what you tell him right away. Maybe I do yell too much. You see down at the station these young boys and girls that are brought in at night because they get into trouble almost always their parents are divorced and I'm afraid maybe a woman can't raise a boy right alone and I guess that's why I punish him more so he won't turn out bad.

Interviewer: He is a sensitive little boy and should never be whipped. When you get angry and loose your temper it does not help him to control his. When he gets a tantrum, quietly put him in another room and close the door until he is over it. Of course, many children do have juvenile court difficulties who come from broken homes but think of the thousands of children who are fine boys and girls who are living with one of their parents.

Mrs. Haynes: I never thought of that.   I guess it's because I never come in contact with the good ones.

Interviewer: I have a book about some of these problems that other mothers have had with their children.   Perhaps you would like to take it home and read it sometime.

Mrs. Haynes: Could I take it tonight?   I'm a slow reader but if I could keep it awhile I'd get through it.

Interviewer: Yes, indeed, bring it to the office when you are through with it.

(The child was sleeping in Mrs. Haynes' car at night beside the police station.   The department was contacted to see if it might be possible to transfer the mother nearer the nursery and on day work.   The report came back that she was an excellent worker when she cared to work but she was lazy and never got along with the workers and was a general problem wherever she went.   The present chief under whom she was working seemed willing to put up with her but if she were changed it might endanger her job.

The child is steadily improving and developing physically and mentally. He has been in the nursery five months.   He has lost all of his former apathy and is even becoming affectionate to the children, teachers and his mother. His eyes are bright and he is showing a charming smile that no one suspected he had the first weeks at school.   His speech grew step by step until now he makes up fragments of sentences "pull—shoe, I do."

The mother is reading and constantly asking questions.   Her voice, at least around the school, is low and gentle and her own attitude more cheerful.   She is watching the teachers and acquiring from them some of the outward forms of proper procedures in habit training for her child.

John's fear of the clinic and nurse has entirely disappeared.   He comes to the nursery now dressed in light cotton suits and underwear with his arms and legs exposed, on hot days he wears a sunsuit on the playground. His fear of scissors has been so reconditioned that he will allow one of the teachers to cut his hair.)

OWN STORY OF ALEX KATINOFF

I was about nine years old when I first remember something about myself personally, but that is not very nice.   I was arrested for trying to sneak into a show.   I knew that if my father ever found out about that he would give me the worst skinning I ever had, and I tried to get out of the police station. I asked the cop to take me to the toilet.   There was a small window.   I climbed through it and jumped an eight-foot wall and beat it home.   But they came after me and put me in Juvenile.   I was so lonesome there.   I cried most of the time,[1] and I felt sorry for my folks.   It's a disgrace to be put in jail.   Well, that passed and in a few days I was out and with a gang again.[2]   There were many nights when we did not go home to sleep.   We

---

[1] Workers in various local and state institutions frequently remark that "Molokan children are more seriously afflicted with lonesomeness for home than is usually the case."

[2] The boy is conscious of the effect of his act upon the reputation of his parents in the community, but he has little choice of companions so long as he remains in the same environment.

had real caves on the banks of the Los Angeles river. It was fun to sleep there. In bad weather we sneaked into an old deserted Pullman coach and slept "in style." Sometimes we would strip these coaches and sell what we could to junk-dealers. . . .

I remember when me and another kid broke into a cellar. We heard that there was a man who had eight-year-old wine. We found his wine and got after it. We pushed the corks in, drank all we could stand. Before we left that cellar we were so drunk we could not stand up. I had left my bicycle outside, and I tried to ride it home. I could not understand why it would not ride straight. I was nearly run over. I met a man and he had four heads. Gee, he is funny, I thought. I looked at a building and it had four walls on one side. The world sure looked lopsided to me. Well, I got home by and by, and gee, was I sick to my stomach. I crawled into bed and every time I had to vomit I stuck my head out of the window. Then my father came! Believe me, I sobered up in a hurry. I was sicker than a dog, and he took a strap and beat the life out of me.

I got drunk like that only one more time in my life. That was at my friend's wedding; not a Russian wedding, of course. I was sitting next to the window and a girl was out on the porch. She passed me a glass of wine and I passed her back the empty glass, and she filled it again and again until I could not drink any more. That was the last time I got dead drunk. Oh, you have to drink with the fellows, but I know my limit now. Everywhere you go there is booze. There is hardly a party without it. You aren't sociable if you don't drink. Sometimes I take a drink when I am blue and tired. I work all day. It gets monotonous. You want to get pepped up and go out, and you take a drink to make you feel better. How it feels? Oh, it does make you livelier, and it feels good. It stimulates you if you know your limit and your stuff. It puts life into you when you want to give up. My father is dead against it, and I try not to have him catch me. I also smoke a lot but never at home. What they don't know they don't worry about, and I don't see no harm in smoking.[1]

I went to church until I was about fourteen years of age. I liked everything about church while I was going. I quit because a bunch of boys and girls were making fun of me. I started to go with a rotten bunch of fellows. Well, they were just rotten. And while I was going with them I was the worst criminal you ever heard of. Oh, we used to do lots of crooked things. I used to break gum-machines, steal things off cars, burglarize stores, steal automobiles. Oh, I quit that a long time ago. I learned my lesson. When you sit in jail, you come to think that there ain't nothin' like freedom, and that they would get you sooner or later anyway. The whole game don't pay.

Well, when I used to run around with the gang we used to do a good many things together, but many times some fellows would pull a job, and I would be standing outside waiting for them, but they would get me just the same. Once a fellow and I started off on Main Street. He went into a hardware store. It was broad daylight, and in about a half-hour he came out with

[1] This boy reflects upon his personal behavior—a practice very uncommon in the traditional Molokan household. He is aware, however, of a conflict of standards and develops a getting-by philosophy.

about a hundred and fifty pocket knives. He gave me half of them, but the owner of the store notified the police and in a few minutes we saw a cop starting after us. I threw away the knives and beat it. I jumped a fence that was about twelve-feet high. Nothing would stop me. Gee, I made a leap for that fence. Well, I got away. The other fellow was caught. A short time afterward he was out again, and he and I went after a Japanese store. He let himself down through the skylight and came out with a bunch of fountain pens. They were worth about $7.00 apiece. We went to the beach to sell them for two bits. . . .

Well, we were caught on that job and laid in jail, and I started to think things over; but when you are out and fall in with the same bunch, you go on doing the same things. Once I was sent to jail when I was innocent. There are really two types of boys who are arrested: those who deserve it, and those who the cops think deserve it. And if you are a Russian, then the cops will "think" very often.[1] . . .

I ran away from home twice. Once because it got a little too hot for me after a fight with the cops. I was advised to stay out of town. And once I ran away because my folks were too strict with me. They are strict Russians and don't know the world. They don't realize all the things that we hear and see and do away from home. . . . Well, it was just the usual run of fights: "shows," "spending money," "church-going," "ball-games," "helping father on rubbish," and a hundred others that all Russian kids fight about with their parents. We get educated in one way, and they want us to get educated in another way. But their way does not suit the city. Well, you fight, and you fight, and you don't want to fight any more. Well, what are you going to do? You run away and knock around a while and then come back home. It sure feels better. . . .

Once a fellow and I started out to bum our way to Frisco in my old Ford. We were planning to work just enough to keep going, but the Ford went on the blink. We got disgusted and started back for home. The Ford wouldn't go. I could have sold the can and bummed my way back; but if I got home without it, there would have been a fuss. We started to look for work again and bought a new second-hand tire and we limped into L.A. about ten miles an hour. . . .

Well, I learned my lesson. I don't bother the cops any more.[2] I quit the bad company too. I met a girl. I thought I really was in love with her. I began to think things over again, but that time I was much older; I was eighteen years. I was working and did not have time for much foolishness. I quit the gang and have kept out of trouble.

Oh, when you get older, kid-tricks don't appeal to you any more. You look around and you realize your parents are getting older and they can't work all of their lives. It's up to us to pay them back now. You realize that after all your mother is your best friend. You may have some trouble

---

[1] This is a very frequent statement made, not only by Molokan boys and their parents, but by urban social service agencies who deal with the Molokan boys. The attitude of the police is: "Well, he may not always be guilty when caught, but he is not caught many times when he is guilty." The situation in itself, however, causes confusion in the boy's mind.

[2] The last entry on his court record was made in 1926.

with her, but she is the only one whom you go to when you're in trouble. You may disagree on religious grounds, but she wants the best thing for you. She and father slaved for us all their lives and always wanted to make good Molokans of us. That's all they know. Why should we fight them? Once I talked back to my mother. We argued about religion. She wanted to hit me. I kind-a talked her out of it and I put my arms around her until she started to laugh; then I bent her arms back and made her realize that I was pretty strong. She never again tried to hit me. I have been grown up ever since. You must know how to get along with your folks. The worst of it is, though, when you lose your temper and start scrapping in earnest.[1]

Suggestions for Further Study

1. Read the entire interview held by Claudia Wannamaker and write a critique on her method of approach to the client, to the problem of social treatment from the standpoint of a client, to the client's attitude; of the interviewing technique, of the manner of asking questions and of interpreting them.

2. In the interview held by Miss Wannamaker which questions need rephrasing? Which are leading questions? Write out the questions you would have asked the client. Indicate why you would ask them. What further questions would you ask the client?

3. Write out a critique of the interviews with Mrs. Salters from the standpoint of the method of approach, the interviewing technique, the analysis of the social situation, of the plan of therapy.

4. The third interview with Mrs. Salters may be of a therapeutic nature. Indicate step by step what your procedure would be if you undertook to hold this interview with Mrs. Salters. What questions would you ask? What statements would you make in an attempt to solve the social problems, family problems, personal problems? Prepare these questions and statements in the form you would present them to Mrs. Salters. Test the success of the interview held by the worker.

5. Write an analysis of the interviews with Mrs. Haynes. What further questions would you ask Mrs. Haynes? How would you interpret the social situation to Mrs. Haynes? What form of therapy did interviewer follow? What further procedure would you adopt in the therapeutic interviews with Mrs. Haynes? Test the success of this interview.

6. Indicate the questions which were probably asked by the interviewer in order to secure the information from Alex Katinoff.

[1] PAULINE V. YOUNG, *Pilgrims of Russian Town*, pp. 193–196. Document 61. Reprinted by permission of the University of Chicago Press.

APPENDIX B

RECORDING OF THE INTERVIEW

It is not within the scope of the present treatise to present any systematic account of case and interview recording. Only a few brief excerpts from the recent literature can here be presented, and the student can follow up the discussion by referring to the bibliographical notes, according to his particular needs and interests.

E. W. Burgess:

Existing case records seldom, or never, picture people, in the language of Octavia Hill, with their "passions, hopes, and history" or their "temptations" or "the little scheme they have made of their lives, or would make if they had encouragement." The characters in case records do not move, and act, and have their being as persons, they are depersonalized, they become robots, or mere cases undifferentiated except by the recurring problems they present of poverty, unemployment, drunkenness, feeble-mindedness, desertion, bad housing.

A simple, but perhaps not complete, explanation for this may be offered. The characters in case records do not speak for themselves. They obtain a hearing only in the translation provided by the language of the social worker. Accordingly they appear as indistinct figures with only here and there, and then often by way of direct quotation, a flash of individuality. The first requisite necessary to reveal to social worker and sociologist the person as he really is to himself would be to *enter the record in his own language.*

To enter the interview in the words of the person signifies a revolutionary change. It is a change from the interview conceived in legal terms to the interview as an opportunity to participate in the life history of the person, in his memories, in his hopes, in his attitudes, in his own plans, in his philosophy of life. Under the legalistic conception of the interview the attention was often focused upon the art of cross examination, upon all the little tricks of technique designed to elicit information which the informant desired to conceal, and upon ingenious methods by which the social worker could impose his will upon an unwilling applicant for assistance. Under the personal, in contrast with the legal, conception of the interview, the social worker aims first of all to put himself as far as possible in the place of the other person, to participate in his experiences, to see life, at least for the moment, as the other person sees it, to enter into his hopes and plans, and to be sympathetic with their realization. . . .

Certain objections are almost certain to be raised against the verbatim method of the interview. There are those who will contend that the remarks

376

of the client are trivial and not worth recording. Some of his statements may be irrelevant, but in so far as they reveal his attitudes and philosophy of life they are important. The right of every man or woman applying for assistance to present his own story in the record should be recognized.

Some one will raise the question whether the record in the first person will not give subjective rather than objective material. He will point out that the record should contain "The facts and nothing but the facts." But what are the facts for sociology and social work? They are certainly not descriptions of the mere external behavior of applicant and of social worker.[1] They are rather, as we have seen, the life history of the applicant, his scheme of life, and his attitude to the problem in question. If these are entered in his own words rather than in those of the social worker the record becomes really objective, and open to anyone to interpret. The verbatim record would go far in removing the effects of the "personal equation" of the social worker and the criticism now frequently made of wide differences in the records of different workers in their characterizations of the same persons.

Another objection that is sure to be raised is the alleged increased length of the record under the new plan. In my judgment the narrative in the first person need be no longer than the record in the third person. In both cases, it is necessary to select the material that is relevant and significant.

A final objection to be considered is the question of the adaptability and skill of the social worker in this new form of interviewing and record keeping. My own belief is that for the great majority of social workers the new technique will be easier to master than the old because it is more human and for that reason more interesting.

The record in the first person has only to be tried out to have its values realized. They may be enumerated briefly as follows:

1. The interview is placed upon the democratic and friendly basis of sharing experience, the worker entering into the inner life of the other and at the same time imparting the wisdom that comes from contact with similar experiences.

2. Each new interview becomes for the social worker an opportunity not only to broaden and deepen his own understanding of life, but also to test out his own intuitions and tentative plans of treatment.

3. Since this form of record provides both a personal document and objective data, the worker on the case, the supervisor, the staff in conference, and the sociologist are all free to make their own interpretation without the ever lurking suspicion of how far the record has been colored and perhaps distorted by the personal equation of the worker.

4. The materials are now provided for a diagnosis in terms of the total situation, rather than with reference to a series of unrelated individual problems.

5. Finally, a current aim, I take it, of social work is to place treatment upon a frankly empirical, experimental plane, so that both the original diagnosis and the method and technique of treatment may be subject to review in light of the acid test of the outcome. To record in the first person,

[1] See MARY RICHMOND, *Social Diagnosis*, p. 94.

by preventing futile attempts at treatment, and by suggesting more individualized planning, will make its contribution to this goal.[1]

Florence Nesbitt:

Our case-workers feel that the interview for the first person record helps them very much in following the mental processes of their clients, getting at their attitudes, their underlying motives and reactions. Thinking the interview through before recording it clears their mind and crystallizes the impression they get out of their client's personality. From the standpoint of the case-reader, it seems to me, that it forms a better revelation of the personality than we can get in any other way and gives a more vivid and definite picture of the client. The case-workers also spoke of this, particularly in its aspect of recalling to them, when they re-read their record, the impression they received at the time of the interview.[2]

Dr. E. Van Norman Emery:

It is our practice to record as accurately as is humanly possible the exact questions that the psychiatrist asks and the exact answers given by the patient. The record is written down in long hand by the psychiatrist at the time that the questions are asked and the answers given. We feel that this is a very essential part of the technique, as we have found it impossible to record verbatim answers in any other way. The psychiatrist is not only interested in the patient's ideas, but is interested in the words which the patient selects in his effort to express these ideas. Many times the way in which the idea is expressed is of much greater significance to the psychiatrist than the idea itself.[3]

From Judge Baker Foundation Case Studies:

No study of delinquents that is either scientific or practical from the standpoint of treatment can be undertaken without getting at the facts which can only be obtained through the individual's own story well guided by sympathetic questioning. It requires more technical understanding and training than perhaps any other part of the study. . . .

The "own story" affords the only means of acquiring knowledge of many facts concerning outside situations as well as factors in the mental life which may be active elements in producing that which we are studying, namely, the tendency to delinquency. There is a much richer psychology concerned with inner mental life, memories, ideations, imageries, etc., with their emotional backgrounds than is dreamed of during an ordinary examination of a delinquent young person. And this is not material of theoretical or academic interest; it is most useful in its practical bearing upon what ought to be done in the case.

[1] ERNEST W. BURGESS, "What Social Case Records Should Contain to be Useful for Sociological Interpretation," *Journal of Social Forces*, VI (June, 1928), 526–528.

[2] Quoted by ERNEST W. BURGESS, *ibid.*, p. 529.

[3] Quoted by ERNEST W. BURGESS, *ibid.*, p. 528.

Some of this material is so deeply buried that it requires considerable skill on the part of the inquirer to overcome inhibitions and forgetfulness so that underlying fundamental truths of the situation may be brought to the surface.[1]

Clifford R. Shaw:

The validity of the statement of attitudes in the life-history seems, in my judgment, to be closely dependent upon the following conditions: (*a*) a document reported in the words of the person, i.e., a written autobiography or a verbatim record of an oral narrative; (*b*) a document representing a free, spontaneous, and detailed expression of past experiences, present aspirations, and future plans; (*c*) a document secured in a favorable situation where the tendencies to deception or prejudices are absent or at a minimum.

Life-histories are original documents. What is more, they are objective documents in the sense that they are set forth independent of interpretation for anyone, whatever his point of view, to analyze and interpret as he will. At any rate, the reader is assured that he is dealing at first hand with the story as told by the youth rather than with material reflected through the mind of another person.

But the point will be raised, even if the narrative is in the first person, will it not, nevertheless, be controlled by the person securing it? Will not the very questions to which the person responds, determine his answers. There is real force to this objection, and it is one that must be squarely faced. Anyone experienced in questionnaires knows only too well what changes in replies may be obtained by the rephrasing of questions. The best way, perhaps, to reduce to a minimum the directing influence of leading questions is to sacrifice them in the interests of the independence of the document. From the standpoint of a document as a free and spontaneous expression of the personality, the ideal would be to obtain it without questions or directions at all. At all events, only a few simple, unguided questions or directions should be given.

At best, of course, a life-history or any other personal document represents a selection from the experience of a life-time. No life-history can be complete, in the sense that it fully records all events in a person's life; if so, a library of books rather than one volume would be required. And where there is selection, there must be factors influencing the selection. Even if the person writes "freely and spontaneously," nevertheless there are factors determining what he includes and excludes, factors of his own personality make-up, of his own interest, what he deems is significant, what he is inhibited from expressing, and also, indeed, the particular situation and relationship in which the writing or telling of his life's story occurs.[2]

Margaret Wead (reporting in emergency relief work):

Summarizing Entries: The plan of reducing the record to a summary instead of dictating after each contact is perhaps the outstanding change

---

[1] Adapted from *Judge Baker Foundation Case Studies*, Case Study No. 1, pp. 29a–31a.

[2] Adapted from CLIFFORD R. SHAW, "Discussion," *The Natural History of a Delinquent Career*, pp. 240–241.

which agencies have made in their record keeping [since the economic depression]. . . . These summaries are usually made monthly. . . . Some of the agencies limit the use of the summary form to their unemployment cases, and dictate chronologically on all others. Other agencies are making use of the summary form even for their intensive cases, especially if the family is well known to the agency. . . .

Some agencies dictate the first interview or the first home visit fully and use the summary method for all later contacts. . . .

A number of agencies find that the summary method is not satisfactory because it leaves little opportunity for supervision of the work done. *Untrained workers have experienced difficulty in determining what material is important to record and in dictating summaries without considerable preparation.* . . .

Topical Recording: . . . agencies find advantages in recording their entries by topics. . . .

Because of the necessity for postponing record writing at times and the need for conserving as much time as possible, our staff has resorted to topical recording almost entirely.

. . . The increasing use of interview outlines would tend toward topical recording, whether a number of entries are summarized or each interview reported in detail. These outlines have been adopted by agencies largely as a guide to new and untrained workers. . . .

Some of the agencies do not find the topical form appropriate for brief unemployment records. . . .

Recording Determined by Treatment and Problem: The detail with which the record is dictated, whether the chronological, topical, or summary form is used, has always been determined to some degree by the type of treatment the agency undertakes. The need for condensing records has concentrated attention on the possibilities of more closely adapting recording to the type of problem and treatment contemplated. . . .

Agencies whose staffs are burdened to the breaking point cannot now give too much thought to how valuable their records will be when the depression is over in revealing the effect the present situation had on families who have received help. They are and must be concerned with using the major portion of their strength and money to relieve the needs of these families. Nevertheless, we would all reluctantly abandon our conviction that records should enable us to contribute information which can be utilized to change conditions injurious to families under our care. If or when another depression comes, we hope that our records will reveal desirable changes in case work practice during an emergency period in order that whatever is of value in our present methods may be studied and made use of. Lacks in the records of 1921 have been glaringly apparent to those workers who have recently turned to them for light as to the situation at that time. But will the records we are writing now be any more helpful?[1]

Pauline V. Young:

Writing a case record in the first person gives the added advantages of eliminating much of the personal bias and interpretations of the individual

[1] Margaret Wead, "Recent Changes in Record Writing," *The Family,* XIII (May, 1932), 74–79.

case worker. Frequently a new worker succeeding the old puts a different interpretation on the "facts" and feels that she must "start all over again" in order to get the right understanding of the family situation. The "own story," if complete and accurately recorded, is a relatively permanent document, free from biases and untimely conclusions of the worker. The client's own story may be regarded in some cases as unreliable; but the situation is within the control of the worker, and does not represent a weakness of the "own story"—it may represent an attempt to mislead or outwit a worker who does not have the confidence of the client. . . .

It is reasonable to assume that the "own story" (1) gives a more accurate picture of the inner life of the client than a report of events, evaluated by outsiders; (2) would eliminate a great deal of duplication of effort of different workers assigned to a given case over a period of several years; (3) would in the end save both time and space; and (4) constitute a valuable and well-nigh indispensable basis for adequate diagnosis.[1]

Mary E. Richmond:

Note taking: . . . The worker who can forget his pencil, visit a family for the first time, conduct a First Interview full of names, addresses, ages and family details, and then come back to his office and dictate a clear and accurate statement, has at his command a better technique than one who is the slave of a schedule or blank form. Beginners often exclaim that this achievement is for them impossible; their memory is too poor and the mere effort to remember destroys all spontaneity of intercourse. Almost anyone can learn to do it, however, and it demands not half the self-discipline that dozens of processes in the other arts demand. If we take our professional work seriously enough, we shall overcome this obstacle without delay. We shall fail the first time that we try, and in successive trials, but gradually, either through visualizing our information or in some other way that comes more natural to us, the memorizing will become easy. The ability to refrain from note-taking does not mean, however, that we should invariably do so. Both methods have their place. When note-taking during the interview has seemed unwise, many workers make rough notes of names, addresses, and main heads as soon as it is closed. If they are going on from one visit to another, they often stop in the nearest drug store, or do this in the trolley car, unburdening the memory of troublesome details before beginning the next interview.[2]

William Healy:

. . . People all look askance when they know what they are saying is being taken down word for word. Of course it is absolutely necessary to take notes in order that there shall be records, preferably verbatim records, for scientific purposes alone, of much that is said in all of these various interviews. We have tried several methods, and are convinced that by far the best scheme is to make little jottings of words and phrases and facts in an apparently careless and irregular fashion while sitting at one's desk, and then

---

[1] PAULINE V. YOUNG, "Should Case Records be Written in the Third Person?" *The Family*, XI (July, 1930), 153–155.

[2] MARY E. RICHMOND, *Social Diagnosis*, pp. 127–128.

immediately after the interview to dictate as nearly as possible the actual words used. After a little practice one uses all sorts of abbreviations that really make up an individual shorthand system and from these one can later dictate accurately the essence of interviews lasting an hour or more. This scheme works very well with us, and rarely arouses any comment from the interviewed.[1]

Beatrice Webb:

Note taking should be discouraged unless the interviewee has achieved a scientific attitude toward the problem and is not disturbed in his recital nor made self-conscious by the taking of notes.

1. Interviewer, if intelligently fortified, will have a rough outline upon which to hang the facts.

2. He must jot down important data: names, addresses, ages, etc. at first opportunity.

3. Memory must be trained to recall data. . . .

I need hardly add that once the interview is over, the first opportunity should be taken to write out fully every separate fact or hypothesis elicited. Never trust your memory a moment longer than is necessary is an all-important maxim. Practice will make it easy to reproduce on paper, that very evening or on the following morning before starting out for the day's work, every phrase or suggestion that needs to be recorded, even of several successive interviews.[2]

Selected Bibliography

1. BRUNO, FRANK J.: "Fitting the Case Record to the Case," *The Family*, XII (December, 1931), 249–250.

   Form of recording should fit particular purposes for which case records are kept—teaching, supervising, self-study, history of contacts with family, and type of problems presented.

2. BRUNO, FRANK J.: "Some Case Work Recording Limitations of Verbatim Reporting," *Journal of Social Forces*, VI (June, 1928), 532–534.

   Maintains that verbatim reporting (1) ". . . will only show up the barrenness of the case worker's technique and would probably throw no more light on the client than the brief summary now contained in records;" (2) will reproduce inaccurately the words of the client.

3. ELLIOT, THOMAS D.: "Objectivity and Subjectivity in the Case Record," *Journal of Social Forces*, VI (June, 1928), 539–544.

   "Objectivity and subjectivity in case records are seen to be reciprocally fertile to each other if their alternating nature is recognized."

4. HAZELTON, MABEL: "The Picture Behind the Record," *The Family*, VII (January, 1927), 283–285.

   Indicates relation between art of short-story writing—compactness, clarity, and unity—and record writing.

5. PALMER, VIVIEN M.: *Field Studies in Sociology*.

   "Documentation," pp. 192–199, and "Analysis and Interpretation of Case Materials," pp. 200–207.

[1] WILLIAM HEALY, *The Individual Delinquent*, p. 49.
[2] BEATRICE WEBB, *My Apprenticeship*, pp. 410 *f.*

6. SHEFFIELD, ADA E.: *The Social Case History*, Russell Sage Foundation, 1920, pp. 109–113; 124–143.

    A treatise on the social case history, with concrete illustrations of how social case interviews should be reported or written up.

7. SWIFT, LINTON B.: "Can the Sociologist and the Social Worker Agree on the Content of Case Records?" *Journal of Social Forces*, VI (June, 1928), 535–538.

    Maintains that material for purposes of sociological interpretation does not necessarily meet the need of the social case worker. Points out several dangers of verbatim reporting. Advocates obtaining client's own written analysis of his situation.

8. WAITE, FLORENCE: "How to Study a Case Record," *The Family*, VII (October, 1926), 186–193.

    Study records with unprejudiced minds: (*a*) the factual basis; (*b*) the analysis of the facts; (*c*) treatment given. Discussion of methods by Helen Myrick.

9. WEAD, MARGARET: "Recent Procedures in Taking Applications," *The Family*, XIII (July, 1932), 168–173.

    The recent procedure in taking applications is a process of elimination and selection, but it should at the same time serve as a determinant of the type of service and treatment needed.

10. YOUNG, PAULINE V.: "Should Case Records be Written in the Third Person?" *The Family*, XI (July, 1930), 153–156.

    A verbatim report as given by a client whose attitudes, problems and philosophy of life can best be learned when reported in her own words.

GENERAL BIBLIOGRAPHY

1. ALEXANDER, S.: *Psychoanalysis of the Total Personality*, Nervous and Mental Diseases Publication Co., New York, 1927.
   A lucid presentation of the general theory of psychoanalysis.
*2. ALLPORT, Floyd H.: *Social Psychology*, Houghton Mifflin Company, New York, 1924, Chap. V.
3. ALPER, MINNIE: "Group Conferences with Clients as a Case Work Tool," *The Family*, XIV (November, 1933), 240–245.
   Methods of giving clients perspective of the agency and community problems to enable them to see beyond their own individual needs.
*4. AMERICAN ASSOCIATION OF SOCIAL WORKERS (Committee of Chicago Chapter): *Interviews: A Study of the Methods of Analyzing and Recording Social Case Work Interviews*, New York, 1931.
5. "An Interview," *The Family*, VI (February, 1926), 303–306.
   A verbatim interview with a spasmodic drinker illustrating the indirect approach to a discussion of a serious problem.
6. ANONYMOUS: "Whittier Social Case History Manual," California Bureau of Juvenile Research *Bulletin*, 1921, No. 10.
   Gives methods of securing information, and of interviewing. Emphasizes need of *rapport* and of note-taking during the interview.
7. BAIN, READ: "The Impersonal Confession and Social Research," *Journal of Applied Sociology*, IX (May, 1925), 356–361.
   "The Impersonal Confession" to a stranger—who supplies the conditions of impersonality, objectivity, and anonymity—tends to reveal facts about one's life rather than the rationalizations and self-justifications which creep into the confession to a friend or acquaintance.
*8. BAIN, READ: "The Validity of Life Histories and Diaries," *The Journal of Educational Sociology*, III (November, 1929), 150–164.
9. BARTON, BRUCE: "What to Do If You Want to Sit at the Boss's Desk," *American Magazine*, XCIII (February, 1922), 19; 28–29.
   Stresses importance of viewing problems and situations from "the other fellow's standpoint."
10. BEDFORD, CAROLINE S.: "Methods of Assembling Material," *Proceedings of the National Conference of Social Work* (1921), pp. 247–249.
    Discusses several methods of summarizing and condensing interviews.
11. BELL, E. P.: "Interviewing: Its Principles and Functions," *Proceedings*, American Society of Newspaper Editors, 169–175, Washington, D. C., 1927.
    Discusses the nature and history of interviewing in journalism.

Note that * means that reference has been annotated in sectional bibliography and may be traced through the index.

*12. BINGHAM, WALTER VAN DYKE, and BRUCE VICTOR MOORE: *How to Interview*, Harper & Brothers, New York, 1931.

13. BINGHAM, WALTER VAN DYKE: "The Personal Interview Studied by Means of Analysis and Experiment, *Journal of Social Forces*, VII (June, 1929), 530–533.

*14. BOGARDUS, E. S.: *The New Social Research*, Jesse R. Miller, Los Angeles, 1926.

15. BOGARDUS, E. S.: *Making Social Science Studies*, Jesse R. Miller, Los Angeles, 1925.
Chapter VI discusses methods of gathering data.

16. BOGARDUS, E. S.: "The Social Research Interview," *Journal of Applied Sociology*, X (September–October, 1925), 69–82.
Discusses problems of securing mental catharsis and principles of procedure in the interview.

*17. BOGARDUS, E. S.: *Sociology*, The Macmillan Company, New York, 1934.

18. BOGGS, MARJORIE: "Present Trends in the Case Worker's Rôle in Treatment," *The Family*, XIII (July, 1932), 158–162.
Stresses the need of "the relationship role" in treatment with the objective of developing an ability for growth in the client.

19. BOOK, MARY VIRGINIA: "As the Andrews Family Sees It," *The Family*, XIV (January, 1934), 307–310.
Relates the author's experience with a frustrated family whose attitude was greatly changed by assigning them responsibilities in the social welfare agency, which they could assume.

20. BORTON, VIENNIE: "Partnership in Relief Giving," *The Family*, XIV (January, 1933), 302–304.
Stresses the importance of reestablishing the self-respect of clients seeking aid by discussing with them the economic situation on the basis of community failure and the clients' responsibility in such a situation.

21. BOWERS, G. A.: "Issues in Research Method," *Journal of Personnel Research*, IV (1925), 155–161.
The interview method is generally unreliable for fact-finding, giving the investigator only a general impression. "At its best the interview is an aid to the discovery or verification through documentary and other sources."

22. BRADSHAW, FRANCIS F.: "The Interview: A Bibliography," *Journal of Personnel Research*, V (May, 1926), 100–103.
A brief bibliography useful particularly in vocational guidance.

23. BRISKEN, ROSE: "Attitudes in Case Work Treatment," *The Family*, XIII (March, 1932), 14–18.
The case worker's attitude toward clients often influences their behavior and enables them to see themselves in the way he reacts toward them. Whatever the case worker approves of in their personality comes to dominate the situation. The case worker who stresses the finer traits and attitudes strengthens these and builds confidence.

24. BRISLEY, MARY: "An Attempt to Articulate Processes," *The Family* (October, 1924), 157–161.

A discussion of the methods used by a group of senior visitors of the Minneapolis Family Welfare Association in their successful interviews with a variety of clients.

25. BROWN, M. R.: *Legal Psychology*, Bobbs-Merrill Company, Indianapolis, 1926.

Chapter IV summarizes the studies made on the reliability of report.

*26. BRUNO, FRANK J.: "Fitting the Case Record to the Case," *The Family*, XII (December, 1931), 249–250.

*27. BRUNO, FRANK J.: "Some Case Work Recording Limitations of Verbatim Reporting," *Journal of Social Forces*, VI (June, 1928), 532–534.

28. BUELL, J. BRADLEY: "Interviews, Interviewers and Interviewing," *The Family*, VI (May, 1925), 86–90.

An account of the methods of interviewing advocated by the Committee of New York Social Workers.

*29. BURGESS, E. W. (Editor): *Personality and the Social Group*, University of Chicago Press, Chicago, 1929, 121–133.

30. BURGESS, E. W.: "Statistics and Case Studies As Methods of Sociological Research," *Sociology and Social Research*, XII (November-December, 1927), 103–120.

The methods of statistics and of case studies are mutually complementary and their interaction fruitful to either method.

31. BURGESS, E. W.: "The Cultural Approach to the Study of Personality," *Mental Hygiene*, XIV (April, 1930), 307–325.

Personality can best be studied and understood when viewed in its cultural setting.

*32. BURGESS, E. W.: "Discussion," in CLIFFORD R. SHAW, *The Jack Roller*, University of Chicago Press, Chicago, 1930, 184–197.

33. BURGESS, E. W.: "What Social Case Records Should Contain to be Useful for Sociological Interpretation," *Journal of Social Forces*, VI (June, 1928), 524–532.

Stresses recording the interview in the first person, which tends to be free from worker's bias and personal interpretation, and the value of friendly interview as opposed to the "legalistic" one.

34. BURGESS, E. W.: "The Study of the Delinquent As a Person," *The American Journal of Sociology*, XXVIII (May, 1923), 657–680.

Any problem child or adult is best understood when studied in the light of the role he conceives himself to play, in the light of his dominant social wishes and his relations to other members of the group.

35. BURR, ANNA ROBESON: *Religious Confessions and Confessants*, Houghton Mifflin Company, Boston, 1914.

An analysis of the motives and underlying principles of the great religious confessions which have been published.

36. BURT, CYRIL: *The Young Delinquent*, D. Appleton-Century Company, New York, 1925, pp. 361–381; 396–399.

Classifies and discusses varieties of children's lies. Discusses very briefly the role of observation, personal interview, and standard personalities in the treatment of problem children.

*37. CABOT, RICHARD C.: *Social Service and the Art of Healing*, Dodd, Mead & Company, Inc., New York, 1928.

38. CADY, HELEN MARY: "On the Psychology of Testimony," *American Journal of Psychology*, XXXV (1924), 110–112.

Maintains that "the most satisfactory method of obtaining accurate testimony is a combination of the narrative and question-answer methods with the narrative preceding."

39. CALIFORNIA STATE UNEMPLOYMENT COMMISSION, *Report and Recommendations*, Sacramento, 1932, Part II.

Verbatim accounts of personal experiences of the new poor.

40. CANFIELD, ALICE: "Are We Degrading the Unemployed?" manuscript, 1933.

Believes that only chronic dependents and defectives and maladjusted should be subjected to old-time type of investigation, while the unemployed employables should be treated much as if they were applicants to employment bureaus.

41. CANNON, MARY A., and PHILIP KLEIN (Editors): *Social Case Work*, Columbia University Press, 1933.

An exposition of modern case work methods with illustrative cases drawn chiefly from private family agencies, stressing psychiatric viewpoints. Has a brief discussion on "A Course in Interviewing."

42. CAVAN, RUTH S.: "Interviewing for Life-history Material," *The American Journal of Sociology*, XXXV (July,1929), 100–115.

A summary of the current literature on the interview. Extensive bibliography.

43. CHAPIN, F. STUART: *Field Work and Social Research*, Century Company, New York, 1920.

An elementary discussion of the approach, scope, organization, and problems of field work in social research.

44. CHICAGO COMMISSION ON RACE RELATIONS: *The Negro in Chicago*, University of Chicago Press, Chicago, 1922, pp. 500 *ff*.

Describes the role of public opinion and stereotype notions regarding the Negro in Chicago—helpful to worker in a Negro community.

45. CLARK, JOHN H.: "Answer Yes or No: Plight Under Cross-Examination," *North American Review*, CCXXVIII (July, 1929), 85–90.

"The plight of the witness under cross-examination, and some rules by which to minimize the ordeal."

46. CLARK, J. P.: "The Interview and the Unimportant," *Journal of Applied Sociology*, X (1926), 368–371.

Stresses the value of recording all items as given in the interview without any attempt to arrange in logical or chronological order, or to evaluate the importance of data, as the apparently unimportant may lead to most significant clues.

47. CLEETON, G. U.: "Estimating Human Character," *Scientific Monthly*, XXIII (1926), 427–431.

A survey of the traditional and modern methods of estimating and measuring human character.

48. CLOW, L. B.: "The Art of Helping: Through the Interview," *The Family*, VI (1926), 129–132.

Summary of two interviews in which treatment was extended during the process of diagnosis.

*49. COLCORD, JOANNA C.: "A Study of the Technique of the Social Case Work Interview," *Journal of Social Forces*, VII (June, 1929), 519–526.

50. COLEGROVE, F. W.: *Memory, An Inductive Study*, Henry Holt & Company, New York, 1900, pp. 246 *ff.*; 264 *ff.*
Hints on how to improve one's memory.

51. COOLEY, CHARLES H.: *Social Organization*, Charles Scribner's Sons, New York, 1915.
Chapters III and IV discuss the role of primary groups and primary ideals in the life of an individual; Chap. VI gives also a profound discussion of the significance of communication and its relation to human nature. The whole volume is important to interviewers, who can gain considerable insight into the processes of the modern life in which the interviewee lives.

52. COOLEY, CHARLES H.: *Human Nature and the Social Order*, Charles Scribner's Sons, New York, 1925, Chap. IV, "Sympathy or Understanding as an Aspect of Society"; Chap. X, "The Social Aspects of Conscience" as related to the problem of confession.

53. COOLEY, CHARLES H.: "The Roots of Social Knowledge," *The American Journal of Sociology*, XXXII (July, 1926), 59–79.
The investigator is concerned with two types of data—spatial or material and personal or social—and discusses how humans acquire knowledge of such data. Very profound, illuminating and original discussion.

54. COVINGTON, FLOYD C.: "The Negro and the Process of Interviewing," manuscript, 1934.
Social background for and techniques of interviewing Negroes.

55. COY, HAROLD: "An Intake Department," *The Family*, XIII (March, 1932), 8–10.
The intake department sifts out and classifies cases and serves as a balance-wheel for the organization and makes possible planned intake for districts.

*56. CRAWFORD, C. C.: *The Technique of Research in Education*, University of Southern California Press, Los Angeles, 1928.

57. DAVENPORT, C. B.: *The Family History Book* (Bulletin No. 7, Eugenics Record Office), Cold Spring Harbor, New York, 1912.

58. DEIHL, NANNIE E., and R. S. WILSON: "Can Listening Become a Case Work Art?" *The Family*, XIV (June, 1933), 99–105.
The interviewer can often apply social treatment more effectively by listening than talking since he provides client an opportunity to unburden.

59. DEJERINE, JOSEPH J., and E. GAUCKLER: *Psycho-neuroses and Their Treatment by Psychotherapy.* J. B. Lippincott Company, Philadelphia, 1915.
Discussion of psychoanalytic techniques in interviewing.

*60. DE SCHWEINITZ, KARL: *The Art of Helping People Out of Trouble*, Houghton Mifflin Company, Boston, 1924.

*61. DEWEY, JOHN: *Human Nature and Conduct*, Henry Holt & Company, New York, 1922.

*62. DEWEY, JOHN, and JAMES H. TUFTS: *Ethics*, Henry Holt & Company, New York, 1908.

62a. DEXTER, ELIZABETH: "The Social Case Worker's Attitudes and Problems as They Affect Her Work," *Proceedings of the National Conference of Social Work* (1926), 436–442.

63. DOUGHERTY, G. S.: *The Criminal as a Human Being*, New York, 1924, Chap. II.

See discussion of the humane third degree and the methods of approaching criminals.

64. DRURY, LOUISE: "Milestones in the Approach to Illegitimacy," *The Family*, VI (April, May, and June, 1925), 40–42; 79–81; 98–99.

Community reorganization, community consciousness, and intelligent public opinion are the real factors involved in the problem of illegitimacy. Useful in interviewing unmarried mothers.

*65. DUNLAP, K.: "The Reading of Character from External Signs," *Scientific Monthly*, XV (1922), 153–165.

66. DUTCHER, ELIZABETH, "When Clients Participate," *The Survey*, LXX (February, 1934), 41–43.

Reports the experiments of client participation in agency planning and organization as a factor in social case work.

*67. ELIOT, THOMAS D.: "Objectivity and Subjectivity in the Case Record," *Journal of Social Forces*, VI (June, 1928), 539–544.

*68. ELLIOTT, LULA JEAN: *Social Work Ethics*, Publication of The American Association of Social Workers, New York, 1931.

69. EMERY, E. VAN NORMAN: "The Integration of the Erotic Component in Man," *The Family*, XIII (December, 1932), 255–266.

Discussion of the role of sensory pleasure, autoeroticism, parental attitudes, changes in the love patterns during puberty, sex, love and the ego, etc.

70. EUBANK, EARL E.: *The Concepts of Sociology*, D. C. Heath & Company, Boston, 1932.

A treatise presenting a suggested organization of sociological theory in terms of its major concepts. Useful in analyzing interviews.

*71. FAMILY WELFARE ASSOCIATION OF AMERICA: *Interviews, Interviewers and Interviewing in Social Case Work*, New York, 1931.

72. FEDER, LEAH: "The Group Conference as a Method of Supervision," *The Family*, XIII (March, 1932), 24–28.

73. FEDER, LEAH: "Why the Professional?" *The Family*, XIII (December, 1932), 275–279.

Training for professional social work implies a knowledge of wide range of facts and keen insight into social and personality problems, a knowledge of community resources, a philosophy of social work, and a certainty of techniques and skills that protects one against short cuts, delays, and indecisions.

73a. FENTON, NORMAN: *A Guide to the Personal Interview with a Child*, California Bureau of Juvenile Research, Bulletin 10, 1934.

74. FISHER, CONSTANCE C.: "Some Factors in Understanding Negro Clients," *The Family*, XII (December, 1931), 245–247.

A worker needs "a knowledge of folkways and of the vernacular of the southern Negro, and a recognition that there are subtle differences among different communities."

*75. FRANK, LAWRENCE K.: "The Management of Tensions," *The American Journal of Sociology*, XXXIII (March, 1928), 705–736.

76. G. S.: "Are Relief Workers Policemen?" *The Survey*, LXIX (April, 1933), 156–157. (*See also* Gertrude Springer.)

Maintains that relief workers visiting families about once a month are not in a position to deal adequately with such problems as bootlegging in the home, drunk and abusive fathers, deserted wives with children "living in sin" with a lodger.

77. G. S.: "How Do We Behave in Other People's Houses?" *Survey*, LXIX (June, 1933), 218–219.

Raises the question: "What about relief investigators, when visiting families: Smoke if they feel like it, holler up stairs, pump children and the neighbors, look under the bed for extra shoes and into the cupboard for food? Bad manners are as cheapening to investigators as humiliating to clients."

78. GEE, WILSON (Editor): *Research in the Social Sciences*, The Macmillan Company, New York, 1929, pp. 38–49.

Chapter I, "Research in Sociology," by Robert E. Park discusses the values and limitations of the life history.

79. GILL, GEORGE E.: "The Case Worker's Approach to Employers," *The Family*, X (June, 1929), 110–111.

A knowledge of industrial conditions; the case worker's responsibility (encouragement of client and keeping him satisfied on job) and opportunity (getting acquainted with industrial conditions of community) enables him to interpret employee to his employer and bring about gradual adjustment.

80. GROSS, HANS: *Criminal Psychology*, Little, Brown & Co., Boston, 1911.

80a. HADER, J. J., and EDUARD C. LINDEMAN: *Dynamic Social Research*, Harcourt, Brace & Company, New York, 1933.

See Chapter IX, "Interviewing as a Technique for Psycho-social Research."

81. HALL, HELEN: *Case Studies of Unemployment*, University of Pennsylvania Press, Pittsburgh, 1931.

Cites numerous case studies of families affected by unemployment of capable, employable breadwinners. Good analysis of case material.

82. HARRINGTON, H. F., and T. T. FRANKENBERG: *Essentials in Journalism*, Ginn and Co., Boston, 1912, Chapter X, "Interviews."

83. HARRIS, RICHARD: *Hints on Advocacy* (American ed.), 1892.

Various suggestions as to how to carry on cross-examination and examination of witnesses, which are applicable to social work situations.

*84. HAZELTON, MABEL: "The Picture Behind the Record," *The Family*, VII, (January, 1927), 283–285.

85. HEALY, WILLIAM: *The Individual Delinquent*, Little, Brown & Company, Boston, 1922.

A pioneering work in the case study method. Chaps. V–VI, "Working Methods"—the observer and his attitude; sources of information; schedule of data concerning delinquents; family and personal history.

86. HEALY, WILLIAM: *Mental Conflict and Misconduct*, Little, Brown & Company, Boston, 1930.

A study of the causes and manifestations of mental conflict.

*87. HEALY, WILLIAM: *Pathological Lying, Accusation and Swindling,* Little, Brown & Company, Boston, 1926.

88. HEALY, WILLIAM, A. BRONNER, AND OTHERS: *Reconstructing Behavior in Youth,* Alfred A. Knopf, New York, 1929, Chap. XVII.

A report of a follow-up study of 500 children placed in selected foster homes to trace the effects of such treatment.

89. HEALY, WILLIAM, A. BRONNER, and ANNA MAY BOWERS: *Structure and Meaning of Psychoanalysis,* Alfred A. Knopf, New York, 1930, Part V.

A review of the modern theories of psychoanalysis, of the cardinal formulations, of the explanation of behavior, of personality formation; the technique of therapy.

90. HELSON, HARRY: "The Psychology of Gestalt," *American Journal of Psychology,* XXXVI (July, 1925), 342–370; XXXVII (January, 1926), 25–62; 189–223.

A general and learned discussion of the principles of "configurationism, configurational structures—resident within perception, thought, action. . . . An unbiased criticism of the several Gestalt theorists and theories.

91. HUEY, KATHERINE: "Problems Arising and Methods Used in Interviewing and Selecting Employees," *Annals of the American Academy of Political and Social Science,* LXV (1916), 208–218.

A statement of the interviewing techniques adopted in one of the pioneer employment offices in selecting workers.

92. JARRETT, MARY C.: "Need for Research in Social Case Work by Experienced Social Case Workers Who are Themselves Doing Case Work," *Journal of Social Forces,* III (May, 1925), 668–669.

Social treatment can develop only through experimental studies made by critical, thoughtful, and experienced case workers engaged in case work practice.

*93. JASTROW, JOSEPH: *The Psychology of Conviction: A Study of Beliefs and Attitudes,* Houghton Mifflin Company, Boston, 1918.

*94. JELLIFFE, SMITH ELY: *The Technique of Psychoanalysis,* Nervous and Mental Disease Publishing Co., Washington, D. C., 1920.

95. KAHN, DOROTHY C.: "Experiment in Selective Intake in a Family Society," *The Family,* XIII (March, 1932), 3–8.

96. KAMMERER, PERCY G.: *The Unmarried Mother—A Study of 500 Cases,* Little, Brown & Company, Boston, 1918.

97. KARPF, M. J.: *The Scientific Basis of Social Work,* Columbia University Press, New York, 1931.

Discussion of what knowledge social workers need, use, and receive, and how they may acquire a scientific basis for their work.

98. KEISER, LAURA J.: "Analysis of an Interview," *The Family,* VIII (March, 1927), 17–20.

Visitor's analysis of her own frame of mind and of the interplay of personalities between worker and client. Report of a verbatim interview and discussion of the technique, which show approach, the interviewing process, plan of therapy, and organization of attitudes.

99. KEMPTON, HELEN: "The First Contact and Social History," *The Family,* XIII (June, 1932), 111–115.

The first contact with an interviewee, barring emergency cases, should be his chance to reveal himself in whatever manner he chooses without hindering him with formal questions or outlines of the social history. Reflections on technique of three contacts.

100. KIMBLE, G. ELEANOR: "Self-consciousness on the Part of the Interviewer and Its Dangers," *Journal of Social Forces*, VI (June, 1928), 565–567.

Present analyses of techniques and thought processes lead to self-consciousness, which endangers clear vision of the goals, and contribute little toward better understanding of interaction and toward teaching how to interview.

101. KIRBY, G. H.: *Guides for History Taking and Clinical Examination of Psychiatric Cases*, New York State Hospital Commission, Albany, 1921.

102. KÖHLER, WOLFGANG: *Gestalt Psychology*, Horace Liveright Inc., New York, 1929.

Systematic discussion of the psychology of configuration.

103. KRUEGER, E. T.: "The Technique of Securing Life History Documents," *Journal of Applied Sociology*, IX (March–April, 1925), 290–298.

The value of life history documents lies in their ability to supply a total picture of the personality and a cross section of one's attitudes.

104. LASSWELL, HAROLD D.: *Psychopathology and Politics*, University of Chicago Press, Chicago, 1930, Chap. XI, "The Prolonged Interview and Its Objectification."

Points out researches in progress for purposes of objectifying the psychoanalytic interview. A good statement of the value of mental catharsis.

*105. LEE, PORTER R.: "A Study of Social Treatment," *The Family*, IV (December, 1923), 191–199.

106. LEVEY, BEATRICE Z.: "The Extent of the Intake Interview," *The Family*, XIV (December, 1933), 268–271.

The intake interview is the pivot upon which subsequent case treatment rests.

*107. LINDEMAN, EDUARD C.: *Social Discovery*, New Republic Inc., New York, 1924.

108. LINK, H. C.: *Employment Psychology*, The Macmillan Company, New York, 1919, Chap. XVIII, "How to ask Questions"; Chap. XIX, "The Observational Method."

109. LOS ANGELES CHAPTER OF AMERICAN ASSOCIATION OF SOCIAL WORKERS: *A Report of the Committee on Standards*, 1929.

Report on ethical standards of social workers to clients, agencies, communities.

110. LUCAS, JEAN M.: "The Interview of Persuasion," *Interviews, Interviewers and Interviewing in Social Case Work*, Family Welfare Association of America, New York, 1931, pp. 26–33.

Persuasion, as a method of changing attitudes, is far removed from coercion or bossing. Persuasion involves real participation of client in the formulation of plans.

111. LUNDBERG, G. A.: *Social Research: A Study in Methods of Gathering Data*, Longmans, Green & Co., New York, 1929.
Chapter VII, "Field Work: The Interview and the Social Survey," is a review of the existing techniques of interviewing.

*112. LUNDBERG, G. A.: "Case Work and the Statistical Method," *Journal of Social Forces*, V (September, 1926), 61–65.

113. LYND, ROBERT S., and HELEN MERRELL LYND: *Middletown*, Harcourt, Brace & Company, New York, 1929.
"Note on Method" (pp. 505–510) discusses techniques—including interviews and questionnaires—for the studying of a community comparable to those of the field anthropologist.

114. MARCOSSON, I. F.: *Adventures in Interviewing*, Dodd, Mead & Company, Inc., New York, 1923.
An account of interviews and methods of "selling the idea" of interviewing to world dignitaries.

115. MARCOSSON, I. F.: "The Part That a Good Memory Plays in Any Achievement," *American Magazine*, XCIV (July, 1922), 49 *ff*.
The advantages of a good memory and how to cultivate one.

116. MARCUS, GRACE: "Psychological Realities and Case Work," *The Family*, XIII (July, 1932), 147–150.
Discusses advantages of the adaptation of psychoanalytic methods to case work.

117. MARCUS, GRACE: *Some Aspects of Relief in Family Case Work*, An Evaluation of Practices Based on Study for the Charity Organization Society of New York, 1929.
A discussion based on concrete case material of the attitudes toward relief held by client and by investigator and of case work problems as related to problems of relief.

118. MARRECO, B. F., and J. L. MYRES (British Association for the Advancement of Science): *Notes and Queries on Anthropology*, The Royal Anthropological Institute, London, 1929, pp. 108–127.
Method of interviewing in anthropological research.

119. MARSTON, WILLIAM M.: "Studies in Testimony," *Journal of American Institute of Criminal Law*, XV (May, 1924), 5–31.
Studies various methods of eliciting testimony.

120. MAULSBY, W. S.: *Getting the News*, Harcourt Brace & Company, New York, 1925.
Stresses importance of listening, of sympathetic interest, of discreetness, of understanding reflections of client.

121. MAYO, ELTON: "The Human Effect of Mechanization," *American Economic Review*, XX (March, 1930), 171–173.
Indicates the value of listening in the interview with employees.

122. McCLENAHAN, BESSIE A.: *Social Case Work—Theory and Practice*, mimeographed. University of Southern California, Los Angeles, 1934.
Comprehensive study outlines and case histories for family case workers. Reports one long verbatim interview.

*123. McCORD, ELIZABETH: "Treatment in Short-time Contacts," *The Family*, XII (October, 1931), 191–193.

124. McCord, Elizabeth: *The Emergency Worker in Unemployment Relief*, Family Welfare Association of America, New York, 1932.
    Discusses the process of investigation, application taking, giving relief, and the training of emergency case workers and their attitude toward clients in an economic crisis.

125. Mead, Margaret: *Growing Up in New Guinea*, William Morrow & Co., Inc., New York, 1930.
    In appendix discusses techniques of research used by anthropologists and stresses importance of learning native tongues and customs.

126. Merrill, Laura A.: "The Case Worker's Rôle in Treatment," *The Family* (July, 1932), 156–158.
    Differentiates between the leadership and the relation phases of treatment and summarizes and analyzes brief cases.

127. Merritt, A. L.: "Human Nature As Seen in the New York Subway," *American Magazine*, XCII (September, 1921), 49.
    Some good hints on how to deal with difficult situations.

128. Miller, A. H.: "A Lawyer's Treatment of His Client," *American Bar Association Journal*, XIII, (January, 1929), 30–33.

129. Moore, Bruce V.: "The Interview in Social and Industrial Research," *Journal of Social Forces*, VII (June, 1929), 445–452.
    An experiment in the objectivity of the interview.

130. Moore, Bruce V.: "Objective Methods in the Personal Interview in Vocational Guidance," *Psychological Clinic*, XIX (June, 1930), 105–115.
    "The interview is most reliable for finding those facts for which records and similar objective forces are least available." Stresses importance of objectivity as an aid to reliability.

131. Moore, Bruce V.: *The Personal Interview*, Personnel Research Federation, New York, 1928.
    An annotated bibliography.

132. Moore, Elow H.: "How Accurate Are Case Records?" *Proceedings of the American Sociological Society*, XXVIII (May, 1934), 45–54.
    Presents in bibliographical form the existing contributions to the experiments of record writing. Limits of attention, of range of observation, of recall, of retention powers, endanger the accuracy of the case records.

*133. Mowrer, E. R.: *Domestic Discord*, University of Chicago Press, Chicago, 1928, Chaps. IX; XI; XII; XIII; XIV; and pp. 54–64.

134. Mowrer, Harriet R.: "Domestic Discord, Personality Adjustment, and the Court," *The Family*, XV (June, 1934), 103–107.
    Domestic discord cases need thoroughgoing study of early life and conditioning, of the sequence of events culminating in conflict. The crucial step in the treatment of domestic discord cases is the interview—highly controlled and of a highly specialized technique—frequently the exact antithesis of the court interview.

*135. Münsterberg, Hugo: *On the Witness Stand*, Clark Boardman Co., New York, 1925.

136. Myrick, Helen L.: "Cross Examination and Case Work Interviewing: An Art," *The Family*, VII (June, 1926), 121–124.

Stresses importance of studies of legal evidence and cross-examination to social workers.

*137. MYRICK, HELEN L.: *Interviews: A Study of the Methods of Analyzing and Recording Social Case Work Interviews* (Committee of the Chicago Chapter of the American Association of Social Workers), New York, 1928.

*138. MYRICK, HELEN L.: "The Non-verbal Elements in the Interview," *Journal of Social Forces*, VI (June, 1928), 561–564.

*139. MYRICK, HELEN L.: "Psychological Processes in Interviewing," *The Family*, VII (March, 1926), 25–29.

*140. MYRICK, HELEN, and ADA E. SHEFFIELD: "Reflective By-products of Social Treatment Interview," *Journal of Social Forces*, III (May, 1925), 657–665.

*141. NEUSTAEDTER, ELEANOR: "The Social Case Worker and the Industrial Depression," *The Family*, XI (January, 1931), 276–281.

*142. NEUSTAEDTER, ELEANOR: "The Rôle of the Case Worker in Treatment," *The Family*, XIII (July, 1932), 151–156.

143. ODENCRANTZ, LOUISE: *The Social Worker*, Harper & Brothers, New York, 1929, Chap. II.
Presents an outline helpful in gathering social case history of a family.

144. ODUM, HOWARD W., and KATHARINE JOCHER: *An Introduction to Social Research*, Henry Holt & Company, New York, 1929, Chap. XIII, "Types of Approach: The Sociological"; Chap. XV, "Types of Method: The Case"; Chap. XIX, "Types of Procedure: Personnel and Common Sense Technique"; Chap. XXI, "Types of Procedure: Exposing the Sources."

145. OLIVER, JOHN R.: *Psychiatry and Mental Health*, Charles Scribner's Sons, New York, 1932, Chap. I.
Indicates opportunities of the priest and church in mental hygiene work.

146. OLSON, EMERY E.: *Credit Management*, Ronald Press, New York, 1925, pp. 63–68.
Discusses technique of interviewing in business.

147. OVERSTREET, H. A.: *Influencing Human Behavior*, W. W. Norton & Company, Inc., New York, 1925, Chap. II, "The Appeal to Wants"; Chap. VIII, "How to Change Persons"; Chap. IX, "The Building of Habits."

148. PALMER, VIVIEN M.: *Field Studies in Sociology*, University of Chicago Press, Chicago, 1928.
Part III, Chap. III, "The Research Interview," its purpose, type, method. Chapter VI, "Documentation," selection of data, technique of recording. Bibliography.

*149. PARK, ROBERT E.: "Behind Our Masks," *The Survey Graphic*, LXI (May, 1926), 135–139.

150. PARK, ROBERT E.: "A Race Relations Survey," *Journal of Applied Sociology*, VIII (March-April, 1924), 195–205.
Life histories are most important and should be recorded in language of person interviewed. Intensity of interviewee's opinions should be noted. Interviewer's impressions should be included separately.

151. PARK, ROBERT E.: "The Significance of Social Research in Social Service," *Journal of Applied Sociology*, VIII (May-June, 1924), 263–267.

The social research worker should seek to learn what social agencies have accomplished not so much along relief or medical lines but along lines of personal and social rehabilitation, of community reorganization, and satisfaction of the social wishes of the person or group.

*152. PARK, ROBERT E., and E. W. BURGESS: *An Introduction to the Science of Sociology*, University of Chicago Press, Chicago, 1921, pp. 50 *ff.*; 344 *ff.*; 893.

*153. PARK, ROBERT E., and H. A. MILLER: *Old World Traits Transplanted*, Harper & Brothers, New York, 1921.

154. PAVLOV, I. P.: *The Conditioned Reflexes*, Oxford University Press, London, 1927.

See particularly the discussion of the origin of the patterned responses and their relation to social influences.

155. PETROFF, LOUIS: *Solitaries and Solitarization* (doctoral dissertation), University of Southern California, Los Angeles, 1934.

An excellent study in social isolation.

156. POTTER, FRANCES M.: "Subjective Elements in Interviewing," *The Survey*, LIX (November, 1927), 226–227.

An attempt to analyze interviewer's actions, reactions, preparation for the interview, and the interviewing process itself.

157. PRATT, GEORGE K.: *Morale*, The National Committee for Mental Hygiene, New York, 1933.

Shows great need of mental hygiene work among the unemployed.

158. QUEEN, STUART A.: "Can Interviews Be Described Objectively?" *Journal of Social Forces*, VII (June, 1929), 528–530.

Raises fundamental questions regarding the terminology, analysis of the "techniques," "processes," and "purposes" of the interviews by the Minneapolis group of social workers.

*159. QUEEN, STUART A.: "Social Interaction in the Interview," *Journal of Social Forces*, VI (June, 1928), 545–553.

160. RANK, OTTO: "Die Analyse des Analytikers und seiner Rolle in der Gesamt-situation," *Psychoanalytic Review*, XVIII (October, 1931), 454–462.

161. RANNELLS, M. E.: "The Psychiatric Social Worker's Technique in Meeting Resistance," *Mental Hygiene*, XI (1927), 78–123.

"Five general causes of resistance are: environmental factors, differences between the social worker and the interviewee, interviewee's intellectual and emotional reaction, habitual reaction pattern of the interviewee, uncertainty of consequences. Factors conditioning the type of response of the interviewee: uncontrollable factors of age, sex, appearance, social and economic status and the like; social worker's personality, mechanical technique. Several interviews with analyses of technique are presented. Also an outline of recording and analyzing interviews and a bibliography." (Walter V. Bingham.)

162. Rasmussen, Knud: *Across Arctic America*, G. P. Putnam's Sons, New York, 1927, pp. 205–210.

Report of several short verbatim interviews with Eskimos and interpretation of data showing problems involved in interviewing a strange cultural group.

163. Reckless, Walter C.: "Suggestions for the Sociological Study of Problem Children," *Journal of Educational Sociology*, II, (November, 1928), 157–171.

*164. Reynolds, Bertha C.: *An Experiment in Short Contact Interviewing*, III, No. 1, Smith College School for Social Work, 1932.

164a. Reynolds, Bertha C.: "The Social Case Worker's Relationship to Clients When the Community Demands Action of a Definite Sort," *Collected Papers on Relationships in Short Contact Interviewing*, National Association for Travelers Aid and Transient Service, New York, 1934.

165. Reynolds, Bertha C.: "Treatment Processes as Developed by the Social Worker," *Proceedings of the National Conference of Social Work* (1926), 400–407.

The treatment processes are: the interview; observation of social phenomena; application of a background of social knowledge to the interpretation of what is seen and heard; application of knowledge of community and personal resources; the coordination and organization of resources; and the education of the individual through his own experience.

*166. Reynolds, Bertha C.: "A Way of Understanding, An Approach to Case Work with Negro Families," *The Family*, XII (November, 1931), 203–208; (December, 1931), 240–244; (January, 1932), 267–272.

167. Reynolds, Bertha C.: "A Changing Psychology in Social Case Work —After One Year," *The Family*, XIII (June, 1932), 107–111.

Reflections on Virginia Robinson's book, *A Changing Psychology in Social Case Work*. Maintains also that not every contact with a person needs social case work. Case work, properly conceived, is a process of educating the client in independence of thought, action, and planning.

168. Rice, Stuart A. (Editor): *Methods in Social Science*, University of Chicago Press, Chicago, 1931, pp. 170–172.

Reviews sociological theories of personality and personality types.

169. Rice, Stuart A.: "Stereotypes," *Journal of Personnel Research*, V (1926), 267–276.

The existence of common stereotypes concerning the appearance of various classes of persons is clearly indicated by experimental methods.

*170. Rice, Stuart A.: "Contagious Bias in the Interview," *The American Journal of Sociology*, XXXV (November, 1929), 420–423.

171. Rich, Margaret: *The Administration of Relief in Unemployment Emergencies*, Family Welfare Association of America, New York, 1931.

Discussion of administrative setup, of procedure in relief giving, of ways of combating discouragement. A few summaries of interviews with unemployed men are included.

172. Richmond, Mary E.: *What Is Social Case Work?* Russell Sage Foundation, New York, 1922.

An analysis of case work practices illustrated by a series of cases; contains a philosophy of social work.

*173. RICHMOND, MARY E.: *Social Diagnosis*, Russell Sage Foundation, 1917.

*174. ROBINSON, VIRGINIA P.: *A Changing Psychology in Social Case Work*, University of North Carolina Press, Chapel Hill, 1930.

175. ROBINSON, VIRGINIA P.: "Some Difficulties in Analyzing Social Interaction in the Interview," *Journal of Social Forces*, VI (June, 1928), 558–561.

Discussion of Stuart Queen's article "Social Interaction in the Interview: An Experiment," in which Miss Robinson points out that "it seems to be far safer to put our emphasis in case work on a deeper understanding of affective changes in individuals and in a freer capacity to identify with a wider range of experience rather than to cultivate further at this point the barren field of technique by which these changes are expressed."

176. ROBINSON, VIRGINIA P.: "Analysis of Processes in the Records of Family Case Working Agencies," *Proceedings of the National Conference of Social Work* (1921), 253–256.

Indicates the need for recording the technique by which the case worker conducted the interview.

177. ROBINSON, WILLIAM C.: *Forensic Oratory; a Manual for Advocates*, 1893. Quoted by J. H. WIGMORE, *Principles of Judicial Proof*, pp. 526–529.

A brief discussion of the problem types of witnesses.

178. ROSANOFF, A. J. (Editor): *Manual of Psychiatry*, John Wiley & Sons, Inc., New York, 1927, pp. 355–369.

179. ROSANOFF, A. J.: "A Theory of Personality Based Mainly on Psychiatric Experience," *Psychological Bulletin*, XVII (September, 1920), 287–288.

See particularly the discussion of the traits of the normal and abnormal personality.

*180. SALSBERRY, PEARL: "Techniques in Case Work," *The Family*, VIII (July, 1927), 153–157.

181. SCHLUTER, W. C.: *How to Do Research Work*, Prentice-Hall, Inc., New York, 1926, Chap. XI, "Collecting the Data and Information."

182. SCHWESINGER, GLADYS C.: "The Significance of Vocabulary in the Interview," *Psychological Clinic*, XIX (1930), 123–130.

*183. SCHWESINGER, GLADYS C.: *Heredity and Environment*, The Macmillan Company, New York, 1933, Chaps. II; V.

184. SEARS, AMELIA: "Outline of the First Interview," *Proceedings of the National Conference of Social Work*, 1921, 249–252.

"Pre-initial interview technique" eliminates the recurrence of "old case," and other "forms of heedless, unplanned effort."

185. SEARS, AMELIA: *The Charity Visitor*, The Chicago School of Civics and Philanthropy, Chicago, 1913.

One of the earliest manuals prepared for the guidance of the field worker.

*186. SHALER, N. S.: *The Neighbor*, Houghton Mifflin Company, Boston, 1904, Chaps. VI; VII; XI.

*187. SHAW, CLIFFORD R.: *Social Factors in Juvenile Delinquency*, National Commission on Law Observance and Enforcement, No. 13, Vol. II, 1931, Chap. I.

188. SHAW, CLIFFORD R.: "Case Study Method," *Proceedings of the American Sociological Society*, XXI (1927), 149–157.

A detailed description of a case study and an interesting family interview.

*189. SHAW, CLIFFORD R. (Editor): *The Jack Roller*, University of Chicago Press, Chicago, 1930, Chap. I.

190. SHEFFIELD, ADA E.: "Identifying Clue Aspects in Social Case Work," *Proceedings of the National Conference of Social Work* (1921), 242–247.

Discusses the relation of the self to three distinct levels of interest; the level of other persons, of institutions, of ideas.

*191. SHEFFIELD, ADA E.: *The Social Case History*, Russell Sage Foundation, 1920.

192. SHEFFIELD, ADA E.: "What is the Case Worker Really Doing?" *Journal of Social Forces*, I (May, 1923), 362–366.

Urges a realistic rather than a moralistic view of a client, and "a behavioristic concern with activities which go on between a client's changing personality interknit with a changing environment."

193. SHEFFIELD, ADA E.: "Three Interviews and the Changing Situation," *Journal of Social Forces*, II (1924), 692–697.

A report and analysis of three interviews.

*194. SIMMEL, GEORG: "Sociology of Secrecy and Secret Societies," *The American Journal of Sociology*, XI (January, 1906), 441–498. Translated by A. W. Small.

*195. SMALLEY, RUTH: "The Social Worker's Use of the Interview with the Child," *The Family*, XIII (December, 1932), 266–270.

196. SMITH, WILLIAM C.: "Contributions of Cultural Sociology to Presocial Work Students," *Journal of Social Forces*, XII (May, 1934), 478–483.

The contributions of the cultural sociologists are gradually beginning to exert an influence upon the social welfare and the psychiatric worker. "In a long-range program of preventive and constructive effort, the cultural approach gives a more adequate understanding of what is cultural and what is biological."

197. SPRINGER, GERTRUDE: "What Price the Power of the Food Order?" *The Survey*, LXIX (May, 1933), 182–183. (*See also* G. S.)

"Dictatorial, censorious attitudes on the part of visitors toward small indulgences by families that have hitherto made their own choices in life inevitably result in a contest of wills and wits in which the visitor, even armed with a grocery order, is the foreordained loser."

198. STEUER, MAX D.: "Cross Examination, Is it an Art or an Artifice?" Address to Missouri Bar Association, St. Louis, October 2, 1926.

199. STRONG, E. K., JR.: *Psychology of Selling and Advertising*, McGraw-Hill Book Company, Inc., New York, 1925.

Several chapters devoted to a sound discussion of the sales interview, of starting the interview (Chap. XXVI), and of the psychology of the sale.

200. STUART, REX: "Getting the 'Extra Percentage' of Power out of People," *American Magazine*, XCII (August, 1921), 36–37.

201. SUTHERLAND, E. H.: "Is Experimentation in Case Work Desirable?" *Journal of Social Forces*, VI (1928), 567–569.
"Findings need to be interpreted with reference to the general surrounding culture of the participants."

*202. SUMNER, WILLIAM G.: *Folkways*, Ginn & Company, New York, 1911.

*203. SWIFT, LINTON B.: "Can the Sociologist and the Social Worker Agree as to the Content of Case Records?" *Journal of Social Forces*, VI (June, 1928), 535–538.

204. SYTZ, FLORENCE: "An Experiment in Student Training," *Interviews, Interviewers and Interviewing in Social Case Work*, 98–105.
Illustrates a method of teaching the social work processes to students in training.

*205. TAFT, JESSIE: *The Dynamics of Therapy in a Controlled Relationship*, The Macmillan Company, New York, 1933.

*206. TAFT, JESSIE: "The Use of Transfer within the Limits of the Office Interview," *The Family*, V (October, 1924), 143–146.

207. TAFT, JESSIE: "The Function of a Mental Hygienist in a Children's Agency," *Proceedings of the National Conference of Social Work* (1927), 392–399.
The therapeutic aspect of the interview with a problem child is more important than the informational content.

*208. THOMAS, W. I., and F. ZNANIECKI: *The Polish Peasant in Europe and America* (2 vols.), Alfred A. Knopf, New York, pp. 1–86; 1853–1859.

*209. THOMAS, W. I.: *The Unadjusted Girl*, Little, Brown & Company, Boston, 1924, Chaps. I and II.

210. THRASHER, F. M.: "The Group Factor, An Element to Be Reckoned with in the Causation and Treatment of Delinquency," *Welfare Magazine*, XVIII (February-March, 1927), 141–147; 314–318.

*211. THRASHER, F. M.: "How to Study a Boys' Gang in the Open," *Journal of Educational Sociology*, I (January, 1928), 244–254.

212. TODD, ARTHUR J.: *The Scientific Spirit and Social Work*, The Macmillan Company, New York, 1920.
Discussion of the need for scientific methods in social work rather than traditional charitable attitudes.

213. TRAIN, A. C.: *The Prisoner at the Bar*, Charles Scribner's Sons, New York, 1908, pp. 224–240.
See Chap. V, "The Trial of Misdemeanors"; Chap. VIII, "Red Tape"; Chap. XV, "Women in the Courts," for helpful discussion of cross-examination under pressure.

214. TRUMP, E. V.: "What Does the Social Worker Do?" *Journal of Social Forces*, III (January, 1925), 268–276.
Good discussion of individual differences of case situations.

*215. VAN KLEECK, MARY: "The Interview As a Method of Research," *Bulletin* of the Taylor Society, XI (1926), 268–274.

216. VAN WATERS, MIRIAM: *Youth in Conflict*, New Republic Inc., New York, 1925, Chap. XI.

Discusses role of personality in relation to work with juvenile delinquents.

217. VLACHOS, ANNA: "Opening the Way," *The Family*, V (October, 1924), 153–157.

Advocates "impressing the client with worker's appreciation of his attitude . . . and with her concern for him."

*218. WAITE, FLORENCE: "How to Study a Case Record," *The Family*, VII (October, 1926), 186–193.

*219. WALLER, WILLARD: *The Sociology of Teaching*, John Wiley & Sons, Inc., New York, 1932, Chap. XXIII.

220. WANNAMAKER, CLAUDIA: "Social Treatment from the Standpoint of a Client," *The Family*, VI (April, 1925), 31–36.

A report of an interview with a client who gives her reactions to various types of interviewers and interviewing.

221. WANNAMAKER, CLAUDIA: "The Recreation Interview," *The Family*, X (October, 1929), 181–186; (November, 1929), 211–215; (December, 1929), 247–252; (January, 1930), 268–273.

Reports of play interests of children in various age groups as revealed through the personal interview.

222. WATSON, JOHN B.: *Psychology from the Standpoint of a Behaviorist*, J. B. Lippincott Company, Philadelphia, 1919.

See particularly his discussion of the various conceptions of personality and the traits of personality; of the patterned responses and conditioned behavior.

*223. WEAD, MARGARET: "Recent Procedures in Taking Applications," *The Family*, XIII (July, 1932), 168–173.

224. WEBB, BEATRICE: *My Apprenticeship*, Longmans, Green & Co., London, 1926.

Appendix B, "The Method of the Interview," depicts the conditions essential for successful interviewing. Appendix C discusses methods of note-taking.

225. WEBB, BEATRICE: *Methods of Social Study*, Longmans, Green & Co., London, 1932, Chap. VI, "The Spoken Word."

226. WEBB, E. T., and J. B. MORGAN: *Strategy in Handling People*, Garden City Publishing Company, Garden City, 1930.

Many practical suggestions regarding handling statesmen, world dignitaries, and "key methods used by the world's greatest men."

227. WELLMAN, FRANCES L.: *The Art of Cross-examination*, The Macmillan Company, New York, 1924.

Discussion of principles of "cross-examination of important witnesses in some celebrated cases."

*228. WHIPPLE, GUY M.: "The Obtaining of Information: Psychology of Observation and Report," *Psychological Bulletin*, XV (July, 1918), 217–248.

229. WHITE, WILLIAM A.: *Forty Years of Psychiatry*, Nervous and Mental Disease Publishing Co., Washington, D. C., 1934.

Progress made by psychiatrists in the transition from the humanitarian to the scientific treatment of their patients. Chapter IX presents "the value of an idea-psychoanalysis."

230. WHITLEY, R. L.: "Interviewing the Problem Boy," *Journal of Educational Sociology*, V (October, 1931), 89–100.
Illustrates cases and interpretation of data.

231. WIGMORE, J. H.: *Principles of Judicial Proof*, Little, Brown & Company, Boston, 1913.
Many sections—on rules of evidence, cross-examination, types of witnesses, and their treatment—of interest to interviewers.

232. WILHELM, D.: "Bearding the Lions," *Independent*, XCIX (July, 1919), 21–23.
Methods of interviewing important political and business leaders.

233. WILLIAMS, J. HAROLD: "Individual Case History Outline," *Journal of Delinquency*, V (1920), 71–82.
Outline of individual case history record used by Whittier State School. "It is not a form or questionnaire, but is designed to be suggestive to the social worker."

233a. WILSON, R. S.: *Individualized Service for Transients* (Pamphlet), National Association for Travelers Aid Societies, New York, 1934.
See part 3, section 2, "Reception and First Interview."

*234. WOODWORTH, R. S.: "Psychological Experience with the Interview," *Journal of Personnel Research*, IV (1925), 162–165.

235. WRIGHT, LUCY: "The Worker's Attitude As an Element in Social Case Work," *The Family*, V (1924), 103–109.
Attitude is an expression of the social worker's philosophy of life and is important in the success of her work.

236. WYSOR, DOROTHY E.: "The Traveler As a Case Work Problem," *The Family*, VI (December, 1925), 239–243.
Discusses the problems, responsibilities, and techniques used by the workers of a Travelers Aid Society.

*237. YOUNG, ERLE F.: "What Type of Personality Should Be the Goal of Social Case Work?" *Sociology and Social Research*, XVIII (November-December, 1933), 123–130.

*238. YOUNG, PAULINE V.: *Pilgrims of Russian Town*, University of Chicago Press, Chicago, 1932.

*239. YOUNG, PAULINE V.: "Should Case Records Be Written in the Third Person?" *The Family*, XI (July, 1930), 153–156.

240. YOUNG, PAULINE V.: "Sociological Concepts As an Aid to Social Work Analyses," *Journal of Social Forces*, VII (June, 1929), 497–500.

241. YOUNG, PAULINE V.: "Interviewing the New Poor," *Sociology and Social Research*, XIX (January–February, 1935), 234–242.

242. ZELIGS, ROSE, and GORDON HENDRICKSON: "Checking the Social Distance Technique through Personal Interviews," *Sociology and Social Research*, XVIII (May-June, 1934), 420–430.
Results of fifteen personal interviews—with children who had earlier answered a questionnaire regarding racial attitudes—tend to establish the validity of the questionnaire method in this type of inquiry.

Note that Nos. 12, 22, 42, 71, 131, 132, 148, 161 refer also to bibliographies.

LIST OF INTERVIEWS AND CASE HISTORY MATERIALS

NAME INDEX

A

Achilles, P. S., 240n
Adler, Alfred, 247, 266, 282
Alexander, S., 16n, 17, 246n, 385
Allport, Floyd H., 249, 266, 267, 385
Alper, Minnie, 385
American Association of Social Workers, 2, 23, 190–192, 197, 198–204, 237, 294n, 385
Anderson, Nels, 243n, 266

B

Bain, Read, 99n, 132, 282, 304n, 307, 385
Barnes, Harry E., 164–166
Bedford, Caroline, 385
Bell, E. P., 385
Bingham, W. V. and Bruce V. Moore, 5n, 6n, 7n, 16n, 23, 50n, 73, 91, 154, 155n, 188, 236, 282, 287, 291, 386
Bogardus, E. S., 1, 2–4, 7, 16, 19, 23, 125, 128, 133, 150, 237, 304–305, 386
Boggs, Marjorie, 386
Book, Mary Virginia, 75, 76n, 386
Borton, Viennie, 74n, 386
Bowers, Anna M., 46n
Bowers, G. A., 282, 386
Bradshaw, F. F., 386
Briggs, Arthur E., 7–11
Brinker, Dorothy, 121, 386
Brisley, Mary, 49, 60, 62, 386
Bronner, Augusta, 246n
Brown, M. R., 387
Bruno, Frank J., 382, 387
Buell, J. B., 387
Burgess, E. W., 7n, 63, 106, 127–128, 238, 250, 254, 255, 267, 298, 306, 315–316, 354, 356, 376–78, 387

Burr, Anna Robeson, 14, 302, 387
Burt, Cyril, 275, 387

C

Cabot, Richard C., 21, 23, 82n, 116, 133, 134n, 184–187, 189, 387
Cady, Helen M., 388
California State Unemployment Commission, 161, 162n, 173, 388
Canfield, Alice, 171–173, 388
Cannon, Mary A., 255, 388
Cavan Ruth S., 257, 388
Chapin, F. Stuart, 6n, 18n, 25n, 388
Chassell, J. O., 197, 236
Christenson, Robert, 157–159
Clark, J. H., 388
Clark, J. P., 388
Cleeton, G. U., 388
Clow, Lucia B., 388
Colcord, Joanna, xv–xviii, 204–212, 237, 389
Colegrove, F. W., 389
Cooley, Charles H., 4n, 83, 94, 96n, 196, 251, 297–298, 307, 354, 389
Couch, Gretchen, 38–41
Covington, Floyd, 142–148, 389
Coy, H., 389
Crawford, C. C., 91, 389

D

Davenport, C. B., 389
Davis, Priscilla Ann, 33–36
Deihl, Nannie, 69, 389
Dejerine, J. J., 16n, 389
Delany, Evelyn, 164
DeSchweinitz, Karl, 294n, 330, 332–335, 341, 343, 345, 354, 355, 356, 389
Dewey, John, 196, 328, 329, 343, 356, 389–390
Dexter, Elizabeth, 301–302, 390

407

SUBJECT INDEX

A

Analysis, of interview, 197–238
Anthropological interviewing, 15–16, 96*n*
Apperception mass, 93, 137, 315
Application blanks, 181
Application interview, 33–36, 183, 192, 376–381
  data for, 102, 168–169, 322
    (*See also* Diagnostic interview, Case history outlines, and First interview)
Appointments, 55–57, 86, 190
Approach, the interviewing, 59–63, 82, 203, 235
Argument, avoidance of, 208
Assimilation process, 136–137
Attention, of interviewee, 271–272
Attitudes, change of, 42, 49, 320–330
  of emergency relief workers, 162–163
  of interviewees, 26, 65, 85, 97, 106, 130, 156, 167–168, 169, 173, 175, 197
  of interviewers, 60–62, 66, 69–70, 71, 81, 82–84, 170, 171, 206, 257, 321, 386 (No. 23)
  of Negroes, 141–142
  in social therapy, 295–296

B

Bibliography, on analysis of interview, 237–238
  on content of interview, 132–133
  on ethical standards, 196
  general, 385–403
  on interviewing special types, 188–189
  on nature and objectives of interviewing, 23–24
Bibliography, on personality problems, 266–267
  on psychological problems in interviewing, 281
  on recording, 382
  on sociological problems in interviewing, 292–293
  on technique of interviewing, 90–91
  on therapeutic interview, 356–357
  on types of interviews, 47
Business interviewing, 6, 71, 77, 150, 152, 154, 403 (No. 232)
    (*See also* Employer)

C

Case history outlines, of a boy, 125–127
  of a boys' gang, 128–131
  of a delinquent as a person, 127–128
  in emergency relief work, 168–169
  of a family, 102–107
  of an immigrant, 138–140
  of individual delinquent, 119–121
  medical social history, 116–117
  of new poor, 167–168
  of problem child, 121–124
  of an unmarried mother, 108–116
    (*See also* Life history)
Catharsis, mental, 41, 203, 302–314, 325, 355
Children, gangs of, 128–129
  habit clinics for, 119*n*
  immigrant, 138, 220–235
  interviewing of, 22, 71, 101*n*, 137, 189
  of new poor, 162
  "own story" of, 98–99
  placement interview for, 179–183

411